Inland Salish Journey

Fur Trade to Settlement

Mike Reeb

Sandpoint, Idaho

www.KeokeeBooks.com

On the cover: Salish people cross the Flathead River on lodgepole rafts containing all their belongings in this Gustavus Sohon watercolor. COURTESY WASHINGTON STATE HISTORICAL SOCIETY

On the back cover: Scouts lead a small column of warriors in search of buffalo in this faithful photographic reproduction of the Charles M. Russell painting "In the Enemy's Country." COURTESY WIKIMEDIA COMMONS

Maps created by Laura Wahl. © 2015 Keokee Co. Publishing, Inc.

Printed in the United States of America

Keokee Books is an imprint of Keokee Co. Publishing, Inc.
Published by Keokee Co. Publishing, Inc.
405 Church Street
Sandpoint, Idaho 83864
208-263-3573
www.keokeebooks.com

ISBN 978-1-879628-47-2

Publisher's Cataloging-in-Publication Data

Reeb, Mike, 1939–

Inland Salish journey: fur trade to settlement / by Mike Reeb

318 p.: ill., maps

1. Salish Indians–History–19th Century. 2. Natives Americans–Pacific Northwest–History. 3. Fur Trade–History.

970.3

Contents

List of Illustrations

Preface

In the days of earliest exploration west of the Mississippi River, French and Canadian fur traders visited the Missouri River country to find an untamed landscape of rolling, grass-covered plains scoured by numerous waterways that reached into the lofty, timber-covered Rocky Mountains. They also rediscovered native people ranging over much of the region, as well as endless herds of buffalo and other four-legged animals. These provided food, clothing and shelter for people who lived there. On return to Eastern cities, the white adventurers spread the word of fabulously abundant beaver and numerous other valuable furbearing animals, thus setting the stage for the Western fur trade era. The Indians did not know the U.S. government was about to purchase a large portion of the vast area from France. The seemingly uncivilized inhabitants had neither knowledge nor comprehension of the transaction nor of how the intruders were about to cause the change that would destroy a centuries-old way of life.

No words in the Inland Salish language describe European concepts of settlement, wilderness and vacant land. Indian people believe they had already settled all the land in North America before white men appeared. White men's "wilderness" was land that American Indians hunted, fished and gathered from for their subsistence, with some areas recognized as "commons" shared by neighboring tribes. Wilderness had no meaning. The Inland Salish people had established home territorial boundaries through war and peace between neighboring tribes long before fur traders entered their lands. Vacant land did not exist.

White men found a different circumstance existed in the upper Missouri plains where the Blackfeet nation struggled unsuccessfully to extend their territorial boundary into common hunting ground used by the Salish, Nez Perce, Kootenai and Shoshoni. Resolution of their land claims and wars with neighbors eventually became a problem for the U.S. government to resolve.

Some 200 years ago, white American explorers from the East laboriously poled boats up the Missouri River system until they could go no farther. Good fortune met there in the form of American Indians who provided the explorers with horses and guides to enable their crossing the rugged mountains that lay before them. They had passed through prairies and heights in search of a route that cut through the mountains to the Pacific Ocean. After many grueling months, the Lewis and Clark expedition reached what most of present-day people know as the Columbia Plateau;

they still had a ways to go before reaching that ocean. Right behind them, Canadian-British and American adventurers, bent on commercial gain, spread throughout the vast region, searching for beaver and other skins. This story details the Inland Salish activities from the fur trade period in Western history and their relationships with the white man through United States' establishment of government in the region.

In their day, the buffalo-dependent Inland Salish returned to home base with winter provisions, overpowered once again by a potent enemy on the plains. At the same time, other members of the family of tribes stayed home to fish, dig roots and hunt local game for survival, free of hostilities. Both factions used primitive stone, bone and wood tools secured by sinew to bring down game and catch fish while their women gathered food from the various in-season corners of Mother Nature's well-stocked pantry. Introduction of white man's means came first with the Canadian fur traders' ready assortment of tools and personal items to exchange for furs and food. In addition to establishing trade opportunities with other natives, new and expanded markets unfolded for the Salish. The fur trade era marked the onset of incredible change for the Indians that eventually overran their lands and imposed huge cultural alterations.

The Salish, who hunted the plains and lived close to the Blackfeet nation out of quarrelsome necessity, eventually benefited from trade guns that equalized weapon advantage held by the enemy. From the start, the Inland Salish and fur men settled into friendly relationships, which lasted until the U.S. government established control over the natives and promoted development. As efficient hunters, gatherers and leather craftspeople, the Indians traded beaver skins, food items, dressed leather, horses and much more to meet their demand for European goods.

The fur trade period spanned 60 years of the Pend Oreille, Kalispel, Spokane, Coeur d'Alene and Flathead tribes' history. Their interaction with the white man was, in the beginning, through Canadian fur trading posts that sprung up near each tribe and were situated to take advantage of water transportation of materials on major waterways. The Canadian-British companies of experienced Indian traders had no competition at first and set values on commodities, but as the period progressed, rivalry from American firms obliged the British to raise the price for Salish products. Competition for skins by organized trapping brigades and the Indians soon put a strain on the resource. By 1840, the worldwide demands for beaver felt hats had shrunk, which corresponded with a stronger demand for buffalo robes.

At the same time, long sought-after missionaries came to Inland

Salish country to teach Christian ideals and attempt to alter Indian lifestyle to mesh with that of the white man. Accepting their Christian training, the Indians continued to hunt and gather to support their food and trading needs; they rejected white man's mode of living. The American-Canadian International Boundary settlement and subsequent peace treaties with some native tribes increased the numbers of plains buffalo hunters from the Columbia Plateau region. Then the friendly relationship between the Indians and whites began to erode midway through the 1850s when the U.S. government attempted to establish reservations for some tribes. A few years later, miners and settlers began to pour into traditional lands then called U.S. territories. This caused a few Inland Salish people to make war on the whites, but the vast majority – downtrodden and disempowered – remained peaceful.

As a career forester and part-time trapper, I worked and played in much of the region involved in this book. A desire to learn more about the early history of the Inland Northwest put this retirement project in motion. Volumes written on the fur trade, for the most part, neither portrayed the important role the Inland Salish played in the success of their business ventures that followed nor reported native activities during this period. The study began eight years ago with source documents left behind by explorers, fur traders, trappers, missionaries, Indian agents and others who lived among the Salish; taken together, they indicated that more could be written on this important period of American history. Many journals contained details on Indians' daily life, travel, hunting and conflict with enemies while others' fleeting remarks required assumptions, so noted in this text. Without Salish records in the time frame, comparison of accounts are impossible; however, white man's notations seem credible in view of the friendly posture between the two peoples. With information in hand, the nonfiction story of *Inland Salish Journey* through the fur trade era to settlement began to unfold.

Research began with source documents found on the Internet; copies of transcribed journals, manuscripts and books now in the public domain led to further study of published material found at libraries and archival research facilities. While reviewing sources, it became apparent that more knowledge of the environs described in the journal notations was necessary. Complications began to arise in the names of places and waterways used in reports, but fortunately, editors of the original papers had sorted out many beforehand. Not so with white man's naming of Indians, which presented a problem in overlapping documents by different recorders, each with a different spelling of the same individual.

The writers of the time mention mostly minor Indian chiefs, of whom there were many, and the head chiefs of the various tribes. Sorting out the individual tribes presented problems; in some cases, note keepers tabbed the Flatheads, Pend Oreilles, and sometimes the Kalispels as Flatheads. The tribe's wintering home territory provided the clue to identifying specific tribes. In a quest to become familiar with former buffalo hunting grounds of the Salish on the east side of the Continental Divide, my wife and I traveled great distances. After driving several hours from our home in Sandpoint, Idaho, to Three Forks on the paved "Salish Road to the Buffalo," we marveled at the natives' persistence in trailing six weeks with their families to dangerous country for food, shelter and trading materials.

Acknowledgements

To all who helped make the task achievable, primary thanks go to my wife, Joy. Her help at home typing the bibliography, making maps, and at research facilities in Montana and Washington has been appreciated, as well as her patient endurance over rough, dusty and/or muddy roads as we followed old Salish haunts to distant places.

Many thanks go to Bonnie Spalding, who signed on to type my handwritten manuscript and soon eagerly assumed the role of writing instructor. I had years of technical writing experience, so I was surprised when I got the draft of the first chapter back with some brightly colored "huhs?" and corresponding suggestions. Bonnie convinced me the reader needed a more full picture. Her help in identifying segments that needed more explanation made the Inland Salish Journey a better read with ample points to ponder and question.

Now, huge thanks go to Mark Weadick for his thorough peer review of the manuscript. His background includes a longtime study of the fur trade era; he is a public speaker on the subject and a participant in the Friends of Spokane House, a fur trade living history organization. His editing suggestions and additional source material have been included to make the book more historically complete. Thanks, Mark, for the kind endorsement.

Deepest appreciation goes to archivist Mark Fitch of the University of Montana for professional direction to help to find photos for the book; Montana Historical Society Collections Manager Aide Amanda Streeter Trum and the staff in the research facility for their guidance in locating desired material; Spokane Public Library and Riva Dean in the Northwest Room for assistance in locating research material and photographs; Gonzaga University Archivist Dave Kingman for helpful guidance through their large collection; Ms. Pat Mueller at Washington State University Library for finding a photographic reproduction of Father Nicholas Point's engraving of old St. Ignatius Mission; and the Colville Historical Society for opening the doors to their facility on a day they are usually closed. Thanks also go to East Bonner County Library and Sue Elsa for finding and obtaining all books requested through interlibrary loans.

A huge thanks to the Keokee Publishing staff for all their work in the production of this book. Publisher Chris Bessler told me right off editing and layout would take time due to prior commitments. With that understanding, editor Billie Jean Gerke kindly added handwritten phrases not in the original manuscript. Billie then began the tedious task of editing the manuscript in between other scheduled projects. A big thanks to Billie for the super editing job. Art Director Laura Wahl did an outstanding job of creating the cover and maps for the book.

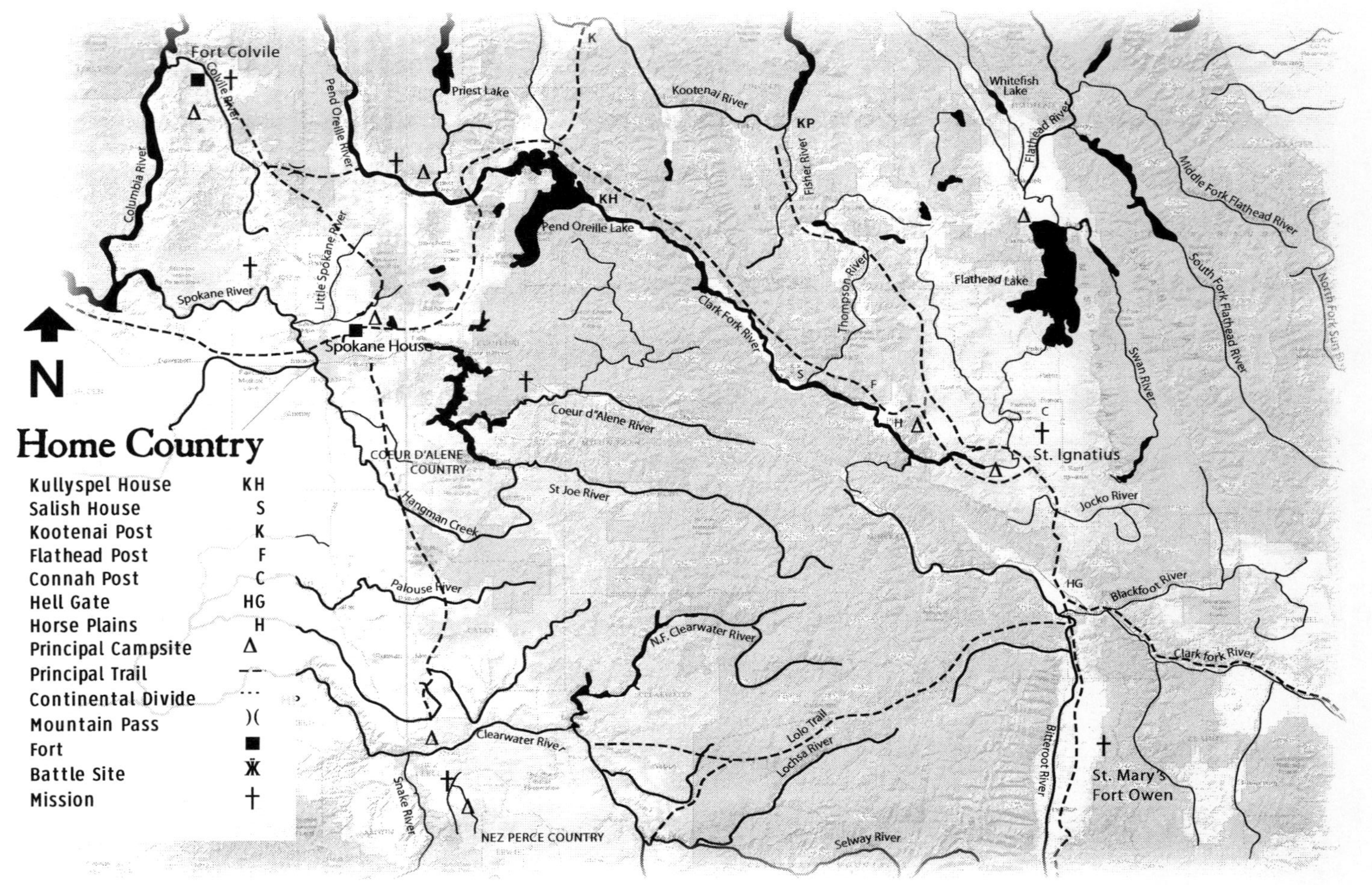
N
Home Country
Kullyspel House KH
Salish House S
Kootenai Post K
Flathead Post F
Connah Post C
Hell Gate HG
Horse Plains H
Principal Campsite
Principal Trail
Continental Divide
Mountain Pass
Fort
Battle Site
Mission
Fort Colvile
Colvile River
Columbia River
Spokane River
Little Spokane River
Pend Oreille River
Priest Lake
Kootenai River
KP
Fisher River
KH
Pend Oreille Lake
Spokane House
Clark Fork River
Thompson River
Coeur d'Alene River
COEUR D'ALENE
COUNTRY
St Joe River
Hangman Creek
Palouse River
N.F. Clearwater River
Clearwater River
Lolo Trail
Lochsa River
Selway River
Snake River
NEZ PERCE COUNTRY
Whitefish
Lake
Flathead River
Flathead Lake
Middle Fork Flathead River
South Fork Flathead River
North Fork Sun River
Swan River
St. Ignatius
Jocko River
Blackfoot River
Clark fork River
Bitteroot River
St. Mary's
Fort Owen

1

Salish Identity

Word spread rapidly among the Inland Salish and neighbors that a white fur trader had built a house on the Columbia River in present-day Canada among the Kootenais. A few brave Salish and Nez Perce men crossed swollen rivers and heavily timbered mountains for a week to tell the trader the advantages of building a house in their land. Soon, the trader, carrying an assortment of wares based on those proven popular with Eastern tribes, arrived on the shores of Lake Pend Oreille to begin the business of fur trading in the wild Salish country.

The following chronology depicts events during the fur trade era that involved the Inland Salish tribes as recorded by white men living and working among them. Speaking the same or similar dialects of the Salishan language, the Spokane, Coeur d'Alene, upper and lower Pend Oreille (Kalispel), Flathead and Colville tribes, central to this account, ruled on a huge piece of real estate rich in wildlife resources essential to their lives. Each tribe under separate leadership had established territories yet lived in peace with one another and their non-Salish neighbors: the Nez Perce, Palouse and Kootenai tribes. All of these peoples, and others of interest, appear in this story where they interacted in a particular occurrence. Buffalo hunters among these tribes traveled many miles in search of prey, to the plains of southeastern Idaho and western Montana, where they encountered elements of their deadly enemy, the Blackfeet Nation.

Salish people had two basic modes of survival. Those who lived solely in their home territory subsisted on fish, local game and roots, such as the Coeur d'Alenes, Spokanes and Kalispels, and were untroubled by hostile tribes. The upper Pend Oreilles and Flatheads depended on buffalo and its by-products and often led groups of downriver cousins in annual hunts where danger lurked. These free and amicable people forged friendly relationships with the fur men that spanned 50 years, until a new economy emerged with a new ruler, and hordes of white settlers came to take their lands.

Within the collective Inland Salish tribes, each group was independently organized and led, shared the same language but with different dialects, and often joined together to hunt buffalo. This close affiliation likely caused a majority of fur men to call them all Flatheads. It is unknown how the smallest of these tribes' name became a reference point in many historical sources. The term "Salish" refers to the linguistic group throughout this text regarding intertribal ventures. Today, the Flatheads prefer the English name Salish; the lower Pend Oreilles, Kalispel; and the upper tribe, Pend Oreille. Chapters unfold to integrate white man's activities in Inland Salish country to provide the reader with a picture of the upper Columbia River system and western Montana history, but first a broad description of the Salish identity.

Long before the 19th century, when white men arrived, the Inland Salish family of tribes occupied lands that came to be known as the Bitterroot, Flathead, Clark Fork, Pend Oreille, Coeur d'Alene and Spokane river systems of today. This forested and mountainous region abounds in numerous lakes, abundant meadowlands in every size and description imaginable, wide flats and rolling hills, and prairies awash with sagebrush and grass. Heavy rains and deep snowfalls characterize the climate in much of the region, with milder patterns relevant to river bottoms and valleys that provided agreeable living quarters for the Indians.

The Flathead tribal home territory was the Bitterroot Valley, while the upper Pend Oreilles lived from Flathead Lake south to the Clark Fork River and down it to Thompson Falls, Montana. The lower Pend Oreille, or Kalispels, dwelt along the same river system downstream to Ione, Washington. South and adjacent to the latter, the Spokane tribe occupied the Spokane River to its junction with the Columbia. The Coeur d'Alenes inhabited lands from Plante's Ferry (Spokane Valley) south to Steptoe Butte and east throughout the drainage system.[1] According to Lewis and Clark, the Flathead population numbered about 500, the upper and lower Pend Oreille tribes each had around 800 souls, and the Coeur d'Alenes and Spokanes numbered approximately 600 people each in early 1800.

Salish is a native linguistic group spoken by "The People" who inhabited inland portions of the British Columbia Interior, eastern Washington, northern Idaho, western Montana and small strips of coastal Washington and Canada. Ethnologist Fredrick W. Hodge identified a minimum of 16 dialect groups within the Salishan family – eight in the inland region and eight in the coastal area. The Flatheads, Pend Oreilles and Spokanes shared a similar tongue; neighbors having more divergent dialects included

1 Hodge, vol. 2, p. 417.

the Coeur d'Alene, Colville and Sanpoil tribes.[2]

Early French fur traders' names of many Inland Salish Indian nations took root over time. The name Spukani (Spokane) comes from the French pronunciation of the Salish word for "sun" meaning "people of the sun." The lower Pend Oreilles, *Glispe* in their language, also known as "camas people" (Kalispel), didn't wear ear pendants as the French word for their name implies. The upper Pend Oreilles preferred *Sctquetkmein*. It is not clear how the Flatheads got their name, as they did not engage in flattening children's heads as rumored. The Coeur d'Alene people preferred *Schitus'umsh*, whereas the French phrase *Coeur d'Alene* means "heart of an awl," which is a sharp pointed tool for making holes in wood or leather. They earned their name by being resolute traders. Other Indian nations important in Salish history received French names, including the Nez Perces (*Nimipu*) who supposedly pierced their noses and affixed ornaments there. The *Atisna* or Gros Ventres, French for "big bellies," and Blackfeet were not descriptive names for those tribes. The Shoshonis, whose various bands were called Sheepeaters and Diggers, were also identified as Snake Indians, during the fur trade. These misnomers prevailed throughout the fur trade era and, in most cases, continue to this day.

Inland Salish Origins

Many historians theorize the Inland Salish migrated to the Columbia Plateau and Rocky Mountains from the Pacific coastal regions, while others take opposing views. A different account suggests these Salish-speakers lived in the interior of British Columbia and spread out from there thousands of years ago[3]. Widespread linguistic similarities make it difficult to substantiate these positions through records or archaeological research or put a timeline on movement. A project conducted on the Kalispel Indian Reservation in Washington uncovered evidence of human inhabitation 3,500 years old.[4] Were they Kalispels or a different people? Early accounts confirm the Salish lived in the previously described region by the early 1700s. If migration originated from coastal regions, it probably occurred in stages and began hundreds of years ago due to food shortages, overpopulation or war. As fish was an essential food source, the salmon and steelhead fish runs from the West Coast to the Spokane River may have lured Indians farther east.

Passed down by many generations, the Salish-Pend Oreille oral tradi-

2 Ibid.
3 Fahey, Flatheads, p. 6.
4 Ellersick Manuscript.

tion declares their people inhabited the Flathead and Clark Fork river valleys following the last ice age, some 10,000 years ago. Stories of tribal creation and origins involve Coyote, who traveled across the land making it safe for the people and those yet to come. Coyote killed monsters that ate humans and animals, the subject of a myth repeated by the Salish, which they only told in wintertime. Archaeological sites near Paradise, Montana, reflect a continuous occupancy of people reaching back to near the end of the last ice age.[5]

Another story told many years ago by the Flathead elder Pierre Adams to Adolf and Beverly Hungry Wolf repeated a legend on the origins of his tribe: "They say there was once a big fight in which Salish relatives and friends killed each other. The fight was over something foolish: two leaders argued about whether flying ducks quack with their bills or their wings. They finally called a truce to the fighting, but one of the leaders set out with his followers to seek a new homeland. They ended up in the beautiful Bitterroot Valley." Adams added, "The Pend Oreilles were already using the Bitterroot Valley for a camping site, but in a show of friendship they agreed to let the Flathead settle there while they moved to another favorite area farther north." Such stories tend to support the notion of the Flatheads coming from the west to their current home territory.

The Horse

During the days before Indians acquired the horse, they used large, wolf-like dogs and their own backs to transport belongings between camps. This limited the size of shelters and amount of possessions they carried over an often uneven and obstacle-strewn terrain. Most lived on the periphery of the vast Missouri plains, venturing out just far enough to hunt buffalo. Resilient braves in pursuit of trading partners, plunder or war made long-distance journeys on foot. Bison hunting in those days was extremely difficult. It involved all able-bodied villagers, who would surround a herd and drive it through a carefully made, brush-lined gap that led into a corral or box canyon where waiting hunters slaughtered them. Where possible, hunters stampeded bison over a nearby cliff. Neither method produced the numbers killed by mounted hunters of the future.

A major cultural change took place as Indians obtained horses. They could travel faster, carry heavier loads and increase range of movement. The Shoshonis had horses before other northern tribes, obtained through trade with southern Indians in the Spanish Territory. About 1720 the Salish began to accumulate sizable herds through trade and thievery

5 Salish-Pend Oreille Culture Committee, p 6-9.

from southern Shoshoni neighbors, who had acquired theirs 20 years earlier.[6] Brought to the Americas by Spanish explorers in the 1500s, the horses were mixed-blood Arab, Barb and Andalusia.[7] Of medium height, strong in heart and limb, in an assortment of dark, light and mixed colors, they transported four times the weight carried by a dog and negotiated steep, rocky terrain with a rider or a load with relative ease. Specifically trained, buffalo-hunting horses were prized possessions that ran alongside stampeding bison so the rider could down two or three with his bow and arrows. The mount needed "horse sense" to dodge prairie dog holes, outmaneuver a wounded or downed and dying bison, and keep its footing. After the introduction of muzzle-loading rifles, they were seldom used for hunting bison, for in the time it took to reload a long rifle, a skilled hunter could ride 300 yards and discharge 20 arrows.[8]

A man of a certain age owned horses, not the tribe, and the number of horses in his herd measured his degree of wealth among Indians. Optimally, each family needed eight to 10 horses to transport possessions and themselves in style. Fur men, who kept records, noted that many Salish possessed in excess of 30 horses each.[9] Steep rocky trails, fallen trees and heavy loads took their toll on horses, requiring replacement of jaded and hoof-sore animals. After each day's travel of eight to 30 miles, depending on the course of travel, Indian ponies were ready to roll in the dust, take a long drink from a cool stream, nibble good grass and relax. Salish men and boys spent a great deal of time tending to and guarding their "wealth" against ever-present thieves. Depending on the severity of a day's travel, or after many days of hard use, weary horses were retired to the herd behind the column to recuperate, and fresh ones were singled out for a new day.

While on the move, a saddle or packsaddle occasionally turned and caused the horse to run and plunge in an attempt to kick free of the frightful thing dangling where it did not belong. Everyone nearby rushed to surround the panic-stricken horse to detach its load. Children age 3 to 5 were lashed to the saddle of a gentle horse and frequently dozed off, slumping forward on thepommel during a long day's ride. Under the age of 3, toddlers and babies were enshrouded in a wicker basket lined with dressed hides and affixed to mothers' saddles. After age 6, most Salish children rode alone and soon excelled as equestrians.[10]

---

6 Harris, pp. 429-437.

7 [I.S.] Horse.

8 [I.S.] Eddin Article.

9 Victor - Bonneville, Ch. 12.

10 Parker, p. 97.

The Salish copied and modified the Spanish-style saddle by stretching a green buffalo hide (rawhide) over a wooden frame to fit their needs. Men's saddles had a short pommel and 6-inch back, with the seat padded with buffalo-hide pillows, and were attached with a wide cinch to keep the saddle securely in place. Women's saddles had a 12-inch front and back. After 1830 women's saddles were adorned with dozens of little hawk bells that tinkled as they rode along – like sleigh bells, only softer. Neither gender used stirrups.[11]

Individual Salish families who had horses in excess of immediate needs let them roam on Horse Plains, Missoula Prairie and other large, grassy areas in home territory. When needed, "wild ponies" were chased by a man riding a well-trained, swift mount close enough for its rider to drop a noose over a head, in a process called "leashing." Once the horse stopped, the caught animal struggled to shake free of the suddenly taut rope while the rider hung onto both rope and mount. Bucking and tugging, within a short time the animal became exhausted and quit fighting. The rider dismounted, fashioned his bridle, jumped on the trembling bronc and dug his heels into its sides to urge it forward. If the horse gave a favorable response, the rider gently patted its neck, but if it spooked and became unruly, a cruel beating followed. After a few days of consistent handling back at the village, even the wildest horse became gentle and obedient. Depending on how long the animals had run wild, after being "leashed," many would follow the mounted Indian back to camp.[12]

Allies

Important allies and neighbors of the Salish included the northern Kootenais, a *Tunaha*-speaking people, and to the west, the Nez Perces who spoke the *Shahaptian* language. Both tribes often joined the Salish on buffalo hunts and shared winter camps; they intermarried and held a common hatred for the Blackfeet nation. The Kootenais lived near the lake and river of that name (spelled Kootenay in Canada) and north to the headwaters of the Columbia River. Tobacco Plains and Libby, Montana, and Bonners Ferry, Idaho, provided key campsites both summer and winter. After acquiring horses, the Kootenais became part-time occupants of the Alberta plains east to Fort Macleod, Canada, until the Piegan (Blackfeet) drove them out near the end of the 18th century. In 1780, the Kootenais numbered about 1,280 souls. The "Great Road of the Flathead," so named

---

11 [I.S.] Spirit Talk News.

12 [I.S.] Ferris Journal, Ch 48, April 13, 1833.

by David Thompson, connected today's Bonners Ferry and Sandpoint areas with the lower Pend Oreille, or Kalispel, Indians' home territory.

The Kootenai road followed the Fisher River south to the Thompson River, then southeast to the Little Bitterroot River, linking the Kootenai people with those of the upper Pend Oreille. Of course, such early "roads" were little more than crude trails that snaked around fallen trees, thick brush and soggy areas. The Indians followed game trails and rode around obstacles rather than hacking out direct line routes.

The large, allied tribe of about 5,000 Nez Perces lived on the Columbia Plateau. Their vast territory encompassed the Clearwater, the lower Salmon and Snake river drainages in Idaho, the northeast corner of Oregon and the southeast portion of Washington.

Most of the larger Indian nations, such as the Nez Perces, lacked centralized organization and divided into several different bands, each with its own independent chief. Three of these bands regularly crossed the mountains to hunt buffalo in Montana and Idaho with the Salish. Chief Cloud Piler, or Kool Kool Tilki, led the Clearwater band; Apash Wyakaikt, Flint Necklace or Looking Glass Sr., led the Washington (Asotin) band; and Chief Hohots Ilopilp led the White Bird (Idaho) band, during the early 19th century.[13]

The Flatheads and Nez Perces had established friendly ties early in the 18th century when the Nez Perce first crossed over the Clearwater Mountains into the Bitterroot Valley. Flatheads taught them various methods of hunting buffalo on the Plains.[14] This relationship led to inter-tribal marriages that formed the Nez Perce-Flathead family groups. Upward of 25 lodges lived nearly full time with the Salish, only returning to their homeland to visit and trade for horses.

The Nez Perces traveled 130 miles from today's Weippe, Idaho, across the heavily wooded and mountainous country via the Lolo Trail to the Bitterroot Valley and Flathead territory. From there hunters continued east or turned south on established trails to the area they intended to hunt. Another route, the Nez Perce Trail, went up the South Fork of the Clearwater River, turned east along a ridgeline, and then descended to Ross Hole in the Bitterroot Valley. From the main ridge, a cutoff trail meandered southeast along a spur ridge to the valley at today's North Fork of the Salmon River, Idaho.

Northern Shoshonis, another ally during the 18th century and first

---

13 McWorter, pp. 181-84.

14 Josephy, p. 19.

decade of the next, were southern neighbors of the Flatheads; they occupied buffalo prairies north to the Bow and Red Deer drainages in today's Alberta, Canada. Formerly a large tribe, their population was drastically reduced by smallpox and conflict with the southerly migrating Piegan tribe. During Lewis and Clark's visit, the tribe consisted of 100 warriors and 300 women and children.[15] From the middle of May to September, remnants of the Shoshonis took up residence in the safety of the Lemhi Valley. In the fall, they crossed the Continental Divide to the Missouri drainage and joined with the Salish and Nez Perces for buffalo hunts and the butchering process. The Shoshonis utilized the upper Beaverhead River for root digging in the spring, returning to the Lemhi in the summer to fish for salmon. Soon after Lewis and Clark visited the northern Shoshonis in 1805, the Indians abandoned their traditional territory. Presumably, the well-armed Piegans had caused further depletion of their numbers. The remaining northern Shoshonis may have been among the Sheepeaters living deep in the rugged Salmon River Mountains, or they may have moved south to the Snake River to join up with the southern Shoshonis or Bannocks. Throughout the fur trade and early settlement periods, the Shoshonis were called Snake Indians.

The Enemy

In the early 1700s, the Algonquian-dialect speaking Blackfeet[16] Nation's three-tribe home territory centered along the Saskatchewan River near today's Edmonton, Alberta, Canada. The Blackfoot (*Siksiká*) lived farther north in the patchy forestland. The Blood (*Káinaa*) tribe occupied the heart of the Blackfeet's domain. Piegans (*Piikáni*), the nation's largest tribe, inhabited the rolling plains south to Red Deer. Fur trader Alexander Henry estimated the number of warriors at 520 Blackfoot, 200 Bloods and 700 Piegans in 1809. These native peoples had access to a variety of animals for meat, but most preferred bison. Sheltered in moveable leather tepees, they spent winters in timbered coves, protected from bitter cold winds common to their country and on its vast plains for the remainder of the year.

Around 1740, the Piegans were busy building a horse herd through trade and thievery from among bordering tribes' horses.[17] Warriors spent

15 Moulton, vol. 5, p. 120, Lewis Journal, August 19, 1805.

16 The reader may stumble on the use of the word Blackfeet when proper English calls for Blackfoot. An effort was made to differentiate between the Blackfeet Nation involved in Salish activities, of which one is the Blackfoot tribe. In other words, Blackfoot does not act as the modifier, or adjective, for Blackfeet Nation.

17 Harris, pp. 229-37.

years collecting many horses ("elk dogs") and learning how to handle the frisky animals. At the same time, they began to acquire a few guns and other European items through trade with neighboring Cree and Assiniboine tribes accessing Canada's trading posts. Toward the end of the century, outsiders opened trading establishments inside Piegan domain.

Many Piegans contracted smallpox in 1781, after stealing personal belongings from a sick and dying northern Shoshoni camp at Red River, Alberta. The disease spread throughout the Blackfeet Nation and to its allies; more than 5,000 died before the epidemic ran its course. Surviving Shoshonis moved south, suffering losses far greater than the Blackfeet, and at the same time spreading the disease to other plains inhabitants. Not ready to surrender productive Bow River hunting grounds, the Shoshonis moved back there in 1784, where they massacred a small party of Piegans and placed sticks painted with snakeheads near each body to claim responsibility.

After discovering the reprehensible deed, Piegans conducted a war council involving the Blackfeet Nation where all agreed on a war of annihilation against the Shoshonis and other plains hunters: the Pend Oreilles, Flatheads, Kootenais and Nez Perces. Their plan called for killing warriors in order to capture and adopt women and children to rebuild populations lost to the odious epidemic blamed on the Shoshonis.

The revenge-driven Blackfeet hunted down the Shoshonis and drove them south toward the upper Missouri and beyond. The part-time residents of the northwestern plains relentlessly pushed the Salish and Kootenais from traditional hunting grounds, causing terrible losses. Their superior numbers, equipped with muskets and iron weapon heads, gave the Blackfeet an advantage over foes that defended themselves with primitive weapons.

The Salish, Nez Perces and Shoshonis' large, high-quality horse herds attracted marauders from great distances to their hunting camps on the plains buffalo grounds. Gros Ventres and Minnetarees (Hidatsa) living along the Missouri River in today's North Dakota, conducted raids periodically in the late 18th century and early 19th century until Blackfeet dominated the region. Equally interested in acquiring slaves, the Minnetarees captured women and children when returning to their home territory. As trappers and traders entered the Hidatsa country, they purchased some of the slave women for wives, as in the case of the famous Shoshoni Sacagawea, married to Corps of Discovery interpreter Charbonneau. In another incident before 1805, Blackfeet captured a Nez Perce girl near a

Salmon River hunting camp and later sold her to white people in Canada. She had a baby, and a stormy relationship with the father caused her to run away, babe in arms, intent on going home to her people. After several moons and the death of the infant, Watkuweis reached a Flathead village, where she received care before some villagers took her home over the mountains to the Clearwater River camp. Watkuweis told her people how well the whites had treated her, making Lewis and Clark's first meeting with the Nez Perces a friendly one.[18]

Records of abductions are rare and surface only when unusual occurrences, as described above, came about. The farming tribes of Hidatsa and Mandan had many slaves to work their fields and process buffalo hides. Young women, some growing up in their villages, became a commodity when white men appeared on the scene. In David Thompson's journey to the villages in 1798, his men bought two slave girls whom they took back to their trading post for resale.[19]

Trade

Before white traders entered Salish territory, all of the neighboring tribes participated in exchange sessions involving primitive weapons, horses, skins, provisions and much more, with some events occurring at great distances from home territory. Very few European goods had found their way to the Columbia Plateau Indians before the establishment of local posts as such items originated in far-off Spanish territories or eastern Canada. Around 1800, small numbers of metal knives, cooking pots and glass beads had filtered through the extensive trading network to the Salish. During hunting excursions to the Three Forks and Yellowstone area in Montana, the Flatheads traded with the River Crow (Absaroka) Indians. Acting as intermediaries, the Crows supplied them with metal tools, cooking pots and other items obtained from the Mandan, who from 1792 had access to European trade goods. The Flatheads exchanged a few dogs, horn bows and many horses they let go cheap; the Crows later sold some of the horses to the Gros Ventres and Mandans at double the price. By 1805, the Absaroka Crows had guns and ammunition, yet traded neither to the Flatheads.[20]

18 Ewers, pp. 28-29.

19 Wood and Thiessen, pp. 218-19.

20 Coues, p 731. According to Alexander Henry Jr., Salish compound bows were made from ram's horn wrapped by successive layers of sinew glued to the thickness of one-third of an inch, smoothed and polished on the inside. The 3-foot bow cast an arrow a long distance. Other bows made of red cedar or willow with an overlay of sinew and glue to measure 4 feet in length were weapons common to the Kootenais.

In 1805, Hudson's Bay trader François Larocque crossed the plains from Manitoba, Canada, to the Mandan villages before going west to Crow lands near today's Billings, Montana. Larocque described the Flatheads as told to him by the Crows: "Elk teeth are ... very ornamental amongst them and they will give a horse for 70 or 80 of them. ... The arrows ... used in war are poisonous and ... much smaller than those made for hunting. They generally fight on horseback and have two bows and two quivers full of arrows with which they defend themselves and greatly annoy their enemies even in flying [as in moving fast]. They are expert horsemen. They represent their country as very good[,] that what fruit trees grow here [Prior Creek, Montana] as shrubs are tall trees [in their country]. Their bows are almost all made of horns of different kinds of deer and of one piece."[21]

Nez Perce bands also crossed the Rockies with horses, beadwork and foodstuff as gifts or for trade. They and the Flatheads formed an alliance with the Crows, thus preserving access to hunt buffalo on the plains of the Yellowstone. The large tribe of River Crows controlled the lower Big Horn and Yellowstone drainages while the Mountain Crows ruled the upper Big Horn to Wind River in Wyoming. The Blackfeet were their enemies, making an alliance with the Flathead and Nez Perce workable. These buffalo hunting tribes from across the mountains received a degree of protection and refuge from the Crow nation. Peaceful coexistence between the Salish and Crows lasted until the mid-1840s when hostilities broke out on the bison hunting grounds.

Cycles of Life

Inland Salish people measured time by the seasons, months by the moons, and days by the rising and setting of the sun. Their calendar began in spring. Salish survival depended on obtaining various food supplies and adequate shelter in the right place each season. In this natural cycle, spring meant the renewal of the earth; root digging, drying and storage took place. Summer and fall embraced travel to and from hunting grounds or fishing spots. During cold and snowy winters, family members turned hides into clothes and moccasins, and fashioned bows and arrows around the fire inside the circular warmth of lodges. With hands busy, conversation rang with hope and a constant need for preparation that often turned to supplementing food supplies until spring. When winter weather closed in, men

---

21 Ibid. The Flathead use of poison arrows in warfare does not appear elsewhere in historical documents the author searched. However, wild iris plants grow abundantly in their hunting areas; after crushing the bulb, mixing it with gall bladders and applying it to arrow tips, a slight wound might take three or more days to kill a man – a painfully slow way to die.

and older boys would hunt local game or go fishing. Regular conflicts with the Blackfeet occurred throughout the year in Pend Oreille or Flathead country while other Inland Salish faced no hostilities. Thus, the cycle of seasons repeated itself over and again throughout their lives until the end of the buffalo.

The lower Pend Oreille, or Kalispel, tribe's principal camping areas included bountiful camas prairies along the Pend Oreille River from Locke upstream to today's town of Newport, both in present-day Washington state. In today's Bonner County, Idaho, some tribal people wintered near Albeni Falls while smaller family groups spread out along the Clark Fork River on the few open, sparsely timbered benches to Thompson Falls, Montana. Spring and summer found the Kalispels digging roots and fishing the region's waters. At Trout Creek and the Clark Fork River delta, fish weirs produced trout, while at today's Heron Rapids, Montana, whitefish were dipnetted in late fall. Members of the tribe made annual trips to Kettle Falls on the Columbia River in Washington State to catch and dry salmon among other tribes at the common place to fish. The Kalispel people depended more on deer and fish protein than did their buffalo-hunting cousins upriver. However, a sizeable number of the tribe made the arduous and long journey to the upper Missouri to hunt and dry buffalo meat and bring back its other useable parts. The Coeur d'Alene, Spokane and Colvilles' tribal life cycles paralleled the Kalispels' in most aspects, except fewer participated in yearly buffalo hunts.

Much of the upper Pend Oreilles' living space above Thompson Falls received less precipitation where expansive prairies emerged, providing year-round horse pasturage in valleys along the Clark Fork and Flathead rivers. Minimal snowfall and early melt-off describes some winter weather conditions along the river below Montana's Jocko River. From April to July, women dug camas and bitterroots, drying what they could carry for winter use. In July, most of the Pend Oreilles traveled to the buffalo grounds to put up winter supplies of meat.

The Flatheads' life cycle paralleled that of their neighbors to the north, whom they often joined to hunt buffalo. Their Bitterroot Valley home contained several vast prairies covered with excellent grasses for pasture. Primary camping areas existed near today's Missoula, Lolo and Stevensville, Montana. The valley also provided several camas and bitterroot meadows in addition to various berry bushes.

Not all members of the upper Pend Oreilles went to the buffalo; a few lived year-round along the Flathead and Clark Fork rivers in small family groups or in single families. They subsisted on mountain game, fish, roots and berries. Many did not own a horse but traveled on foot or by bark canoe. Each year around December 1, families considered poor by some of their tribe met at Horse Plains (today's Plains, Montana) to trade with Hudson's Bay Company and other Indians. The Pend Oreille sought dried buffalo meat from other Indians in exchange for dried roots and berries.

Trapper Warren Ferris described the breakup of one such trading session: "I was greatly deceived in the canoes for the squaws would lift them from the water onto the bank, and again set them into it, with such ease that I imagined [the canoe] must be quite insufficient to the transportation of any heavy burden. Some of them, however appeared loaded until there was no longer room for anything more, and still floated securely. They were managed by the squaws, who with paddles, direct their course with great steadiness, astonishing rapidity and apparent ease and dexterity."[22]

The Inland Salish clothing, shelter and customs varied little from other Columbia Plateau and Rocky Mountain plains Indians in the 19th century's first half. In writing about their experiences in the vast Western mountains, fur traders and trappers held high regard for the Flatheads and Pend Oreilles collectively, and rated their character superior to other Indian nations in honesty, hospitality, bravery, leadership, morality and cleanliness. Qualities that separated the Salish from other natives during the fur trade follow, after a brief look at their living conditions.

Dress

William Clark noted Flatheads' appearance at his late summer meeting with the tribe in 1805. Men tied (cowed) their shoulder-length hair with otter skin strips. Women's hair fell loosely over their shoulder and face "promiscuously" and they wore ankle-length skin dresses belted at the waist and colorfully decorated with a few dyed porcupine quills and beads.[23]

Trader Ross Cox[24] and trapper Warren Ferris described Salish dress based on observations made in 1813 and 1832 respectively. During this time span, the influx of trade goods had minimal effect on their basic garments, except more beads, hawk bells and ribbons decorated clothing. According to Cox, both sexes were fair-skinned and remarkably well-made and slender. Men's winter attire of tanned deerskin leggings reached from the ankles to the hips, fastened by a leather belt. A shirt of dressed deerskin with loose hanging sleeves fell to their knees with leather-strip fringes on

22 [I.S.] *Ferris Journal*, Ch 45, December 13, 1833.

23 Moulton, vol. 5, *Lewis and Clark Journal*, p. 188.

24 Cox, p. 122.

Mat lodges were utilized by many Kalispels, Spokanes, Colville and Coeur d'Alene Indians. COURTESY MANSFIELD LIBRARY, UNIVERSITY OF MONTANA

both leggings and shirts. Women wore loose robes of dressed sheep or deerskins that reached from neck to feet, ornamented with fringes, beads, porcupine quills and thimbles. Highly prized trade items of European cut-glass beads found their way to the Salish in late 1700s through barter with other tribes. No permanent covering for the head existed, except in cold weather, when a buffalo robe wrapped high above the neckline sufficed. Both sexes used local pipe clay[25] to clean clothing regularly, and everyone had two or three changes. During hot weather, men stripped down to a breechcloth that covered their privates. Buffalo hide moccasins to mid-calf provided footwear for all.

Twenty years later, Ferris provided his description:[26] "Salish features are seldom ugly, often pleasant and smiles exhibit beautiful white, even teeth. Of medium stature, straight and well-proportioned, black hair flowing over their shoulders and for a few longer yet." Ferris noted leggings and shirts ornamented with small blue and white beads, a few human hairs taken from enemy scalps dyed various colors, and leather fringe along seams. Wealthier braves and some women began to wear brightly colored cloth tops made from trade fabric and wool blankets in the mid-1830s.

Women's garments differed in the number of large beads used to decorate long gowns around the neck and shoulders. Sometimes dresses were loaded with 8 to 10 pounds of large cut-glass beads. Leggings and tops of moccasins also had beadwork, and some added a leather belt around their waist.

25 Ibid. Pipe clay, common to the Indians' territory, originated from finely ground glaciated soil and often whitish mixed with water into a thick solution to be rubbed on the skin garment and allowed to dry in the sun, after which it is rubbed until pliable and soft. When complete the garment takes on the color of the clay and is free of all soil and grease spots.

26 [I.S.] *Ferris Journal*, Ch 51, December 13, 1833.

"Water for Camp," a photographic reproduction of a painting by Charles M. Russell, shows lodges typical of the buffalo hunting Inland Salish. The arrangement of tepees, the men sitting in a circle playing games while the women carry water for preparing dinner was a common scene in an Indian camp. COURTESY WIKIMEDIA COMMONS

Shelter

Most Flatheads and Pend Oreilles lived in buffalo, elk or moose hide tepees, or lodges as the fur men called them. These conical structures, supported by 12 to 14 lodgepoles depending on size, provided spacious and comfortable quarters in wet and cold weather. The interior had a central firepit for cooking and heating that vented through a small opening at the top of the lodge. Clean and dressed hides covered the ground around the fire pit.

In moving camp, a travois of two bundles of four to six lodgepoles attached to a saddled horse dragged personal belongings wrapped in hides and lashed to these poles. When terrain allowed, one horse could transport a load of 150 pounds this way. When crossing rough country, packhorses carried belongings. Eight to 10 horses and several travois were required to move family possessions. Indian camps with tepees, each set up on 65-foot centers, required nearly 20 acres of flat terrain near water and wood to accommodate a village of 120 lodges. The Salish moved all their belongings to and from regular campsites according to the season in quest of food, pasturage, safety and wintering grounds. The non-buffalo-hunting elements of the Coeur d'Alenes, Kalispels (lower Pend Oreilles) and most of the anadromous fish-dependent Spokanes lived in semipermanent structures made of wood frames covered by tule mats of cattail reeds. Residents of these abodes, principally near Fort Spokane, periodically abandoned them for several weeks each year to hunt deer and socialize, gamble and dance with other Indians. Upon return, hunters could easily repair those dwellings needing upkeep.

Foods

Upon white man's arrival, Salish lands provided ample provisions that included deer, elk, moose, bighorn sheep, goats, ducks, geese and fish. Despite abundant foodstuffs in their region, Salish members of all five tribes made annual trips to the prairies on the east side of the Continental Divide to hunt buffalo. There, they dried the meat and transported the 80-pound sacks on packhorses, back to home territory for winter use and trade. Non-buffalo-hunting Coeur d'Alenes lived on fish, roots and venison in their home territory. The Spokanes dried fresh foodstuffs for winter use and depended on homeland salmon and steelhead runs for a large portion of their food supply. The Salish did not farm until white men taught them how, and then only sparingly. Throughout their territory, the Salish gathered various root crops and berries from wide and wet prairies thick with indispensable stands of the blue-flowered camas plant.[27]

Women dug the camas roots each summer, a staple they boiled or baked in earthen ovens before stoning it by crushing it to a coarse meal, then formed cakes and dried them on split wooden frames.[28] The bitterroot plant produced a small white bulb women boiled to a jelly-like state to which they added berries to make a rather stiff mixture they then baked into cakes. The common wild onion and carrot, when used to garnish meats, proved more palatable to white man's tastes. Branches on old-growth fir often provided a lichen growth used to make a type of panbread. Many varieties of berries rounded off their diet: hawthorn and huckleberry, service and snowberry, chokecherries and whortleberries. Rare wild plum trees grew only along the Jocko River in one grove that provided a delicacy for the locals who got there first. Cooking involved boiling or roasting. Most white fur men never developed a taste for lichen bread or bitterroot concoctions. John Wyeth said of Flathead preparation of one meal: "They will pick a goose or brant, and run a stick through its body, and so roast it, without taking out its entralls [*sic*]. They are, according to our notions, very

27 Camas is a plant with grassy leaves and an edible bulb. Blue and white flowers grow in clusters. Native to North America, its Latin name is *Camassia quamash*.

28 Boas and Teit, p. 57.

nasty cooks."[29]

Regardless of the variety of all food resources in their backyard, for meat and other uses, most Flatheads and Pend Oreille favored bison and its many practical parts, so they traveled hundreds of miles over mountains into hostile country to harvest them. Each summer all able-bodied men, women and children, accompanied by other Inland Salish, made the seasonal trip to bring back thousands of pounds of dried buffalo meat, fat and other parts for winter use and trade.

Language

Most Indians, from the Crows and Blackfeet in the Western Plains to the tribes near the Pacific Ocean, could communicate in a Salish dialect in its simplest form. White men who worked to master the language, such as Jesuit Priest Gregory Mengarini, found it complicated. He wrote, "[It's] brevity of expression carried to an excess."[30] For instance, *Skumcne* means "Waters of the Pocket Gopher" which in English is the "Big Hole." Salish for the Bitterroot River, *Nstetee x etk*, meant "Waters of Red Osier Dogwood."[31]

Mengarini found the Indians' pronunciation of individual words difficult to understand, and when two to four words were combined to make a phrase, a further obstacle in mastering the language emerged. The Salish spoke to Indians of other tribes and white men using a word or two, which constituted a simple phrase; however, among themselves, their speech was broken, and extremely terse to the white man's ear. Once "the language is fully understood," Mengarini wrote, "it has richness in vocabulary unequaled by other languages."[32]

The Inland Salish people always spoke slowly and carefully in a low voice and rarely showed emotions, as they considered a loudly pitched voice to show anger and melancholy – an ill-bred behavior. Among equals or superiors one might interject little jokes, which may bring a smile, but rarely would they laugh aloud.[33] When speaking to people with a different language, the Indian was somewhat solemn, pronouncing each word in a proper tone, accompanied with hand gestures, synchronized with thoughts as sign language. In this way, individuals of different dialects or languages

29 [I.S.] Wyeth, John, Ch. 4.
30 Mengarini, p. 145.
31 Salish, p. 40.
32 Mengarini, p. 146.
33 Point, p. 147.

could make themselves understandable to each other.[34] In many ways, their style of dialogue reflected a serious, analytical and resolute character. Women conversed in a similar manner. Despite having immense responsibilities and hardships, they seldom showed impatience.

Music

Similar to other tribes, the Salish had their own music that distinguished them from distant or different local tribes. A simple series of quarter notes, with little variance in pitch, each given the same emphasis to the beat of a drum, formed the foundation of their music. Besides drums, they used the flageolet,[35] a small flute blown from the end with two thumbholes for creating notes. Mengarini suggests musicians played moderately fast. The Salish relished dances in which women participated, such as the Blue Jay, Scalp, and Profit or Skull Bounce, without words or structure. Singing in the simple vowels a, i and e, either in combination or individually, in one four-note phrases may be "ie, ie, ie, ie," followed by three notes "e, ia, a" and then four notes, "a-i-i-e." The war dance inspired courage among braves when preparing to fight their enemies.[36]

Salish Culture

Basic duties of the sexes varied little among Rocky Mountain tribes. Men provided leadership and protection, hunted and carried in game, tended and packed horses, and made weapons for war. All other village duties fell to women. When men completed their daily tasks, they sat around camp, played games and raced horses. Salish men were incurably addicted to gambling, to the extent individuals often lost everything they owned. Women's chores included putting up and taking down the lodge, drying meat, gathering roots and berries, preparing meals, processing hides, and nurturing younger children. Salish women endured much and worked hard from quite young, and by age 35, they looked worn out for their years.

Father Nicolas Point described women's role in traveling to and from the hunting grounds between December 29, 1841, and April 1842. Their route followed the Clark Fork River. "During the march to the hunting grounds, the women are in charge of the baggage. To keep the pack animals together and moving forward, they were obliged to run up and down along the line of [the] march. All the while, the women must

34 Ibid.

35 Flageolet is a musical instrument of the 16th and 17th centuries, resembling the flute.

36 Mengarini, p. 200.

also care for the children who are too young to fend for themselves. When a pole works loose, or a horse stumbles, becomes mired or loses his load, the women must dismount and take care of the problem. Dismounting is in itself complicated by the fact that the saddles are raised [front and back], by a sort of platform more than a foot high. When the company reaches a campsite, the women are obliged to erect the lodges, cut the wood and prepare the food. They must do this in spite of fatigue, injuries, illness or even increases in their families. But, remarkably, during the entire course of the hunt, a period of three months, not ... one of them showed any impatience. ... After the women, the Great Chief has the most responsibility on his shoulders."[37]

Mothers of most Salish children gave their newborns the name of the first object they touched after birth, such as dry wood, sand, old shoe, or on rare occasions an ancestral name. The child carried the name until he or she found an individual spirit power and then assumed the name of that animal or object as his or her lifelong guardian. Individual Salish boys went into seclusion for a few days to find their guardian or spirit. Girls did the same but under guard for protection. During the course of several days of contemplation, a vision appeared in the form of an animal, natural object or event. The guardian spirit told the child it had taken pity on him or her and would be its protector. The spirit described the powers granted and what to put in his or her sacred bundle or medicine bag.[38] The child, having received its "spirit power," returned to its family and forever after carried the small leather pouch containing articles prescribed by the guardian spirit around its neck. The white man called these very personal and private items "medicine," but the Indians did not.

Entertainment

Nathaniel Wyeth noted in his journal: "The Indians appear to enjoy their amusements with more zest than the whites, although they are simple. They are great gamblers in proportion to their means, bolder than whites."[39]

Trapper Warren Ferris described the Flatheads' favorite game, called "Hand" by fur hunters: "Bettors, provided with small sticks, beat time to a song in which they all join. Four or more players and bettors seat themselves opposite to their antagonists, and two players, one on each side, who are provided each with two small bones, one called the true, and other false, open the game. These bones were shifted from hand to hand a

37 Point, p. 145.
38 Cebula, p. 14.
39 [I.S.] Wyeth Journal, May 1, 1833.

few times, with great dexterity, and then each player held his closed hands stretched out in front, for his respective opponents to guess 'which one' by pointing a finger. Should one of them chance to guess right and the other wrong, the first is entitled to both true bones and to one point in the game. Points are marked by twenty small sharp sticks, which are stuck into the ground and paid back and forth until one side has won them all, and the game ends. The lucky player, who has obtained both true bones, immediately gives one to a comrade, and all the players on his side join in a song with the bones concealed in closed hand. Should the guesser on the opposing side miss both the true bones, he pays two points and tries again; should he miss only one, he pays one point. When he guesses them both, he commences singing and hiding the bones, and so the game continues until one or other of the parties win."[40]

Women also relished gaming and played Hand and another game, exclusive to their sex, but at much lower stakes. Four 8-inch-long bones were marked on one side with common figures and thrown forward on a spread-out buffalo robe. If the unmarked sides of all four landed up, they counted four points and were thrown again. If two sides of the same figure and two unmarked ones landed upright, they counted two points. If only one figure turned upright, they counted nothing, and the opposing party took the bones and repeated the process. The winner became the player who got the prearranged number of points first.

Another game portrayed by both Ferris and fur trader Nathaniel Wyeth,[41] named "Roulette" by French trappers, involved two players, and a 2- or 3-inch ring with beads of various colors fastened to the inside. A third man had to roll the ring along a course 15 feet long by 3 feet wide, while the two players, opposite each other, kept pace with the rolling ring and tried to throw an arrow behind and/or under the ring. When the hoop stopped, it rested on one arrow. Each colored bead on the ring had a different value and only counted when directly over the arrow. The third man counted points by small sticks, which he laid on the ground or held in his hand, until reaching the predetermined number, which in turn determined the winner.

Expert equestrians, the Salish people favored horseracing in a dangerous manner far different from today. In shorter races attention did not focus on the start, but on the rider who came in first – the winner. Sometimes longer races involved only a finish line with no pre-determined route

40 [I.S.] Ferris Journal, Ch. 15, May 30, 1831.
41 [I.S.] - Wyeth Journal, April 30, 1833.

established. He who took the lead set the route, until another passed him. This rider might change the route until another passed, and so on, until the finish. These risky races usually went in favor of horsemanship, rather than the horse's speed. Group races often involved many mounted horses running to a certain point and back, with the foremost rider winning all bets.

Organization

Salish government operated under leadership of separate tribal head chiefs and councils of subchiefs and elders when fur traders arrived in 1809. Usually hereditary, head chiefs made decisions on campground arrangements, led tribal movement, addressed personal moral issues and, in most cases, provided leadership during war; otherwise, they did not give orders. Mengarini defined their government as "anarchic-monarchy,"[42] in a tribal venture or not. White men, particularly missionaries involved with a well-defined pecking-order type organization, had a difficult time coping with the Indian form of democracy.

Subchief authority was in name only, except for those at the head of several family groups – sometimes referred to as a band. Tribal elders acted as advisers to the head chief when asked. Selected from the best in the tribe, 20 young warriors were always prepared to follow the war chief or hunt master. All of these positions had subtitles. Laws concerning good and evil and codes of conduct were familiar to Salish citizens from an early age, passed on by family members and leaders. Most citizen Indians adhered to such verbal traditions and were submissive toward their leaders. Penalties for infractions ranged from public scolding by the chief to flogging with a whip or paying goods to the wronged person. Otherwise the individual was absolute master over himself. Strong Salish leadership accepted many of the white man's laws and Christian ideals throughout the fur trade period, thus expanding their unwritten law.

Due to constant warfare with the Blackfeet on the buffalo grounds, the Flathead established the elected position of war chief. Tribal members voted each year after the fall hunt for the warrior who showed the greatest wisdom, strength and bravery combined. This arrangement lasted throughout the fur trade era. In 1814, a 35-year-old upper Pend Oreille who held this position five years won the election for another year.

He had killed 20 Blackfeet in various battles and proudly displayed their scalps on the door of his lodge. Ross Cox described his position: "This 'war chief,' as they termed him, has no authority whatever when at home,

---

42 Mengarini, p. 201.

and is as equally amenable as any of the tribe to the hereditary chief; but when the warriors set out on their hunting excursions to the buffalo plains, he assumes the supreme command, which he exercises with despotic sway until their return. He carries a long whip with a thick handle decorated with scalps and feathers and generally appoints two active warriors as aides-de-camp. On their advance toward the enemy, he always takes the lead; and on their return brings up the rear."[43] The war chief used his whip in an impartial manner when a man breached discipline. Both the recipient of the drubbing and other braves considered this treatment a public duty and never complained or attacked in retaliation.

Leadership

The Salish people had strong and effective leaders all through the fur trade period. Acquisition of guns during the period and development of defensive techniques checked the powerful Blackfeet enemies from committing wholesale slaughter of the Salish. By joining forces, tribes and allies discouraged thunderous attacks of the past. During trader David Thompson's time, the Salish adopted a policy to fight only a defensive battle and never be the aggressor. Taught from an early age, warriors were "never to go out and hunt their own graves."[44] Adhering to this policy, their excellence in bravery, skill and devotion proved superior in warfare. Father Mengarini wrote, "Flathead bravery and openness in war have always rendered them as formidable opponents to their enemies, whatever nation they might be."[45]

Big Hawk (Skuti-hlá) is the earliest known head chief of the Flathead who led during the last decade of the 1700s, before braves had guns. A Kootenai by birth, Big Hawk and his mother settled among the Flathead after smallpox decimated his band.[46] His tenure was short-lived. The Piegans treacherously murdered Big Hawk at a supposedly friendly meeting on the buffalo grounds of the upper Missouri.

About 1795, when left without a leader in dangerous country, the Flathead council met and elected Three Eagles (Chihiz-Skalyimi) to lead them, who was possibly the son of Big Hawk. He and his tribe met with explorers Lewis and Clark in the Bitterroot Valley in 1805,[47] and afterward guided them during the early years of the fur trade. It is unknown when

---

43 Cox, p. 122.
44 White.
45 Mengarini, p. 160.
46 Curtis, vol. 17, p. 44.
47 Moulton, vol. 5, Lewis Journal, p. 187.

Three Eagles died or a transfer of power occurred.

Big Face (Tjolzhitzy)[48] so called because of an elongated face, followed as principal chief of the Flathead. He guided his people during some of the tribe's most difficult years, never giving up their ancestral hunting grounds to the Blackfeet. Blessed with natural piety, wisdom, patience, courage and cool disposition in the hour of danger, he won the respect and obedience of his followers. Big Face was the first Salish baptized (Paul) by Father Pierre-Jean De Smet at Pierre's Hole. Orphaned as a child, soon after birth when his mother died, he was nurtured by another woman. Possessing gratitude, the young man, more than once, placed his trust in the Great Spirit (Kyleeyou) to help with a predicament. His prayer was, "Oh Great Spirit, you who see all things and undo all things, grant, I entrust you, that I may find what I am looking for; and yet let thy will be done."[49] The great old chief lived into his late 80s and died in 1841.

Fur men coined names for the Indians, usually in the French language, often based on a personality or physical feature. In 1810, David Thompson named a principal chief of the lower Pend Oreille Le Bon Vieux (Good Old Man), another head chief Cartier (a Canadian acquaintance) and a subchief Orator, who together guided the upper Pend Oreille tribe.[50] Thompson used the Salish vocabulary only once to identify Cartier as Chinalamal.[51] Among the upper Pend Oreille's earliest leaders, according to Big Canoe, were Head Chief Celp-Stop (Crazy Country) and War Chief Big Smoke.[52] John Work mentions Flathead Chiefs Gros Pied (Big Feet) in 1825 and Grand Visage (Big Face), while Wyeth and Ferris in their time called the upper Pend Oreille Head Chief Walking Bear "Guignon" (French for "bad luck").[53]

Victor (1795-1870), called Mitt-to (Many Horses) by the Indians, followed as head chief of the Flatheads in 1842 and led them through most of the buffalo-robe portion of the fur trade. Mitt-to, a son of Three Eagles was a good-sized boy when Lewis and Clark passed through in 1805. He rose to that position by election of his tribe, which admired his leadership in the first year of the Catholic St. Mary's Mission in the Bitterroot Valley. Father Pierre-Jean De Smet, who established the mission, believed he won the vote "for no other reason" than "for the noble qualities, both of heart

48 [I.S.], Chittenden & Richardson, vol. 1, p 326 - De Smet.
49 Ibid. p. 226.
50 Jack Nisbet, The Mapmaker's Eye, p. 121.
51 Ibid. (or Chemalamale) p. 79.
52 Ronan, pp. 73-76.
53 [I.S.] Wyeth Journal, May 10, 1833.

and head, which they all thought he possessed."[54] Victor died of sickness on a summer hunt near Three Buttes, Montana, in 1870. His son, Charlot, or Charlo, succeeded him.

During much of the fur trade era, Walking Bear led the upper Pend Oreille. Father De Smet baptized him Peter[55] at Pierre's Hole in 1840, at a gathering of nearly the entire Salish nation. Before his baptism, De Smet urged the old chief to repent of his sins. The chief said: "When I was young and even as I became old, I was plunged in profound ignorance of good and evil, and in that period I must no doubt have displeased the Great Spirit; I sincerely implore pardon of him. But every time I have perceived that a thing was bad, I have at once banished it from my heart. I do not remember ever in my life to have deliberately offended the Great Spirit."[56] Estimated to be in his 80s, Walking Bear's death occurred before the end of 1840, soon after the baptism.

Walking Bear's successor appears to have been Selpisto, baptized Constantin by Father De Smet. In November 1846, Priest Nicolas Point reported he met with both the former and current great chiefs of the Pend Oreilles. Constantin, a religious man, had led his people to several victories over the Blackfeet, during which he lost two sons in battle. Shortly afterward, Constantin judged another man more worthy and capable than himself to be head chief and resigned in favor of Pierre George.[57] In 1890, Indian Agent Peter Ronan named Joseph as preceding Great Chief Alexander,[58] indicating that two men held this position in a six- to eight-year span.

Alexander (Tum-cle-hot-cut-se, or No Horses) succeeded to leadership of the upper Pend Oreilles in 1848. Selected by his tribe and mission priests, Alexander participated in both the Blackfeet and Flathead Treaty negotiations in 1855. Considered by his people as a courageous, aggressive and strict leader, he was never challenged by any tribal member. He was born in 1809, of a Shoshoni father and a Pend Oreille mother, and died in 1868.[59]

Standing Grizzly Bear (about 1790-1856), baptized Loyola by Priest Joseph Joset, led the lower Pend Oreilles (Kalispels) through much of the early fur trade.[60] He and many of his people made annual treks to buffalo country, joining up with Salish cousins upriver. After Catholic missionaries

54 Bigart and Woodcock, p. 69.
55 [I.S.] Chittenden & Richardson, p. 318.
56 Ibid. vol. 1, pp. 226-27 & 325-26, De Smet Letters.
57 Point, p. 206.
58 Ronan, p. 73.
59 Bigart and Woodcock, p. 69.
60 Ibid. pp. 68-69.

established St. Ignatius near today's Usk, Washington, he gave up buffalo hunting to tend his small farm.[61] Poor soil and severe winters made farming difficult, prompting missionaries and many of the tribe to relocate the mission to Montana in 1854. The great chief clung to his ancestral home, as did some of his followers. The area around Cusick eventually became a small Kalispel reservation. Standing Grizzly Bear and some of those closer to him refused to move, saying God gave them this land and they ought to keep it.[62] Victor (Pitol), who is not to be confused with the Flathead Chief Mitt-to, succeeded Standing Grizzly Bear as chief of the Kalispels. Chief Masselow followed Victor.

When Spokane Chief Garry was a young man of 14, his father, Head Chief Ileum, sent him with Governor George Simpson of the Hudson's Bay Company to attend school at Red River in Canada, where he learned to read, write and practice agriculture. When Garry returned to his people in 1830, he attempted to teach them what he had learned, but most of the Spokanes resisted the move to white man's culture. Soon, the discouraged Garry stopped trying to teach reading and writing and took up old ways. He had better luck teaching agricultural means to the tribe, for many took to raising potatoes and other vegetables and grain. As white settlers made inroads in the region, the Spokanes feared they would take away their lands and began talk of war. Garry, in an 1855 council meeting with Territorial Governor Isaac Stevens, eloquently laid out the regional tribes' concerns and what could be done to prevent war. Garry's warning to fellow tribesmen not to make war on powerful white men fell on deaf ears for a part of the tribe. The conflict that followed had a disastrous effect on the entire tribe and their Coeur d'Alene allies.

Two noteworthy Coeur d'Alene head chiefs, Stellam and Andrew Seltice, played different roles in the tribe's history. The former was a leader in the losing war effort and gave up his status to a more peaceful Andrew Seltice, who negotiated an agreement that established the Coeur d'Alene reservation.

Subchiefs and shamans all rose to their positions through merit of deed and tribal or band members' greatest respect. Among important qualities that determined a leader were good sense and equally good verbal communication skills, piety and patience, honesty and courage. Theoretically, any young Salish man had the opportunity to rise to tribal leadership. Every chief possessed "good medicine," meaning he maintained a correct,

---

61 [I.S.] Ellersick Manuscript.

62 [I.S.] Ellersick Manuscript.

natural relationship or harmony with all things, including men. Each possessed at least a few medicinal traits such as spiritual leader, prophet and primitive doctor.

Some Indians possessed more spirit power than did others and became shamans, or medicine men and women. The use of herbs in remedies and of sweat baths often cured mild illnesses. A more serious malady may have involved a ceremony staged at the patient's lodge, where spectators sang and beat lodgepoles with sticks. At the same time, the medicine man chanted, poked and prodded the patient, sometimes bending over to suck out the sickness or bad spirits. These processes could go on for days until the patient regained his health or died.[63] Wood used to immobilize fractured limbs often proved successful. Pelchimo, a Flathead subchief and well-known warrior, also held prestige as a horse doctor/medicine man. Major John Owen, who purchased St. Mary's Mission when it closed in 1850, entrusted Pelchimo to treat his sick and injured horses. Owen and fellow tribesmen utilized his expertise in training horses.

Spirit power among a few shamans enabled them to predict future events. The Flathead Bear Track was one such medicine man who, during an unsuccessful buffalo hunt, told the people to erect a long tent. Making his medicine, he said to the audience: "My power [spirit] I received from a white buffalo calf. The buffalo are coming, and that calf will be in the lead." The next day a herd of bison appeared, led by a white calf. Tradition says that Bear Track had the power to foresee approaching enemy horse thieves so he could warn his people in advance, and he could predict results of battles.[64]

A few other native leaders mentioned in this text follow:[65]

Flatheads: Crawling Mountain, Moise (1794-March 1868), Ste-it-tish-lutse baptized Moses by De Smet and called "Bravest of the Brave" by him. He likely became a lead warrior in the 1830s.

Little Chief, Red Feather, Insula (about 1800-1860) was the son of a Nez Perce mother and Flathead father. Small in stature, brave at heart, with exceptional verbal skills, he led his people in battle and religious events in numerous instances. Asked to be head chief of the Nez Perce Salmon River band, he refused, saying he was born among the Flatheads and would die with them. De Smet had baptized him Michael.

Five Crows, baptized Ambrose (died about 1870) was a composed, brave warrior and lead buffalo hunter of the Flathead tribe.

Big Canoe, In-er-cul-say (1790-1882) was the upper Pend Oreilles'

---

63 Cebula, p. 14.

64 Bigart and Woodcock, p. 89, footnote Teit, 1930, pp. 384-85.

65 Ibid. pp. 76-77.

most celebrated war chief, who likely rose to that position in the 1820s. His battles against enemies would fill a volume.

Salish Character

The friendly character and demeanor of the Salish distinguished them from many other Indian nations in fur trading areas. Clearly recognized by both British and American interests, these Indian tribes stood out as favorites of the white men in the Mountain West and Plains. From the first meeting with Lewis and Clark in 1805 until the 1860s, the Salish neither harmed nor killed a white man. No member of any other tribe was trusted to deliver important letters several hundreds of miles away through hostile territory to an uncertain location, or to watch over a valuable storeroom of trade goods for months on end. Nor were other tribes hired to transport thousands of dollars' worth of hides from distant trapping areas to a safe base. Fur men never sought other tribes for refuge and protection from marauding Blackfeet while in hostile trapping lands. The Salish's trustworthy performance helped British and American fur traders profit from business operations.

Fur men, in writing their own personal experiences with the Pend Oreilles, Flatheads and Kalispels, held the highest regard for their character. Both the British and Americans, who lived with them for three weeks or more, noted traits that separated the Salish from other tribes with whom they dealt. A curious consistency exists among the various writers' remarks throughout the fur trade period. Examples of distinct Salish qualities follow in each journalist's own words.

Upon his return from the long trip in 1806, a member of the Lewis and Clark expedition, Sergeant Patrick Gass, commented on Salish morality, "To the honor of the Flathead, ... we must mention them as an exception; as they do not exhibit those loose feelings of carnal desire, nor appear addicted to the common customs of prostitution; and they are the only Nation on the whole route where anything like chastity is regarded."[66]

Under similar circumstances, David Thompson of the Canadian North West Company, in 1810, offered the following on Salish and their personal values: "[They] ... are a very different race of people from those on the east side [of the Continental Divide]. Those on the west side [of the Divide] pride themselves on their industry and their skill in doing anything and are as neat in their persons as circumstances allow."[67] Years later the

66 Mac Gregor, p 170, Gass Journal, March 21, 1806.

67 Hopwood, Thompson Travels p. 262.

following lines from his memoirs speak for him, "They were a fine race of moral Indians, the finest I had seen, and set a high value on the chastity of their women, adultry [*sic*] is death to both parties."[68]

While living with the Salish during the winter of 1813-14, NWC trader Ross Cox wrote: "The Flathead have fewer failures than any of the tribes I ever met. ... They are honest in their dealings, brave in the field, quiet and amenable to their chief, fond of cleanliness and decided enemies to falsehood of every description."[69]

Trader Nathaniel Wyeth wrote in 1833: "They [the Pend Oreilles and Flatheads] have a mild playful laughing disposition and their qualities are strongly portrayed in their countenance. They are polite and unobtrusive and however poor never beg except as pay for services and in this way they are moderate and faithful, but not industrious. ... When one speaks the rest pay strict attention. When he is done another assents by yes or dissents by no and then states his reasons that are heard as attentively. ... The more peaceable dispositions of the Indians than the whites are plainly seen in the children. I have never heard an angry word among them nor any quarrelling altho [*sic*] there are here at least 500 of them together and at play the whole time at football bandy and the like sports which give occasion to so many quarrels among white children."[70]

Catholic missionaries and Jesuit priests Nicolas Point and Gregory Mengarini both commented in their memoirs on Flathead traits during the period of 1841 to 1850. On separate occasions, each accompanied the Salish on summer and winter buffalo hunts in addition to their duties at the mission. After eight years among the Flatheads, Father Mengarini summarized their customary traits: "[Treachery] is unknown to them. [They have] a horror of theft and lying, vices innate in other savages; fine moral qualities, hospitality, generosity and justice."[71]

Mengarini also noticed the Flathead nonacceptance of European cultural traits and values taught by the missionaries that involved "hatred, revenge, jealousy, inconsistence, insubordination, gluttony, gambling, sloth and disregard for the education of their children."

Father Point's assignments included two years with the Flathead, a

68 Ibid. Thompson Travels, p. 264.

69 Cox, p. 121. Cox calls the Salish "Flatheads." The NWC Salish Post was located in upper Pend Oreille territory. His contact with other tribes included the Kootenais, Nez Perce, Okanogans, Sanpoils, Yakamas and coastal tribes.

70 [I.S.], Wyeth Journal, April 30, 1833. Wyeth came to the mountains with a full complement of men and supplies in 1832. His experience with Indians during his first year included Shoshonis, Bannocks and Salish.

71 Mengarini, p. 170.

four-year mission among the Coeur d'Alenes and nine months in Blackfeet country. Based on experience among the three nations he wrote: "Among the Blackfeet and the Coeur d'Alene there are many who are in no way inferior to the generally superior Flatheads. However, it would undoubtedly be correct to maintain that among the Flatheads one rather usually finds the virtues of modesty, frankness, courage, goodness and generosity. On the contrary, the Coeur d'Alene are noted for dissimulation, egotism and criticism. The Blackfeet are notorious for being bloodthirsty and ... well-known for pillaging. These are the principle [*sic*] traits which have earned for the Flathead the appellation of 'the nation of chiefs' and for the others, the opprobrious [disgrace attached to shameful conduct] name still applied to them."[72]

Fathers Point and Mengarini abhorred the way men of all Indian nations treated women. Mengarini wrote that men generally had but one wife, but "changed them so casually as another might change a pair of shoes which hurt his feet."[73] A Salish-style divorce involved a wife simply leaving her husband with all her possessions, including the lodge and everything in it, except weapons and his *Sumesh*, or medicine, bag. Though not wide-spread, polygamy occurred more often during the fur trading days before missionaries arrived on the scene, done so for status and economic reasons. Influenced by a desire for white man's goods, the practice also supplied more women's hands to process hides for eventual trade.[74]

Married women's rigorous role in Salish society coupled with a harsh or cruel husband led to occasional suicides. Most of these tragic events ended with the woman hanging herself. Incidents of this nature occurred more often among women in plural marriages. Canadian fur trader Peter Skene Ogden callously noted such an event while on a trapping expedition in 1825: "[On] this day one of our [Flathead] guides' wives, as he has three and can afford to lose one, in a fit of jealousy committed suicide by hanging herself. This is the second instance of this kind since we started. This woman has left four young children who no doubt will experience the inconveniance [*sic*] of being without their mother."[75]

Honesty

Honesty, a longtime and ingrained virtue of the Salish, earned special notice from early white men who placed integrity at the top of their

72 Point, pp. 11-12.
73 Mengarini, p. 170.
74 Ibid. and Turner- High p. 89-96.
75 Rich, p. 70, Ogden Journal, July 30, 1825.

attributes throughout the fur trade period. In initial years of trade with NWC, the American fur trader Charles Courtin and a party of Flatheads had just departed on a buffalo hunt when the Blackfeet attacked and killed Courtin. The Flatheads contacted David Thompson, who adjudicated Courtin's estate[76] by dividing the hides among the employees. In similar situations, tribes other than Salish appropriated the property.

In 1832 at Pierre's Hole Rendezvous, trapper John Ball and others had purchased horses from the Salish, of which Ball wrote: "When we had purchased a horse and it ... got back into the immense herd, we could never have reclaimed it, or perhaps known it if seen, but they would bring them back to us, and again and again, if needed. And if any of our property, tools or camp things seemed lost, they would bring them to us. [They] were in all things orderly, peaceful and kind."[77]

John B. Wyeth, a packer and cousin of Nathaniel Wyeth, came to similar conclusions at the same rendezvous. "The Flathead Indians are a brave and, we had reason to believe, a sincere people. We had many instances of their honesty and humanity."[78]

Numerous participants in the fur trade wrote of thievery and murder committed by Indian tribes on whites, such as the Blackfeet, Crows and Snakes (Shoshonis). At the 1832 rendezvous, trapper Zenas Leonard commented, "[C]ustoms of the Snake Indians are very similar to those of the Flathead, with the exception of stealing, which they consider no harm."[79]

Finally, Trapper Warren Ferris summed up Salish qualities of honesty and decency in an 1831 journal entry: "They are the only tribe in the Rocky Mountains that can with truth boast of the fact that they have never killed or robbed a white man, nor stolen a single horse, how great soever the necessity and the temptation. I have since the time mentioned here, been often employed in trading and traveling with them and never known one to steal so much as a[n] awl-blade. Every other tribe in the Rocky Mountains holds theft rather in the light of virtue than a fault, and many even pride themselves on their dexterity and address in the art of appropriating, like the Greeks deeming it no dishonour to steal, but a disgrace to be detected."[80]

---

76 White, Thompson Journal, March 3 and 10, 1810.

77 [I.S.] Ball, Ch. 3.

78 [I.S.] Wyeth Journal entry at Pierre's Hole Rendezvous.

79 Leonard Narrative.

80 [I.S.] Ferris Journal, Ch. 15, May 30, 1831.

Piety

The first to mention Salish devotion to their God as the "Great Spirit," was NWC trader Ross Cox. While spending the winter with them in 1814, he wrote: "The Flathead believe in the existence of good and evil spirit, and consequently in a future state of rewards and punishment. They hold that after death the good Indian goes to a country in which there will be perpetual summer; that he will meet his wife and children; that the rivers will abound with fish, and the plains with the much-loved buffalo; that he will spend his time in hunting and fishing, free from the terrors of war, or the apprehensions of cold and famine. The bad man, they believe, will go to a place covered with eternal snow; that he will always be shivering with cold and will see fires at a distance which he cannot enjoy, water which he cannot procure to quench thirst, and buffalo and deer which he cannot kill to appease his hunger. [His surroundings will be] thick woods full of wolves, panthers and serpents. Their punishment is not eternal and, according to their crimes, they are sooner or later emancipated and permitted to join their friends in the Elysia field."[81]

Typical of all American Indians, the Salish had their share of superstitions. For instance, in Cox's time the people believed the beaver to be a fallen race of Indians, and their wickedness provoked the Great Spirit; consequently, all were condemned to their present status. However, they would be restored to humanity in due time. Furthermore, they witnessed male beavers talking with each other in council with an offending member.

The medicine man, as the spiritual leader, perpetuated illusions of this nature; however, through close relationships with traders and trappers, the Salish abandoned many superstitions. Some falsehoods prevailed, even to the time Christian missions were established in the 1840s. Beliefs such as the bravest warrior's being immune to an enemy's musket ball and the Great Spirit's will causing success or failure in a battle or buffalo hunt continued. Time and Christian teaching changed these beliefs among most Salish people.

In 1832, a party of Pend Oreilles, likely led by Chief Walking Bear, visited Captain Benjamin Bonneville's winter quarters near Salmon, Idaho. Bonneville wrote: "This tribe ... evinces strong and peculiar feelings of natural piety. Their religion is not a mere superstitious fear, like that of most savages; they evince abstract notions of mortality; a deep reverence for an overruling spirit, and a respect for the rights of fellow men. ... Like most savages they are firm believers in dreams and in the power and efficiency of

81 Cox, pp. 126-27.

charms and amulets, or medicines as they call them. Some of their noble braves, also, who had numerous hairs-brea[d]th scrapes ... are believed to wear a charmed life, and to be bullet-proof.[82] ... Simply to call these people religious would convey but a faint idea of the deep hue of piety and devotion which pervades their whole conduct. Their honesty is immaculate and their purity of purpose and their observance of the rites of their religion are ... uniform and remarkable. They are certainly more like a nation of saints than a horde of savages."[83]

In Nathaniel Wyeth's travels with the Salish in 1833, he made several journal entries on Indian piety and religious practices. Unlike Bonneville, Wyeth seems less inclined to religious beliefs, but his remarks provide information on their practices.

April 30: "During the whole time Sunday there is more parade of prayer. Nothing is done Sunday in the way of trade with these Indians nor in playing games and they seldom fish or kill game or raise camp while prayers are being said. On weekdays, everyone ceases whatever vocation he is about, if on horseback he dismounts and holds his horse on the spot until all (prayer) is done."

May 5: "Sunday according to our reconing [*sic*], there is a new great man now getting up in the camp and like the rest of the world covers his designs under the great cloak [of] religion. His follow[ers] are now dancing to their own vocal music in the plain. Perhaps 1 to 5 of the camp followed him. When he gets enough followers he will branch off and be an independent chief. He is getting up some new form of religion among the Indians more simple than himself. Like others of his class he works with the fools' women and children first. While he is doing this the men of sence [*sic*] thinking it is too foolish to do harm stand by and laugh, but they will soon find that women, fools and children form so large a majority that with a bad grace they will have to yield. These things make me think of the new lights and revivals of New England."

May 10: "This moment Chief Guignon (Walking Bear) is saying the usual afternoon prayers. I observe that he first makes a long one which is responded to by the usual note in accord, then a short one followed by the same note on horseback, the whole time walking about the camp, hat on, in an audible voice and directed as though addressing the men below rather than him above."

May 12: "Being Sunday remained in camp."

82 [I.S.] Irving, Ch. 10. Bonneville.

83 Ibid. Ch. 13, Bonneville.

A faithful photograph of Charles M. Russell's "For Supremacy." This painting represents a typical early battle between Salish and Blackfeet warriors. The enemy, on the left, is armed with muskets, and the Salish, on the right, are armed with bows and lances. COURTESY WIKIMEDIA COMMONS

May 19: "Same camp. Snowed by fits most of the day. Being Sunday the medicine chief had devotional exercises with his followers. He formed them into a ring, men, women and children, and after (giving) an address they danced to a tune. In dancing they keep the feet in the same position, the whole time merely jumping up to the tune keeping the hands in front of them. At intervals he addresses them."

This concludes a broad description of everyday life of the Kalispel, Pend Oreille, Flathead, Spokane and Coeur d'Alene peoples as judged by white men who lived among the tribes. The following pages will describe year-to-year activities of the Salish people in their friendly relationship with fur traders and troubled years of conflict with the Blackfeet Nation. Routine travels of the people to the buffalo will take the reader across the wilds of today's Washington, Idaho, Montana, Wyoming and Utah. Interactions between white men and Indians, both material and economic, along with major events changed their lifestyle. The fur trade period in the Pacific Northwest begins in Inland Salish country.

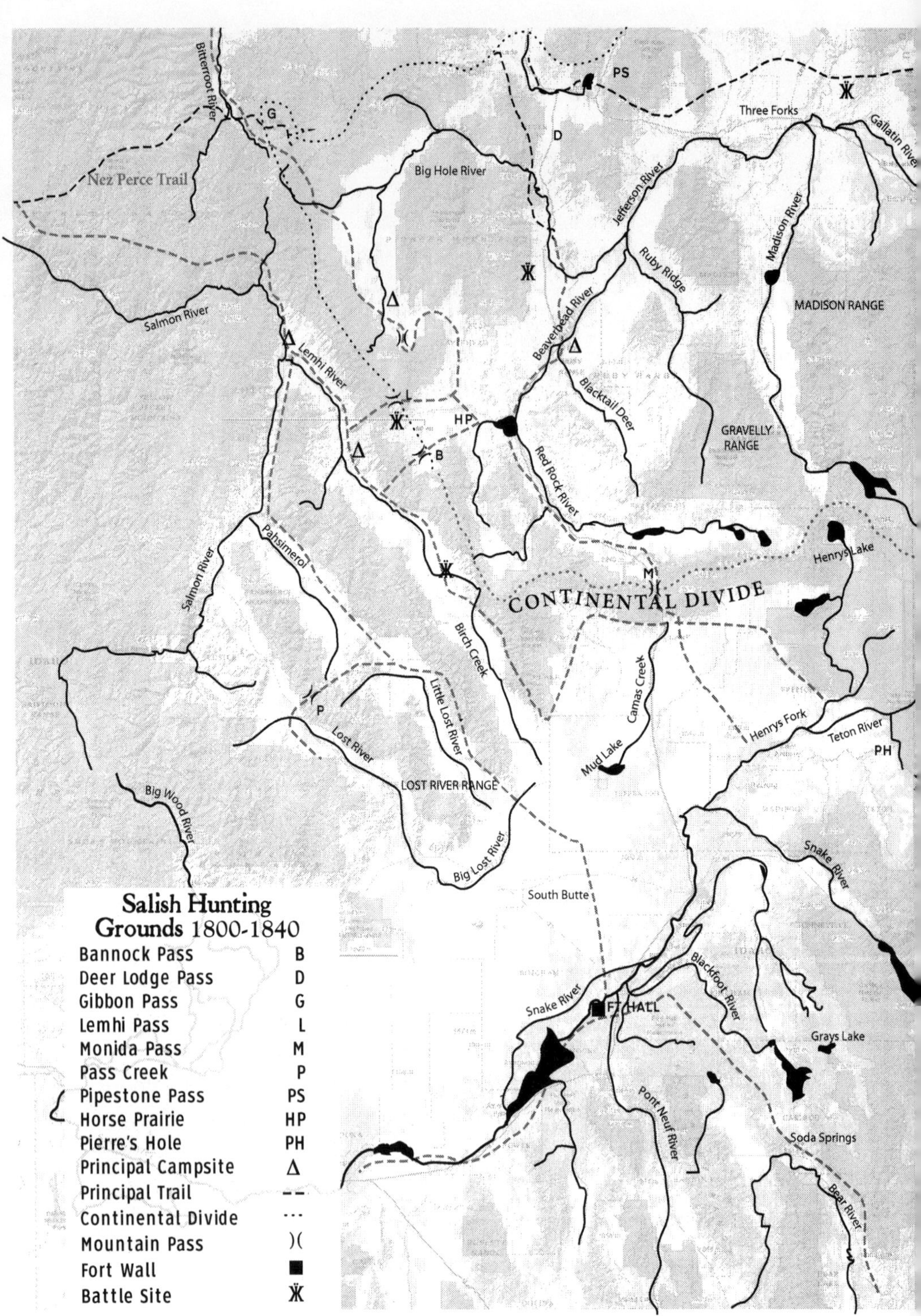
Bitterroot River
Nez Perce Trail
G
PS
D
Three Forks
Gallatin River
Big Hole River
Jefferson River
Madison River
Ruby Ridge
MADISON RANGE
Salmon River
Beaverhead River
Lemhi River
Blacktail Deer
L
HP
B
GRAVELLY RANGE
Red Rock River
Henrys Lake
M
CONTINENTAL DIVIDE
Pahsimeroi
Salmon River
Birch Creek
Camas Creek
P
Little Lost River
Lost River
Henrys Fork
Teton River
PH
Mud Lake
LOST RIVER RANGE
Big Wood River
Big Lost River
Snake River
South Butte
Blackfoot River
Snake River
FT. HALL
Grays Lake
Pont Neuf River
Soda Springs
Bear River
Salish Hunting Grounds 1800-1840
Bannock Pass B
Deer Lodge Pass D
Gibbon Pass G
Lemhi Pass L
Monida Pass M
Pass Creek P
Pipestone Pass PS
Horse Prairie HP
Pierre's Hole PH
Principal Campsite Δ
Principal Trail – –
Continental Divide · · ·
Mountain Pass)(
Fort Wall ■
Battle Site Ӝ

2

Muskets, Blankets and Beads

1805-1825

Peoples of the Pend Oreille, Flathead, Nez Perce, Kootenai and Shoshoni tribes with sizeable herds of horses had established themselves as residents on the buffalo plains by the last quarter of the 18th century. Their peaceful association occupied and hunted Three Forks, Helena and Sweet Grass Hills along the waters of the Missouri and north to the Highwood River on Alberta Plains, where seas of buffalo grazed. Living conditions soon changed when the much larger Blackfeet Nation advanced southward and eventually to the upper Missouri from traditional homelands above Calgary, Canada, in search of horses to build their herds and to make war against their enemy, the Shoshonis.

Brandishing imported muskets, iron-pointed lances and arrows obtained through trade with Hudson's Bay Company traders on the Saskatchewan River, the Blackfeet overwhelmed all native people they encountered on their southerly path. Armed with only primitive, stone-pointed weapons that often broke on impact with a shield, the Salish and other tribes retreated from the hunting grounds west across the mountains. By the end of the century, the Blackfeet dominated the northern plains from the North Saskatchewan River southward to the headwaters of the Missouri River and from Battle Creek in Montana westward to the Rocky Mountains.[84]

By the time Lewis and Clark made contact with the Flatheads on September 5, 1805, the tribe had suffered severe losses in people and horses on the plains and had withdrawn to the safety of the Bitterroot Valley. Despite setbacks, the Salish and allies continued to hunt buffalo in the upper drainages of the Missouri River and southeast Idaho. In 1840, Flathead tribal elders estimated their population at 800 families or about 4,000 souls before Blackfeet aggression and a smallpox epidemic.[85] When white man arrived, the population of the Pend Oreilles and Flatheads had

84 Ewers, p. 30.
85 [I.S.], Mengarini, p. 193.

declined by half since reaching a high in the mid-18th century.

Trapper Warren A. Ferris recalled an 1833 conversation with a Flathead known to trappers as Faro, who told of his people's terror of the Blackfeet and meeting with the Corps of Discovery: "A great many snows past when I was a child, our people were in continual fear of the Blackfeet who were already in possession of firearms of which we knew nothing, save by their murderous effects. During our excursions for buffalo, we were frequently attacked by them, and many of our bravest warriors fell victims to the thunder and lightning they wielded, which we conjectured had been given them by the Great Spirit to punish us for our sins. In our numerous conflicts, they never came in reach of our arrows, but maintained at such a distance that they could deal death to us without endangering themselves, sometimes indeed their young warriors closed in with us, and were as often vanquished; but they never failed to repay us fourfold from a safe distance. For several months we saw our best warriors almost daily falling around us, without our being able to avenge their deaths. … We were utterly powerless to oppose them."[86]

In early September 1805, Head Chief Three Eagles' tribe of about 400 Flatheads with 80 warriors and 500 horses were camped at Ross Hole, when scouts brought word of an armed party of bearded white men and a black man approaching. You can well imagine their apprehension, as the group might have been allies of the dreaded Blackfeet. The black one could have indicated war paint. Three Eagles watched as the party advanced down the valley and decided they were not a war party. Again, Flathead Faro's childhood memories recalled this historic meeting to trapper Ferris, "[M]any of our people were now exceedingly terrified, making no doubt but that they were leagued with our enemies the Blackfeet, and coming jointly to destroy us."[87] After much discussion, Chief Three Eagles convinced his warriors to follow him to the Lewis and Clark heavily armed camp.

William Clark's diary describes his impressions of the people: "[T]hey are stout and light complected more so than is common for Indians. … I was the first white man who ever wer [*sic*] on the waters of their river."[88]

Expedition member Joseph Whitehouse added his thoughts: "They received us as friends and appeared to be glad to see us. … The natives are

---

86 [I.S.], Ferris, Ch. 16, June 1, 1831; Major John Owen Journal, February 26, 1862. The Shoshonis and Bannocks killed and scalped a well-known Flathead named Faro and a woman on the Clark Fork River near today's Drummond, Montana. Earlier, Father Mengarini mentioned Little Faro who led a faction of Flathead opposed to the missionary. Their descriptions described the same man.

87 Ibid.

88 Moulton, Clark Journal, September 5, 1805.

light complected decent looking people, the most of them well cloathed [*sic*].[89]

Faro added: "After such dismal foreboding imagine how agreeably we were disappointed, where, upon arriving at the strangers' encampment ... they found a few strangers ... who treated them with great kindness, and gave them many things. ... The Flathead have been ever since the friends of the white man. The strangers accompanied the chief and his warriors back to the village, and there was peace and joy in the lodges of our people."[90]

The Corps of Discovery spent a day with the Salish and then continued on to the Pacific Ocean, guided to Lolo Trail by three Flatheads, while the Salish broke camp the next day and crossed over Gibbon Pass to meet the Shoshonis for a buffalo hunt at Three Forks. Thus began the friendly relationship between the Salish and the whites on the upper Columbia Plateau. The buffalo-dependent Flatheads and Pend Oreilles had hunted the animal in their home territory in the ancient days before the introduction of the horse. The plains areas from Kalispell to Arlee and the Bitterroot Valley all held buffalo, according to Duncan McDonald, an HBC man and resident on the Flathead resevation.[91] Other nearby prairies supported bison herds long before Lewis and Clark's expedition made contact with the natives. A direct route over the Mission Mountains on the Jocko River trail and pass provided easy access to the buffalo and camas grounds on the Blackfoot River, Little Blackfoot River and farther east to the Missouri Plains. Its use as a convenient shortcut trail ceased after the Blackfeet occupied the area late in the 18th century.[92] At that point in time, the Salish tribes, Kootenais and Nez Perce formed an alliance and trailed farther east to hunt via trails along the Clark Fork and Bitterroot rivers.

Indians' preference for the more useful and tasty cows severely disrupted the buffalo's reproductive cycle, which eventually led to its demise. Remnants of once widely spread bison herds were evident in the first third of the 19th century. Snake River Brigade leader Peter S. Ogden observed a "band of buffalo" in 1825 running off to the southeast near today's Drummond, Montana.[93] In November 1832, John Work, a brigade leader of the Hudson's Bay Company, found only bulls on the Big and Little Blackfoot rivers, killing three there and another one near present-day Deer Lodge, Montana. He recorded his disappointment, "The meat is very indifferent,

89 Moulton, Whitehouse Journal, September 5, 1805.
90 [I.S.], Ferris, Ch. 16.
91 Kingston, p. 169. Duncan McDonald letter to Kingston, author of the article. McDonald reported finding skeletal remains in such places.
92 White, p. 215. Thompson Journal, March 1, 1812.
93 Rich, p. 74. Ogden Journal, August 18, 1825.

but never the less acceptable as provisions are very scarce with us."[94]

Fur traders found their way to Salish country soon after the Corps of Discovery had passed through on their return trip to St. Louis. British and French entities dominated the fur trade in Eastern and Central Canada for a century before advancing westward on rivers and lakes to the Rocky Mountains. By the end of 18th century, two multinational enterprises in the British Colony of Canada, the London-based Hudson's Bay Company (HBC) and the Canadian North West Company (NWC) competed for the North American Indian trade. At intervals along the North Saskatchewan River to the base of the Rocky Mountains, both corporations established trading posts, some side by side. In the early 1800s, the NWC built the Rocky Mountain House to capture resident Piegan trade, which soon became the supply depot and point of departure for crossing the Canadian Rockies to the Columbia River.

HBC began exploration for a route across the Rocky Mountains in 1792 when fur traders joined a band of Piegans and trailed to the Bow River foothills. Pete Fidler's journal entries describe Piegan and Bloods' concerns in trading with the Kootenais and Salish. At a large village near the river, fur men met with head chiefs to learn of potential travel routes and discuss business. The chiefs complained of trading guns to the Kootenais, for they took them over the mountains and exchanged with their enemy, the Salish. As the traders began to leave the camp, a chief advised them to be on watch for the Flatheads hovering around the foothills to steal horses and raid small, weak parties. Fidler and his group took the chief's advice, chose defensible positions for campsites and took turns guarding the horses from attack by the Flatheads. As the HBC men would soon learn, the Piegan chiefs had described their own modus operandi with other Indians.

The NWC began a similar search in the fall of 1800 under the leadership of Duncan McGillivray and David Thompson, but they focused on finding the Kootenais. They traveled south from Rocky Mountain House to the forks of the Red Deer River, where they met seven lodges of Piegan hunters. These Indians knew exactly where the Kootenais were, as they had taken horses from them the day before. Thompson departed early the next morning with a few men and two of the Piegan horse thieves and traveled about 23 miles west up a fork of the river where he found 26 men and seven women with 11 horses. The Kootenais had furs to trade and Thompson agreed to escort them to the trading post. By the time the group

94 Lewis and Phillips: Work Journal, November 4, 1831.

reached Rocky Mountain House, the Indians only had three horses, due to the lurking Piegan thieves. Two days after the Kootenais traded their furs, they began their long journey home by traveling up the heavily timbered North Saskatchewan River. Six years later, this became the traders' route across the mountains to the Columbia River.

The North West Company (NWC)

The adventurous North West Company's David Thompson expanded the company's trading operations in 1807 to the Columbia River system in Kootenai territory, and later among the Salish. For a number of years, their HBC competitors had confined their operational area to lands of the Blackfeet Nation and other tribes east of the Rockies. An early attempt by the British company to extend operations west of the mountains erupted in threats of hostility from important Blackfeet customers. The Kootenais and Salish welcomed NWC traders to the country, which escalated hostilities between longtime enemy tribes. The Blackfeet perceived the NWC's move into its adversarial quarter with trade guns and iron arrowheads as threatening to their dominance on the Missouri River buffalo plains. That bold advance of NWC into Kootenai and Salish country came at a critical time in their history.

With a strong American and European demand for felt hats, made with hair from beaver furs, the NWC fur men expanded their trading operation to untapped and fertile fur-bearing lands. Crossing the rugged Rocky Mountains, where snow persisted on mountain passes most of the year, to the Columbia River with men and supplies presented huge logistical problems. Crude Indian foot trails choked with downed timber and rapid rivers obstructed with waterfalls did not stop the adventurers from establishing trading posts in Kootenai and Salish territories. Beaver pelts, profit and friendly natives devoid of European goods drove the company men deep into the Columbia Plateau regions. Other animal skins, such as mink, marten, muskrat, ermine, otter, wolf and buffalo also had demand and value but nothing like the seemingly endless numbers of beaver. Harvesting them was not as simple, easy nor quick as one might think.

Fur traders depended on the Indians and a few white and/or mixed-blood, French Canadian fur trappers to deliver pelts to their posts in exchange for supplies and personal items. The trapper captured the animal in a hand-forged, heavy steel trap or patiently waited pond-side to shoot it. Once skinned, it took up to an hour of fleshing to remove fat and meat from the furless side of the hide. Fur trappers' Indian wives usually bore the brunt of that work, after which they stretched the skin to a circular willow hoop with a sack needle and rawhide cord, stitched carefully at regular intervals so the pelt would dry evenly in a rounded shape. A large, dried and cleanly fleshed beaver pelt in prime condition weighed up to 2 pounds, yielding top trade value; the average hide weighed 1.5 pounds. Grading individual hides as to quality and size rested with a trader's judgment. When the valuable beaver skin market finally took root in Salish country, the natives quickly learned white man's standards of hide preparation.

Four years had elapsed from the time of Lewis and Clark's visit with the Flatheads before the fur traders brought equalizing guns to Salish country, during which time their nemesis, the Blackfeet, dominated their hunting grounds. Despite the Salish and allies possessing only primitive armaments, they always put up a good fight. Perhaps that was why in the summer of 1807 a delegation of Blackfoot, Bloods and Piegans rode west to talk peace with the Salish. The Blackfeet met up with a band of Kootenai and Salish hunters on their way to a new trading post at the head of the Columbia River. Talks of peace went well until a young Piegan brave tried to steal a Flathead's horse. That led to an immediate skirmish in which several Flatheads, a Kootenai, and a dozen Piegans lost their lives. Armed with bows and arrows against the Blackfeet with their iron weapons, most of the Salish turned back for home and missed their first meeting with the fur traders.[95]

Disregarding Blackfeet superior strength, the next summer the Salish launched a large contingent of buffalo hunters to the Three Forks area. A trapper-spokesman for the American Missouri Fur Company, John Colter, fell in with the Salish; apparently, he planned to lead them to Manuel Lisa's trading post on the Yellowstone at the mouth of the Big Horn River. En route, a large force of Piegans jumped the party on the Gallatin River near today's Bozeman, Montana. A fierce battle ensued, in which the Piegans rapidly gained the upper hand. The noise drew the attention of a band of Crow hunters, who carried guns, and they readily joined the Salish attack against their common Piegan foe. This band and Colter's sure aim undoubtedly secured the Salish a costly victory. Wrote Thomas James, who worked with Colter two years after the battle, when he passed the site: "Where skulls and bones were lying around on the ground in vast numbers. ... Called 'the Arabs' of this part of the 'Far Far West,' the Blackfeet were at length repulsed, but retired in perfect order and could hardly be said to have been defeated. The Flatheads, a noble race of brave, generous and

95 Nisbet, Thompson Journal, p. 45, and Nisbet, Sources of the River, p. 96.

hospitable men – might easily be termed the Spartans of Oregon."[96] In retaliation for this 1808 summer setback, a young Piegan war party from the North Saskatchewan River raided the Salish home territory during the winter of 1809. After returning home in the spring, the Piegans told the NWC Fort Augusta trader about killing a number of Flatheads, and they had the scalps to prove it, along with roughly 200 horses.[97] Meanwhile, trappers traveling from the Red River District in Canada and St. Louis had begun to operate near Mandan Indian villages along the Missouri River.

Between 1807 and 1809, fur hunters, traders and an agent of General Wilkinson, then governor of the Louisiana Territory, found their way to the Bitterroot Valley. Presumably, the Salish and Nez Perce buffalo hunters led the way in returning home from the Missouri Plains. In July 1807, 42 men arrived in the valley, according to the count by the Flatheads who met them.[98] Ex-military Captain John McClellan rode at the head of this diverse group of white Americans, French Canadians, mixed bloods and Iroquois Indians.[99] Navigating up the Missouri River in a keelboat in 1806, McClellan had met Lewis and Clark on their return voyage from the Pacific Ocean. Captain McClellan told Clark of the group's speculative mission directed toward Santa Fe to explore a trade route to the area. After wintering with the Yankton Sioux, however, McClellan moved upriver where he connected with some 30 trappers at the Mandan Indian villages. The captain changed plans there, opting instead to form a larger party by joining the trappers on their way to the dangerous yet beaver-rich country of the upper Yellowstone River. Names of the men known were François Rivet (Revais), Michael Allaire, Charles Loyer, Jacques Pierre Hoole, Louis Pacquin, Andre Ballanger, and Lolo and Iroquois Indians Pierre, Jacques, Joseph and Iqnace.[100]

All played a role in the Salish fur trade years. Three Flatheads, two Nez Perces and four lodges of Kootenais carried word of McClellan's arrival in the Bitterroots to David Thompson at his trading post in today's British Columbia. McClellan's crew had built a small fort near the vicinity of today's Missoula, Montana, and explored the Clark Fork River downstream during the winter. In the spring of 1808, Captain McClellan and 12 men left the area for the hostile Blackfeet's territory on the Missouri River

96 [I.S.] James, Ch. 1, Undoubtedly, Pend Oreilles accompanied the Flatheads on this hunt. The name Flathead applied to all tribes of the Salish Nation during this time frame.

97 Coues, p. 598, Alexander Henry Journal, May 10, 1810.

98 Nisbet, Thompson Journal, p. 45.

99 Jackson, Children, David Thompson Journal, pp. 9-10.

100 White, Thompson Journal, November 1, 1809, to April 10, 1810.

in an attempt to broker peace with that nation.[101] No records exist of the McClellan party's fate, leading historians to believe Blackfeet killed them.

Missouri fur trader Charles Courtin and a few of his trappers were in the Bitterroot and Flathead valleys before 1810. The licensed American trader had moved trade goods up the Missouri by keelboat, passing by the Lewis and Clark expedition on their own return trip.[102] In the summer of 1807, reports indicated Courtin planned on going to the Three Forks, Montana, area.[103] Based on a letter from Finan McDonald to George McTavish in 1824, Courtin had built a small fort in 1807 between the Jefferson and Madison rivers, one-half mile below where the Manuel Lisa Fort[104] would later stand. It is likely he had troubles with the Blackfeet and joined up with the McClellan party when they passed by his post.

At least one historian told of Courtin and independent trappers in 1809[105] arriving with some Salish hunters returning to the Bitterroot. Then in February 1810, Piegans killed Courtin and one Flathead and wounded two Indians near Hell Gate on the Clark Fork River. Salish Chief La Breche managed to salvage Courtin's 450 beaver pelts and returned them to his trappers camped on the Flathead River near Dixon, Montana. Afterword, David Thompson of the North West Company (NWC) impartially divided the beaver hides belonging to the deceased among trappers Michael Bourdeaux (Bourdon), François Sans Facon, François Gregoire and Registre Bellaire.[106] Thompson then rewarded the chief for bringing in the skins, and a free trapper for his lost time in searching for him. After Thompson's time, Hell Gate earned its name from trappers who learned from the Salish of the many deadly encounters at the point where the Clark Fork River cuts through the mountains to the Missoula Plains.

Two lofty mountain ridges squeezed the floor of the river valley down to create an ideal ambush site for Blackfeet raiders, but also made a fine defensive formation for the Flathead camp about five miles from the river canyon. Lieutenant John Mullan, while passing through Hell Gate

---

101 Jackson, Columbia Magazine.

102 Moulton, Clark Journal, September 14, 1806.

103 Nisbet, p. 81.

104 Morgan, pp. 123 and 396; If McDonald's observation is correct, Courtin was the first American fur trader to enter the beaver rich upper Missouri, one year before the Manuel Lisa venture.

105 Jackson, Columbia Magazine.

106 White, Thompson Journal, March 4, 1810. This is the first mention of Flathead Chief La Breche, a trader's name meaning breach, flaw or opening, and probably referred to a physical feature or injury. Possibly this man is referred to as Cut Thumb, Grand Visage and finally Big Face by various journalists in later years. If so, the Flathead principal or head chief was about age 50 when Thompson met him.

canyon for the first time in 1853, listened as Indian guides told of an entire advance party of 11 wiped out there, which caused the main body of Blackfeet to retreat to their home territory.[107] Thompson called the river above Hell Gate "Courtin's Defile." Ten years later, Alexander Ross referred to it as Piegan River. By the 1830s, Hell Gate became a regular reference point for the fur men and later for white settlers.

After the death of Courtin and the McClellan party's disappearance, about 25 trappers remained among the Salish on the Bitterroot and Flathead drainages. With a trading post in the area and plentiful beaver in the waterways, the trappers made the area home. Most married Salish women. David Thompson put some of the Iroquois in the group to work building birch bark canoes for him, while other freemen supplied meat or moved supplies and hides to and from the post's main depot. Bourdon and Rivet, both experienced free trappers, very soon became part-time employees of NWC during the off-season.

As the fur trader, geographer and surveyor for NWC, David Thompson had crossed the Canadian Rockies in the summer of 1807 and established Kootenae House at the head of the Columbia River near Lake Windermere in British Columbia. The Kootenais occupying the area welcomed the trading post and white man's goods that eliminated the need to cross the mountains to posts on the Saskatchewan River.

Their neighbors from east of the mountains, the Piegans, visited regularly but soon turned hostile as the Kootenais began to wield muskets. Thompson received visitors and messages from far away, delivered by the Salish and Nez Perces who encouraged the trader to come south to their territory. The Salish made another attempt in May 1808 to meet Thompson near current Bonners Ferry, Idaho, but due to flooding, only three kept the appointment. Another year would pass before the Salish ceremonially greeted fur traders upon arrival in their country.

On September 5, 1809, 16 Salish men with two dozen horses met Thompson and his crew at Bonners Ferry and then escorted them south on the Lake Indian Road to Kootenai Bay on Lake Pend Oreille. Indians waiting in canoes loaded some of Thompson's trade goods and started for the mouth of Pack River to meet the gathered Salish people. Windblown waves forced the canoes to shore after traveling just three miles, where the party camped for the night. They resumed their journey the next morning and arrrived at the large encampment of 54 Kalispels, 23 Coeur d'Alenes, four Kootenai men and some families waiting at the mouth of Pack River to

---

107 Annual Report of Commissioner of Indian Affairs, 1853, p. 61.

present Thompson's party with gifts of berries, fish and deer meat.[108] Those who brought furs desired iron goods: guns, arrowheads, kettles, knives, ammunition and powder. Women preferred awls and needles to replace the primitive bone tools used in making leather clothes, tents and other items. Blue beads stirred little interest at the time, as the Indians favored necessity over decoration. During the first month of trading in the area, the Thompson crew acquired five packs of beaver primarily from Coeur d'Alenes, along with provisions that included fish and berries. Thompson had told the Salish "to procure these advantages they must not pass days and nights in gambling but be industrious in hunting and working beaver and other furs, all which they promised."[109] Right away, the traders selected a site on the Hope Peninsula near the lake and began construction of a small, two-story cabin that Thompson named Kullyspell House.

Before completing construction, Thompson and two men rode off with a Kalispel guide to explore the country east along the Clark Fork River that flowed west into Lake Pend Oreille. Utilizing the Salish Road to the Buffalo that crowded between steep hillsides on the north and the river, they moved through ancient timber stands where little sunlight caught grass for horse feed. Thompson studied the river and thought it navigable by canoe, save a few rapids that would require portage. After crossing the Vermilion River, the trail became rocky in spots, with varying grades across spur ridges, further weakening their horses. The fourth day they passed a waterfall, later known as Thompson Falls, and discovered a "mile-long prairie dotted with about 40 unattended horses."[110]

The Pend Oreilles had left extra horses to graze while off hunting buffalo, evidently feeling they were quite safe from thieves. Thompson and his men then rode upriver to Horse Plains, where they left the Road to the Buffalo and turned north along the "Kootenai Road" to the Kootenai River.[111] By chance, they met the company supply caravan coming downriver in canoes from Rocky Mountain House, with whom Thompson then joined. At today's Bonners Ferry, the party obtained packhorses from the Kootenais, loaded their trade goods and trailed south to arrive at Kullyspell

108 Elliott, WHQ, vol. 11, no. 4, Thompson Journal, September 9, 1809. Thompson referred to the Kootenai band of Indians that lived at Bonners Ferry as Lake Indians.

109 Hopwood, p. 261, September 11, 1809.

110 White, p. 48, Thompson Journal, October 30, 1809.

111 Ibid. p. 48, Thompson Journal, The 448-mile-long Kootenay River rises on west slopes of Rockies in southeastern British Columbia, flows south as Kootenai River in northwestern Montana, west through Idaho, back north into British Columbia where it enters Kootenay Lake from the south to join the Columbia beyond Nelson, British Columbia. The Kootenai tribe's principal encampments were scattered throughout the river system with one on the uppermost Columbia. In Idaho's Bonners Ferry, north to Kootenay Lake, Libby, Tobacco Plains and north of Flathead Lake in Montana all provided the best wintering conditions.

House October 30 in a snowstorm. During their absence, Finan McDonald traded for about two packs of furs and three horses from 44 Coeur d'Alene men who had learned of the new trading post.[112]

The Salish Road to the Buffalo, serving the Coeur d'Alenes, Spokanes and Kalispels, passed through Horse Prairie (today's Plains, Montana), an important Pend Oreille winter camp that supported many horses on its 13,000-acre grasslands. The river-grade trail there turned northeast at the prairies' edge before climbing 1,200 feet across the grasslands to a timbered ridgetop, where the road followed the ridge before turning southeast down a wooded draw to the Camus Creek basin. The trail continued down the creek, south to a ford across the Flathead River. From there, Indians trailed upriver to turn southerly up the Jocko River and then dropped down to Hell Gate and the crossroads. Travelers took either the Clark Fork River or the Bitterroot Valley route that crossed the Continental Divide to the buffalo.

On November 2, 1809, Thompson and some six men returned to the mile-long prairie above the falls (Thompson Falls, Montana) and began construction of a small, two-room cabin-warehouse. With them came trade guns and iron arrow points that would improve the odds for Salish and neighboring Kootenais in battles against their common Blackfeet enemies. Before "Salish House" reached completion, Indians and free trappers of the McClellan-Courtin groups turned up to swap provisions and beaver skins for various goods. Hides filled the warehouse and attached living quarters by April, causing Thompson to move into his tent. During the winter, as Thompson observed the shooting ability of the men who had just obtained guns, he declared them much better marksmen than most Piegans. They practiced downing deer at ranges up to 120 yards, a much smaller target at a longer distance than a buffalo.[113]

On April 14, 1810, a delegation of Pend Oreille and Nez Perce chiefs arrived to bid the traders adieu as they departed with furs in the new canoes for Kullyspell House. Stopping briefly at Kullyspell House, Thompson directed the clerk, Finan McDonald, to manage Salish House. After a round-trip by water to explore navigability of the Pend Oreille River to Box Canyon (Metaline, Washington), Thompson had furs loaded on packhorses and trailed to the Kootenai River where they found the previously stashed canoes and repaired them for the long, arduous voyage to Canadian depots. On May 17, 1810, the fur men set off with 46 packs of pelts and

112 Elliott, vol. 23, p. 24.

113 Hopwood, Thompson Narrative. .

eight bags of pemmican.[114]

Before setting off for Canadian depots, Thompson rehired Jaco Finlay as an interpreter and clerk and assigned him to locate and construct a new post among the Spokanes. Finlay and a few men rode away to select a place to build Spokane House near a principal Indian village of 44 families at the confluence of the Little Spokane and Spokane rivers. The proximity of the village and fish runs influenced his decision to build there. In the late fall, after threats of a Blackfeet attack at Salish House, Finan McDonald and crew left their post to help Jaco put the finishing touches on the small, crude log building named Spokane House. NWC traditionally called trading posts "houses" no matter how big or how small.

Meanwhile, the upper Pend Oreilles returned from the Crow country buffalo grounds in mid-November[115] of Thompson's first winter at Salish House. Old Chief Gros Veau's (Big Calf) band set up camp at Horse Plains along with a few Kootenais, and a larger encampment of Pend Oreilles established winter quarters on an open plain near the confluence of the Flathead and Jocko rivers. In late March 1810, before the river got too high, both camps packed up, forded the river and moved to Camas Prairie to dig for roots.[116]

The Salish had looked forward to the 1810 summer buffalo hunt after having accumulated some 25 muskets and several hundred iron arrowheads through trade. They invited Salish House trader Finan McDonald and two of his men, Baptiste Bouche and Michael Bourdon[117] to participate. About 130 Salish warriors with their families and the NWC men rode up the Clark Fork River across Deer Lodge Pass to the buffalo plains near today's Dillon, Montana, where they set up camp.

On the third morning, while camped in the open, scouts reported sighting the enemy nearby. The Salish quickly built a barricade of tent poles and baggage, behind which women and children laid down flat near the horses standing in the rear. Armed with 12-foot lances, some 170 Piegans formed a mounted file and charged the line of defense, but near the barricade, a surprising volley of musket fire and iron-pointed arrows put them to a skidding halt. Wheeling, they retreated 400 yards away, where the war chief put them in order for a second attack. Advancing to within 30 yards of the Salish line, they again had to pull back from a heavy

114 Elliott, vol. 11, p. 163. July 1920. A 90-pound pack held about 60 skins at that time. As the fur trade commenced, the size and/or weight per hide diminished

115 White, p. 61, Thompson Journal, November 9, 1809. The Salish very likely hunted the Three Forks area again, taking advantage of their Crow allies' proximity.

116 Ibid.

117 Jackson, p. 11.

barrage. The Piegan chief rallied them a third time but stayed just beyond arrow range as the warriors decided to save their horses. McDonald thought the fight was over, but the shrewd old Salish chief told him the battle had only begun and would not finish before sunset.

The Salish warriors then formed a line on a low, open grassy ridge ahead of their previous position. Within a few hours, dismounted Piegans moved slowly toward the line, stopping 150 yards beyond musket range when both sides dropped to the ground. Minutes later the determined enemy warriors rose up and began to advance at 6-foot intervals, singing and whooping until within gun range but too far for arrows.[118] At this point, the Piegans began jumping up and down and from side to side. McDonald tried to get the Salish to shorten their musket range, but they held back. By himself, he closed in to kill one Piegan and wound another, firing 45 times. At sunset, the Piegans carried off 13 wounded and seven dead; the Flatheads had five killed and nine wounded. After returning to their Saskatchewan home, the Piegans reported that most of their wounded died, for a death toll of 16.[119]

Coureur de bois in typical dress. These Frenchmen became involved in the 1650s in the fur trade. Woodcut by Arthur Heming (1870-1940). COURTESY WIKIMEDIA COMMONS

Later, NWC trader Alexander Henry Jr. lived among the Piegans and wrote of their nature: "War seems to be the Piegans' sole delight; their discourse always turns upon that subject; one war party no sooner arrives than another sets off. Horses are the principal plunder … obtained. Formerly the Flathead and other tribes became easy prey, and were either killed or driven away like sheep, but within a few years they … acquired firearms and became formidable."[120] The last half of 1810 and the winter of 1811 brought misery to the Salish wintering in home territory on the Flathead and Clark Fork rivers. Seeking revenge for the summer defeat, a large force of Piegans struck with fury. Participation of white traders both in the fight and by supplying arms to their adversaries provoked the humiliated Piegans to strike against the Salish and NWC Columbia operations. The imperfect victory had its consequences before the Salish left the hunting

118 Ibid.

119 Coues, p. 644, Henry Journal, October 8, 1810.

120 Ibid. p. 726; The Henry Journal covers 15 years of experience in NWC operations in southwestern Canada, where he dealt with the Piegans, Bloods and Blackfoot tribes on the Saskatchewan River.

grounds. Henry's journal entry of November 28, 1810, noted the Piegans and Gros Ventres had returned home with 60 Flathead horses and a captive Gros Ventre woman who had escaped from the Salish. He also assumed correctly that Finan McDonald "must have left his house" to escape the onslaught. For upward of 30 years after, the three tribes of the Blackfeet Nation and allies raided trapping outfits and native hunters on the upper Missouri and in southeastern Idaho, which fur men termed the war zone.

Fur trader Nathaniel Wyeth learned of a battle site from a native guide that may have been linked to the previous Flathead fight with the Piegans. The guide pointed out a ridge east of their campsite on Camas Creek prairie, where 200 Flatheads, Pend Oreilles and Kootenais lost their lives fighting the enemy.[121] From that place, other onslaughts continued down the valley of the Flathead and Clark Fork rivers until the Piegans turned back at "Bad Rock" below Horse Plains, stopped cold by the Pend Oreilles. At Salish House, a few miles downriver from "Bad Rock," Finan McDonald and his crew fled west in late fall to the still-under-construction "Spokane House" to avoid the very real possibility of death. The Piegans persisted in their determination to stop traders from supplying the Salish and Kootenais with firearms. While at Rock Mountain House, Alberta, Canada, in mid-September 1810, loading fresh supplies destined for Salish House, a Piegan chief visited David Thompson to warn him of the danger in going farther up the North Saskatchewan River and over Howse Pass. Thompson wrote, "[If] they proceeded upward, there was four tents upon the River, they would send them back, that we should not take any further supplies to the Flathead and company."[122] Thompson listened and decided to take the much longer and more arduous route over Athabaska Pass. Meanwhile, Hudson's Bay Company (HBC) clerk Joseph Howse and his party holed up with two NWC men at Kootenae House due to a Piegan blockade near Canal Flats.

Earlier, Howse and 13 men in two canoes had passed NWC Rocky Mountain House loaded with trade supplies that included kegs of watered-down alcohol, powder and balls bound for Salish country.[123] In order to proceed, Howse smoothed the Piegans' ruffled feathers by giving food and alcohol to the guards at Canal Flats. Moving his supplies from Kootenae House to the head of Flathead Lake on Ashley Creek, Howse began construction of a cabin and opened trade with the Pend Oreilles and Koote-

121 [I.S.] Wyeth Journal, April 23, 1833: The number of fatalities is likely inflated. Also: Hopwood, Thompson Journal, August 21, 1811: David Thompson added that La Breche and another Salish Indian arrived at their Kettle Falls camp with news of their war with the Blackfeet.

122 Nisbet, p. 87.

123 Coues, p. 605, Henry Journal, June 19, 1810.

nais. In December, he and two men accompanied the Indians on a hunting expedition to the headwaters of the upper Missouri and returned to the cabin in February 1811.[124]

According to HBC trader James Bird Sr., the Piegan chief at the Muddy River post declared, "[I]f they again meet with white man going to supply their enemies, they would not only plunder and kill them, but ... they would make dry meat of his body."[125] HBC heeded the warning by not returning to the Columbia country for 11 years. In that summer, Piegan raiders struck the Flathead River valley again, only to find most of the natives off hunting with their horses. Along their path, the Piegans murdered an entire Kootenai family and pillaged three Iroquois, stripping the men and sending them off with their families destitute. In what may have been the first occasion, they crossed the undefended Bad Rock to sack NWC Salish House.[126]

Thompson and crew again used Athabaska Pass to move trade goods to the Columbia River, where they paused to build canoes to complete the journey to the river's head. They shoved off in early spring in what quickly became a hellish effort that involved portages around rapids and ice jams alongside 5 feet of hard-packed snow just to gain 40 miles of river to the usual Howse Pass launching point. The remainder of the trip by water and land to Salish House, a distance of more than 300 miles, involved nearly the same amount of time, 21 days, as the initial ordeal. Thompson arrived at the vacated and partially destroyed Salish House on May 27, 1811, when he wrote a "few lines in charcoal on a board in case the Americans should pass – purposing we had left the HO [house] on acct of the War with the Piegans."[127] Thompson likely intended the message for the free trappers in the area.

The widely traveled fur trader continued to Spokane House with all the trade goods, where he stayed but two days organizing the books and duties of the staff. Thompson then gathered up tools and some men and moved north to Kettle Falls on the Columbia to construct another, larger, cedar plank canoe for the trip to the Pacific Ocean. After completing their craft, a crew of nine men, including hunters Michael Bourdon and François Gregorie, joined Thompson to paddle down the Columbia River to the ocean. In just 10 days, on July 15, 1811, they pulled the canoe

124 White, Thain, Research Collection, Montana Historical Society, Helena, Montana, Howse House study. February 9, 1843, Joseph Howse Letter to Governor George Simpson describing activities.

125 Nisbet, Thompson Narrative, p. 96.

126 White, Thompson Journal & Thompson Narrative, p. 178

127 Ibid. Thompson Journal, p. 172.

ashore where Americans of the Pacific Fur Company had nearly completed construction of Fort Astoria.

Pacific Fur Company

Earlier, in April 1811, American opportunist John Jacob Astor's organization, the Pacific Fur Company (PFC), had arrived by ship at the mouth of the Columbia River, where their fur men began construction of a supply depot. Other members of the Astor enterprise experienced numerous problems in traveling cross-country from St. Louis to the new Fort Astoria, most arriving in early 1812. During the first two years of operation, they built and supplied several interior trading posts, including a supply depot at Fort Spokane adjacent to the NWC Spokane House, to offer new trading opportunities to the Salish and Kootenais. In a head-to-head competition, company clerks and a few men from both NWC and PFC left those adjacent depots in October for Kootenai and Salish posts with a broad selection of goods at highly competitive prices.

One spring, at a Spokane House Rendezvous, two Kootenai Post traders, Pillet (PFC) and Montour (NWC), decided to settle differences with a pistol duel at six paces. Company tailors came to the rescue with needles and thread, after a ball tore the collar of one's coat and the other's pant leg. After the duel, they decided in favor of becoming friends. Leaving from Fort Spokane, PFC clerks Ross Cox and Russell Farnham took 12 men up the "Salish Road to the Buffalo" to build a trading cabin on the Clark Fork near Salish House. The party stopped 20 miles short of their objective on November 10, 1812, when they came upon a small Kalispel camp of old men, women and children waiting for their buffalo hunters' return. Finding adequate grass in the area and friendly Indians eager to trade, the fur men decided to build the post there. Before the cabin was completed, the buffalo hunters returned to camp with dried meat, beaver skins and important news.

Their chief said that most of the Indians had camped upriver near Salish House to trade with NWC. Soon after, Farnham and six men took the trade goods upriver while Cox and six men finished the cabin and returned to the Fort Spokane.[128] Staying through the winter, Farnham tagged along with Indian buffalo hunters and then returned to Fort Spokane in May with many furs. During the same time, another PFC clerk and two men made their way, without competition, to the Coeur d'Alenes; however, their canoe upset when crossing the Coeur d'Alene Lake and spilled the goods to the bottom. After righting the craft, they dove into

128 Cox, pp. 102-03.

the frigid water until they had recovered the entire load and went on to make contact with Indians. According to Alexander Ross, they "made a very good and very cheap trade."[129] The ambitious American company hurt NWC returns, for on May 25, 1813, the fur men left Fort Spokane with 28 horses loaded with furs.[130]

Elsewhere in the region, PFC's Donald Mackenzie attempted to open trade with a Nez Perce band located at the confluence of the Snake and Clearwater rivers (today's Lewiston, Idaho) where he built a small post. He soon learned the Indians would not trap beaver as they thought it the work for women or slaves. The Nez Perces obtained white man's goods primarily through trading horses from their numerous herds. The newcomers sorely needed horses, but Mackenzie experienced many problems with the local band that included a stolen cache and a sharp rise in horse prices, both of which prompted reprisal on his part. The fur man got most of his stolen trade items back and a reduced prices for horses, then pulled out of the area with 80 horses. Leaving behind a disgusted band of Nez Perces, the giant of a man and his crew of 18 returned to Fort Astoria in 1813, where negotiations for the sale of PFC to NWC were progressing.[131] PFC competed aggressively for Indian trade until the British-American War of 1812. Threatened by the arrival of British war ships and a losing war effort on the East Coast, PFC chose to sell its assets and supplies to the Canadian NWC and finalized the deal in October 1813[132] at Fort Astoria. Most PFC employees who were originally NWC men easily transferred to the new owner.

The war-ending treaty between the United States and Great Britian in 1818 established a joint occupancy region that included the Columbia River system, less the modern-day Canada portion. Trappers, traders and settlers from both nations took advantage of this agreement, which remained in effect for 30 years. The area included the beaver-rich Snake River drainage, which fur men flocked into along with the adjacent Spanish lands on the Green and Bear rivers. Spanish authorities, 600 miles away at Santa Fe, New Mexico, were unable to patrol the area due to an overload of enroachments near their administrative site. Both British and American firms ignored the Spanish claim and trespassed as they pleased. Lands east of the Spanish jurisdiction and the Continental Divide belonged to the United States through purchases from France and required

129 [I.S.], Ross Adventures Ch. 13.
130 Cox, p. 106.
131 [I.S.], Ross, Ch 13.
132 Chittenden, vol. 1, p. 222.

White traders bartering with the Indians.

Woodcut by an unknown artist circa 1820. A trading session probably along the Missouri River.
COURTESY WIKIMEDIA COMMONS

a license from the goverment to occupy the territory and hunt. British and Canadian firms did not have permission, but before the rush of American trappers, they ventured into area, traps in hand.

Meanwhile, David Thompson returned to the Salish House in the winter of 1811-12 to trade with locals and to make a detailed exploration of the region. His journal entries during that period identify most of the upper Pend Oreille tribes' winter campsites. In late December before the brunt of winter, Thompson and two men set out from Salish House on horses to investigate the Clark Fork River upstream from its union with the Flathead. Upon reaching the narrow, rocky river canyon, they continued upstream about 10 miles, killing eight of the numerous deer found along their course. Arriving at a hemmed-in meadow along the river, they came upon nine tents of Pend Oreilles eating quite well on the many deer. Thompson learned their horses could not pass by the cliffs next to the river above their camp a few miles above Quinn's Hot Spring. The Thompson trio returned to Salish House with loads of venison to sit out most of the winter.[133]

When winter began to ebb, Thompson focused on procuring provisions for his trip to the Canadian depots. Setting out from the trading post again in mid-February 1812, Thompson took 10 men in two canoes to trade with Indians upriver. Stopping first at Horse Prairie, they found Cartier's sizeable camp with little meat to spare, so Thompson bought a mare from the Indians and slaughtered it on the spot. Continuing upriver, the voyageurs came on an old chief's camp of 12 lodges below the confluence

133 White, pp. 187-88, Thompson Journal.

of the Clark Fork and Flathead rivers at today's Paradise, Montana. With no provisions to trade, the Northwesters resumed their voyage up the Clark Fork. Beginning at the Flathead River ford near Camas Creek, they stopped at tribal camps scattered along open benches upstream to the Jocko River. The largest village of 60 lodges, 20 of which housed widows and old men, along the Flathead River below the joining and another 20 a short distance up the Jocko, all formed the bulk of the upper Pend Oreille tribe.[134]

Trading began shortly, with Thompson obtaining a canoe-load of provisions. Before leaving the village, Head Chief Cartier asked him to attend a council meeting with tribal elders to ponder a Piegan peace offering. In early 1812, five "respectable" Piegan elders rode into a Flathead camp to request a meeting to discuss peace. A Flathead chief responded by stating that a conference of Salish representing the entire nation and its allies would convene at their discretion, after which the Piegans would receive notification within one moon. The council took place at the large Jocko encampment February 29, 1812, with several men from each of the Salish and Kootenai tribes, two Nez Perces, and David Thompson attending.

First, the Pend Oreille head chief described the purpose of the meeting and then asked the elders to "speak truly the mouth of your people." All spoke of Piegan treachery and doubt of a lasting peace. The head chief stood up and advised the council that everything had changed since white man brought guns, ammunition and iron arrowheads to their country. He spoke of what happened after the last battle, which obliged the Piegans to give up much of their lands for bison hunting. He emphasized, since Piegan allies did not accompany those who asked for peace, they would not be bound to terms of the agreement. Then he added, "Let us hear what the chief of the white man says."

Thompson said their answer should be "[T]hat you claim by ancient rights the freedom of hunting bison, that you will not make war upon any of them, but shall always be ready to defend yourselves."[135] The Pend Oreille head chief said the advice was good, but the younger men in attendance argued for a more aggressive approach if there was to be no agreement. He reminded the young men that the tribe did not have the warriors they once had but should prepare for war as they would hunt buffalo in August and surely cross trails with the Piegans. Two days later the head chief advised a trader at Salish House of summer plans, who in return warned him to be careful, reminding him that he already had 20 lodges of

134 Ibid. pp. 200-201, Thompson Journal.

135 White, Thompson Narrative, Footnote, pp. 209-210.

widows and aged to maintain.[136]

The policy adopted at this council of only to defend themselves and not be the aggressors in war continued throughout the fur trade period. Afterward, Thompson received information on the American fur traders' activities from Salish buffalo hunters.

The Pend Oreilles hunted the Three Forks area during the summer and early winter of 1811-12. While there, they discovered that "Meadow Indians" (Blackfeet) had destroyed a white man's fort the previous fall, which they described in detail to Thompson. The residue illustrated the level of ferocity and firepower of the Piegans in the only attack on a log-walled fort during the fur trade era. According to secondhand information from other Indians, the Piegans' surprise attack in the fall of 1810 struck the weakest side, having portholes in the perpendicular log wall and bastion. They managed to tear down a section of the wall before the trappers inside the fort building discovered the assault. Responding from the cabin a few yards away, the trappers opened fire on the Piegans, who were protected only by the partially destroyed log wall. Numerous balls embedded in the house and log wall, and debris showed the intensity of musket fire from both sides. At length the Piegans retired from the scene with their dead and wounded. Surviving trappers buried their dead in a single hole, covered them with stones and placed a single cross on top. Later reports from other sources had the grave containing 10 white men and said nothing of what became of the wounded. The surviving fur men escaped in the dark of night, quickly traveling south up the Madison River to clear themselves from the Piegans camped nearby. They arrived in Shoshoni country on the Snake River dejected and starving.[137]

In mid-March of 1812, the Thompson outfit loaded Salish House furs and 2,500 pounds of dried meat, then paddled off on the Clark Fork River, winding westerly for many miles through Lake Pend Oreille to Seneacquoteen on the Pend Oreille River, where they transferred goods to packhorses. They continued overland to Spokane House where Thompson and George McTavish tallied the season's returns. The latter, Thompson's replacement, and his outfit had wintered at the post after delivering supplies there the previous fall.[138]

Due to Piegan hostility, NWC had decided to transport the pelts

---

136 Ibid. Thompson Narrative, p. 211.

137 White, pp. 212-213. Thompson Journal, February 29, 1812, American Andrew Henry and about 30 trappers built Fort Henry in the spring of 1810, only to be driven out by the Piegans in the fall. The survivors crossed into Idaho and wintered on Henrys Fork of the Snake River.

138 Elliott, WHQ, vol. 19, No. 4, Thompson Journal, March 20, 1812.

over the long and difficult route via Athabaska Pass. Late in March 1812, the Thompson and McTavish outfit trailed overland to Kettle Falls where they cut down enough old-growth cedar trees to make six plank canoes. A month later, the hardy adventurers shoved off upstream with about 129 packs of pelts, provisions and gear (or 11,000 pounds), entering the Columbia River just above the falls near Kettle Falls, Washington. The arduous, 17-day voyage against the current ended at Wood River in British Columbia, where waiting horses would begin the ascent to the Athabaska Pass and Rocky Mountain House. David Thompson led the way on snowshoes on his last venture to Columbia country.[139]

Back in Pend Oreille country, August indicated cow bison were fat, so in 1812 a large Salish hunting party of about 150 warriors and families came together to head for the hunting grounds. Both free trappers and part-time NWC employees, Michael Bourdon and Michael Kinville accompanied that party. They went up the Middle Fork of the Flathead River and Nyack Creek and crossed the divide at Cut Bank Pass.[140] On the way down to the plains, they rode into the Piegans guarding eastern approaches. A terrific battle ensued on a grassy ridge with no woods nearby. After a series of minor feigned attacks, the Piegans formed a single line, shoulder to shoulder and 3 feet apart, singing and dancing in an advance. Within about 150 yards of the Salish, the Piegans ceased their hype, raised their voices in war whoops, and rushed the hunters. The Salish had a line on a low ridge and met the attack boldly. The Piegans could stomach but one deadly charge, and with great difficulty, gathered their dead and wounded and left the field. Kinville lost his life, as did many Indians on both sides. Notwithstanding the setback, the Salish continued the hunt with fair success until the Piegans surprised their camp, killing several warriors and taking many prisoners. The wife of a Pend Oreille war chief became a captive in the attack.[141]

During the 1813 fall hunt on the upper Missouri, the Pend Oreilles retaliated by capturing Piegan prisoners, who were taken back to the Pend Oreille winter camp near Salish House. Stationed at that post in the winter of 1813-14, NWC's Ross Cox described the treatment of these captives. Tied to a tree, one brave man suffered repeated burns to his body from a red-hot gun barrel. Receiving no cries for mercy, Pend Oreille warriors cut flesh from about his head and began removing fingers, joint by joint. Seem-

139 Nisbet, p. 129.

140 Hopwood, Thompson Travels, p. 320 and Glacier Park Administrative History. Thompson did not identify the battle site in his writing. However, park historians do, but their sources are unknown to this author. Thompson also listed Michael Bourdon as killed in the fight, which was not the case.

141 Cox, pp. 102-103.

ingly unfazed, the captive taunted their inability to torture. Addressing one warrior in particular, the captive said he shot the arrow that blinded his one eye. The brave jumped up, scooped out the Piegan's eye and nearly slashed his nose off in the process. The bloodied man turned to another brave, saying he killed his brother and scalped his old fool father. Within seconds, that man avenged his family by scalping the captive. The badly butchered captive did not change his tone when speaking to the war chief: "It was I that made your wife prisoner last fall; we put her eyes out – we tore out her tongue; we treated her like a dog. Forty of our young warriors … "[142] Before he finished, the war chief shot him dead, ending the gruesome spectacle.

Atrocities practiced on female prisoners, in which Salish women assisted, were even more shocking. Cox wrote that details were too revolting for publicity. Stunned by such barbaric acts, the traders, through interpreters, protested such unmanly and disgraceful cruelties to prisoners, saying that if they did not cease at once, the white man would quit their country forever. Their words had the desired effect, for the female prisoner was set free to join fellow Piegan captives. Yet, an old Pend Oreille medicine woman furiously called the young braves cowards and fools without the heart of fleas.

The traders spoke to the war chief about how Europeans treated their prisoners, where only warriors were captured – never women – and that an exchange of captives may have saved his wife. At first, he refused to accept such ideas, but on further pressure from the traders, he agreed to try that strategy, provided the head chief and tribe had no objections. A day later, the war chief told the traders: "My white friends, you do not know the savage nature of the Blackfeet; they hope to exterminate our tribe. They are a great deal more numerous than we are. … We shall now, according to your wishes, send back the prisoners, but they will laugh and never spare anybody of our tribe." In March, the fur traders furnished the Piegan prisoners with horses and provisions and sent them back to their people.[143]

According to a December 17, 1817, letter from Alexander McKenzie to Ross Cox, the NWC and Salish merciful action had no effect on the Piegans' malicious behavior. Two years later they attacked the Pend Oreille homeland and advanced to near Salish House. That created an anxious few days for clerk James McMillan's crew. However, a strong response by the

142 Ibid. pp. 118-119; Ross Cox became an employee of NWC after PFC sold its interest to that firm.

143 Ibid. p. 120.

Salish and a lack of provisions caused the Piegans to retreat. The Salish troubles with the Blackfeet Nation continued for many years, but there is no recorded incident of Salish commiting lethal torture on the captives. Instead they imposed the death penalty for horse thieving and in battle rarely took prisoners. Later documented cases of captive-taking involved beatings or cropping the ears of male culprits and immediate release. Female prisioners were not regularly taken unless they participated in a raid with their men. They were then punished in an intense, hateful manner by Salish women in the scalp dance circle and then set afire.

Backtracking downriver to a more peaceful environment, we return to Thompson's travels in Salish country from 1809 to 1812 among the Kalispels and neighboring tribes. While exploring by horse or canoe, Thompson describes his interactions with the dispersed Kalispel family groups living along the Pend Oreille Lake and River from Kullyspell House to the "root meadows," a major encampment at today's Cusick, Washington. His initial horseback excursion from Kullyspell House late in September 1809 trailed westerly along the unpopulated north bank of Lake Pend Oreille until a few tents of Kalispels appeared near Indian Island on the Pend Oreille River. Five men, two women and three boys graciously greeted the trader, followed by a speech given by the leader, Good Old Man (Le Bon Vieux), so called by Thompson.

After this, he presented gifts of two cakes of root bread, 12 pounds of roots, two dried salmon and boiled beaver meat to the travelers, who had subsisted on waterfowl on their four-day journey. Thompson reciprocated by giving the chief four 6-inch strips of tobacco and the other men two strips each. After smoking, Good Old Man told Thompson the area had plenty of beaver, but with only sticks and snares, they could not kill many. Furthermore, he said there was not an ax or chisel among them or with the neighboring tribes. Thompson got information on the navigability of the river and borrowed a canoe to continue his exploration. On his return to the Kalispel camp to get his horses, the old chief sold him a saddle and more than ample provisions that included 50 pounds of dried salmon, 15 geese and a deer to take back to the post.[144]

On another occasion, traveling by canoe, Thompson met up with several tents of Kalispels a few miles above the "root meadows" and was greeted by two natives he called Old Chief and Haranguer. During their smoke and conversation, the subject of war came up, wherein the two natives described their tribe's preparation and motivation for war. Unlike

144 Elliott, WHQ, vol. 23, no. 1, p. 21, Thompson Journal, September 30, 1809.

their buffalo hunting cousins upriver, most Kalispels during Thompson's time had not engaged in war. The older men knew of conflicts that occurred infrequently with neighbors during the late 1700s that always resulted in all making peace. Their idea of war involved the sacrifice of blood to the Great Spirit, whether their own or that of the enemy. Usually revenge sparked the affair that induced warriors to cover their heads with white chalk. Before combat, and in anticipation of the shedding of blood, each warrior, upon rising in the morning, prayed to the Great Master of Life in a low, grief-stricken voice for success in slaying his man.

Their war party always feared smaller groups of the enemy, as they did not have the strength for an open frontal attack but relied on cruel, stealthy, hit-and-run tactics.[145] At another time, while at Spokane House, Thompson attempted to defuse a war the Coeur d'Alenes and Nez Perces had planned against the Okanagans by providing the chiefs with tobacco and telling them to prepare instead for the Blackfeet, who had recently breached the Bad Rock obstacle. His efforts seemed to pay off, as there is no record of a conflict.

Transportation of trade goods and furs over the Canadian Rockies, as in Thompson's day, ceased after acquisition of the Pacific Fur Company by NWC in 1813. Large canoes transferred cargoes of persons and goods via the Columbia River from the Fort George seaport to the mouth of the Spokane River. From there packhorses carried loads 60 miles across prairies to Spokane House, the district supply depot at the mouth of the Little Spokane and Spokane rivers. NWC had abandoned their adjacent building for the more elaborate facility of Fort Spokane after purchasing PFC but referred to it as Spokane House in reports. In supplying outposts, fort workers led the packhorses east across the Spokane Prairie, then turned north via Hoodoo Creek Valley to the Pend Oreille River and Seneacquoteen portage, today's Laclede, Idaho.

Voyageurs in cedar plank canoes from the portage moved cargo up the Pend Oreille River to Lake Pend Oreille and Kootenai Bay. Here, employees and packhorses moved supplies north by trail to a Kootenai Post located near today's Bonners Ferry, Idaho. Meanwhile, the canoe men continued east across Lake Pend Oreille and up the Clark Fork River for 90 miles, portaging at Cabinet, Heron, Noxon Rapids and Thompson Falls to Salish House; this transfer route prevailed until 1826, when a move north from Spokane House to Kettle Falls (Fort Colvile) took place. By the time trade goods arrived from England at remote outposts, there was a huge

145 Ibid, vol. 23, p. 174, July 1932, Thompson Journal, June 7, 1811.

markup and corresponding profit for NWC. The Salish had no knowledge of the original cost of items; they simply knew they wanted what the traders supplied. In 1813, a good trade gun was worth 20 beavers, which cost North West Company about one English pound, seven shillings, while the average value of 20 beaver pelts was about 25 English pounds.[146] Other items, such as ammunition, metal cooking pots and utensils, knives, traps, axes, and awls were expensive but desired. Personal items included tobacco, blankets, ribbons and beads.

The Spokane House assortment of trade goods, particularly ammunition, had evaporated by September 1814 when the supply train finally arrived with more than expected. The inventory included a cock, three hens, several goats, three hogs and a cook who eventually used the offspring for dinner. Such strange critters amused the Spokanes who immediately associated them with wild bills of fare. Hogs became the white man's bear, and to demonstrate similarities they brought a baby bear to the fort. The Canadian voyageurs took to the cuddly little fellow by becoming its substitute mother. They fed and taught the cub a variety of tricks not of the type a mama bear would have. The Indians enjoyed watching the little cuss perform antics, satisfied the hogs could never duplicate.[147]

Spokane Tribe

The People of the Sun spoke a similar Salish dialect as the Coeur d'Alenes, Kalispels, upper Pend Oreilles and Flatheads. Interaction between the latter two tribes was limited to buffalo hunts when they traveled with the Kalispels and the Coeur d'Alenes to the Bitterroot Valley. A peaceful tribe when white traders came on the scene, the Spokanes had regular contact with southern neighbors, the Nez Perces and Palouse, and their northern neighbors, the Colvilles; however, before that time, the Spokanes engaged in hostilities with other tribes.

In the last half of 18th century, the Spokanes and closely allied Kalispels had occasional conflicts with their Coeur d'Alene neighbors. Most often, the Kalispels initiated the war effort by covering their heads with white chalk, then trailing to a Spokane village to drum up recruits for the cause.[148] The joined forces then elected a war chief and rode off to war. Conflicts erupted over petty matters between small parties with few casualties that usually ended by the adversaries smoking the peace pipe. During that same time frame, the Spokanes invaded their western Okana-

146 Ibid, p. 105.
147 Cox, p. 348.
148 Ruby and Brown, p. 11.

gan neighbors and drove them north into Canada before being chased back to home territory.

A smallpox epidemic in 1782 took a far greater toll than did wars when half the population of 1,400 succumbed to the disease.[149] Each village had one or two older men who assumed the title of chief; however, the "chief" exercised little rule or control over other men in the village. Names of Spokane chiefs during the fur trade operations in the area are sparse in company records. According to Ross Cox, "Chief Illin or Son of Sun, a leader of the tribe in 1813, received agreement from both trading companies that no liquor would be given to his people."[150] Nahutuwhlk, called Erect Hair, succeeded the above chief and served until 1833, when Garry returned from HBC's Red River School to become the figurehead chief of the tribe.[151] Like the Kalispel neighbors to the north, they had no trouble with Blackfeet raids. The tribe's richness lay in their massive horse herd.

According to chief factor Alexander Kennedy, the Spokane Indians and hosts of NWC Spokane House numbered about 210 families or 840 souls in 1822.[152] About 60 families of the middle band maintained a village a quarter mile from the fort; most living in pole-framed huts covered with a mat of hand-stitched tule grass they called "flags." A few hide-covered tepees completed the village scene. The upper Spokanes occupied both sides of the river at Spokane Falls to Plante's Ferry in Washington on the border of Coeur d'Alene country. Downriver below Little Falls (Tum Tum), the lower Spokanes inhabited both sides of the river down to the Columbia, maintaining their largest camp on a bench below today's Dentillion Bridge.[153]

The tribe's primary sources of protein and predominant trade item were spawning whitefish and suckers speared in late winter and early spring, along with steelhead trout and salmon caught from late June to October, all taken from the Spokane River and its tributaries. Dried for winter stores, fish alternated with a freshly killed deer, as well as locally dried roots and berries added variety to abundant provisions. They ingeniously caught fish by building barriers made of willow sticks slanted downriver at pools below sets of rapids. Behind each barrier, men planted stakes to enclose an area of about 35 yards square, into which salmon naturally swam upstream through the wicker basket funnels placed in the barrier into the enclosure. After

149 Ibid.
150 Cox, p. 104.
151 Ruby and Brown, p. 82.
152 Nisbet, 1822-23, Spokane House Report.
153 Pacific Northwest Quarterly (PNQ), vol. 30, pp. 133-35, Ray. Today Plante's old ferry is located in Spokane Valley, now a state park.

entrapment, anglers closed the funnel escape route with brush and then speared the fish with a harpoon-shaped piece of bone lashed firmly to a pole that was a foot long and 2 inches in diameter. The hooked spearhead was tied loosely to a long pole so that under a thrust into a fish the harpoon broke loose from the pole. Depending on the size of a pool, one or more persons waded in, or from a canoe, speared a fish and pulled it in by the cord attached to the pole.[154] Daily catch during the peak of the salmon run ranged from 220 to 620, with some weighing more than 30 pounds each.[155]

Cold weather required warmer clothing that included a pair of deerskin leggings and a fur robe of wolf, bear or buffalo wrapped around their body. The Spokanes made robes from locally caught muskrat hides, which they cut in strips and wove into a light, warm garment. They used the robes for blankets at night, even though some only covered their hips when standing. Obtaining necessary skins for clothing and shelter required the Spokanes to venture far for game or furbearers, simply because there were few animals in their domain. Organized hunts for congregated wintering deer normally did not supply the tribe's needs for dressed skins; however, trade with the Kootenais and Kalispels and Spokane House met those needs.[156]

Each year around August 1, a few neighboring Nez Perces and Palouses joined some Coeur d'Alenes and Spokanes to hunt buffalo on the plains with the Salish Pend Oreilles and Flatheads. Mostly adventurous young men made the long, arduous trek via the Salish Road to the Buffalo along the Clark Fork River and faced danger from the Blackfeet on the prairies. If successful, the young braves' economic and social status improved considerably.

The Spokanes hosted regular get-togethers to play games, dance and gamble for a week or more at various times of the year. Sometimes, high stakes grew to the point one village would take all other attendees' horses and property, after which a serious quarrel often erupted. One such gambling quarrel ended in a double homicide in front of the unfinished Fort Colvile on August 12, 1829, where a Spokane chief and one of the representatives of the Kootenai tribe both lost their lives. An earlier, friendly powwow exploded into a six- or seven-minute battle, in which five more Indians died. The following morning the Spokane, Coeur d'Alene and Nez Perce attendees lined up for war against the Kootenai and Senijextee (Sanpoil) tribes. Traders John Work and John Dease stepped between

154 Davies, pp. 82-83, David Douglas Journal, August 4, 1826.
155 Nisbet, Spokane House Journal, 1822-23.
156 Ibid. Kennedy, 1822-23.

the opponents and negotiated a peaceful settlement. As Work turned to walk away, Charlie, a Nez Perce horse trader, pointed a gun as if to shoot, but backed off when he noticed other Indians and HBC men watching him.[157]

The Spokanes wanted to keep their land, food resources, horses and recreation they already had, but NWC management expected more effort put into bringing in furs. White man's relentless need to "work hard to get more" disrupted the Indians' more relaxed lifestyle. Trader Kennedy labeled the Spokanes indolent, lazy beggars in his 1823 district report that included the complaint, "The tribe does not bring us 100 skins in the course of a year."[158] While recommending a move to Kettle Falls, he criticized expenses incurred by the Spokanes in return for allowing the post on their land. Kennedy thought Spokane House's high rent, a complete set of clothing each year for the three local village chiefs and filling continuous requests for tobacco – plus other river bands' requests for tobacco, ammunition and medicines – was too much. However, the company would find rent and gratuities changed little after it moved north to Kettle Falls (Colville) in northeastern Washington. Kennedy's report provided a broad description of tribes with which the company did business in the Spokane District: "The nations within this district are brave and independent, their wants are few and easily supplied, and they live constantly on what nature bestows, without giving themselves much trouble to improve their state which [work] might enable them to do."[159]

From NWC's commencement in Kootenai and Salish lands until 1818, Spokane House depended entirely on the Indians and about 25 free trappers for their furs. However, about that time, the freemen had whittled down the beaver resource in the region and joined with their buffalo-hunting relatives to trap the waters of the upper Missouri. The largely aging freemen, some being ex-employees with large families, lived on borrowed money in the form of advances for supplies. Some had little credit left after exchanging their furs. Free trappers had established homes among the upper Pend Oreille and Flathead tribes, some since 1807. Known as "the Flathead Freemen," this independent group of primarily Iroquois, mixed-blood French Canadians (Métis) and whites married and had children with Salish women. Freemen regularly out-produced their hosts in fur numbers,

---

157 John Dease letter to McLaughlin, August 15, 1829, and John Work letter to Edward Ermatinger, March 19, 1830. The Senijextee, (or Lakes tribe, a Salish speaking people), occupied the Columbia River from Kettle Falls north toward Arrow Lakes in Canada.

158 Nisbet, Kennedy Spokane House Report.

159 Ibid.

but some turned in lower quality and poorly handled pelts taken in the heat of summer. Many Salish did not take to trapping, preferring instead to supply buffalo products, dried fish and roots for trade.

During this period, the freemen endured the problematic Blackfeet while hunting beaver with other Indians both on the plains and locally. Among the 14 known, earliest freemen to arrive in the area, no fewer than five died at the hands of the Blackfeet. Others, such as Métis Charles Loyer, managed to sidestep such trouble while taking part in five consecutive Snake River trapping expeditions. Canadian by birth, François Rivet moved at a young age to St. Louis, where he worked as a subsistance hunter on the Mississippi and lower Missouri rivers. HBC considered him an American by virtue of the many years he lived in the area. Lewis and Clark hired him to move freight up the Missouri to the Mandan Indian village on their initial voyage in 1804. He was at first a free trapper and then later an NWC engagee, as an interpreter-caretaker of a Flathead post, and an HBC packer and a farm supervisor. He retired at age 74 from Fort Colvile after 30 years in the Salish country.

Métis Jaco Finlay, a Canadian free trapper, and his family followed David Thompson to the Clark Fork River to spend a winter hunting beaver on a river that today bears his name, the Jocko River. Thompson engaged Finlay as a clerk to locate and build a trading post among the Spokane tribe, which he accomplished with Finan McDonald's help. Three years later, Finlay resumed free trapper status until retiring to the abandoned Fort Spokane where he died in 1828. Jaco had nine sons by several different Indian wives, of which three were a Cree, a Pend Oreille and a Spokane. All of Jaco's sons participated in the fur trade until its profitable end, when five, along with their Salish wives, returned to the Flathead and Bitterroot valleys.

Some of the Fort Spokane management personnel also took Salish or Kootenai women for wives, and many committed to lifelong relationships. Upon transferring to other stations, the ex-fur traders brought their families to faraway outposts or, in retirement, to eastern Canada where children received the white man's education. The same applied to many company engagees and freemen. Notable and lasting country marriages included Finan McDonald and Margaret (Pend Oreille); William Kittson, who married McDonald's daughter Helen; François Rivet and his wife Therese (Pend Oreille) and his stepdaughter Julia (Pend Oreille), who wed Peter Skene Ogden; and John Work and Susette Le Grace (a half-blood Spokane). A small number, perhaps 10 percent, of HBC men and free trappers abandoned their families when they left the mountains. The abandoned women, with or without children, often married other fur men or returned to their tribes, were welcomed and well cared for, and many times remarried within the tribe.

In 1818, NWC expanded operations by launching a company-financed Snake River trapping expedition from the newly constructed Fort Nez Perce at the Walla Walla-Columbia rivers' joining in today's Washington state. Staffing this expensive operation required importing hunters, since free trappers working in Salish country were not interested in the risky venture. Workers recruited for the operation included hundreds of Iroquois-Canadian trappers, who had either migrated south on their own or were led by NWC traders to the Columbia Department, and 60 Hawaiians transported by ship to Fort George. The company engaged many as trappers for the Snake River expeditions, while others toiled as boatmen or laborers working out of its posts. Led by former Astorian Donald Mackenzie with ex-Flathead freeman Michael Bourdon as his conductor of trappers, they discovered rich beaver country in southeastern Idaho, northern Utah and western Wyoming. However, the enterprise proved unprofitable due to the unruly and unproductive Iroquois engagees and troubles with Snake and Bannock natives. After three years of operation and the merger of NWC and HBC in 1823, Fort Spokane became the supply depot and Flathead Post the embarkation point for Snake River expeditions.

In September 1820, the chief trader at Spokane House equipped about 50 Iroquois to trap in the Salish and Kootenai country.[160] In new country and with no help from the natives or corps of existing free trappers, the Iroquois' attempts turned into a huge disappointment for NWC. Added to the mass of beaver hunters was a group of Saskatchewan free hunters whom Jaco Finlay had persuaded to come to Salish country. About the same time, NWC moved its trading operation upriver eight miles from Salish House (Thompson Falls, Montana) to what is now a railroad siding at Eddy. The Flathead Post contained six huts linked together under one roof, with one of the bays enclosed for living quarters. One cabin affixed to the structure in 1825 provided a residence for the chief trader, while the other enclosed bay became a sleeping and storage area.[161] The post site had more grazing land and better protection from Blackfeet raids on the east, by a cliff called Bad Rock[162] that extended into the water.

160 [I.S.] Ross, Adventurers, Ch. 13.

161 [I.S.] OHQ, 1824, vol. 14, Elliott, Ross Journal.

162 White, Thompson, Journal October 15, 1809; Others to describe Bad Rock were Warren Ferris, Nathaniel Wyeth, Father De Smet and John Mullan.

Fort Spokane

NWC abandoned the log cabin trading post called Spokane House in 1813, for the more substantial and adjacent Fort Spokane, purchased from PFC. After completion of additions by 1824, the compound contained a chief trader's residence, servants' cabin, two storage sheds and a warehouse that occasionally served as a dance hall, all enclosed by a log stockade with bastions at opposite corners. During North West's tenure, the new location appeared in journals as Spokane House, but after HBC acquisition of the company, it became Fort Spokane. The 1822-1823 Spokane House Journal kept by Finan McDonald and James Birnie provides insight on the Indian trade conducted there among the four local tribes. As the hub of the Spokane District, Fort Spokane received most of their furs and a substantial amount of provisions from Kootenai and Flathead outposts; however, local tribes brought their trade items directly to the fort.

The Spokanes primarily supplied dried fish, roots and horses for exchange due to scarce furbearers and game in their area. The few Spokanes who teamed up with Nez Perces and Coeur d'Alenes infrequently to hunt the Missouri Plains had buffalo saddlebags and blankets to trade on occasion. The Coeur d'Alenes dealt mostly in dried fish and roots, fresh deer, muskrats, fox, wolf, and a few beaver. Sent on a five-day round-trip north to the Kettle Indians (Colvilles), employees brought back beaver, dried fish and roots. Frequently a few members of the Palouse and Nez Perce tribes visited the fort, primarily to gamble and socialize with the nearby Spokanes. The much sought-after Nez Perce horses mostly went to the Spokanes rather than to the fur men. North West Company and later HBC maintained 60 head of horses for packing goods. In a one-time, rare trading opportunity, James Birnie acquired two fine packhorses and noticed inequality among whites and Indians in the fort journal. "The Nez Perce do not seem much inclined to trade with the whites, but they are trading with the Spokanes."[163]

The traders considered the lower Pend Oreilles (Kalispels) the more industrious of local tribes, as they brought many furs and dried roots in for trade. On one occasion, they exchanged 30 kegs[164] of roots and 25 beaver pelts, and at another, eight kegs and 78 beaver. The Kalispels also liked to gamble with the Spokane at these sessions. The total number of furs from the 1823 walk-in trade was small: 43 beaver pelts in January, 160 in September and 72 in December, plus some muskrat, otter and other

163 Nisbet, Spokane House Journal, August 10, 1822.

164 Wooden barrels of less than 10-gallon capacity.

small animal furs.

In mid-July 1822, Indians from various tribes had converged on the Spokane River to catch salmon and trade for the same from the Spokanes. Unexpectedly, a band of Kootenais arrived at the fort on a peace mission with local tribes. Well-known as friendly, the Kootenais were permitted by HBC to sleep in the fort while arranging the peace council. Two days later a band of Coeur d'Alenes, traditional enemies of the Kootenais, set up camp some distance from the trading post. Apprehensive of the Coeur d'Alenes being "disposed to attack them treacherously,"[165] fort employees geared up to protect their guests. HBC people went to the Coeur d'Alene camp to advise them of the Kootenais' objective. The following morning the peace parley got under way in the fort with much ceremony and exchange of gifts between tribes. Chiefs of individual tribes expressed appreciation to the whites for bringing about the desirable event. The peace conference ended in the evening but not before plenty of smoking and talk had taken place. All of the Indians but the Spokanes left the vicinity of the trading post July 20. The Kootenais returned to their territory where, later in the summer, they made peace with the volatile Piegans, which was temporary at best!

Around 1820, after many deadly setbacks in the heart of Piegan country, the Salish hunted farther south into extremities of enemy territory. The Big Hole and Beaverhead drainages in Montana, Lemhi and Lost rivers in Idaho, and the upper Snake River Plain became their annual hunting grounds until 1840. Along with Nez Perce allies, they occupied the vacated territory of the Lemhi Shoshoni tribe, who had moved south to the Snake River. The area held huge herds of buffalo and many beaver rarely trapped by former native inhabitants. The Piegans soon found the Salish enemy hunting regularly on their turf, the region claimed by power of conquest as their own. The Small Robe band of Piegans found the task of driving the allies and white trappers out of the region overwhelming and required help from northern bands of their own tribe plus Blood and Gros Ventre warriors. Despite many setbacks, the Salish precariously maintained their presence for some 20 years in what trappers considered as Flathead country and the war zone.

The transition to the more southern hunting ground got off to a bloody start along the regularly used Clark Fork River trail to the buffalo. According to Peter Ogden's September 22, 1825, journal notation, four years earlier a large Blackfoot war party struck the Salish hunters' camp

165 Nisbet, Spokane House Journal, July 18, 1822.

near present day Deer Lodge, Montana. The Blackfeet lost 38 men. During the battle a prominent Flathead war chief was killed while leading the warriors to a victory at today's Cottonwood Creek. The Indians then named the creek Little Chief Fork, which became a regular campsite and landmark for trailing Indians and fur men. The powerful response to the attack by the Salish encouraged a peace agreement with the Piegans two years later.

Fur mens' journals rarely mention the northern or Lemhi Shoshoni dwelling in the upper Missouri or the mountain valleys of Idaho south to the Snake River region after 1824. Something unrecorded must have happened to the estimated 400 Shoshonis found earlier during the Corps of Discovery years. Pressure from the Piegans forced a move south after a number of deadly encounters. American trappers, the last to enter the region in 1823, called it "Flathead Country," while HBC counterparts dubbed it the "War Zone." They hunted remote sections of the area, noting small family groups of Shoshonis in places like Stanley Basin, Yellowstone Park and the upper Salmon River, but none seems to have existed on the buffalo ranges north of the Snake River. In remote regions, some had horses while others had none, making them less likely prey for Blackfeet raiders.

Shoshoni historian Brigham Madsen suggests that within two decades of Lewis and Clark's crossing of Lemhi Pass, the Shoshonis had consolidated into two large bands, one of which included Bannock people and leadership[166] with home territory near American Falls. With plenty of buffalo in the area, the Snake Indians rarely ventured into the "War Zone" to hunt. While in the Little Lost River valley in November 1827, Peter Ogden complained of no buffalo nor a blade of grass, a condition he credited to overuse by 300 tents of 1,500 Shoshoni hunters and their families. In June 1831, Warren Ferris, a trapper with the American Fur Company, recorded the massacre of six lodges of men, women and children on the Salmon River, as reported to him by two surviving Shoshoni hunters who had returned to camp and found the ghastly scene.[167]

Earlier in 1824, Alexander Ross penned, "The Blackfeet had made a war excursion against the Snakes, killed eight, taken some slaves and a good many horses."[168] The Lemhi Shoshoni tribe, as an independent band, ceased to exist soon after Ross' notation. Perhaps a story told by an old Shoshoni man to a pioneer merchant in the Lost River Valley explains their disappearance from traditional native soil. The old man said his people had a great battle with the Piegans near the prominent Red Butte on

166 Madsen, Lemhi, p. 28.
167 [I.S.], Ferris Journal, Ch. 17, June 22, 1831.
168 [I.S.], OHQ, 1913, vol. 14, Elliott, Ross Journal.

Horse Prairie Creek. Armed mostly with primitive weapons, the Shoshonis were no match for the Piegans, and survivors fled their homeland.

The largest band in the Piegan tribe, the Small Robes, historically rendered the most havoc upon the allies and continued to do so after the Salish changed hunting grounds. However, the Salish and their allies, well armed at that time, had created a balance of power. The Small Robes lived at a greater distance from their supply source in Canada and regularly left the southern buffalo grounds to resupply. Consequently, their tactics changed from rushing in with overwhelming numbers and arms to stealthily waiting for opportunities to strike small parties. Bold and expert horse thieves, elements of the three Blackfeet tribes continually raided Salish herds while on buffalo hunts and occasionally at home in the Bitterroot and Flathead valleys.

North West Company's 11-odd years among the Salish proved beneficial for both entities. The natives came to depend on white man's various trade goods and understood the labor needed to obtain each article. Safety improved with the acquisition of muskets, which played a role in saving the Flatheads and Pend Oreilles from extinction at the hands of the Blackfeet. Everyone had a want list: metal tools, cooking utensils, tobacco and, in prosperous times, personal items. Competition from PFC helped bring down prices for goods, but until American traders came on the scene, natives' return for beaver skins and provisions remained well below market value. The Salish people realized little change when one-time competitors NWC and HBC merged, as many of the same traders stayed and prices on trade items remained essentially the same. The new company gradually adopted cost-cutting measures and appointed tough-fisted managers to field positions where they faced stiff competition from American fur traders for skins in the Snake River country. The British firm adjusted quickly to rival tactics and price structures to outperform the Americans in capturing the majority of Salish trade.

3

Hudson's Bay Company (HBC) 1821-1825

The Montreal, Canada-based North West Company (NWC) merged with the British Hudson's Bay Company (HBC) in July 1821 to form a huge company that spread from coast to coast in Canada and in the Pacific Northwest of today's United States. North West Company had enjoyed nine years without any competition in the Columbia River drainage, but even with that advantage, it did not make a profit in its last four years of operation.[169] Returning to profitability fell on the shoulders of HBC's new officers, made up from both firms' members and directed by Governor George Simpson. The process of identifying problems that required solutions and placing men in the field to implement new policies took three years. The Columbia Department and Spokane District had functioned according to the previous policy under chief trader John Lewes at Fort George (Astoria, Oregon). During the new company's reorganization phase, the Spokane District produced exceptionally good returns in 1821, with natives and free trappers working buffalo grounds near the upper Missouri and Snake rivers to collect 70 percent of the Columbia Department skins. The chief trader's letter to Governor Simpson read in part: "Spokane Department, consisting of three posts, it is from this last department that the greatest number of furs are made, and which are of the best quality provided in the Columbia … the returns from there are 134 packs."[170]

Alexander Kennedy, a profit-sharing officer of the newly reorganized HBC, arrived at Spokane House on October 18, 1822, as the chief factor of the Columbia Department. Before traveling on to his headquarters at Fort George, Kennedy sought reasons for NWC's lack of profits in previous years. Although the Spokane Department carried the district, he identified ways to improve its profits. Prime concerns in Kennedy's recom-

169 Merk, p. 175. Simpson Letter, February 22, 1822.

170 Merk, Appendix p. 177, Letter from John L. Lewes, April 22, 1822; the three posts: Spokane House, Flathead and Kootenai. [I.S.] Chittenden, vol. 1, p. 42, wrote that a 90-to 100-pound-pack held some 10 buffalo robes, 14 bear, 60 land otter, 80 beaver, 80 raccoon, 120 foxes or 600 muskrats.

mendation to the governor involved moving the Spokane Department hub to Kettle Falls to have better control over the freemen. In his 1823 report, Kennedy wrote: "The beaver [pelts] produced from there ... [Flathead freemen] form the major part of our returns, but they are of very bad quality [and] purchased at a dear rate. These freemen are supplied with goods at much lower prices than the natives [received], and allowed greater prices for their furs, which [were] taken from them by the pound weight instead of fur skins[.] [T]his they turn to their advantage by leaving a good deal of flesh on the skin of the beaver [that] adds considerably to the weight, [plus being] killed out of season, ill stretched, and hastily dried."[171]

Before Kennedy arrived at Fort Spokane, company officials had called on the Snake River Expedition leader, Donald Mackenzie, to take a new position in Canada. That change in management brought on the reassignment for Michael Bourdon (Bourdeaux), a conductor of trappers on prior expeditions, to organize freemen from the Flathead, Kootenai and Spokane posts for the 1822 company hunt. Bourdon left the Flathead Post in early spring 1822 with 45 trappers and families, mostly Iroquois, taking the Bitterroot Valley–Big Hole–Lemhi Pass Trail to the Snake River beaver country.

Bourdon's party endured several skirmishes with the Blackfeet during the southward journey and lost two men, with another two wounded, to the enemy while putting down seven of the foe.[172] Hunting south to Bear River, known as Bourdon's River for a short time, the party turned north to trap the southern tributaries of the Snake River. At the eastern Snake River Valley, perhaps in Swan Valley, Idaho, nine Iroquois and five white and mixed-blood trappers refused to go through the hostile country but agreed to return to Fort Nez Perce. After the dissenters started west toward the fort, Bourdon had to cache 700 skins due to a shortage of packhorses. Down the trail a few days, the defectors turned east toward the Big Horn River and Mountain Crow country.[173] The frustrated leader and remaining trappers returned safely to Flathead Post loaded down with all the beaver pelts their horses could carry. Bourdon did not learn of the Iroquois' failure to report to Fort Nez Perce until months after his return to Spokane House.

171 Nisbet, Spokane House Journal, February 22, 1822. The fur industry bought dried beaver skins based on the weight of each pelt. A No. 1 skin weighed 1 pound when dried, or one point toward an exchange. Smaller beaver and other furs had a similar point value. When Indians or fur men traded furs, they received a total point value that allowed selecting from a variety of articles, each with a point value.

172 Nisbet, p. 121, Spokane House Journal, September 1822.

173 Jackson, Childner, pp. 56-57.

Not wanting to miss the 1822 fall beaver hunt, Bourdon planned to deliver the furs to Spokane House and resupply, and then return to the post to conduct the fur men on an expedition to the upper Missouri under the protection of their buffalo-hunting Salish kin. He left forthwith from the Flathead Post with seven men in canoes loaded with skins: 985 from freemen, 167 from Indian trade, and 80 damaged hides the Iroquois had left behind two years earlier. He reported to the HBC chief trader that more than 2,200 beavers had been secured in the "best beaver country west of the mountains." Within a week, Bourdon had obtained the supplies and left to rejoin the freemen to resume their hunt. Results of the fall foray are inconclusive, but in April 1823, François Rivet and his crew transported 42 packhorse loads of hides and dried meat from Seneacquoteen Landing that had originally come from Flathead Post.[174]

Meanwhile, the Pend Oreilles, Flatheads and Kootenais had an exceptionally good spring and summer beaver harvest in 1822 and traded 1,669 skins.[175] Yet, HBC traders complained of the many lower quality pelts and poor preparation, but proper training would correct that. The Pend Oreilles near Flathead Post had 16 free trappers work their way down from Saskatchewan by way of Spokane House to settle in with them.[176] The unexpected Canadian immigrant trappers traded 500 beaver caught along the way and agreed to join the Snake River Brigade the following spring. Today, three of these mixed-blood men, Antoni and Louis Valli and Keyakik Finlay,[177] have descendants living on the Montana Flathead Reservation.

Chief Factor Kennedy arrived at Fort Spokane two weeks after Bourdon had resupplied and departed for the fall hunt. Upon hearing post personnel's unhappy stories of the cached furs and defections among the expedition crew, he decided a new, more assertive headman was in order. He had one within the fort in his clerk, Finan McDonald, whom he considered an experienced, stern leader who was not linked to Flathead freemen like Bourdon.

In the spring of 1823, McDonald[178] took charge of the Snake

174 Ibid. SHJ, April 13, 1823.

175 Ibid. SHJ, November 30, 1822.

176 Ibid. SHJ, October 11, 1822.

177 Kennedy, 1822-23 Report.

178 Finan McDonald, at 6 feet, 4 inches, was a giant of a man who came to the Northwest with David Thompson as a clerk in 1809. He headed Spokane House at the time of his appointment as Snake River Brigade commander, his first and last such assignment. In 1827 he retired from the company and with Margaret, his Pend Oreille wife, moved to Ontario, Canada.

River Brigade, with Michael Bourdon as the conductor of the free trappers. McDonald had dual objectives: to reclaim the cached furs and to improve returns. Leaving Flathead Post, the brigade of about 50 men and their families used the Bitterroot Valley Trail to access southern beaver country. Trouble with hostile Piegans began soon after reaching the Big Hole, in today's Montana, where one freeman trapper died from their attack. Several days later, the trappers crossed through Lemhi Pass into today's Idaho where 75 Piegans attacked his party. A pitched battle began in which the trappers drove the enemies, who were low on ammunition, into a thick patch of timber and surrounded them. The fur men set fire to some timber to force the Piegans out in the open, where they shot down all but seven. The widely experienced Michael Bourdon and four other men lost their lives, while 68 Piegan bodies remained for wolves in the bloodiest encounter of the fur trade era.[179] After burying their dead, the trappers continued through a wide swath of beaver country to Bear River before reversing their course toward the north.

In a herculean effort, the trappers worked the upper Missouri drainage to Three Forks and ended their excursion at Great Falls in Montana. In the area of the falls, McDonald met up with Piegan trappers accompanied by a white HBC trader, Hugh Monroe from Fort Edmonton in today's Alberta, Canada, who was on special assignment with the Indians. McDonald penned a letter to fellow HBC men at the Canadian post, which Monroe delivered. A part of the message conveyed, "Piegans have made peace with the Flatheads although parts have not sanctioned it."[180] Despite harassment and skirmishes with Blackfeet along the trail, McDonald returned to Spokane House with 4,393 skins that likely included the 700 cached skins – a record never equaled in future Snake country operations. The organized HBC expedition deep into American lands was the last such venture conducted by the firm, because the undetected trespassing event posed likely political troubles for the British. Back at Spokane House, McDonald told HBC management that beaver would have "Gould Skins" before he would return to Snake River country.[181] Spokane House's returns peaked in 1823 with approximately 9,000 beaver skins brought in from all sources. Regional beaver harvest by local Indians and freemen declined steadily thereafter due to overtrapping, which prompted many free trappers to join Snake River brigades. The following spring Finan McDonald wrote George McTavish: "The Flathead Cuntre [*sic*] is rount [*sic*, ruined] of Bea-

179 Morgan, pp. 124-25.
180 Jackson, Piikani, Edmonton House Journal, p. 95, November 28, 1823.
181 Ibid. p. 122.

ver for Free men to hunt."[182]

Alexander Ross drew the 1824 beaver expedition and led 43 free trappers, many coming from a variety of posts on the Columbia Department and Canada, who joined the venture with local freemen. Iroquois Indians made up more than half of the Ross party that included 10 representatives of the Flathead, Kalispel, Kootenai, Spokane and Palouse tribes. Ross had his hands full with the widely mixed crew and unusually deep snows that blocked the crossing at Gibbon Pass and stranded the party for nearly a month at a place later named Ross Hole. Yet, their long-distance hunt to the Boise River and back reaped 4,000 beaver, but many hides fell below prime. HBC management criticized Ross for his lack of control over the unruly group of Iroquois and American trappers that tagged along to Flathead Post.

These events and others in Ross' long career caused the new governor of HBC operations in the West, George Simpson, to appraise him as "self-sufficient empty headed" and criticize his reports as "full of bombastic and marvelous nonsense."[183] After Ross' return and downgrade to a trader at Flathead Post, he drew the assignment of schoolteacher at Red River in Canada.

Ross compared the tribes he did business with in the winter of 1824-1825. The Flatheads wanted guns, ammunition and tobacco. Ross considered them clean, fond of whites, easy to trade with and moderate in demands. On the other hand, the Pend Oreilles were poorly clothed, not in any degree as clean and tidy as the Flatheads, but they did possess a sound knowledge of the trade. They also had many wants and constantly asked for more. The Kootenais fell into a kind of middle position, more particular than the Flatheads but less troublesome than the Pend Oreilles, and their tribal dress was ordinarily black from pitch pine, blood and grease.

In comparison, Kootenai men were smaller than the Pend Oreilles with an "effeminate countenance." By contrast, Ross thought the Nez Perces appeared as "manly, bold, assuming, well dressed, and independent, but stingy and little acquainted with the rules of trade."[184] Ross' ranking of the natives reflected the ease or difficulty he had in trading with them. He followed HBC's "rules of trade" that included company price for furs and goods, as well as size, quality and preparation of each pelt. His onetime observation of physical and personal traits of the various tribes was whimsical conjecture.

182 Morgan, McDonald Letter, p. 123, April 5, 1824.

183 Merk, pp. 45-46.

184 Ross Journal, 1824-25. HBCA, B.69/a/1/2F.

After HBC Governor George Simpson had analyzed each district's performance for a three-year period, he set out with a small group from Montreal in 1824 for the Columbia Department with a list of concerns and probable changes. A captain of industry, aggressive and severe in his judgments, Simpson roared into Spokane House on October 28, 1824, with the conception written in his journal the evening before: "The Columbia Department from the day of origin to the present hour has been neglected, shamefully mismanaged and a scene of the most wasteful extravagance and the most unfortunate dissention."[185] He got right down to business after meeting the district's management people and introducing Dr. John McLaughlin, the new chief factor of the Columbia Department. The governor stayed one day at the post to lay out concerns before moving on to visit other HBC operations and finally to Fort George.

Simpson returned to Spokane House April 8, 1825, after eight months of examining departments; in the course of three days, he outlined changes. To the chagrin of all concerned, Simpson replaced management, lowered wages, cut employees, and closed or moved unprofitable posts. He ordered the primary supply depot at Fort George closed and relocated along the Columbia across from today's Portland, Oregon, later called Fort Vancouver. Further directives that upset the Spokane tribe involved the movement of men and material north to Kettle Falls, Washington, where a new depot, Fort Colvile, was to be constructed.

The Kalispels appreciated the move as it provided them with more part-time work as packers and caretakers of HBC canoes, horses and supply caches on the Pend Oreille River. A change in the Snake River Expedition from the embarkment point at Spokane and Flathead posts to Fort Nez Perce incited district engagees and free trappers to grumble among themselves. Seasonal management people realized the post's relocation would cut district returns in half and cause a significant loss of work force. Free trappers who previously wintered comfortably at Flathead Post among family and friends faced a move to the new location or a long commute back to home at Flathead Post.

Simpson scorned the Flathead Post free trappers, many of whom were Iroquois, and noted in his journal: "This band of Freemen, the very scum of the country and generally outcasts from the Service for misconduct, are the most unruly and troublesome gang to deal with."[186]

Simpson deplored men laying around from November to February

185 Merk, p. 43, Simpson Journal, October 27, 1824.
186 Merk, Simpson Journal, p. 45.

at the posts when they should be trapping. To correct this situation, he changed the timing of the Snake River expeditions to fall departure and summer return. His alterations improved Salish business opportunities with HBC by terminating the import of European provisions to forts and posts. He included a promise to send pigs, cattle, seeds for vegetables and grain to complement potatoes already produced at Fort Spokane. However, the protein element of the employees' diet did not materialize for several years. Simpson's revisions put native wild meat and dried fish in strong demand at higher prices.

After reorganization, Fort Colvile employees needed to implement local methods to feed one chief trader, two clerks, four summer men and 14 voyageurs[187] and their families. Incredibly, the acquisition of domestic animals in any quantity would not materialize for 15 years. Before leaving Spokane on April 12, 1825, Simpson met with eight chiefs of the Pend Oreilles, Spokanes, Kootenais and others to explain the new company's policies, after which the governor said, "all appeared much pleased" and "promised well."[188] A Spokane chief and a Kootenai chief each sent off a son[189] with Simpson to be educated at the missionary school at Red River (Manitoba, Canada). In addition, all of the chiefs had requested missionary instructors for their tribes, which Simpson agreed to take up with British authorities, but with no profit in providing missionaries for the Indians, it is doubtful Simpson took the matter further. Nine years later, when the Americans sent missionaries west, the company gave full support to the effort. On his way east, Governor Simpson stopped at Kettle Falls to personally line out the new fort site, named it Colvile, and penned a letter to John Work ordering him to dispatch men to the new location and begin construction. At that time, the governor also dropped off seed potatoes and advised everyone that they were not for eating but planting, to meet his expectation of 30 to 40 bushels a season. He encouraged the trader to lay up "abundant stock" of fish and other provisions, as imported food from the Pacific Coast would not be available.[190]

Although Simpson addressed John Work in regard to his removal from Spokane to Kettle Falls, the latter did not take command at the new location. In a letter from York Factory in July 1825, the governor advised

187 Merk, Simpson Journal, p. 70.

188 Merk, Simpson Journal, p. 135, April 19, 1825.

189 Ibid. p. 138, The Kootenai lad, Pelly, died at the missionary school a few years after he arrived. Spokane Garry returned to his people, but rather than teaching them to read and write, because they "jawed" about it, he sank back to Indian ways.

190 Lewis, vol. 16, no. 3, pp. 102-103. Originally named Fort Colvile, the spelling evolved over time to Colville.

the chief factor, Dr. John McLoughlin, that he had decided to appoint John Warren Dease as the chief trader at Fort Colvile and John Work as the clerk at Flathead Post.

Construction of a storage building and residence began in August but progressed slowly due to unproductive labor and the time it took to saw timber into boards for the buildings. In March 1826, a blacksmith and cook stripped all the iron they could find at Fort Spokane, including all door hinges for the Kettle Falls buildings. Soon after abandonment, Jaco Finlay and his family moved into a stripped-down building at the old fort and made it their home until Jaco's death in 1828. Construction of Fort Colvile took several years to complete; however, a productive farm took root at the onset of the project that, 10 years later, produced 5,000 bushels of wheat and corn grain plus 55 head of cattle and 150 pigs.[191]

Furs from Flathead Post and elsewhere went through Fort Spokane until 1827, when the shift to water transportation down the Columbia River from Fort Colvile took place. The change in supply depots eliminated some 60 miles of moving goods by packhorses and made operations more cost effective. Canoes carried goods to and from the Flathead Post to the bay at Cusick, Washington, on the Pend Oreille River, where packtrains negotiated a steep, timbered trail over a 4,000-foot pass to the well-beaten Colville River Indian road and then north to the fort. During the height of winter, deep snows made the trail unusable to horse traffic and required men to backpack articles on snowshoes.

Liquor

Both North West and Hudson's Bay companies traded and dispersed spirituous liquors to Indians at their forts on the east side of the Rocky Mountains, and both companies provided "grog or high wine" – a strong, double-run, distilled spirit diluted with water up to eight times – to Indians when they brought in furs. The fur men considered liquor their most profitable trade item. David Thompson abhorred trade of alcohol to Indians and vowed not to give it to the Kootenais when he crossed the mountains to the Columbia in 1808. However, upon loading trade items on packhorses at Rocky Mountain House, superiors insisted he take two kegs. Mighty grumbles and grunts accompanied his loading them on a "vicious" and spooky packhorse that, by noon on the trail, had reduced the kegs to saturated kindling wood.[192]

191 Cole, p. 123. McDonald, Archibald Letter to John McLeod, January 25, 1837.
192 Hopwood, Thompson Travels, p. 256.

There is no evidence of using alcohol as a trade incentive during the tenure of NWC in the Columbia Department. However, after HBC assumed control, the management at Fort Vancouver instigated the Canadian custom of serving alcohol to local Indians near that post. It is unknown if Fort Spokane followed suit, but whatever attempts to trade alcohol to the Columbia Department Indians may have taken place ended after two years, when Governor George Simpson traveled to the district. Simpson had witnessed the injurious effects of spirits on natives while in Canada.[193] Dr. John McLoughlin, the HBC chief factor for the Columbia Department, in 1829, during the time of increased competition from American fur hunters, wrote, "If the Americans give no liquor to Indians, neither must we."[194] British traders at outposts and trapping brigade leaders provided a "dram," equal to about one ounce, on holidays and before trading sessions began.

On one occasion while trading at Flathead Post, John Work commented on the effects a small amount of rum had on a Kootenai and a female shaman dressed as a man (Qánqon): "The chief it seems has been occasionally accustomed to get a dram on his arrival, and on asking for it got a glass of rum mixed with water, which, little as it was, with the smoking took him by the head and made him tipsy. A woman who goes in men's clothing and is a leading character among them was also tipsy with three-quarters of a glass of the mixed liquor and became very noisy, ... other ... leading men who got a little were not affected."[195]

American fur companies transported alcohol from St. Louis, beginning in 1825, to their annual summer rendezvous for trappers' use. Various stories of drunkenness among mountain men at rendezvous, at which Indians attended and traded, appear in historical accounts, but none involved Indians. Scant trade records of the period do not indicate availability of the commodity as a trade item to natives. However, ornithologist John Townsend, who traveled west with Nathaniel Wyeth in 1834, indicated that Indians obtained alcohol through trade. He wrote: "Camp is crowded with a heterogeneous assemblage of visitors. The principal of these are Indians of the Nez Perce, Bannock and Shoshoni tribes, who come with the furs and peltries which they have been collecting at the risk of their lives during the past winter and spring, to trade for ammunition, trinkets, and 'fire water.' "[196] Whether Townsend actually witnessed Indians trading

193 Merk, Simpson, p. 110.
194 Barker, p. 60. McGlauglin Letter to James Birnie October 6, 1829.
195 Elliott, WHQ, vol. 5, no. 3. Work Journal, December 12, 1825.
196 [I.S.] Townsend, Ch. 5.

for alcohol is questionable, as he may have misjudged mounted natives "constantly dashing" into and through their camp, yelling like intoxicated fiends. However, American mountain men may have given Indian friends a drink out of their jugs.

In the early 1830s, the American Fur Company (AFC) had opened trading posts on the Missouri River in Piegan and Blood country and realized the need to adopt HBC's alcohol practices or lose trade to nearby competitors in Canada. Early on, Indians had received small amounts of liquor during trade ceremonies, but as the fur market shifted from beaver to buffalo robes toward 1840, the commodity became a necessary trade item.[197] Consequently, alcohol abuses among the Blackfeet Nation worsened and resulted in bloody disputes and persistent demand for the product among native customers. However, the Salish, in doing business in the HBC Columbia Department and with American firms, had little exposure to liquor until the late 1850s when smalltime white traders invaded their home country.

In July 1832, the United States government initiated a law that absolutely prohibited importation of liquor in any form to Indian country. American fur industry leaders argued against the law, saying such restraint would make competition with HBC impossible, and asked for leniency on upper Missouri operations. Despite industry pleas, government regulators attempted to enact and enforce a law that barred all exceptions, but inadequately policed the overall situation. As a result, alcohol smuggling became widespread, with incidents of bribery and/or trickery a regular practice by American fur businesses.[198] AFC's Kenneth Mackenzie, seeking a way around the ordinance, imported a still to Fort Union and turned Indian corn into alcohol. All went well until downriver travelers to St. Louis alerted authorities who soon shut the operation down.

Fragile Truce

The Blackfeet Small Robes (Inuksik) band of Piegans roaming from the Musselshell River to the upper Missouri and beyond were regular adversaries of the Salish and trappers. Centered at Three Forks, the band represented more than 40 percent of the entire Piegan population, some 150 lodges, until the 1837-38 smallpox epidemic, of which about half survived. Not one of the other 13 to 15 northern Piegan bands came close in size, averaging only about 25 lodges. The Small Robes kept to themselves,

197 Lepley, p. 74.
198 Chittenden, p. 29.

seldom meeting with other northern bands of the tribe.[199] Occupying the beaver bonanza of the upper Missouri, the Small Robes Piegan band consistently produced more skins than all other Blackfeet groups that Canadian HBC posts purchased. In 1824, the band traded more than 1,000 pelts at faraway Edmonton House. The Small Robes' great distance from a trading source, coupled with Salish equalization in hostile events, caused many in that band to consent to an imperfect peace agreement with the Salish.[200]

The tenuous peace failed to include the Small Robes' allies: Northern Piegans, Bloods and Gros Ventres who stole Salish horses throughout the period. Yet, general warfare and scalp hunting by non-peaceful entities during the period remained minimal. Independent, small groups of 10 to 40 marauders, intent on increasing their herds, frequented the Salish hunting area to steal horses.

Although buffalo and beaver hunts on southern reaches of the upper Missouri and upper Snake grew less deadly, the Salish and their allied American fur hunters continued to lose men, horses and equipment to prowling Piegans and allies. At the time of peace, the well-armed Salish and their allies more than matched the raiding Piegans by moving about in large, multitribal groups. The McDonald trouncing of the Small Robes no doubt redirected their violent behavior to decide a truce.

Moreso, resupply of arms, ammunition and other essentials remained difficult to obtain for the Small Robes Piegans, as they lived more than 300 miles from a supply source. Their origins of supply included the allied Cree, Assiniboine[201] and Gros Ventres, but munitions came from HBC posts on the Saskatchewan River. Unable to discourage Salish buffalo hunters after decades of warfare, the Small Robes Piegans chose peace. An anonymous fur trader wrote about the Salish-Piegan peace parley that occurred on the broad plains along the meandering Beaverhead River in 1823.[202] The course toward peace began as young Flathead warriors planned a raid on the Piegans in revenge for stealing a great many horses; war chief Red Feather suggested they try instead for peace. Old Head Chief Cut Thumb (possibly Big Face), supported the well-respected war chief's advice to young warriors.

The two Flathead chiefs and lead warriors went to the Small Robes'

199 Ewers, p. 185.

200 Jackson, Piikani, p. 25.

201 Signifies "stone boilers," a name applied by the Chippewa Indians to a Siouan tribe, who formerly inhabited the territory between the Missouri and the Saskatchewan.

202 Anonymous Fur Trader, pp. 11-22. Most credit this 1853 portrayal of Red Feather's exploits to Peter Skene Ogden, as various chapters in the book match places and events in Ogden's career with HBC. Ogden did not mention that name in his journals; however, William Kittson referred to Red Feather twice in his journal.

camp, peace pipe in hand. After smoking, the two adversaries aired their grievances. Central to the discussion was the Salish complaint about horse stealing, while the Piegans lamented the killing of warriors in revenge. Red Feather's presence aggravated the Small Robe leader because in the previous year, the Salish had cut off "20 of our men attempting a raid and Red Feather carried three of their scalps now."[203] Nevertheless, at council's end, the Piegan and Salish foes agreed to make peace.

HBC's Edmonton House actions had indirectly brokered conduct of the ceasefire by assigning 10 freemen with their Blackfeet wives to accompany the northern Piegan and Blood bands on their beaver hunts to American lands on the upper Missouri.[204] The freemen at HBC agreed to split up in parties of two or four men and accompany the various bands to inspire the Indians on the ease of taking the valuable animal for trade. Furthermore, the company traders strongly encouraged the freemen to lead the Indians with their furs back to Edmonton House for exchange. Making trappers out of the Piegans had marginal results, as many of the young men found it more desirable and profitable to steal horses from the many trappers and Indians traversing the area. The company's scheme improved its returns for a few years and at the same time eased violent encounters among the Blackfeet, the Salish and HBC trappers.

Alexander Ross provides information on the truce in his June 19 journal during the 1824 Snake River trapping expedition. While camped along the Wood River near the future Hailey, Idaho, a band of 40 mounted Piegans made a surprise visit. Initially, the fur men expected trouble, but the Indians exhibited peaceful intentions to meet and smoke with the Ross crew. As night fell, the Indians entertained the trappers with music and dance. A Piegan chief told Ross they had left their land in the spring to conduct an "embassy of peace" with a Snake Indian tribe; however, while passing the peace pipe, a Shoshoni brave shot their chief, an act that provoked a Piegan to kill two of their young friends. The chief ended his story by saying, "We are now on our way to meet our friends the Flatheads" whose party of 100 strong was not far off.[205]

Later in the year, while conducting the annual winter HBC trading session at Flathead Post, Ross recorded the presence of Piegans. Writing November 29, 1824, Ross indicated that attending were 128 lodges of natives with 1,850 horses encamped at Horse Plains to await their turn to trade. Counting men, women and children, there were 306 Flatheads with

203 Ibid.
204 Jackson, Piikani, p. 97.
205 [I.S.] OHQ, vol. 14, pp. 382-84, Elliott, Alexander Ross Journal.

180 guns, 247 Pend Oreilles with 40 guns, 212 Kootenais with 62 guns, 66 Nez Perces with 20 guns, and 30 Spokanes with six guns. Each tribe had its own day for trading. First, the Flatheads exchanged 324 beaver pelts, 159 buffalo tongues and a large portion of the 11,072 pounds of dried buffalo meat that HBC purchased during the season. Second, the Pend Oreilles traded 198 beaver pelts December 3. Then the Kootenais, accompanied by 10 Piegans, traded 494 beaver and 509 muskrat pelts. Ross' journal of that day explained, "The Kootenai don't belong here but are driven from fear of the Piegans."[206] Ross evidently thought they should trade at Kootenai Post; however, the Tobacco Plains band north of Flathead Lake was closer to Flathead Post. In keeping with the fragile truce, the Salish people camped with the Piegans at Horse Plains.

Journals kept by Peter Skene Ogden and his clerk, William Kittson, provided information on Salish activities during the year and insight on conditions of the fragile truce. Ogden led the 1825 Snake River Expedition from Flathead Post with the largest number of trappers in the company's record; yet by its end only about half the men and material returned to the starting point or to Fort Nez Perce. The journey began with 58 men, 65 women and children, and 268 horses transporting gear over the Bitterroot Trail toward the Bear River in Utah. Salish peace with the Small Robes and Salish protection salvaged the fur men's expedition.[207]

In an earlier start than usual, in late April 1825, the Flatheads and a band of Kootenais led by old Chief La Breche[208] left the Bitterroots for the buffalo grounds. The old chief and a subchief had been entrusted with delivering an important letter from HBC Governor George Simpson at Fort George to the Snake River expedition leader Peter Ogden at an unknown location in southern Idaho or northern Utah. Company employees carried Simpson's letter and others to Flathead Post and transferred them to the Indians who agreed to find Ogden. The two chiefs' payment for services rendered included two pistols, 200 balls and powder, and 2 pounds of tobacco.[209] Chief La Breche and his people took a direct route to southeastern Idaho, where he chose the site for their 38 lodges on the Teton River near its junction with Henrys Fork of the Snake River,[210] and

206 [I.S.], Elliott. Ross Journal, December 3, 1824. Fur men considered buffalo tongues a delicacy and paid high prices for them.

207 Ibid. December 20, 1824.

208 Old Chief La Breche's name, given him by the French-speaking fur men, was most likely Big Face; this Indian head chief would have been in his 70s during this time frame. He should not be confused with old Chief La Buche (Rough Hewn) who is also in this text.

209 Rich, pp. 251-252. Alexander Ross Letter.

210 Rich, p. 61. Ogden Journal.

dispatched scouts to find Ogden. Within a few days, 40 tepees of Small Robes Piegans arrived and encamped near the Flatheads in a demonstration of the peace agreement between the two former enemies. The poorly armed Piegans had intended to help themselves to Snake horses that summer. Warned by the newly arrived Piegan neighbors that a group of the Bloods, Northern Piegans and Gros Ventres were on the warpath, the Flatheads sent men to pass on their warning to the Little Lost River band of hunters that had separated earlier to find meat.

Meanwhile, short-handed after the desertion of half his men to American fur traders near Salt Lake, Ogden made a hasty retreat north to the Snake River. Directing his course toward the Lemhi and Salmon country with just 20 trappers, their families and a valuable haul of beaver hides, he thought the Salish buffalo grounds safe enough to continue hunting. After they crossed the Snake River near today's Blackfoot, Idaho, and traveled 10 miles northwest toward the Lemhi, Flathead scouts arrived, to the good fortune of Ogden. The Indians informed Ogden of their camp just four days' distant on Henrys Fork with plenty of beaver nearby and letters for him that old Chief La Breche had carried from Flathead Post. Ogden wrote June 7: "I was glad to learn the Flatheads were at Henrys Forks as that quarter is[,] I believe[,] still rich in Beaver but being the general rendezvous of all the War tribes and our party being weak, I did not dare attempt going in that direction. … I shall lose no time in reaching it as we [s]hall have the Flat Heads to protect us."[211]

The Flathead scouts and Ogden's HBC trapping party broke camp late the following day; the messengers made a beeline for their Henrys Fork camp, and the brigade began a seven-day trapping jaunt up the Snake River through a sagebrush and grass plateau toward the Flathead camp. On the second day out, Ogden's party met up with 25 friendly Small Robes with only four muskets amongst them that left camp with the Salish, outbound to steal horses from the Shoshonis, or Snakes. Two days later at the southerly bend of the Snake River, two Flatheads, a Kootenai and a Piegan, all chiefs, rode out to meet Ogden and join his party. Chief La Breche handed Ogden the letter from Governor Simpson that ordered him to return to Fort Vancouver via the Umpqua River, rather than to his original Flathead Post starting point.[212] Two and a half days later, after turning up Henrys Fork, Ogden's crew and the chiefs reached the combined Piegan-Salish

211 Rich, pp. 57-58, Ogden's Journal, June 7, 1825.

212 Ibid. p. 60, Ogden's Journal June 12, 1825, HBC officials and Ogden thought the Umpqua River originated in Utah rather than in its actual location west of the Cascade Range in Oregon.

camp at the mouth of Teton River and pitched their tents.

The highland plain of dry sagebrush and grass gave way to a lush green valley, its waterways lined with cottonwoods and willow – ideal habitat for beaver and buffalo. Leaving the Small Robes behind, the Flatheads broke camp on June 16 and moved northwest up Henrys Fork for three days to trail buffalo while the HBC men trapped beaver. The large group had limited success on dispersed hunts until they crossed Fall River, where both parties found and killed many buffalo near today's Ashton, Idaho. The Indians required three days to process their kill, during which time trappers worked the river and streams to the east. Ogden had relaxed his rules and allowed his men to spend the night away from camp near set traps, but few availed themselves because of the region's hostile standing.

A sign of peace occurred on June 20, when 40 Northern Piegans from a distant camp of 45 lodges appeared at Ogden's location to request a trading session. In a show of goodwill, the Piegans returned a horse the trappers had lost in early spring. Ogden felt concerned that if he refused the request, "their furs would soon find their way to an American camp." He completed a trade for 112 beavers and three horses, but he refused demands for ammunition: "We have already too many enemies in this quarter already too well provided in arms and ammunition without adding to the quantity."[213] Denied their appeal for ammunition, the Piegans settled for tobacco and beads; despite paying the outrageous price of four and a half skins for tobacco, they rode off in good spirits. Four days later on Sunday, the day for worship and rest for the Flatheads, Ogden and his men had time to visit and join in their games.

Later Ogden recorded his take on the tribe's trapping efforts: "The Flatheads exert themselves to Kill beaver but they have only seven traps"[214] among them, and that "bad and dear" were their words for how well a trap secured a beaver. "Bad" meant a severed foot or a lost beaver if the anchored trap was not set firmly in the water; and "dear" meant it was like a fist grasped and held firmly. Ogden understood, for he wrote, "Scarcely a day passes without a loss." Other Flatheads shot the furry rodent while still in its pond, hoping to recover the carcass without excess wading or diving into the water. Sunday afternoons, Indians and trappers held foot and horse races, during which the Salish prevailed. Ogden's clerk, William Kittson, found the events important enough to include them in his journal and summed up a footrace by writing, "One of our young men came up with [the

213 Ibid. p. 62.

214 Rich. Kittson Journal, June 26, 1825.

best] of the Flathead Indians."[215] Apparently, a young white trapper came close to winning the footrace, but an exuberant Indian took first place.

Leaving Henrys Fork June 25, the outsized trappers' camp skirted the ridgeline through a rock-strewn sagebrush and grass prairie toward the northwest, to the head of Camas Prairie, where they spotted a northern Piegan camp of 50 lodges a mile off. Expecting an attack, the Flatheads prepared for battle and approached the camp singing a war song. Gesturing as friends in an obviously docile manner, the Piegans rode out and invited the trappers to share their camp and food, but the Flatheads held back. It took the return of a stolen horse and 70 beavers in trade to Ogden before the skeptical Flatheads encouraged the trappers to move on.

After traveling nine miles west a day later, the Flatheads and trappers encountered 150 Piegans and Bloods and three Canadian free trappers. Avoiding perfidy, Ogden only invited leaders into the trappers' camp. Riding slowly into camp, the entourage followed with one chief bearing the English flag. All sat down to smoke and discuss interests. A Piegan chief expressed interest to trade at Flathead Post in the fall, as the great distance to Edmonton House had been blocked by their enemy the Assiniboines. Afterward Ogden traded tobacco for 39 beavers. The Blackfeet compatriots had secretly contracted to HBC Edmonton House on a mission involving travel with the Piegans to harvest pelts on American ground for the company. Somewhat distressed Ogden penned a letter to the "Gentlemen of the East – York Factors," outlining his troubles in the sector and the potential for active American competition in the future.[216]

Early the next morning, as the Blackfeet Nation's Piegan-Blood party broke camp, Ogden gave the letter to freeman Maurice Picard for delivery to a Canadian HBC post. The next morning, the Flatheads and Ogden moved across a pass into American territory where all of the HBC men continued the company's illegal beaver trapping activities unbeknownst to rising American competitors. Having previously met with the 800 or so unpredictable Blackfeet without serious incident to date, the Flatheads and fur men decided not to press their luck and pushed north toward the main Salish camp at Horse Prairie, tributary to the Beaverhead River. Some of the Camas Prairie band of Piegans had joined the Flatheads' procession, while others followed behind, loaded with cords to capture horses. The night before the crossing at Monida Pass to safer country, thieves struck and helped themselves to several Flathead horses and two from the

215 Ibid. p. 63, June 26, 1825.

216 Rich, p. 64. Ogden's Journal, June 28-29, 1825, Maurice Picard and James Bird Jr., both half bloods, and white man Hugh Monroe accompanied the Blackfeet.

fur men. Horse stealing aside, considering the number of customary enemies the Flatheads and fur men had encountered since leaving the Snake River, indeed, the fragile truce seemed real.

After crossing the Continental Divide, the Flatheads with Ogden's trappers in tow moved down toward Red Rock River where they found abundant buffalo and killed many. The procession reached the 70 lodges of Flatheads and Pend Oreilles[217] on July 3 at Horse Prairie Creek encampment at its union with Red Rock River that forms the Beaverhead River. Moving toward home, old Chief La Breche and 36 lodges of Flatheads-Kootenais separated from Ogden and the large, primarily Pend Oreille encampment for their destination at the Big Hole, which increased the load of dried meat already carried by their horses. Chief Red Feather remained in charge of the encampment. According to Kittson, he was a "good looking Indian commander.[218]

Two days later, Ogden and his crew departed the camp to trap the headwaters of Horse Prairie Creek and its tributaries that would indirectly lead them toward the Big Hole River Valley and, again, link up with La Breche. Just as the trappers completed their trek, Red Feather and his Pend Oreilles and Flatheads tied in with them near the head of the valley with the news of a great herd of buffalo grazing there. The chase soon got under way as the trapper and Indians killed 300. During the chase, the horses under a couple of young Pend Oreille hunters spilled their riders. One Indian did not wake up after the tumble.

After a day of drying meat, Ogden separated from the busy-at-the-same-task Indians, pushed on to the mouth of Gibbon Pass where Chief La Breche and his people had camped, and prepared to return home to the Bitterroot Valley. From there, Ogden dispatched Kittson and two men on July 16, 1825, to deliver 18 horse loads of furs to the Flathead Post and Fort Spokane. Led by Flathead Chief Gros Pied and 10 lodges, the pack string followed a day behind La Breche's long caravan of Indians like a string of beads rolling over the pass in the heat. After leaving Kittson safe at Lolo Creek, Gros Pied and a few braves rode four days west over the Lolo Trail to trade for horses with the Nez Perce. The travel-weary chief returned to Kittson's camp below Thompson Falls in just 19 days' time, well pleased with his exchange.[219]

Previously, at Horse Plains on the Clark Fork River, Kittson had

217 Rich, p. 242. Kittson Journal, July 3.

218 Ibid. This Red Feather is likely a different chief than Insula, or Michael, who also went by Red Feather.

219 Ibid. p. 245, July 21.

transferred to a company canoe while his packers transported the furs to his campsite. Kittson made a brief stop at the old Flathead Post and found it in good order before going on downriver to Thompson Falls and spent a hungry two weeks waiting for the new Flathead Post Trader John Work and supplies to arrive.[220]

Meanwhile, Ogden's crew had continued trapping with six engagees, 17 free trappers and several Flatheads, while their children played as their mothers minded campfires, kept the stewpot filled and fresh-aired robes ready for bed. For the next two months, a few Salish guided the trappers to an area beyond the security of a large, well-armed, friendly encampment nearby while making a loop route in country less frequented by hostiles. From the valley, the men trapped northwest, crossed the Continental Divide at Sugarloaf Pass and down it to the head of the Clark Fork, and then west toward the present-day Phillipsburg, Montana, valley.

Sporadic harassment from small groups of Blackfeet had not interrupted trapping the valley streams as Ogden's trappers worked down Flint Creek to the Clark Fork River. At the mouth of Flint Creek on August 17, Ogden laid out plans for his trappers to work the Little Blackfoot River – very near Piegan country – which stirred up all kinds of loud and profane displeasure at the idea of risking life or limb to non-peaceful, northern Piegan visits. Several freemen actually defected for friendlier ground but promised to return when Ogden and the remaining 16 men returned to Salish protection. Near the entrance to the Little Blackfoot a few days after departure, two freemen scouts reported the Piegans had trapped that river out. Although that was an unlikely account, Ogden chose to accept it and turned south along the Clark Fork River to complete the loop back to the Big Hole.[221] While making this loop, the trappers endured many successful and unsuccessful attempts to steal horses by small groups of two to eight Blackfeet. On a few occasions, with the help of Flatheads in the party, they chased down the robbers and reclaimed their horses. Great numbers of Blackfeet and their allies usually stayed clear of the area at that time of year as buffalo were scarce[222] and Salish horse herds few.

Ogden and the Salish Flatheads faced raiding parties that operated in small groups acting independently from the central leader of the tribe. Blackfeet culture promoted horse thievery as a means of gaining property

220 Rich. Kittson Journal, pp. 244-248.

221 Rich, Ogden Journal, p. 73.

222 Ibid. Ogden Journal, p. 74, August 18, 1825. Near Drummond, Montana, Ogden spotted the buffalo, hunted to near extinction by the Salish before fur traders' appearance. The upper Clark Fork drainage was the only ideal habitat near Salish home territory. Many fur men in the mid-1830s reported the bison never lived west of the Continental Divide.

and status within their ranks. Being poor, these Indians simply wanted to build a horse herd in the least risky way. Using stealth rather than force, the majority tried hard to avoid a fight by slipping quietly into a camp in the darkest of nighttime to snatch a few horses. Both Small Robes Piegans who had honored the truce and the thieving northern Piegan and Blood camps were scattered about the Big Hole when the trappers returned. Eight Piegan horse thieves loaded down with cords[223] and provisions met up with a few trappers to say they intended to rob the Flatheads, whose camps were not far away. The friendly leader of the party informed the men that raiders had just returned to their camp of 150 lodges with 53 American horses stolen on Bear River. After receiving the report, Ogden sent two men to warn the friendly Indians and the deserters he thought were in their camp. For six days, fur men moved gingerly about the mid-Big Hole with ears tuned to unfamiliar sounds, one eye on trapping, the other to spot unannounced and wily Blackfeet.

Also on August 17, Chief Gros Pied and six HBC trapper employees left Flathead Post with supplies and extra horses for Ogden, whom they expected to find in the Big Hole,[224] and he carried letters for Ogden along with responsibility for securing horses during the journey. The Gros Pied party found signs in the Big Hole and surmised Ogden had moved off toward the head of the Big Hole River. Three of the HBC men rode slightly ahead of Gros Pied with two men, each trailing horses when, crossing a dry gully, 27 dismounted Blood and Piegan marauders suddenly jumped the men and tried to seize their horses. Two were so surprised and shaken they forgot all about their own property, HBC goods and packhorses in their care. The other fellow resisted his attacker and hung on to everything he had because he kept his head, remembering the chief was right behind them.

Within minutes, Gros Pied and the other trappers burst on the scene to drive the renegades away with what plunder they had in hand. In their haste, raiders got off three shots without effect. Gros Pied aimed straight and sent a shot through the body of a Blood thief, killing him on the spot. The surviving Bloods and Piegans put heels to their mounts and thundered away with two guns, 17 traps, 18 horses, 20 pounds of ammunition and miscellaneous other items. The evening of September 7, after inventory of materials brought in by the ill-fated packers, Ogden lamented in his journal "the many serious losses … sustained during the unfortunate

223 Many leather strips or cords used (as ropes) for tethering horses indicated potential thievery.

224 Rich, p. 248. Kittson Journal.

voyage I now begin most seriously to apprehend that we shall never reach the Columbia."[225] The afternoon following notification of the robbery, a Pend Oreille chief arrived at Ogden's camp to offer his influence among Blood chiefs to recover the stolen property, as soon as his camp of some 1,200 arrived in the valley to start the fall hunt. It is likely the Blood chiefs had no control over the raiders. His efforts, if made, failed to produce results. Five days later, 172 lodges of Pend Oreilles and a few Flatheads began arriving at Ogden's camp in the Big Hole, along with 10 tardy free trappers, of which six had agreed to rejoin Ogden to trap along the way to Fort Nez Perce. Blackfeet horse thieves acted like magpies drawn to a big slaughter.

Despite strong security, within a few days 30 horses disappeared from the Salish herd, along with some belonging to trappers. Soon after that, the Pend Oreilles caught three Piegan thieves near the edge of camp, administered a severe beating to each and cropped one's ear before turning them loose. With buffalo scattered all over the valley, the Salish raised camp to find better opportunities elsewhere and moved east with Ogden over Beaverhead Pass to Grasshopper Creek Valley. Hunting there was no better. It only prompted another move to the Beaverhead River plains near today's Dillon, Montana. The large procession entered the valley late on September 21, 1825, only to find 200 tents of the Bloods and a handful of Gros Ventres and Piegans encamped near where they had intended to hunt. Stopping a mile away, the Salish and trappers set up tents.

Later in the evening with peace pipes in hand, the Indians went to the enemy's encampment to see if they would accept a visit. They would not. After returning to camp, the Pend Oreilles and Flatheads prepared for the real possibility of a fight. Ogden wrote: "All bustle and strong guard, [during] the night no appearance of fighting."[226] The following morning, notwithstanding 10 horses' disappearance overnight, the Salish chiefs repeated their peace pursuit while others broke camp. After several hours in cold rain and the possible return of stolen horses, traditional adversaries again parted as friends – at least for the day. The session ended at noon when the Indians and trappers trailed southeast across the level prairie of Blacktail Deer Creek. The encounter and subsequent powwow exemplifies Blackfeet respect for Salish warfare abilities, and perhaps, horse stealing aside, they became a part of the fragile truce. Ogden did not get his HBC property back.

---

225 Ibid. p. 78, Ogden Journal, September 7, 1825.

226 Ibid. p. 83, Ogden Journal, September 21, 1825.

After three long days along a narrowing trail, the Indians and fur men descended into the Red Rock River plains where many buffalo were killed and the meat dried. Overcrowding with men, women, children, dogs and horses within the camp prompted Ogden to move off a few miles to prepare his meat for the trek to Walla Walla. Before leaving, he ordered two HBC employees to remove and return fur caches left along the way back to Flathead Post. Ogden's crew dwindled when five free trappers refused to leave the Salish sanctuary for Fort Nez Perce.[227] Dutifully, he and 18 men trapped their way some 500 miles to the Fort.[228]

Ogden took his family along on expeditions whenever possible. His wife, Julia, goes down in history in at least one recorded incident of bravery and ingenuity in dealing with life-threatening happenings with her children on her husband's 1825 expedition.

While camped at Mountain Green, Utah, Julia found herself and her children, including 6-year-old son Charles and infant Michael, in the middle of American leader Johnson Gardener and her husband arguing over deserters. Hastily, she gathered her children from harm's way. First, she put 8-month-old Michael in the saddle pouch of her horse and returned for the others. When she came back, baby and the horses were gone – cut loose by a deserter.

Julia followed their tracks that led to the American camp about a half-mile away and marched right through the middle of camp and grabbed her horse with her baby still attached. She noticed one of the company packhorses loaded with beaver. After mounting her horse, she seized the packhorse by its halter and led it back through camp.

Mountain man Joe Meek retold the story of what happened next to his biographer. "At this undaunted action, some of the baser sorts cried out, '[S]hoot her, shoot her[!]' [While] the majority vehemently disagreed: '[Let] her go; let her alone; she's a brave woman. I glory in her pluck."[229] Julia and her children traveled with her husband on five trapping expeditions in the Pacific Northwest, Utah, Nevada and northern California. Michael became an HBC trader at Fort Connah, located south of Flathead Lake, Montana.

Considering Ogden's experience in the war zone and the fragile

---

227 Elliott, WHQ, vol. 15, no. 4. Work Journal, December 21, 1825. The five freemen: Charles Loyer, Jacques Beauchamp, Charles Groslouis, Antoni Paget and Jean Baptiste Gadawa turned in their furs at Flathead Post.

228 Rich, p. 84. Ogden Journal, September 28, 1825.

229 {I.S.}Victor, Ch 5, Meek was not in the mountains at the time of the event. He no doubt heard this story in a campfire confab

truce, his Snake River expedition fared reasonably well despite engagees and freemen desertions. William Kittson and his HBC crew transported part of their catch of 44 packs that contained 2,700 beaver skins and arrived August 1 at Thompson Falls[230] on the Clark Fork River to wait for canoes coming from the Seneacquoteen landing on the Pend Oreille River. Over the next two months, more Snake River hides dribbled into Flathead Post and Fort Nez Perce for a total count of 3,694 beaver and 47 land otter,[231] all destined for Fort George on the Columbia River.

The newly appointed Flathead Post trader John Work and several men pulled in at Thompson Falls with four large canoes on August 14, 1825, and met Kittson with the Snake River skins. Non-buffalo hunters and early returning Kalispels, Coeur d'Alenes, Spokanes and Kootenais awaited his arrival to trade their goods. In a half-day trading session, Work added 468 beavers, some provisions, saddle blankets, saddlebags, robes and dressed skins to his load.[232]

Four days later, HBC men transported the cargo downriver to Seneacquoteen landing, then sent off for packhorses at Spokane to complete the journey to the fort, a process that took 39 days. A few weeks later, Work and his trading crew turned around to conduct the regular fall trading session at Flathead Post, arriving there November 24. They found the building floorboards ripped up by Indians looking for anything worthwhile that may have fallen through the cracks. A fire built in the middle of the traders' residence had gone out due to dampness in the log structure that required minor repairs. Likely, the vandals were Blackfeet raiders making their rounds between the time Kittson passed the post on July 30 and when the traders arrived nearly four months later.[233]

As Work got things tidied up a bit and his goods unpacked, customers began showing up, led by three chiefs, the Pend Oreilles, a few Flatheads and Spokanes; they traded 518 beaver pelts, 11 otter pelts, 4,094 pounds of dried meat and fat, for mostly guns, ammunition and tobacco, in the first five days. The Indians complained that Work was more difficult to deal with than his predecessors, moreso on his first mission as Flathead Post trader and being a stranger to the Salish. Apparently, this trading tactic occurred whenever a new man took the post, yet Work wrote, "[They] seemed well pleased not withstanding that not a single item of their [price]

230 Rich, Appendix, p. 246. Kittson Journal, August 5, 1825.
231 Merk, John McLoughlin Letter of account to George Simpson, March 20, 1827.
232 Rich, p. 247. Kittson Journal, August 16, 1825.
233 Elliott, WHQ, vol. 5, no. 3. Work Journal, November 24, 1825.

demanded would be abated."[234]

Major items obtained by the Indians during the trading session included 115 pounds of balls, 78 flints, 37 pounds of powder, 14 muskets, 2 pounds of shot, three and a half dozen gun worms (a corkscrew-type device to removed unused wads or balls from a gun barrel) and three beaver traps, 41 scrapers, 11 dozen folding knives, files, axes, 79 thimbles and 18 and a half pounds of brass and copper kettles. Personal items included 20 hawk bells, 2 and a half yards of green transparent beads, 12 looking glasses, a half pound of vermillion, and lots of tobacco. Work noted that gun worms, awls, flints, and some tobacco and knives generally were free to those Indians bartering furs. According to the Spokane House Standards of Trade, 60 pounds of dried meat bought an Indian a good blanket and a scalping knife, or 3 pounds of gunpowder or 2 and a half pounds of twist tobacco. A common trade musket required 310 pounds of dried meat and fat.[235] Work paid three and a half pluis (plews) per 60-pound bale for lean and dried meat, back and inside fat.[236]

Kalispel women arrived at the post with much-needed tule mats to trade on December 8. After completing business, the men set about using the mats to cover leaky roofs of residences and fur storage areas. A day later, 20 Nez Perce buffalo hunters arrived ahead of their Flathead hunting partners, riding gaunt horses. Following the customary musket salute to the fort and like response from the traders, they told Work the Flathead would be along later as their mounts were sorefooted and underfed, too. The Nez Perces traded only 18 beavers, being more inclined to hunt buffalo and trade its many parts for mostly tobacco and ammunition. Four days later, 60 to 80 Kootenais from the upper river band arrived at Flathead Post.

An interesting member of the leadership group included a woman, Qánqon, dressed in men's clothing, who had a female traveling companion. Respected by her tribe as a shaman and well versed in the Salish language, she served as interpreter for the post fur traders. [237] The Kootenais had brought in many furs: 981 beavers, eight otters, 1,200 muskrats, six fishers,

234 Ibid. November 26, 1825.

235 Merk, p. 173.

236 Elliott, WHQ, vol. 5, no. 3, p. 186. Work Journal, November 30, 1825.

237 Ibid. November 29, 1825, Qánqon grew up below Kootenay Lake, where she met and married trader Augustin Boisverd in 1809. Kootenae House became her home place for a short time until David Thompson asked Boisverd to send her back to her people, due to "loose conduct." Returning to her tribe, she claimed her white husband transformed her into a man and henceforth wore that attire. When Thompson made his canoe voyage to the mouth of the Columbia River, Qánqon, and a female companion had been camped near Fort George for two weeks, providing spirit talk to local Chinook natives. After returning in their canoe to home country, the couple settled in with the upper Kootenay Band. She had many other adventures, finally meeting her end in 1837, attempting to broker peace between the Blackfeet and Flatheads. See *Sources of the River* by Jack Nisbet for more on Qánqon.

seven minks, 10 martens, 21 elk skins, 27 deer skins, nine saddlebags and 31 fathoms of cords, in exchange for 12 guns, three blankets, a few kettles and, above all, ammunition and tobacco.

In early December, the old Salish Chief La Buche (French for "rough hewn") and eight attendants visited Work at the Flathead Post. Work invited the old chief to stay with him in his residence. Their visit lasted five days, in which time the two established a friendly relationship that would last throughout Work's career in the Columbia Department. Records show Work always identified the old chief as a Flathead, but the La Buche camps were located at Horse Plains and farther up the Flathead River in the then upper Pend Oreille territory. Hudson's Bay Company men often called Indians living near the post and upriver from Lake Pend Oreille "Flatheads" as both tribes spoke the same language, hunted together and traded at Flathead Post.

On December 17, 1825, after inching a long pack string of horses over Bad Rock in cold rain, three chiefs and 60 to 70 Flathead braves rode up to trade at Flathead Post, singing and firing their guns in the air above the British flag carried by a chief. Head trader John Work stepped outside to observe their approach, ready to invite the chiefs into his cabin to smoke while his employees and the braves unloaded, filled the other cabin, and opened storage bays to prepare for business the next day. Continued nasty weather into the evening left all those who wanted to stay dry with little choice but to bed down inside tight quarters.

The air had turned dry and frosty by morning when Work instigated trading, and by noon they had finished. His count tallied 222 large and 107 small beavers, one otter, four buffalo robes, 72 buffalo saddle blankets, one elk skin, 18 packsaddles, 113 fathoms of cords, or leather horse leashes, four hair bridles, 52 bales or 3,122 pounds of dried meat, 119 fresh and 23 dried buffalo tongues, two bosses (hump fat), and 10 pounds of castorum (beaver-scent glands) used in the manufacture of perfume.[238]

At the end of the trading session, Work paid 20 balls, powder and 2-foot lengths of tobacco to each chief and the same to Gros Pied for bringing in brigade leader Peter Ogden's Snake River furs. Gros Pied's braves also earned powder and balls. In the afternoon, the Flatheads left for their winter camp with horses worn sore from chasing buffalo all summer. Work's journal entry grumbled at the amount of dried meat and fat exchange needed to feed employees at the new Fort Colvile. The Indians argued they

238 Elliott, WHQ, vol. 15, no. 4. Work Journal, December 17-19, 1825. Cords were about six feet in length. A measurement made by the length of a man's outstretched arms from fingertips to fingertips, or about 113' x 6'= 678 feet.

had reserved the rest for their own use as bad trails ruled out a winter hunt and they had a mind to winter over to trap beaver until spring.

Other fur men's journals provide evidence of peace between the Salish and Small Robes Band of Piegans. Their joint presence at the fall and winter trading session at Flathead Post would not have occurred in times of conflict. On August 17, 1825, trader John Work wrote: "Flathead, Kootenies [*sic*], Ponderas [*sic*] [Pend Oreilles] and Piegan[s], of the latter there are but very few. A considerable number, 30 tents were coming, but from some cause turned back." December 23 he added: "The Pend Oreille blamed for stealing some ... Kootenai horses. It's reported that the Piegan stole seven of the best horses from the Pend Oreille that went first off to the Buffalo."

Later, after returning from a horse-buying trip to the Nez Perces, Work noted on July 30, 1826, from Palouse Prairie: "A few young men arriving in the evening from the buffalo, from them it was heard that the F Heads are now on their way to meet us to trade. Peace is again made between them and the Peegans [*sic*]." Piegan supply problems also became apparent to Peter Skene Ogden on his second Snake River expedition in March 1826. Close to camp near today's American Falls, Idaho, he and his men encountered 90 mounted Piegan warriors. Ogden met the Indians on neutral ground and recognized their chief as one he had traded with on the Saskatchewan River in Canada years before. They had been on a horse stealing expedition against the Shoshonis. Ogden noticed how poorly armed they were, only 15 guns and ammunition almost gone. Some warriors did not have so much as a bow or arrow. As the 90 turned away, the Piegan chief warned Ogden "to stay on guard."[239]

American fur men also noted the "fragile truce" in August 1827 when William Sublette's command prepared for a hunt on upper Henrys Fork in what they dubbed Flathead country. It was probably near Henrys Lake in August where the Americans had a visit from the first friendly party of Blackfeet since entering the mountains when the Small Robes Piegan Chief As-As-To came to asked if Sublette could send a trader to build a post in the Beaverhead River country. When Sublette asked if any of his men would volunteer for the mission, just three volunteered. The far darker, mixed-blood James Beckwourth, with but one year of experience in the mountains, agreed to lead the party. Supplied with trade goods, the Americans rode several days north with Piegan guides to their unidentified encampment not far from a cluster of Flathead lodges.

239 [I.S.] Elliott, Ogden Journal, March 29, 1826.

While there, an altercation broke out during a scalp dance in which Piegan warriors celebrated the killing of three white men from an American trapping outfit. Beckwourth had clubbed his Piegan wife, who disobeyed his order not to dance with the Indians, which infuriated the celebrators, who all thought the mountain man had killed her. The Piegan Chief As-As-To saved Beckwourth's life by reminding the warriors of the rights a man had to discipline his wife. A number of Salish and a Flathead were in the Piegan camp at the time of the incident. After Chief As-As-To had cooled the Piegan warriors down, the Flathead chief complimented him for his action and said it would be war if any Americans died. Late in the evening Beckwourth's wife crawled into their tent with an aching head.

After 20 days of trading, the Beckwourth party of four left the Piegan camp, with 39 packs of beavers and extra horses, for Sublette's camp. Many Piegan warriors led them to within two days of Sublette's camp when concerned Flathead braves[240] joined the caravan. Peace or truce aside, the Salish did not trust such an escort of unpredictable Piegans. Traders and hides did arrive safely at the trappers' camp, but that was the last time the Rocky Mountain Fur Company (RMFC) had friendly dealings with the Piegans.

Fragile truce or Piegan supply problem, whichever the case, the Salish and their allies engaged in no major battles with their longterm Piegan enemies until 1831. Yet, small groups of roving Piegans continued to steal horses – a legitimate activity in their society. Then again, the Salish regarded horses as personal property obtainable only through purchase or exchange. Often in rebuttal, the Salish pursued Piegan thieves to recoup a few or as many horses as they could lay hands on. Such unfriendly exchanges eventually led to violence and demise of peace.

240 [I.S.] Beckwourth, Ch. 10. The storytelling Beckwourth's account of his stay with the Piegans and trading success is likely embellished, but it illustrates the fragile truce at work at the time.

4

Beaver, Buffalo and Blackfeet

1825-1831

With the exception of one long year, the Inland Salish tribes had but one trading outlet in their region; however, that changed for the buffalo hunting faction when the American fur men entered the mountains. Besides beaver and other furbearers, a large portion of Salish trade items included various provisions purchased by HBC to sustain employees throughout the year. An unlimited market for dried buffalo meat and the animal's many by-products drove a large part of the Salish people to work hard to harvest and process the large beast in excess to their own survival needs. The business involved many obstacles, not the least of which was long distances to transport goods to the marketplace in all kinds of weather conditions, all the while harassed by Blackfeet raiders. As American fur men arrived in the mountains, new trading options appeared right on the Salish hunting grounds. Within a few years, no less than four competing firms operated in the area, all seeking their business primarily for beaver skins and horses. Americans' new supply source allowed over-wintering on the buffalo grounds, which some Flatheads, Pend Oreilles and allied Nez Perces took full advantage; it was like having a convenience store nearby.

After American concerns began to make inroads in capturing Salish trade, HBC raised the price for beaver pelts to match competitors and maintained lower prices on trade goods. Such changes, with most Salish hunters returning home to a nearby trading post, limited American trading effectiveness. As the era progressed, all competitors employed other measures to corner the Salish business, much to the consumers' delight. HBC prevailed due to the Americans' high cost of transporting goods from St. Louis and subsequent prices for items at rendezvous. American traders who operated in Snake River country had a small advantage over HBC, as they needed only half the number of horses and men to handle them, due to HBC's longer distance from supply depots, thus lowering costs. Nevertheless, when the Salish needed essentials on the hunting grounds, such as powder, balls or tobacco, one or another of the numerous American firms was at hand and eager to supply them. The tireless quest by brave and rugged men in quest of profits, in effect, amounted to waging war against the beaver.

When fur traders entered the far Western mountains, all waterways of less than 4 percent gradient supported large beaver populations. Unhindered by modern-day roads, bridges, farms and other developments, the beaver dammed creeks at will, built wood lodges and dined, primarily, on the bark of streamside shrubs. In northern heavily timbered regions, prime habitat was mainly of far less desirable woody mix. However, the upper Missouri, Snake and Bear rivers' drainages and prairie valleys were cut by meandering streams lined with willow, aspen and cottonwood that supported large populations of beaver. As the widely traveled free trapper Michael Bourdon reported in 1822 to superiors, the country "is the best for [b]eaver this side of the mountains." Fur hunters concentrated efforts in the region that included Salish hunting grounds for more than a decade.

Trappers and their native families conducted business in large groups for protection from menacing Blackfeet raiders. Operating out of a single camp, the men split up in pairs, often traveling several miles to set and check their traps, all the time looking over their shoulders. Upon capturing the usually drowned beavers, trappers quickly skinned them and carried the pelts back to camp for fleshing and drying. Before competition from rival trappers, HBC moved rapidly through a drainage area, staying no more than one or two nights in one spot, and not harming the fur resource. However, rivalry led to overtrapping when Americans came on the scene, because both sides tried to catch every beaver before another guy got it. After intensive trapping pressure, the prolific beaver developed the habit of retiring to its lodge or burrow for several days which prompted trappers to move on to greener pastures. Fur hunters either bypassed overtrapped waterways or struggled to make poor and unprofitable returns. Both company and Salish trappers employed similar methods in capturing beaver, but that is where the similarity ends. Very few natives took to trapping even though their trade numbers at Flathead Post appear high. In one of the better trade years, some 200 potential Flathead and Pend Oreille trappers exchanged 522 beaver skins for an average of two beavers per man. Salish and Kootenai pelt production remained steady for a number of years, but according to Peter Ogden, the Indian trade had diminished by 33 percent in 1828 in the Columbia Department as a whole.

American Fur Hunters

Opportunistic American fur traders challenged the lower Missouri River system shortly after the Louisiana Purchase from France in 1803. Initially small groups of independent trappers worked the river and side streams up to the Mandan villages. Within a few years, organized firms joined the rush by establishing trading posts along the river, and then extended their reach to the Yellowstone River and beyond. Forts established in Blackfeet territory at Three Forks had overwhelming troubles with the natives and closed down almost before completion. The southern migrating Blackfeet received their supplies from British establishments north along the Saskatchewan River in Canada. The new American adventurers had difficulty establishing their business in the hostile country until they followed HBC's example and employed large, well-armed trapping parties to penetrate the dangerous country. A little over two decades after the land purchase, competition between rival American firms peaked, which led to fierce bickering, deceit and business failures. Meanwhile, the HBC monopoly, a company of Indian traders with many years of experience, held a great advantage over the Americans.

HBC realized the Americans would soon set traps in the Snake River country after the 1818 treaty partly specified lands be joint occupancy in Oregon Country west of the Continental Divide. First, in July 1824 the HBC London committee ordered the chief factor of Columbia department to "get as much out of Snake Country as possible for the next few years."[241] Their objective was to create a buffer zone or fur desert to discourage American hunters. Governor George Simpson reiterated the committee's directive during his October 28, 1824, meeting with the staff of Spokane House. His journal of that day reads: "If properly managed no question exists that it would yield handsome profit as we have convincing proof that the country is a rich preserve of Beaver and for which political reasons we should endeavor to destroy as fast as possible."[242] Political issues involved British leaders' desire to add portions of Oregon Country to their colony of Canada. The strategic plan overwhelmingly failed because numerous American trappers poured into Snake Country over the next several years. American fur men would outnumber HBC brigades by more than 3-to-1 and had more to do with the eventual beaver population decline than HBC.

The founder of the American Fur Company and subsidiary Pacific Fur

241 Merk, p. 46.

242 Ibid. p 242.

Company John Jacob Astor's brilliant attempt to establish permanent trading posts on the Columbia River failed because of the war of 1812 with Great Britain. Had the enterprise succeeded, the fur business climate in the Pacific Northwest would have been far more equitable. After the fact, he persistently worked to improve the American competitive position on issues of liquor trade to Indians, where operations overlapped, and of import duties. In a letter dated January 29, 1829, to U.S. Senator Thomas Benton, Astor wrote in part: "It is known that none of the goods for Indian trade such as Indian strouds, and cloth of particular descriptions, are as yet manufactured in this country. We are obliged to import them from England and it just so happens that those are just the articles paying the heaviest duty. The English traders have theirs free of duty, which enables them to buy ... goods 60 percent and over cheaper than what we pay.... But this is not all ..., they send their furs [to New York] ... and undersell the American Traders ... free of duty, which we, if we send any to British Dominions, are obliged to pay 15 percent."[243]

The subject of an import duty system did not deter ex-Lieutenant Governor of Missouri William Ashley from opening a new business he called Rocky Mountain Fur Company (RMFC). Instead of zeroing in on the Indian trade, he hired and equipped large crews of men in St. Louis to hunt beaver farther west. The first to enter the beaver-rich country of Wyoming's Green River in 1824 were American fur hunters employed by Ashley, who separated into groups to explore and trap tributary waters of that river. One of Ashley's lead men, Jedediah Smith conducted six trappers northwest to the Bear, Portneuf and Blackfoot drainages, learning new country and trapping beaver. In mid-September, Smith stumbled on 12 destitute Iroquois without weapons and with a few horses, near today's town of Blackfoot, Idaho. The detached HBC group camped, hunted buffalo and gambled there during the heat of summer with the Shoshonis rather than go after beaver as ordered. After a while, a gambling quarrel erupted where the Shoshonis robbed them of personal belongings and ordered them to leave camp. With only the clothes on their backs, the destitute Iroquois paid Smith 105 cached beaver pelts to take them to Alexander Ross' HBC's camp. Unfamiliar with the country, Smith received directions from the Iroquois around the impassable lava flows on the Snake River Plain that opened to productive beaver country. The explorer-trapper not only got paid but gained hard-to-come-by knowledge of the country that otherwise would have been costly or difficult to achieve. He and the delinquent Iro-

243 Chittenden, vol. 1, pp 20-21. Strouds were British-manufactured wool blankets of various plain or striped colors.

quois arrived at Ross' camp in mid-October.[244]

From Lost River, the Americans joined the HBC brigade and received a guided tour of fertile beaver country all the way to the Flathead Post. Smith's crew included two future legendary mountain men, William Sublette and James Bridger, all of whom stayed nearly a month at the HBC post. The Americans studied details regarding camp organization, resupply tactics, and security measures relevant to prowling Blackfeet. After observing HBC's profitable trade with the Salish, Smith planned to tap the Indian source of furs in the future. However, his firm of Rocky Mountain Fur Company made no progress in that direction for two years.

Of those wretched Iroquois Smith rescued, Old Pierre Tevanitagon was the leader of the lot that included troublesome Ignace Hatchiorauanqsha (John Grey) of half-white and half-Iroquois birth. As an outspoken representative of the Iroquois, Grey habitually rubbed British brigade leaders the wrong way with many threats and complaints. British brigade leaders all vented frustration over the self-regulating Iroquois' easy distractions from hunting beaver when buffalo or other natives crossed their path.[245] Effective as trappers, they were difficult to control as a group. Most Iroquois preferred free trapping while Old Pierre's group became engagees under contract to the British brigade. The Americans left Flathead Post with the outbound Snake River Brigade of 75 men and their families, led by Peter Skene Ogden. Both parties traveled together for three months on the prior guided route, until late in March 1825 when Smith separated his RMFC outfit from the HBC fur hunters in Lemhi Valley to head south.[246]

Ogden's HBC brigade worked south to Cache Valley, Utah, with fair success in gathering beaver hides. In May 1825, they crossed south over a low divide into the headwaters valley of today's Ogden River in untrapped virgin country within Spanish Territory. After several days of exceptional beaver harvests, 30 Americans under the truculent Johnson Gardner happened upon the brigade and set up camp nearby. He and others in his group offered the British trappers more for their hides and better prices on supplies. Desertions from British ranks began immediately. By the fourth day, Old Pierre with 13 engaged Iroquois and 10 freemen quit to join the Americans. Many defectors kept their hides, ignoring their debt to the company; however, during subsequent years HBC would recover many of the losses. Reduced by more than half, Ogden's party broke camp en route

244 [I.S.] Elliott, OHQ, 1824, vol. 14, p. 385, Alexander Ross Journal October 15, 1824.

245 Jackson, Children, p. 10.

246 Morgan, p. 137.

to the Snake River.[247] In a year, as new employees in Ashley's outfit, the defectors would, through purchase, become part of Rocky Mountain Fur Company d.b.a. Smith, Jackson and Sublette.

Peter Ogden waited nearly three years to obtain details of what motivated the defection of half his men. For three weeks spanning New Year's Day of 1828, his expedition shared a snowbound camp with a few RMFC trappers near the mouth of the Portneuf River led by Samuel Tulloch. Ogden nearly choked when he learned the competition paid $5 per skin for both large and small sizes, a wide difference from HBC's rate, which, at that time, was $2 for large and $1 for small. The trappers also could choose to deliver the furs to St. Louis and obtain $5.50, of which about one-third of the Americans took advantage. The trapping majority that chose to get their goods at the rendezvous paid at least 150 percent of the supplies' cost, "dearer than we do," Ogden noted in his journal.[248] Without knowing HBC's markup, it is impossible to know the full economics involved in the defection, but with Americans swarming all over Snake River country, Ogden realized change was already in the works.

Furious over the defections, HBC made plans to meet the anticipated American competition for Salish furs and realized it would only be a matter of time before Americans made a trading contact with them. Dr. John McLoughlin, chief factor of the Columbia Department, wrote trader John Work at Spokane House regarding the likelihood of Americans operating in Flathead country. In a letter dated August 10, 1826, McLoughlin directed: "in case the Americans come to the Flathead country, they must be opposed as much as we can, but without a waste of property. ... It is not in our interest to spoil the Indians; however we must do so if necessary and treat them as liberally as [do] the Americans."[249] Even before Work received the letter, three Pend Oreilles reported some Indians were gathering near Thompson Falls for the fall trade session, but most were still on the buffalo grounds with the Americans and "indifferent" to trade. The information and directive put Work and crew in motion toward Flathead Post with an assortment of goods. The party traveled by horse to the Pend Oreille River, transferred to canoes and arrived at Flathead Post on August 24, 1826, but no Indians; three days later, Work and two men set off for the Horse Plains campsite. Upon arrival, they found 50 lodges of Flatheads and Pend Oreilles led by Chiefs La Buche (Rough Hewn), Gros Pied (Big Feet), Grand Visage (Big Face) and Bourge (Pimples), a Pend Oreille.

---

247 Rich, Kittson Journal, May 23, 1825; and Ogden, May 23-20, 1825.
248 [I.S.], Elliott. Ogden Journal, June 5, 1828.
249 Merk. McLoughlin Letter, p. 281.

Work, the chiefs and principal braves sat together to smoke and exchange news. The chiefs reported a small collection of provisions and furs to trade, because other native hunters (Nez Perces) overran the buffalo grounds. There had been no wars, but while engaged in a horsestealing episode, a Pend Oreille and a Piegan lost their lives. Accordingly, a large party under Grune (Little Crane) and Red Feather remained at Rivière de Mer (River of the Sea) with nothing to trade and weakened horses that prevented their coming.[250] The Indians told Work a party of Flatheads had gone with two HBC Snake River deserters, Iroquois Jacques Ostiserico and John Grey, to several American camps while on the buffalo grounds and accompanied the hunters back to Horse Plains. Familiar with the Salish language, Jacques spoke of two trading companies with large shipments coming to the mountains, each with 150 or more packhorses. Stretching the truth a bit further, Jacques reported three American ships had set sail for the Columbia with trade goods. Grey presented tobacco and some scarlet cloth to Chiefs Gros Pied and Grand Visage, making it clear the gifts were from American leader William Ashley. The HBC deserters went on to say he wanted to see them when he came from the east with supplies. In all, 22 Flatheads, Nez Perces and Snakes, of which there were two, went with Grey and Jacques to the American camps.[251]

Throughout chronicles of American operations in the Rocky Mountains, a few Flatheads and Nez Perces are so-called members of various groups. Newcomers to the mountains not only utilized them as trappers but tapped their knowledge of the country, trails, beaver locations, etc. Few Indians were interested in the pursuit of full-time trapping. Perhaps 16 of these Flathead fortune seekers were part of an American party that told campers at the 1828 Bear Lake Rendezvous of RMFC Robert Campbell and his party's whereabouts and shortage of ammunition.[252]

Salish chiefs voiced concerns to Work about a young Indian's report that a white man had told him Americans would soon "get the country." Those words spoken on the southern buffalo grounds spread among the Salish, causing them to wonder if the current trading session might be the last. Work reassured them by first scheduling the next session, then telling them the white man was likely a deserter. Work suggested the Indians bring in any deserter among them. Returns from the trading session fell far

250 Elliott, WHQ, vol. 15, no. 4. Work Journal, August 24, 1826: Rivièr de Mer (River of the Sea) location is unknown but is likely the Salmon River. An unnamed author wrote about Chief Red Feather's exploits and death in the book *Traits of Indian Life and Character*. This Red Feather is not Insula, who sometimes went by the same name Red Feather.

251 Ibid.

252 [I.S.], Bonner. Jim Beckwourth, Ch. 9.

below usual: only 221 beavers, 990 bales (7,200 pounds) of dried meat, 66 saddle blankets, a few cords, dressed leather and five lodges.[253] Competition for Salish skins had begun, as the American traders had intercepted a portion of the beaver pelts on the buffalo grounds.

A faithful photographic reproduction of the Charles M. Russell painting "The Buffalo Hunt No. 39." COURTESY WIKIMEDIA COMMONS

In the summer of 1827, RMFC Robert Campbell was given charge of 18 men, all former HBC employees that included Old Pierre, his Iroquois and a few others, each familiar with the Salish territory and its people. Trailing north from Bear Lake, the Campbell group trapped Henrys Fork, Beaverhead, Clark Fork, the Bitterroot rivers and finally the upper Big Hole River. At the latter, they tied in with Salish and Nez Perce buffalo hunters in late fall. Bison were abundant in the valley, but the Indians refused to allow trappers – then short on provisions – to shoot any. The Indians had planned a "surround" of the herd and did not want it spooked. The Salish preferred that method of hunting buffalo when the right conditions prevailed.

Trapper Joseph Meek described just such a hunt when he and a few companions joined the Salish and Nez Perces near Red Rock Lake, Montana, in 1837. Like other mountain men, Meek had a propensity to embel-

253 Elliott, WHQ, vol. 15, no. 4. Work Journal, August 26, 1826.

lish his take on the hunt.

> We started slow: nobody war [*sic*] allowed to go ahead of camp. In this manner[,] we caused the buffalo to move before us, but not to be alarmed. We war [*sic*] eight or ten days traveling from the Beaverhead to Missouri Lake [Red Rock Lake] and by the time we got thar [*sic*], the whole plain around the lake was crowded with buffalo and it was a spledid [*sic*] site. In the morning the old chief haranged [*sic*] the men of the [Indian] Village, and ordered us all to get ready for the surround [*sic*]. About nine o'clock every man war [*sic*] mounted, and we began to move.
>
> That war [*sic*] a sight to make a man's blood warm. A thousand men, all trained hunters, on horseback, carrying their guns, and with their horses painted in the height of Indian fashion. We advanced until within about a half mile of the herd: then the chief ordered us to deploy to the right and left, until the wings of the colume [*sic*] extended a long way, and advance again.
>
> By this time the buffalo war [*sic*] all moving, and we had come to within [*sic*] a hundred yards of them. Kowesote [Nez Perce hunt leader] then gave us the word, and away we went pell mell. Heavens, what a charge! What a rushing and roaring – men shooting, buffalo bellowing and trampling until the earth shook under them. It was the work of half an hour to slay 2000 or maybe 3000 animals. When the work was over[,] we took a view of the Field. Here and there and everywhere, laid the slain buffalo. Occasionally a horse with a broken leg war [*sic*] seen, or a man with a broken arm, or maybe he had fared wurse [*sic*], and had a broken head. Now came out the women of the village to help us butcher and pack up the meat. It was a big job; but we war [*sic*] not long about it. By night the camp war [*sic*] full of meat, and merry. Bridger's camp which was passing by that way traded with the village [Indians] for 1500 buffalo tongues.[254]

Packing up their meat, Campbell and the trappers, two Flathead warriors and one of their wives all headed south for winter quarters.

Near the head of the Red Rock River in today's Montana, they came upon a Piegan village and set up camp nearby. Then, several Iroquois trappers went to the Piegan village for a visit, only to find fortifications built up for protection, which seemed to the trappers to indicate a war party. The Piegans quickly repaid the social call – maybe to size up a raid – raising suspicion among the trappers. Early the next morning, Campbell and party left for Henrys Fork with the Piegans not too far behind, who after following some 60 miles attacked the party on the Teton River. Pierre, who had edged too close to the Piegan line, lost his life to a well-placed ball, as did

254 [I.S.] Victor, Joe Meek, Ch. 19. Meek called Red Rock Lake, Missouri Lake. The headwaters of the Jefferson, Madison and Henrys Fork of the Snake all came together above this lake.

the married Flathead brave. Cheering him on, the wife had followed him into battle. After the fight, Campbell found only a part of the old Iroquois chief's body – a foot – in the Piegans' deserted camp. The skirmish occurred in what became "Pierre's Hole" in today's Teton County, Idaho.[255]

A few days after the fight, several Iroquois shot down two Piegan horse thieves and scalped them in the presence of a horrified Campbell. The Indians put a foot on the dead body, fastened fingers in the hair with one hand, ran a knife around the skull above the ears with the other, and yanked the scalp off in an instant. Balking at going farther south for fear of more Blackfeet attacks, the Iroquois and two others returned to the Salish buffalo hunters and finally to Flathead Post. Campbell, the surviving Flathead and a Frenchman continued south to winter in Cache Valley, Utah.[256] During the winter they lost four horses to Mountain Crows who gathered them up after a visit with a nearby Snake camp. In a brave attempt to recoup the lost, the Flathead offered to go down to the Shoshoni camp in the night, but Campbell dissuaded him. Within a few weeks, the wintering party departed for Bear Lake to meet a company trapping party and raise a cache of supplies.

From there Campbell separated from the Flathead and trappers to retrieve the Iroquois and furs. Campbell and two mixed bloods struggled through deep snows on snowshoes to reach the usually snow-free country at the mouth of the Portneuf River, where they found conditions much the same for the two trapping outfits that had holed up there for the winter. Nonetheless, the trio left them behind and began a 44-day snowshoe trek with mixed bloods' packdogs for Pend Oreille country. The only tent carried on the grueling trek housed the dogs at day's end.

Meanwhile, the Iroquois toasted their shins around the fire, enjoying a cozy winter at a part-time camp on Horse Plains, stuffed with lip-licking colt meat when Campbell found them. During that same time, 14 former HBC employees showed up at Flathead Post to trade for essentials.[257] Disrupting the Iroquois' comfortable reunion with the Pend Oreilles, Campbell urged his party of 30 men, women and children on to the summer rendezvous at the south end of Bear Lake, taking many beaver along the way.

Campbell and party had a pack string loaded with cached and newly trapped beaver when they crossed the Snake River. Nearing the

255 [I.S.], Campbell Narrative 1825-35.

256 Cache is a fertile valley in the Wasatch Mountains of Utah and Idaho, watered by the Bear River.

257 Morgan, p. 427. Dr. John McLoughlin Letter to George Simpson, July 10, 1828.

Bear Lake rendezvous site, Campbell sent word with 16 passing Flatheads, also en route to the same destination, that they were in desperate need to replace inferior ammunition. Fortunately, by nightfall of the next day they had obtained some powder and balls from four trappers dispatched from the rendezvous, who remained with Campbell. The next morning and still 18 miles from their objective, Campbell noticed a large band of unidentified natives tagging along behind. Unconcerned at first, he assumed they were friends that regularly attended the annual affair; yet, as they got closer, one of Campbell's Flathead's recognized their chatter as Blackfeet. The trapper contingent ran for cover of a willowed spring surrounded by rocks, with the enemy hot on their heels, and a standoff firefight began.[258] Four hours later, two trappers raced through enemy lines toward the rendezvous site for help. Consequently, the hostiles retreated but took $5,000 worth of beaver furs and 40 horses with them. The encounter led to the camp cook's death, and two trappers and a child were wounded.[259]

The Bear Lake Rendezvous broke up late in July 1828, with two fur trading companies setting sights on Pend Oreille country. Rocky Mountain Fur Company (RMFC) partner David Jackson and his party, including his clerk Thomas Fitzpatrick, trapped their way north. Supplied by American Fur Company (AFC), newcomer Joshua Pilcher and crew followed Jackson's more experienced crew closely. By early December, both parties arrived at Flathead Lake, where Pilcher pitched camp on its shores to wait out the winter while Jackson's trappers worked the Flathead, Clearwater and Kootenai river drainages. Winter's deep snows and thick timber cover made for tough going; horses were of little use. In early winter both outfits, tired of eating beaver flesh, made contact with the Pend Oreilles and HBC Flathead Post to trade for provisions.

The December 1828 trading session at Flathead Post turned into a big disappointment for HBC Trader John Warren Dease and his eight men. Upon arrival, he found only a small band of Pend Oreilles and some free trappers waiting to swap furs but no provisions. A few days later, the Flatheads arrived with 40 Americans; most were in David Jackson's RMFC and a few in Joshua Pilcher's outfit.[260] The Americans carried very few trading items other than cloth, tobacco and some "iron works." Dease

258 [I.S.], Campbell Narrative: Bear Lake spans Idaho and Utah border. The powder brought to the previous rendezvous was of poor quality. Over the course of the year, Blackfeet had learned of the American weapon problem and charged Campbell's party, assuming they had not resupplied.

259 Morgan, p. 298, Ashley Letter.

260 Dease Letter to the Governor and the Council of Northern Depot, HBC Archives D.4/122/11tf.

learned they had exchanged most of their inventory to natives along the way for horses and provisions, at a cost of five packs of furs or 300 skins. Dease did acquire half the American skins for such things as rum, sugar, coffee and a few other necessaries.[261] HBC's ban against giving alcohol to the Indians did not apply to the Americans. By that time, Pilcher and his company had such poor luck, the newcomer quit the fur business, sold his traps and transferred his men to RMFC.[262] The winter of 1828-29 was lean for HBC Fort Colvile employees, as the Salish traded only 2,040 pounds of dried meat and fat and 117 tongues, or less than 10 percent of their usual production.[263] The Flatheads told Dease they had a poor year on the buffalo grounds due to Piegan problems throughout the entire hunt. Following the Salish to the Bitterroot Valley, the fragile truce ended as Piegan marauders revived their practices of robbery and murder. Just two days from that trading post, the Flatheads lost two in an attack.

Separated from his partners for two years and thought dead, RMFC partner Jedediah Smith ran into Jackson on the upper Flathead River in early spring of 1829. His disastrous trapping venture to the West Coast suffered the loss of 19 men on the Umpqua River in Oregon, massacred by Indians, and temporary loss of horses, supplies and hides. After making his way with two other survivors to the British fort at today's Vancouver, Washington, the kindly HBC chief factor Dr. John McLaughlin helped recover his property from the Umpquas. They purchased Smith's hides and excess supplies, and informed him of other Americans trapping the Flathead country. Extending their courtesy, HBC transported them up the Columbia by canoe to Fort Colvile where they purchased horses to complete the journey. Smith found Jackson and his crew near today's Whitefish, Montana, in an unexpected yet fortunate reunion. With their trappers, RMFC partners Smith and Jackson left the Salish and Kootenai country in April, never to return. The firm's returns for the year amounted to a modest 45 packs plus whatever Smith sold to HBC at bargain basement prices.[264]

After the 1829 rendezvous at Pierre's Hole, Smith expressed his appreciation of HBC's assistance to their firm and asked his partner, William Sublette, to withdraw their trappers and traders from the western side of the mountains for the present so as not to come in conflict with that company. Sublette reluctantly consented and issued orders for moving east over the mountains to trap and set Wind River Valley in Wyoming as

261 Ibid.

262 Morgan, pp. 269-71.

263 John Work, Colvile District Report, April 1830, HBC Archives, B.45/a/3/15.

264 Gowans, p. 49.

wintering grounds.[265] That arrangement lasted a year as the partners sold RMFC to Milton Sublette (William's brother), James Bridger, Jean Gervais and Henry Fraeb.

HBC expected more rival American trappers to arrive in the Salish home territory and hunting grounds, thus affecting returns in Indian trade, so they adjusted prices to meet competitors head-on. In an 1829 letter to Chief Factor Dr. John McLoughlin, an optimistic Governor George Simpson outlined steps to meet the opposition: "We shall soon be masters of the Field as those people [American firms] we know to be needy adventurers, existing on a bad credit who cannot afford to follow up a losing business." McLoughlin's and Colvile district's orders read: "Mr. Dease at Flathead Post is to sell to Indians at the American tariff; also to have on hand a larger stock of luxuries than usual to meet the demands of the American trapper. … In that way a considerable part of their hunt can likewise be secured."[266]

The governor's plan to capture American trade did not materialize, as few trappers ventured into Flathead and Pend Oreille territory. However, Salish furs bought more goods at HBC posts, which encouraged the Indians to transport their catch to the post. HBC returns for the year remained steady in 1829, for in late March it took eight men in three canoes to transport pelts and meat to the drop point at Usk on the Pend Oreille River.[267] In the same month, John Work's 1829 Colvile District follow-up report contained a census of Indians living within his trading area. Collected over an unspecified period, the numbers began with John Dease's work a few years earlier, when he listed only men. Work expanded the count to include women and children, information presumably obtained through trade dealings and communication with the Indians. The count is unusually precise.

Tribe	Men	Women	Boys	Girls	Totals
Spokane	222	241	111	130	704
Colville	96	110	61	74	341
Pend Oreille	283	248	207	185	923
Kootenai	182	215	118	115	630
Flathead	150	180	164	169	663
Coeur d'Alene	157	112	60	75	404

Clerk John Work, as acting chief trader, wrote the Colvile annual report due to chief trader John Dease's illness and removal to Fort Vancou-

265 Victor, Ch. 2.
266 Merk, p. 308. Simpson Letter, March 15, 1829.
267 Work, Answers to Queries and Samuel Black, Ft. Nez Perce District Report, 1829.

ver. Afterward, a promotion put the energetic Work in charge of the 1830 Snake River Brigade. Francis Heron then assumed the chief trader position at Fort Colvile district. The changes in key fort personnel led to the assignment of Clerk William Kittson as trader at Flathead Post.

Letters from Francis Heron to the Kootenai and Flathead traders addressed policy for the pending sessions: "You will trade at the tariff of last year, and treat the Indians all together as they have hither to been treated. If however the Americans cast up in your quarter, your scale of trade must of course be regulated by circumstances. Get the skins in that case as cheap as you can, but let not one fall into the hands of an opposition that can be purchased at any price. ... The Indian [Salish] ought to be made to understand the impolicy [unwise act] of allowing Americans to hunt on their lands." Heron's reference to "last year's tariff" reflects the major price adjustments for goods made by management to counter American competition for the Indian trade. The company reduced the price on the most popular items: Indian trade guns went from 18 large beaver to three and one-point blankets from five large beaver to one. All other goods lowered in value, the same proportion as above. Chief Factor McLoughlin lamented to top management that the Indian furs in the Columbia department cost five times more than in the past.[268] The change in price structure paid off immediately, for both the company and Salish, for Flathead Post exceeded the previous year's returns by 300 beaver, numerous buffalo by-products and more than 6,000 pounds of dried meat. Similar results occurred among the Kootenais and other tribes; all were inspired to work harder to capture beaver. The changes brought on by competition for Indian skins thwarted American firms' attempts to capture Salish trade.

Clerk William Kittson, no stranger to Flathead Post, embarked with eight men from Fort Colvile on November 2, 1830, to conduct the fall and winter trading session. After arrival at the post, storage sheds began to fill up with Pend Oreille skins, and, at the same time, snow began to pile up in the usually sheltered valley. The Flatheads did not arrive with their harvest until Christmastime when weather conditions turned brutal.

Deep snows engulfed the whole of Salish country that caused widespread death and fatigue to area horse herds. In response to a prior directive, Kittson dispatched five men in canoes from his post in mid-January

268 Baker, pp. 23-24. McLoughlin report to London committee, August 5, 1829. Indian blankets varied in color from white, scarlet and blue, often striped with bands of a different color. Grades were determined by weight and according to a point system from one to five. The one-point blanket, addressed above, weighed three pounds and measured two feet eight inches wide and eight feet long.

with a letter, three bales of meats and two small bales of leather. His letter reported a good trade, but deep snows would make it difficult for natives to trap beaver as planned and requested sorely needed trade goods. The canoe men had a difficult voyage down the Clark Fork and Pend Oreille rivers due to 23 ice jams that required portages to reach Pend Oreille Bay near today's Cusick, Washington. Exhausted and nearly frozen, the voyageurs found half of the 11 packhorses starved to death and the others too weak to tackle such deep snows, so they cached the larger portion of supplies, donned snowshoes, and trudged 50 miles through deep snow over a mile-high pass to the Colville River valley and on to Fort Colvile.[269]

Kittson had ordered trade goods for his post, but nasty weather put off sending the requested items and retrieving the cache at Pend Oreille Bay until mid-February 1831. Flathead Post men and four hired Colville Indians led three horses loaded with goods up the Colville River valley to the snowy mountain trail where they transferred the packs to their own backs and crossed to Pend Oreille Bay on snowshoes. After returning to Fort Colvile from the bay in 10 days' time with the meat and leather, the four Indians received pay of five beaverskins for their choice of trade items that equaled two medium blankets.[270]

With ice jams nearly gone, on April 2, 1831, the Flathead Post cargo canoes pulled into Pend Oreille Bay loaded down with hides, exceeding the previous year's returns. Most furs came from the Salish's preceding fall hunts as this spring's trade amounted to a trifle. Among the assorted furs were 878 large and small beaver, 170 buffalo fur saddle blankets, 54 dressed skins and only 690 bales of dried meat. The Pend Oreille and Flathead women spent the nasty winter dressing skins, while the men killed snowbound deer and elk. The company's new price structure for goods had inspired the Salish to bring in more beaver than in the past and more than the usual from the high-producing Kootenais. The achievement won the Pend Oreilles and Flatheads HBC's "Good man as hunter of beaver status."[271]

Starting in 1831 and for nine years thereafter, the Salish had lots of company on their hunting grounds. Fur companies operated 30- to 80-man crews that represented HBC, RMFC, AFC, Bonneville and Wyeth, who periodically trapped throughout the area. These men often camped and traveled with the friendly Flatheads, Pend Oreilles and allied Nez Perces and shared the favored winter quarters at the confluence of the Lemhi and Salmon rivers

269 Fort Colvile Journal, April to December 1830, kept by Wm. Kittson and Francis Heron.

270 Ibid. February 1 to 24, 1831.

271 Ibid., n.d.

and mid-Lemhi River country. Both sites were usually free of deep snow with plenty of game nearby; frequently, Salish hunters returned to home territory in early December with large supplies of dried meat for trade and winter use. For several years, smaller bands or families of the Salish Nation wintered in the region; those left behind had bison nearby should dried supplies run short. Periodically, some 300 American and British beaver trappers passed through Salish hunting grounds and nearly destroyed the resource in less than a decade. Fur men initially depleted beaver populations in drainages south of the Snake River before moving north to the beaver-rich Blackfeet region centered on the upper Missouri River system. American firms dominated the scene, each having large numbers of armed men and trade goods. An influx of competitive traders into the region made life easier for the Salish by eliminating the need to travel back home to HBC's Flathead Post.

Ambitious American traders cut into the British fur profits from 1826 to 1831 until the longtime Salish suppliers put men in the field to travel with Indian hunters. That move put an end to any substantial American trading opportunities with the Pend Oreille tribe. However, some Flatheads and Nez Perce allies continued trading with the Americans both in the field and at rendezvous. Buffalo populations in the upper Missouri and Snake river drainages continued to decline throughout the decade as Indians and fur men overwhelmingly killed cows. Preferred for its flavor, tenderness and hide, the slaughter of cow bison diminished or eliminated herds in many areas. As regional butcher shop operators, the Salish hunters would have to move to new hunting areas by 1840.

Menacing Piegans had not been powerful enough to check Salish hunters or white fur men, as all operated in large, well-armed groups. Only when assisted by the Blood and tribes of the Blackfeet Nation did their Piegan cousins dare to execute a major battle. Operating in groups of 20 to 50 braves, the marauders camped in secluded, spring-drained canyons and scouted for opportunities to easily steal horses and other items. Likely ambush locations involved brush-covered streams that trappers worked, travel routes close to cover and edges of large encampments. Most ambushes were committed on foot. Nighttime raids required stealth rather than brute force. Hobbled horses were stolen next to the victim's lodge. The Piegans kept the Salish and trappers on the alert, looking over a shoulder and sleeping with one eye open to safeguard lives and property.

After entering the Lemhi Valley in early November 1830, HBC John Work's Snake River brigade exercised extreme security measures to protect his men and property from lurking Piegan horse thieves. He posted not only extra guards at night but among trappers in the field. His sizeable group of men spent more time running raiders off than they did trapping beaver. While hunting upriver and in a hurry to exit the valley of thieves, the harried trappers met old Chief La Buche with a few Nez Perces and several Flatheads, whereupon all shared campsites for three days. Before leaving the hostile area, Work wrote in his journal: "Everyone is glad to meet these people who are our real friends, what a difference between a people and the murderous Blackfeet though both Savages and inhabiting the same country. The Blackfeet short ago stole above [Horse Prairie] 30 horses from the F. Heads."[272]

A faithful reproduction of a watercolor by Charles M. Russell called "Roping by Moonlight" depicts a common tactic of Piegan horse thieves that troubled the Salish and trappers alike. COURTESY WIKIMEDIA COMMONS

The allied hunting grounds of the Salish and Nez Perces encompassed a vast swath of land in today's southern Idaho, north of the Snake River and east of the impassable lava rock flows. Annually, scouts traversed the area in search of bison herds and assessed the presence of trouble-causing Blackfeet. River valleys of the Lost, Little Lost, Pahsimeroi, Lemhi, Henrys Fork and Birch Creek, all broad plains framed by lofty mountains, supported substantial bison herds. Besides the allied Salish, Nez Perces and white fur hunters, Shoshonis and Bannocks worked southern portions of the region in

272 Work Journal, November 17, 1830, HBC Ref. B 239k 1 p. 292. Horse Prairie offered a regular camping area for the Salish, protection from wind and the Blackfeet, and abundant pasturage for horses all in close proximity to large herds of buffalo. It provided winter grounds for the Salish during portions of the decade.

peaceful coexistence. In earlier times, the latter controlled the area, but by 1830, they were too few in number to expel the Salish and Blackfeet.

Nez Perce buffalo hunters from two Clearwater bands in Idaho regularly spent winters in the Salmon River valley and camped 10 miles north of the fork where the Lemhi joined the Salmon. Known to the fur men as Grand Camp, this three-mile-wide valley surrounded by steep, grassy hillsides provided good pasturage for horses and fair protection from Piegan thieves. During the 1830s, lower Horse Prairie Creek served segments of the Pend Oreilles and Flatheads as a winter quarters when weather conditions cooperated; otherwise, they joined their allies at the Grand Camp.

Flathead Chief Insula, or Red Feather – called Little Chief by the trappers due to his stature – led one such mixed band of Salish that often hunted and wintered with the Nez Perces. Having a Nez Perce mother and a Flathead father, and being a brave lead warrior with a pleasant personality, made Insula a logical choice as chief for this detached band of the Salish and Nez Perces.[273] So much so, when asked to be their chief, Insula gracefully declined the offer saying: "By the will of the Great Master of Life I was born among the Flathead and if such be his will, among the Flathead I am determined to die."[274]

For a few years, the Salmon winter grounds overflowed with people and horses, putting a strain on food resources. In 1831, several trapping outfits chose the site for winter quarters, adding an extra 150 people and their horses to live off the surrounding land. Already in place, the Salish owned more than 1,000 head of horses, with the Nez Perce having a like number.[275] Game soon grew scarce, as did forage for horses, which caused some people to move in the dead of winter. Alternative sites for the trappers lay 200 miles south on lower Henrys Fork and the confluence of the Snake and Portneuf rivers, but the Indians stayed put or moved partway up the Lemhi River.

Piegan horse thieves fared better than usual during the years of overcrowding at the Salmon. Moving about with only 10 to 15 warriors, they could sneak into camp, pick 20 to 30 horses and quietly lead them from the village. Unlike the fur men, Indians did not regularly post nighttime horse guards in winter unless traveling, staking their best hunting horses next to a lodge, where the sleeping occupants' dogs were supposed to bark a warning if anyone happened to come close. However, the crafty Piegans distracted the ever-hungry dogs by dropping small chunks of meat

---

273 Bigart and Woodcock, pp. 84-87.
274 [I.S.], Chittenden & Richardson 1905, vol. 1, p. 321.
275 [I.S.], Irving. Bonneville, Ch. 12.

they carried just for that purpose.[276]

In mid-April 1831, 40 lodges of Flatheads and a few Pend Oreilles set off from the Bitterroot Valley for the buffalo grounds in southeastern Idaho. Traveling the usual trails south, they crossed the grass-covered divide at Bannock Pass, dropping into the Lemhi Valley where they tied in with a few Nez Perces. The combined party moved south to Birch Creek's grassy valley, preceded by a reconnaissance party to locate buffalo and possible Blackfeet. On May 26, the lead scouts happened on a trappers' camp on Camas Creek belonging to the experienced traders Lucien Fontenelle and Andrew Dripps, who held a complicated business agreement with AFC.[277]

A faithful photographic reproduction of Charles M. Russell painting "In the Enemy's Country" of scouts leading a small column of warriors in search of buffalo. COURTESY WIKIMEDIA COMMONS

The scouts told the traders of a skirmish they had had a few days before with the Blackfeet, of whom they killed two. Alarmed over the news of their most persistent nemeses close by, the fur men planned extra precautions. Eager to establish trade relations with the Flatheads and secure protection from marauders, the new company[278] invited the entire village

276 Ibid.

277 [I.S.], Ferris Journal, Ch. 15, May 28, 1831. Birch Creek, a willow-and-aspen-lined stream, was called Cote's Defile during the fur trade, so named for Astorian Joseph Cote after his death there in 1828 by Blackfeet trapping with William Sublette's outfit.

278 American Fur Company entered the Rocky Mountain fur trade in 1830, operating the first season south of the Snake River where beaver were scarce due to prior trapping. Engaging three experienced Iroquois from rival RMFC, they branched out in early spring hunting Henrys Fork and west where they met the Salish.

to come trade with them. The Flathead scouts hurried away with gifts from the traders for their chief to deliver the message. During the scouts' absence, the trappers moved camp westward to Medicine Lodge Creek, with eyes open for the enemy, where they killed numerous buffalo, but only one in 12 was fat enough to be palatable.

Meanwhile, the allied Indian villagers moved toward Medicine Lodge Creek after receiving word of the pending trading session, which the chief eagerly accepted. After three days, several young Flathead men showed up ahead of the village to report to the traders that yesterday the Blackfeet had killed one of their people and assaulted a woman some distance from camp. They had brutally raped her, cut off her hair and sent her home. The atrocities committed by the Blackfeet and Flathead reprisals spelled the end of the Fragile Truce. Revenge ruled both camps for several years.

On June 1, 1831, 50 lodges of Flatheads, Pend Oreilles and a few Nez Perces arrived at the AFC camp and settled in. Warren Ferris described the meeting: "Unlike other Indians ... we have seen, they advanced to meet us in a slow orderly manor [*sic*] singing their songs of peace. When they had approached within fifty paces they discharged their guns in the air, reloaded, and fired them off in like manner. Our party of course returned the salute. The Indians now dismounted, left their arms and horses, and silently advanced in the following order. First came the principal chief bearing [an] English flag, then four subordinate chiefs[,] then a long line of warriors, then young men and boys who had not yet distinguished themselves in battle and lastly the women and children. The chief then grasped the hand of the head trader [Andrew Dripps], raised it high as his head and muttered a two-minute prayer. The rest followed his example in the order of rank. The whole ceremony occupied about two hours at the end of which time each of us had shaken hands with them all."[279]

279 [I.S.], Ferris, Ch. 15, June 2, 1831.

A faithful photographic reproduction of the Charles M. Russell painting "Buffalo Hunt." COURTESY WIKIMEDIA COMMONS ⓓ

The allied chiefs produced pipes and sat in a circle with leaders of American Fur to discuss trade. Later, Ferris wrote of their manner and character: "They call themselves in their beautiful tongue Salish and speak a language remarkable for its sweetness and simplicity. They are noted for humanity, courage, prudence, candor, forbearance, integrity, trustfulness, piety and honesty. They are the only tribe in the Rocky Mountains … that have never killed or robbed a white man."[280]

The Americans and the Salish camped for three weeks on Medicine Lodge Creek, where some of the people trapped nearby streams and others hunted buffalo and dried meat for a pending trip to St. Louis. Women dug camas roots on nearby meadows as their men chased buffalo. On June 19, 1831, Fontenelle and Dripps, 30 employees, 20 hired Flatheads and Nez Perce escorts left the encampment for Cache Valley in today's state of Utah to recover cached hides.[281] From Cache Valley, the traders

280 [I.S.] Ibid. Warren Ferris, trapper and small scale trader, spent four years in Salish territory, often traveling and camping with them, making these observations in his publication after retiring from the fur trade. The Salish greeting of American fur men was a standard practice the tribes engaged in before a trading session. Ferris commented on the simplicity of the Salish language, indicating he conversed in the simplest form.

281 [I.S.] Ibid Ch. 17, June 19, 1831.

and crew transported the furs to St. Louis, a journey of some two months. Eight of the Indians accompanied the eastbound traders, of which four went to the city. Only two of the Indians' names, Nez Perce Worn Out Horns and Flathead Paseal, were known.[282]

Tales of Four Indians

Many historians consider the four Indians to be the first of four delegations sent to St. Louis by their tribes seeking, information of the white man's "Great Spirit." The event best deserves remembering as the Protestant church's initial promotion to establish missions among the far western Indians. Church leaders had invented a rendition of the Indians' purpose in making the long trip along with the inconceivable notion that they had crossed 1,300 miles of hostile territory alone, without a guide. Nez Perce historian L.V. McWhorter asserts that the Indians made the journey on the will-o'-the-wisp.[283] Beginning in 1908, he collected oral histories from older tribal members. One of his interviewees said his paternal great uncle "Worn Out Horns" made the trip east and returned, only to be killed a year later in the Lemhi Pass Massacre. It seems that, by early September 1831, Fontenelle and four Indians had reached St. Louis where the former delivered their furs and went about acquiring supplies. Within a few weeks, the traders accomplished their tasks and by about October 1 had barged the supplies 400 miles upriver to Bellevue in today's Nebraska.[284] While in St. Louis, the four Indians received good accommodations, a variety of white man's food and a tour of the town by General William Clark.[285] Two of the Indians, a 44-year-old Flathead and a younger Nez Perce-Flathead-mix, fell dangerously ill shortly after arriving in the city. The sick men received a visit from two Catholic priests who also baptized them as Narcissa and Paul, respectively. Both died and were laid to rest in the parish cemetery on October 31 and November 17, 1831, respectively.[286]

More than two years after the two surviving Indians vacated St. Louis, the religious press contrived its history of the event. In 1833, a Methodist publication, Christian Advocate and Journal, published a touching but totally fabricated story of the four poor Indians who wanted missionaries to "come over and help them," written by a letter-writing, plagiarizing and rich "merchant of New York City" named G.P. Disoway.

282 McWhorter. Ch. 24, pp. 29-30, Ferris.
283 Ibid. Ch. 24, pp. 29-30.
284 Hafen, Fontenelle Letter to Pierre Chouteau Jr., p. 335.
285 Chittenden, vol. 2, pp. 634-35.
286 Paladino, p. 10. The Indians names were not known.

This dogooder-on-a-crusade invested particular "interests in the labors of Christian missionaries to save the souls and to do something to improve conditions of the Indians." Disoway, who supposedly wrote of the Indians' plight, had met the highly educated, Christianized, Wyandot half-blood William Walker. Disoway copied a letter written by Walker and sent it to the Advocate as if he had written it, indicating his interests favored spiritual welfare for Indians; neither man ever met one of the four Far-Far West Indians. Walker had called on William Clark at St. Louis, who related the four-Indian story to Walker, who sent Disoway his version of the Flathead visit. Neither knew much about the four visitors except they were Indians, they were poor and they were sick.[287]

Catholic and Protestant writers differ in the Indians' purpose in making the long journey and in tribal bloodlines. The Catholic leaders wrote of the Indians' desire to obtain teachers, while Protestants based their premise on a speech by one Indian who said his people wanted the "White Man's Book of Heaven."[288] The Catholics insisted the Indians were Flathead or half-blood Nez Perce; the latter considered them Nez Perce. The language barrier prevented whites from establishing a clear intent or bloodlines in the visit.

To reinforce the cry for missionaries, the press also published a supposed speech made by one of the Indians at a banquet on the eve of his departure. Indeed, if it did happen, the fabricated speech contained fashionable rhetoric of the period certainly not credited to an illiterate Indian, be he Flathead or Nez Perce. However, the writer of the supposed talk, in essence, did stress the Indian's inability to obtain the White Man's Book of Heaven while there.[289] Regardless of falsehoods surrounding these events, it provided the match that lit the fire to the Protestant missionary movement flaming across the country to the Pacific coast.

Absent during the four Indians' experience in the city, St. Louis Catholic Bishop Joseph Rosati wrote a letter to the Association of Propagation of the Faith based on information received from attending priests. His letter dated December 31, 1831, contained the following summation: "Some three months ago four Indians who live across the Rocky Mountains ... arrived at St. Louis ... they came to see our church. ... Unfortunately, there was no one who understood their language, and the other two attended and acted very becomeingly [*sic*]," – meaning the two survivors had attended the service and could not have departed with Fontenelle, as he had left for Bellevue, Nebraska, in October.

---

287 DeVoto, pp. 6-10.

288 Ibid.

289 Ibid.

His letter ended with the bishop saying that one of his priests "offered ... to go to them the next spring with another (priest)."[290] Nonetheless, lots of dialogue would pass between St. Louis and Rome before the Catholic Church would sanction sending "Black Robes" to the Far-Far West.

Another player in the fate of four Indians, American artist George Catlin, painted pictures of two alleged Nez Perce Indians while traveling up the Missouri River on the American Fur Company steamboat's maiden voyage in the spring of 1832.

In Catlin Letter No. 48, written several years after the fact, he named the two Indians No Horns On His Head and Rabitskin (*sic*) Leggings and then described their attire at the time of painting as "beautiful Sioux dresses," being presents from that tribe. Catlin believed the Nez Perce men were part of a delegation that crossed the Rocky Mountains to St. Louis to learn more about the white man's religion. The delegation hoped to find the truth of what white men amongst them said about "our [whites'] religion was better than theirs, and that [the Indians] would all be lost if they did not embrace it." Catlin wrote that one man died at the mouth of the Yellowstone River while the other had "since lived to arrive safely among his friends," and concluded his letter by complimenting the "many Reverend Gentlemen" based on missionary reports he had heard. He, "like thousands of others, ha[d] the satisfaction of witnessing the complete success that crowned the bold and daring exertions of Misters Lee and Spalding."[291] There is no question that Catlin painted the two Indians' picture. However, it is highly unlikely that the men in the picture decked out in beautiful Sioux clothing were truly Nez Perces, traveling on a steamship's maiden voyage up the Missouri River to their homeland. The two Nez Perces would have returned home the same way they got there, with the fur trader pack outfit.

Yet another and more plausible explanation appears in Dr. Marcus Whitman's report to the Presbyterian Board of Directors in regard to trader (Lucian) Fontenelle's account of events upon his return from the mountains. Accordingly, eight Indians, three Flatheads and five Nez Perces accompanied Fontenelle and Dripps to Council Bluffs, all intent on "gaining religious knowledge." From Council Bluffs, Fontenelle, with furs, escorted two Flatheads and three Nez Perces, one a youth, to St. Louis while Dripps headed north to Bellevue with two other Flatheads and a Nez Perce that declined the venture to St. Louis.

The remainder of Dr. Whitman's report agrees with Catlin and

290 Paladino, pp. 11-12, Bishop Rosati's secondhand information contains other inaccuracies not reported here.

291 Catlin Letter no. 48, pp. 379.

Bishop Rosati's account of the fate of the four Indians, except for the extra young Indian whom Fontenelle took to St. Louis, who supposedly survived and returned home with his three comrades via the westbound fur traders.[292] On October 1, 1831, Andrew Dripps and at least three of the four Indians in question left Bellevue with the packers and supplies for the mountains.[293] Hampered by a late start, jaded horses and little forage along the route, the caravan halted at the mouth of the Laramie and Platte rivers for the winter. Dripps dispatched four men from there to advise his trappers camped on the Salmon River of his plans.[294] One messanger was likely Nez Perce Worn Out Horns. Their dispatched departure date is unknown; however, they reached the large Salmon River Nez Perce-trapper encampment in early spring to find Dripps' men gone, so they settled in with the Indians.[295]

Dripps' trappers had moved to the Pahsimeroi Valley to winter with a few Salish, finding many buffalo and mild winter weather. In early February, the trappers broke camp, trailing toward the Bear River area by the main travel routes where they expected to find Dripps and the supplies already set up for business. In early spring, the Dripps packtrain continued their journey, arriving at Muddy Creek near Evanston, Wyoming, in April 1832. Ferris' journal entry for April 24 reads: "We recrossed Bear River and encamped on the easterly margin, during the afternoon a well-known Flathead named Paseal, who had accompanied Fontenelle and Dripps to St. Louis last summer, returned with the agreeable intelligence that Dripps at the head of forty-eight was encamped at the entrance of the Muddy."[296]

Back in June 1831, after the Dripps pack string left Medicine Lodge Creek for St. Louis, the allied Salish and remaining 25 trappers, which included five ex-HBC Iroquois, broke camp to begin a 175-mile journey westward in search of buffalo and beaver.[297] Skirting the mountains that faced the Snake River Plain in a westerly direction, they turned north to ascend Little Lost River Valley where the Indians harvested a few bison. Reaching a gentle divide, the hunters descended 35 miles down the Pahsimeroi River. Finding poor hunting, the half-mile-long column turned southwest up Double Spring Creek, crossing the 9,000-foot pass into a

---

292 Young, OHQ, no. 4. Dr. Whitman's 1835 Report to the Missionary Board.
293 Hafen, p. 335: Contributed by Harvey Carter, Fontenelle Letter to Pierre Chouteau.
294 [I.S.] Ferris Journal, Ch. 24, April 24, 1832.
295 [I.S.] Ferris Journal, Ch. 25, May 14, 1832.
296 [I.S.] Ferris Journal, Ch. 24, April 24, 1832.
297 [I.S.] Ferris Journal, Ch. 17, June 19, 1832. Mountain men knew the Little Lost River as Day's Defile, named for NWC trapper John Day, killed there on camp guard duty by Indians in 1820. Lost River, tabbed Godin's Defile, was named for Iroquois Thierry Godin, who explored the valley and was later killed there by Blackfeet in 1828.

headwater stream of Lost River. Downward along the creek on July 1, lead scouts sighted numerous buffalo grazing on the valley floor, where both the Indians and trappers went right to work, bringing down many fat cows to butcher and dry. The fur men prepared provisions for 14 days, enough for a trapping expedition to Stanley Basin at the headwater of the Salmon River, while the allies continued the hunt. Separating from the main encampment, the trappers and a few lodges of Salish followed a Snake Indian guide through some of Idaho's most rugged mountains to reach the basin – supposedly loaded with beaver – while the Salish and their allies chased bison around Lost River from Copper Basin to present-day Mackay, Idaho.

The 50 lodges of 350 natives had a productive summer hunt in the most picturesque valley of Idaho's highest mountains, free of Blackfeet problems. When the trappers returned to the allied camp on August 11 with a disappointing catch, they found the Indians packing dried meat in preparation to move on.[298] After everyone was ready to go, the company of dark and white retraced the route back to the head of Little Lost River, killing several grizzlies along the way. At the river's head, they took an extremely tough course east over the mountains on Pass Creek trail to Birch Creek Valley, where they turned north toward the Lemhi River and Gilmore Pass.

A few miles before crossing the Continental Divide, the Indians spotted a large smoke cloud south on the plains; they thought it might be a signal fire set by Flatheads who had earlier gone to Cache Valley with the traders.[299] Although answering the signal from an unknown sender might be risky, the chiefs felt confident their strength would hold off any Blackfeet attack, so a few Indians climbed to a high point to set a patch of fallen timber on fire in answer to the smoke signal. There is no record of who the signal senders were or of any Flatheads returning. The itinerant Indians and trappers continued north another day before they separated August 25, when trappers took the Bannock Pass trail. The Salish continued north to fish favorite holes on the lower Lemhi River where king salmon returned each year to spawn in shallow gravel beds along waterways of the Salmon and Lemhi rivers, also in August. The Salish and Nez Perces made a habit of spending a week between the summer and fall hunts to stock up on fish.

Unlike the Spokanes' unique method of catching fish, the Salish used sticks, rocks, arrows and an occasionally tomahawk, as well as the most-efficient lance. Women and children, young and old men took part

298 [I.S.] Ferris Journal, Ch. 18, June 28, 1832: They crossed rugged Lemhi Range via Uncle Ike and Pass creeks.

299 [I.S.] Ferris Journal, June 28, 1832.

in the annual event, armed with preferred weapons. The lancer waded in the shallows with his lance poised to strike a downward blow, followed closely by two or three boys carrying forked sticks. The lancer pinned a fish to the bottom, which the closest boy quickly hooked through its gills, before hurrying to shore where a waiting old man killed the fish with a tomahawk or rock. Fish stunned by rocks or shot in the head with a musket or arrow were retrieved in the same manner. Women split the fish and girls hung them above smoking fires to dry. Warren Ferris, who partook in one of these affairs, said: "We were compelled every few days to move camp to other shoals, in consequence of the offensive epheria [euphoria] of stinking fish. ... Some of us fancied that our camps had a fishy smell for months afterward."[300]

Salish woman drying meat using the jerking process. COURTESY OF SPOKANE PUBLIC LIBRARY, NORTHWEST ROOM

300 Dallas Herald, December 14, 1872, Ferris quote.

5

Competition and Conflicts

1831-1834

On the move, a grand Indian village needed acres of real estate spread over a mile or more, especially when squeezed in by wilderness obstacles. The main trail through Hell Gate and over Deer Lodge Pass varied from a few feet to today's divided, four-lane freeway in open plains country. Where vegetation, rocks and goat slopes constricted trail width, travelers followed a single-file path tromped permanent by thousands of hoofbeats over untold years. The Indians transported everything they owned by packhorses where terrain refused the width of a travois made of tepee poles connected to the saddled horses. Horses also transported 150 pounds of camp gear wrapped in hides and secured to a packsaddle. The head chiefs and war chiefs rode up front, followed by young warriors, spare horses, and women tending pack- or travois-horses. Children and dogs brought up the rear.

Trappers of an American Fur Company (AFC) outfit entering the plains from Sugarloaf Pass, alarmed by the sight of a small group of Indians riding their way, prepared for trouble, only to meet friendly Pend Oreille lead scouts. The Indians told the trappers that the entire Pend Oreille village would move up the valley the next day and camp nearby. When the nearly 1,000 villagers actually arrived and began setting up camp on September 10, 1831, their conditions caused the trappers a different kind of concern. They quickly learned they had been short on meat and had had to rely on root crops for primary food while on the trail. Their starving dogs headed for the trappers' camp to find something to eat and grabbed anything that smelled like leather left unattended or not hung high in a tree.

Early the next morning, the ravenous Pend Oreilles and dogs set out with the trappers for buffalo country with visions of many kills to silence hunger pangs. That evening, trapper Warren Ferris recorded the Pend Oreille village of 100 lodges on the move through grass covered plains, east of today's Anaconda, Montana.

> Three thousand horses of every variety size and color with trappings almost as varied as their appearance [is] either packed or ridden by 1,000 souls from squalling infancy to decrepid [*sic*] age, their person fantastically ornamented with scarlet coats, blankets of all colours[.] [B]uffalo robes painted with hideous little figures, resembling grasshoppers quite as much as men for which they were intended, and sheepskin dresses garnished with porcupine quills, beads, hawk bells and human hair.
>
> Imagine these humans crowned with long black locks gently waving in the wind, their faces painted with vermillion and yellow ochre. Listen to the rattle of numerous lodgepoles trailed by packhorses, to the various noises of children screaming, women scolding and dogs howling. Observe occasional frightened horses running away scattering their lading over the plains. See here and there groups of Indian boys dashing about at full speed. ... Yonder see a hundred horsemen pursuing a herd ... hungry dogs chasing ... timid rabbits. ...
>
> Imagine these scenes and sounds lighted by the flashes of hundreds of gleaming gun barrels ... you will have a faint idea of the character of our march, as we followed old Guignon over the plains on the sources of the Clarks [Fork] River.[301]

After 12 miles across open prairie, the Pend Oreilles set up camp near today's Butte, Montana, where the chiefs decided to split forces in the morning. One group trailed south over the grassy Deer Lodge Pass to the Beaverhead River, while the others with the trappers struck off to the southeast to Jefferson River. The latter group ascended a narrow, grass-willow-and brush-lined creek bottom, closed in on both sides by steep, timbered hills and crossed Pipe Stone Pass before descending to the Jefferson River plain; those two days over the mountain further sapped their strength, but the plains were alive with buffalo. After killing many and wolfing down steaming fresh meat, the Pend Oreilles could do little more than sprawl about rubbing overstuffed bellies, but by morning, all felt eager to carry on with vigor.

All went well until September 19, 1831, when the trappers brought the body of a French Canadian back to camp from the river where he had set traps. Shot twice and stabbed in the chest, his body had been stripped and left in the water, unscalped. It was a brutal warning that the stealthy enemy retained an unhealthy presence in the area. The following night, Piegans cut loose eight horses in the very center of camp, which did not miss the attention of a Piegan who had joined the Pend Oreilles and who now cried a warning that raised the sleeping village. The would-be raiders fired a volley at the alarmist, missed him, but put holes in several lodges

301 [I.S.] Ferris Journal, Ch. 20, September 15, 1832. Guignon means "bad luck" in French, the name a trapper gave Chief Walking Bear.

before scuttling away in the dark. The probability of enemies had become present and dangerous. These episodes caused Pend Oreille Chief Walking Bear to back down on his promise to guide the trappers to the beaver-and-bison-rich Three Forks area. Consequently, and wisely so, he knew his reduced numbers neither protected themselves nor the trappers in the heart of Piegan territory. The trappers headed south – less several horses – the day after the latter incident, leaving the Indians to finish the hunt and meat processing.

Meanwhile, the Pend Oreilles who had taken the Deer Lodge Pass route made tracks for buffalo near the famous Beaverhead rock landmark where they set up camp. Reunited with the Jefferson River hunters within a few weeks, the Pend Oreilles presented a formidable force the Piegans, by themselves, dared not to attack. Nevertheless, the skulking horse thieves and ambushers continued their constant harassment of the hunters throughout their stay. On one occasion, in pursuit of a dozen raiders, the Pend Oreilles killed, scalped, stripped and pinned one Piegan to the ground with an arrow. Red pantaloons cast to the side of the body belonged to an AFC trapper who had disappeared a year earlier, providing evidence the dead Indian had murdered him. On the first of October the Indians broke camp to hunt their way to the Big Hole and home.

After the pause in August to fish for salmon on the Lemhi River, the Flatheads and some Nez Perces moved up to Horse Prairie to hunt buffalo. Four RMFC men under trade-leader Jean Baptiste Gervais joined the Indians to set up a paltry collection of goods in a largely unsuccessful, 10-day trade session that failed to win the natives from their hunt. In November, the Indians moved back down to the Salmon River wintering grounds to find a mass of humanity and thousands of horses. The entire RMFC 100-plus-man outfit and 30 AFC trappers had moved into the valley, intending to winter there. Adding to the growing community, Henry Fraeb and 30 men arrived with RMFC's much needed supplies. Ferris found the competitors' winter rendezvous on the Salmon River a "confused scene of rioting debauchery for several days after which, however, the kegs of alcohol were bunged [corked]."[302] which he probably joined for a few beaver skins. After sobering up, and flush with trade goods, the trappers bought all the dried buffalo meat the Indians could spare and a few buffalo robes, plus some squares of fur on buffalo hides used for both bedding and saddle blankets.

Too soon, it was apparent that nearby game to feed the large encampment and forage for 3,000 horses would not last through the winter.

302 [I.S.] Ferris Journal, Ch. 21-22, November 4, 1832.

Consequently, a small group of Flatheads and AFC trappers left first for the sheltered, Blackfeet-free Pahsimeroi Valley and its small herds of buffalo. Shortly, a band of Nez Perces moved 30 miles down the Salmon to its westerly bend in a small valley where deer and mountain sheep were ample. Other Nez Perces stayed put on the Salmon a few miles below the confluence of the Lemhi River, well stocked with plenty of dried meat. Two weeks before Christmas 1831, the Flatheads and some Nez Perces began moving up the Lemhi, followed later by James Bridger and the RMFC outfits. They stayed in joined camps along the river at good horse feeding sites a few miles below today's Tendoy, Idaho.[303]

They passed the rest of the winter fending off Blackfeet and hunting buffalo along the way to the headwaters of the Lemhi. Within a few weeks of arrival, prowling Piegan rustlers got away with 20 horses, taking them over Lemhi Pass. The Flathead and Nez Perce allies, regular victims of horse thieves, reacted vigorously to each occurrence by alertly watching for signs of mounted riders leading or herding unmounted horses. On one such occasion in mid-November, a hunting party moving up the Lemhi Valley located the fresh trail of obvious raiders. Diverting from their planned hunt, the allies pressed after the Piegan thieves and soon recovered some stolen horses along with two scalps.[304]

Trapper Warren Ferris described a daring raid at the joint camp on January 28, 1832: "Soon after dark a party of Blackfeet [Piegans] approached camp and several of them boldly entered at different points, cutting loose horses on their way. One of them rode a beautiful horse and slowly rode through both encampments. During his progress he was challenged by the guard, but gave the usual Flathead answer and passed on: soon after his departure, the owner of the horse discovered that he was missing, and imagining that he had broke loose, departed with a companion in quest of him. They proceeded silently about fifty yards from camp and met a [Piegan] Blackfeet who came running up to them, thinking they were some of his comrades: but quickly discovered his mistake and fled. They brought him to the ground, however by a well-directed shot and about twenty others immediately sprang up from the sage and fled into the woods bordering the river. The Flathead raised his scalp."[305]

Although more cautious, Piegan raids continued throughout the winter, assaulting detached pairs, individual trappers, or Indians and killing five of the fur men and several Flathead scouts on horseback. By March 1,

303 [I.S.] Ferris Journal, Ch. 22, January 25, 1833.
304 [I.S.] Ferris Journal, January 27, 1833.
305 [I.S.] Ferris Journal, January 28, 1833.

1832, Bridger and his men had enough; they packed up camp and headed east over Lemhi Pass in quest of safer country and beaver hides.[306]

Beaver and buffalo in the upper Missouri and southeastern Idaho took a big hit during the summer and fall of 1831. At least 1,300 Pend Oreilles, Flatheads, Kalispels, Coeur d'Alenes and Nez Perces, 800 Piegans, Bloods and Gros Ventres, and roughly 300 transient trappers made the area home. The many mouths to feed necessitated the occupants to kill hundreds of buffalo and other animals to survive. The region, known as the war zone, also supported the largest beaver population remaining in the Rocky Mountains and a substantial herd of buffalo. The centerpiece of the fur trade for three years drew the attention of all competing fur companies and Indian hunters who seriously depleted the sought-after resources.

Guided by old Pend Oreille Chief La Buche and his son, John Work and his 35 HBC Snake River trappers moved to the lower Big Hole River-Beaverhead Valley in mid-November 1831 via Deer Lodge Pass. Plagued earlier by Piegan marauders, trapped-out territory and dwindling provisions, the fur men looked forward to better luck on the buffalo grounds. For a month, they camped on the Beaverhead, killing more than 70 bison, some fat cows, which they dried for use in winter quarters. Freezing temperatures with minor snow cover soon put an end to beaver trapping. The ice cover made it difficult to capture the animal that stayed snug in its lodge, coming out from under the ice only to bite off a stick from its previously gathered food pile and return home.

Work's outfit, well supplied with meat, headed for winter quarters in the Lemhi Valley through wickedly slick terrain, with snow depths increasing the farther they advanced. Passing through the mid-Horse Prairie Creek basin, they encountered several Blackfeet raiding parties with Salish and Nez Perce horses hightailing downcountry toward their home territory. One group fired on the trappers' camp at night, seriously wounding a horse guard and causing the HBC men to stay put five days to treat the man. While camped, horse-thieving parties of 27 men to as few as two passed at a distance with their booty. Old Chief La Buche led an advance party to check on pass conditions. Along the way, they put two thieving Blackfeet leading four horses on the run. By pressing them hard, they caused the Blackfeet to release two of the horses, which the chief caught and took back to camp. All together, Work's trappers observed five raiding parties returning home from the Salmon wintering grounds with 15 allied horses. The fur men, with La Buche in the lead, crossed Lemhi pass through 2 feet of snow on December

306 Alter, p. 118.

16, 1831, and descended to the valley.[307]

Upon reaching the Lemhi valley and proceeding north a few miles toward the grand encampment, Work's outfit tied in with 33 lodges of Flatheads and Nez Perces who had vacated the overcrowded location. The chiefs told Work that no buffalo ran downriver in the direction of the "grand encampment," and their people were short of provisions. Therefore, the two parties moved up the Lemhi Valley in light snow showers, hoping to run across scattered bull bison. Finding good grass on Mill Creek's junction with the river, they made camp and spent several days.[308]

On New Year's Day 1832, John Work wrote: "Fine mild weather. This being Sunday and New Years day neither our people nor the Indians went in pursuit of buffalo. ... The men and some of the principle [*sic*] Indians were treated with a dram and some cakes in the morning, from a small quantity of rum that had been brought from the fort for the occasion."[309] Discouraged by buffalo scarcity and increased numbers of hunters from "Grand Camp," John Work's crew and about 25 lodges of Flatheads left for the Beaverhead River on January 4.

En route, they forced several suspected Blackfeet horse thieves into a thicket of willows along Horse Prairie Creek and fired on them. A Blackfeet woman with the Flatheads spoke to the concealed warriors, who told her that an American fort on the Missouri[310] had traded great quantities of arms and ammunition to them, and a large force was readying for a strike on the Flatheads in the spring. The Flatheads quit their watch at nightfall, allowing the Piegans to escape, but not without serious wounds as a morning inspection revealed. Two Salish had wounds: one in the breast, the other on the thumb. John Work wrote, "Here we had an opportunity of seeing the Indian mode of fighting."[311] Leaving the skirmish site, the hunting party rode downstream to the Beaverhead River through light snow, still searching for food. Breaking out of the river canyon into the broad plain near Dillon, Montana, they caught sight of many bands of buffalo. Spirits lifted, the hungry hunters initiated a slow, deliberate hunt down the valley, moving camp every few miles.

In nine days, they harvested many animals in the face of ever-increasing Blackfeet raids for horses. By the time they reached the Birch Creek tributary to the Big Hole River, the Salish lost 11 head and Work's

307 Lewis and Phillips, Work Journal, pp. 105-114.
308 Ibid. Work Journal, pp. 114-115.
309 Ibid. Work Journal, p. 116-119.
310 Ibid. p. 123, AFC Post's Fort Piegan was at the Marias-Missouri Rivers' junction.
311 Ibid. Work Journal, p. 122.

party eight. The five Americans who had tied in with them three days earlier lost six. While camped on Birch Creek, the Americans left for the Lemhi Valley. At the same time, a dozen lodges of Flatheads quit the hunting party to join the larger Pend Oreille camp, probably near today's Twin Bridges, Montana. Twelve to 15 tents of Flatheads and HBC's 35 men remained in the buffalo-rich – and Blackfeet overrun – grasslands. On January 30, 1832, loud gunshots followed by war cries jarred the Flatheads and HBC men awake at dawn to find an estimated 300 Blood and Gros Ventre warriors attacking their camp. They promptly held the attackers back by heavy musket fire and three shots fired from the HBC small cannon. At one point, the enemy had the camp surrounded; yet, the hunting party broke their line and sent them scuttling into a nearby patch of timber. Old Chief La Buche had two horses killed under him.

Nearly all hostiles had plenty of ammunition and fired on their camp continuously for five hours. At noon, the enemy retreated. A Blood chief leading a charge lay dead among the many killed and scalped. The hunters lost one Flathead and six horses, while three were wounded. The HBC outfit had four people seriously wounded, two of whom later died, and five horses killed. The next day, four lodges of Flatheads on their way from the Pend Oreille camp to join the hunters ran headlong into the retiring Bloods. Before the leaderless Blood troublemakers hurried away with Flathead baggage, the adversaries engaged in a brief conversation at a safe distance apart. The retreating Blood warriors told the Flatheads that a Small Robes Piegan chief had earlier refused to accompany their now-deceased chief on the raid because he desired to make peace with the Flatheads the next summer. Wherein the Blood chief had boasted to the Small Robes, "They would find only their bones to make peace with."[312]

Snow fell as the Flatheads made a failed attempt to recover their friends' plundered goods; however, they were able to capture the Bloods' packdogs and bring them back to carry the plunder of shoes, other small articles and ammunition. On February 4, the hunting party raised camp to retrace their previous route for the next five weeks, hunting buffalo free of Blackfeet harassment. Snow covered much of Horse Prairie Creek, and having jaded horses made hunting many bison in the valley difficult. Frequent snowstorms, bitter cold and limited hunting success prompted the party to head for the Lemhi Valley. Crossing Bannock Pass in deep snow nearly put the horses down, but fortunately they found a well-beaten

312 Ibid. p. 128. The small cannon barrel burst after the third shot; the Bloods did not know that.

buffalo trail to the river. On March 10, the Indians and trappers settled in on snow-free Texas Creek that offered good horse feed and a place to rest.[313] A week later Piegan raiders found the Flatheads' camp and absconded with four horses tied to their tents and four jaded HBC mounts left ungrounded.

An attempt by two young Flatheads to recover the horses ended when they caught up with two Piegans leading the HBC horses, and a fight broke out. The Flatheads killed and scalped the two thieves but could not bring back such weakened horses due to the proximity of the Piegan camp of 40 men. A day later, all but two lodges of the Salish left their camp, followed by Work's brigade trailing downriver for three days to the Grand Camp of Flatheads and Nez Perces at Bohannon Creek. John Work and his crew remained in that camp for three days, anticipating the recovery of two very ill children of trappers, but both died. After their burial, Work obtained information from the Indians on his planned route to Fort Nez Perce. The HBC outfit then hurriedly left Grand Camp, of which John Work remarked in his journal, "We are glad to get away from them for the Nez Perce[s] are really an annoyance."[314] The fur men continued their hunt south along the Salmon River to Lost River and beyond

Due to stiff competition for American trappers' furs, HBC matched the opposition in 1831 by raising the price of beaver to $5 per pound for a large, prime skin. Payment in goods, adjusted for the British money exchange rate of 11 shillings, became the standard.[315] The increase gave HBC a competitive edge as their trade items cost less. The company expected the move would lock in acquisition of American trapper furs and secure its trade relationship with the Salish. For 13 years, British companies had staffed Flathead Post with traders and laborers to conduct late fall and spring trading sessions with the Indians. Increasing numbers of American fur men entering Salish hunting grounds intercepted some of the trade, creating the need for a new system. Also in 1831, Francis Heron, the chief trader at Fort Colvile, proposed sending two men and trade goods with Salish hunters. After Chief Factor McLoughlin's approval, engagees Nicholas Montour and old François Rivet agreed to give it a go.[316]

American law prohibited foreign countries from trapping or trading east of the continental divide, a matter overlooked by HBC prior to the influx of American fur hunters in the area. To supersede this hurdle, the

313 Ibid. pp 126-137.

314 Ibid. pp 137-138.

315 Barker, McLoughlin Letter, p. 199, June 28, 1831, to Francis Heron at Fort Colvile.

316 Baker, p. 212. McLoughlin Letter, September 9, 1831. Nicholas Montour, a half blood son of a partner in NWC, held various clerk positions with that company and HBC. Discharged from service in 1823, he joined the Snake River Brigade as a freeman in 1824.

company engaged Montour and Rivet to travel with the Salish into the plains in American territory during their winter hunt. For some unreported reason, the two men stayed put at Flathead Post. McLoughlin labeled Montour "indolent" in a letter to the chief trader at Colvile, suggesting Rivet replace him if he so desired.[317] In the meantime, Rivet broke his leg, rendering him ineligible and temporarily disabled/unfit for duty.

Assuming the job as traveling trader with the Salish in the spring of 1832, Francis Ermatinger transported goods from Fort Colvile to Flathead Post and then joined in with the Indians hunters.[318] During the first of five annual forays, he and four engagees accompanied the Salish to the Salmon River and returned with 400 skins. In the years to follow, and while on the upper Missouri and Snake rivers, he secured about 1,000 beaver a year, tops for the Colvile district. Archibald McDonald wrote in a letter to York Factory, "Tis from this quarter we look for our main return, but the swarm of American adventures and vagrants all over the country now have deranged everything."[319]

Contrary to American law, HBC had set aside trade conduct east of the Continental Divide. This operation proved highly successful in trading away the Indians' "hunt" before the Americans had a chance, along with obtaining some opposition furs.[320] Ermatinger timed his jaunts with the Salish from April to November, when he returned to the Flathead Post to trade with the freemen and Indians who stayed home instead of accompanying organized hunts or staying late on the buffalo grounds. Most free trappers working out of Flathead Post at the time were the sons of fur men who had come to the region years ago, such as Jaco Finlay, Antoni Valli, Charles Loyer and Antoine Plante. Being well acquainted with beaver country from childhood, these mixed-blood Salish ventured into Blackfeet country as a group or with Ermatinger and tribal hunters.

The Blackfeet Nation and allied Gros Ventres' resupply difficulties lessened when AFC expanded their trading operation in 1831 by establishing a post on the Missouri at the mouth of the Marias River in the heart of Piegan country and nearby Bloods. With rearmament supplies 200 miles closer to the upper Missouri, Fort Mackenzie proved an easier means for the Piegans to loot hunters in the region. Encouraged by ready access to arms and ammunition, these plunderers stepped up assaults on the Salish, their allies and trappers in the upper Missouri and Snake rivers. It took beaver pelts to finance their war, which some Piegans aggressively went after. AFC

317 Ibid. p. 280.

318 Cole, p. 116, Archibald McDonald Letter, April 18, 1836.

319 Ibid. p. 161, March 11, 1833.

320 Governor Simpson Letter to York Factory, July 1834. HBCA B.223/44/22ft.

presented opportunities for the majority of the tribe of non-trappers by purchasing buffalo robes, a commodity readily obtained from Indians and processed by women's labor. The new arrangement brought grief for several years to Indian hunters and fur men throughout the region. A long way from home in 1831, the Gros Ventres lacked strategic ability but had the fortitude to tackle the Continental Divide to make raids in the Bitterroot Valley. The marauders likely passed through Hell Gate in the dark and followed along the Jocko-Horse Plains trail across wide-open prairie to within five miles of the Flatheads' main encampment. The hell-bent-for-trouble war party bivouacked at the first timbered draw above the mouth of O'Keefe Canyon and the Missoula Prairie. It was likely the next morning when the warriors decided to watch the busy trail for potential victims. In a poor choice of location not far from Hell Gate, the Gros Ventres attacked an HBC packtrain transporting Flathead furs.

Chief trader William Kittson and some of his outfit were following the packtrain about a mile in the rear when they heard gunfire and sped back to the Flathead camp for help. War Chief Wears Hair in Ringlets (later baptized Adolphe) and Arlee collared enough warriors for a force and advanced on the enemy. They found two slain packers and the Gros Ventre camp. The Flathead force devastated the marauders' camp, killing and scalping about half. Surviving raiders made a hasty retreat east up the ridge toward their home territory.[321] Years later, Flathead Post trader Francis Ermatinger pointed out the battle site to Reverend William Henry Gray in 1837 while traveling through the area.[322] As grass began to green in April 1832, the wintering Lemhi River Flatheads, Pend Oreilles and Nez Perces moved their Tendoy camp upriver near today's Leadore.

On May 17, several hundred Piegans and Bloods attacked the village with annihilation in mind. Initially they stormed the camp, cut up several lodges and wounded inhabitants. Surprised, but quick to respond, the Flatheads formed a defensive parameter around their camp and killed several. A standoff followed during which the Blackfeet taunted, "[We're] going to destroy you root and branch and fight until we get our stomachs full."[323] Words conflicted with limited ammunition, which caused the Blackfeet to sneak away, but they managed to round up many scattered Flathead horses and drive them south up the valley. The following day the Flatheads went to find their horses but, instead, met the returning Blackfeet at the narrows near the head of Birch Creek and drew them into a fierce battle. Outnum-

321 Ronan, Peter, pp. 76-78.
322 Johnson, Donald, Gray Journal, p. 28.
323 [I.S.] Ferris Journal, Ch. 25, May 22, 1832 & Dallas Herald, January 27, 1873.

bered 3-to-1 in an expression of superior courage and determination, the Salish drove the enemy from the field while killing and scalping 16. Twelve Flatheads died in two days, with 40 wounded, but the Blackfeet did not lift a scalp, and had to return empty-handed to a distant camp.

Three days later, trapper Ferris, an unnamed Iroquois and Flathead Paseal, searching for their camp, passed through the bloody battle site to find nothing but fly-infested Blackfeet bodies.[324] Continuing 20 miles north of the site, the men came upon a band of Indians, at first thought to be Blackfeet, and prepared to die fighting, but as the equally suspicious Indians drew closer, Paseal recognized them as Flatheads. The buffalo-bound hunters turned around and escorted them back to camp, nearly without ammunition, grieving dead kindred and tending the wounded. If the Blackfeet had known their perilous condition, they surely would have wiped the Salish out. Ferris and his company had orders from AFC leader Fontenelle to locate the allied camp and encourage them to attend the upcoming rendezvous at Pierre's Hole. In meeting with the Flathead Chief Big Face at his camp, Ferris explained his mission, presented gifts, and divided his company's powder and balls with some of the warriors while he waited for the chief and his council's decision. Within a few hours, Big Face agreed, but said the journey would be slow because of their many wounded.

On May 22, the village broke camp and moved south, up the valley, carefully trailing 10 severely wounded warriors on buffalo hide litters lashed to lodgepoles attached to and dragged by horses. Following close behind, many young men on foot saw to the needs of the suffering. One of the wound-tenders had a grossly swollen knee, gunshot caused, but showed no expression of pain. Undoubtedly, infection caused his death 11 days later, and his body was buried on the margin of Henrys Fork. After passing the battle site, villagers continued down the willow-and-aspen-lined Birch Creek, toward the Snake River Plain, troubled by too little ammunition and food. Near Willow Creek, the hungry party passed the abandoned Piegan-Blood campsite and judged it covered three times the space of the Nez Perce-Flathead camp. Many fresh gravesites spoke for the bloodthirsty adversarial casualties, which prompted Big Face to say the living had "had their stomachs full of fighting."

On May 24, while trailing down Birch Creek, the earlier dispatched buffalo hunters tied in with the convoy that carried fresh buffalo

---

324 Ibid. Dallas Herald, January 27, 1873. Ferris describes this incident in his journal and newspaper article some 40 years after the event. Most details track in publications, except in the exact location of the decisive fight. Ferris' journal indicates the conflict was not at the Salish camp on Texas Creek where the fatalities actually occurred.

meat, which lifted their worn spirits. The valley from that point down to the plains held many buffalo that inspired the natives to spend a few days hunting. Two days later, the long caravan reached the sinks where Birch Creek disappears into the Snake River Plain. Here, three wounded warriors died. Each one was tenderly wrapped in skins and lashed securely, then buried in the earth. Little humps of stone placed on grave tops marked each hero's final resting place. Turning away to the southeast, the survivors would not speak their names again. The Indians and three trappers began the three-day journey across the dry, sandy and rock-strewn plain to a crossing on Henrys Fork of the Snake River. Before leaving Birch Creek, the natives filled all vessels and buffalo-bladder containers with enough water for the next leg of the journey. During the march, young braves rode ahead to Henrys Fork to fetch water back to the column of caretakers and wounded. Upon reaching the wide and spring-swollen river, some 400 Indians crossed in half an hour using a unique technique.

Already packed with belongings, individuals took each lodge and rolled it into a ball with a rope attached to the top. Women and children mounted each ball, towed by a brave clenching the towrope tight between his teeth while seated atop a horse as they crossed. The swift current swept the makeshift boats and passengers half a mile downstream to the opposite shore. Four balls with lodgepole travois lashed to each top transported six to eight wounded across. On the opposite bank, within an hour and a half, women had stretched tepee skins around lodgepoles and bent over cooking pots fixing supper.[325] Beyond camp, untouched by progressive human hands, tall grass flourished. Chief Big Face decided it was a good place for horses, wounded and everyone else to rest several days. The fur man, Ferris, and six young Flatheads left the next morning on a mission to bring back ammunition and to tie in with AFC's large camp of 100 men on the Teton River.[326] After a few days, the villagers, resupplied with powder, also struck out for the rendezvous, stopping three days along the way to kill and dry buffalo meat. In mid-June 1832, the Flatheads arrived at the Pierre's Hole Rendezvous near today's Tetonia, Idaho, and set up 80 tepees near those of 120 Nez Perces. Approximately 1,000 people and 2,000 to 3,000 horses and mules gathered in the picturesque valley, rimmed on one side by the Three Tetons[327] at one of the largest, most scenic American rendezvous ever held.

The first such affair was attended by scores of Salish and Nez Perces. Traders representing RMFC and AFC newcomers Nathaniel Wyeth

325 [I.S.] Ferris, Ch. 25, & Dallas Herald, 27 Jan 1873.
326 Ibid.
327 Gowans, p. 66.

and Alexander Sinclair, along with 350 trappers, packers and camp cooks, assembled in the lush valley.[328] Finding their furs, dried buffalo meat and horses in demand, the Flatheads enjoyed a productive trading session. Although under some obligation to AFC, they exchanged with several other companies in the encampment. Various trappers needed fresh mounts to replace overworked horses, for which Indians allowed something in trade. Purchasers thought the horses cheap, costing but one blanket and a knife. After the trappers took their fresh horses back to camps, many returned to the grazing herd. Repeatedly, the Flatheads brought every wanderer back. Such honesty impressed the trappers, who certainly could never find particular mounts among the scattered thousands.[329]

Fur men attending the rendezvous for the first time marveled at the Flatheads' piety that included images and objects of worship common to the white man. It appeared to the newcomers that they had a sense of conscience and justice unlike other tribes encountered while crossing the plains. John Ball shared his observation of a Salish Sabbath, "[T]here is a day on which they do not hunt nor gamble, but sit moping all day and look like fools."[330] Through an interpreter, he wrote of the daily moral lectures the chief gave his people. "In the evenings, the Chief [Big Face] mounted his horse to lecture his people in a high tone on several dos and don'ts that included the need to be punctual in dealings with whites and orderly among themselves."[331] The mysterious religion practiced by the Flatheads puzzled the white men, but they did recognize its effectiveness.

Meanwhile, numerous trappers at the rendezvous sought Flathead women for wives, and it appears William Henry Vanderburg did also. Leading a detached AFC outfit of 50 men, Vanderburg joined Fontenelle and Dripps at the Teton River camp in mid-June to attend the rendezvous. Vanderburg had hunted during the previous winter in the Bear River and Cache Valley region. He took a Flathead bride during the rendezvous, a relationship that would be short lived due to his premature death at the hands of the Blackfeet. A 1905 Flathead Reservation census report verified his widow gave birth to a son, baptized Louis with the European surname of Vanderburg.[332]

The rendezvous began to break up on July 17, 1832, as the RMFC trappers, along with Wyeth's men and Sinclair's group, headed upvalley for the fall hunts. After spending the night near present-day Victor, Idaho,

---

328 [I.S.] Newell Narrative.
329 [I.S.] Ball, John, Across the Plains to Oregon, 1833.
330 [I.S.] Wyeth, J, Oregon, a short history, 1832.
331 [I.S.] Ball, Across the Plains to Oregon.
332 [I.S.] Malouf, p. 327.

the trappers arose to see many Indians entering the valley from the south. When they noticed the white men, they charged, stopping only after realizing they faced a greater number than expected. The chief was a lone rider coming forward with a peace pipe in his hand. Having recognized him as a Gros Ventre, an enemy of the fur men, half-blood Antoine Godin and a Flathead rode out to meet the chief as if to talk. When the chief extended his hand to Godin, the Flathead shot him dead; the two men stripped off the chief's decorated scarlet blankets and raced back to camp in a hail of bullets. Thus began the Battle of Pierre's Hole.[333] The trappers immediately dispatched men back to the rendezvous to seek help that would take several hours to arrive. As they watched and waited, the Gros Ventres constructed a small fort in an aspen grove by a nearby creek. When reinforcements of nearly 100 white trappers with about 150 Nez Perce and Flathead warriors rode in, the entire force attacked the makeshift fort.

The enemy had effectively built an impenetrable wood barricade with gun pits behind "cribbed up" small logs through which to fire. Advancing trappers and Salish fell under barrage from the fort. White men then decided to burn the fort, but the Flatheads and Nez Perces vetoed the idea on grounds it would destroy the plunder. As evening fell, the fur men and Indian allies backed off, believing they had the fort surrounded. In morning's first light, they saw to their dismay that the enemy had slipped away in the night, leaving three dead comrades, 24 dead horses and all cooking gear. After the Nez Perces and Flatheads helped themselves, they followed the trail of blood and found seven more bodies, but the Gros Ventre had made good their escape, mostly on foot. Estimates of casualties vary among those who left written records, from hearsay to those who took part in the conflict. Robert Campbell and Nathaniel Wyeth offered similar figures: three white men dead and eight seriously wounded, 10 Nez Perces lost, eight Flatheads dead, with both having many wounded.[334] The Gros Ventres reported 50 men, women and children died on the way home.

Most casualties occurred during the brave charge on the fort by the Indians and a few trappers. Hallalhotsoot, a mixed-blood Flathead-Nez Perce, received a minor wound during the attack, where he first demonstrated leadership skill. Young and shrewd, he later was called Lawyer due to his ability in an argument.[335] Part of his family's band lived on the

333 Victor, pp. 111-18, Joe Meek. No less than seven participants describe this battle; it's not surprising that accounts and casualties vary.

334 [I.S.] Robert Campbell Letter; Lewis Fork July 18, 1832, and [I.S.] Wyeth Journal; numbers of casualties vary in all accounts.

335 Josephy, p. 69.

Clearwater River, but he grew up with the Flatheads in the Bitterroot and Salmon regions. Lawyer participated in the Nez Perce Treaty council and soon after was recognized head chief of the Nez Perces by the U.S. military. On August 1, the Flatheads left the rendezvous site with plenty of white man's goods and headed northwest, transporting their wounded as they hunted along the way via the Monida Pass route to the Beaverhead River. They joined the Pend Oreilles and other Salish allies on the broad, lush plain near Beaverhead Rock and established a village of 150 lodges, an imposing force if a Piegan raider should show up.

HBC's Francis Ermatinger, several engagees and on-site traders had accompanied the Pend Oreille contingent from Flathead Post. His presence discouraged AFC's Andrew Dripps and his American party, so much so, they passed the Indian camp without displaying their goods. The stealthy Piegans had made their camp up Ruby River where on October 14 they killed AFC leader William H. Vanderburg and trapper Pilou. Surviving fur men fled to the Salish camp and asked if some of their men might provide protection while they buried the two men. They did, and the party found and buried the trapper but found no trace of Vanderburg's body. A month later, the Pend Oreilles found his bones in Ruby River, where the Piegans had thrown him.

Meanwhile, prompted by the AFC's established trading post in their country, the Piegans invented a new strategy involving their conduct toward American trappers. Toward the head of Red Rock River, in mid-October, 70 warriors approached a large RMFC camp under James Bridger. At first, ready for a fight, the trappers were surprised when two unarmed Piegan chiefs approached them. Unveiling pipes, the chiefs said they wanted to make peace and trade with the white fur men. Skeptical, the fur men sat down with their longtime enemy to smoke and exchange news. While passing the pipe around the parley, the two chiefs sent word to the Flatheads to warn of a planned visit in the spring to, if possible, exterminate their race. The meeting ended with the chiefs receiving gifts from the trappers, and the chiefs giving Bridger a word of caution that 100 Blood warriors a few days ahead might "show fight," but they neglected to tell him of the Bloods' role in the new strategy. The fur men had no way of knowing that a few days earlier, Piegans had killed the AFC leader William Vanderburg and Pilou, 30 miles away on Ruby River.[336]

Bridger and his crew separated from the Piegans to head south over Monida Pass toward the Snake River and, sure enough, ran headlong into

336 [I.S.] Ferris Journal, Ch. 33, October 24, 1832.

the Bloods. An immediate exchange of musket fire erupted, when suddenly the enemy stopped shooting and two chiefs raised a white flag. Trapper guns went silent as an unarmed pair approached to tell Bridger that the white chief at Fort Union said the flag would lead to peaceful trade with the fur men. The two chiefs said they desired friendship not bullets; they truly wanted to bury the hatchet and smoke the peace pipe. After receiving gifts from the outnumbered fur men, the Bloods rode off to raid the Shoshonis.[337] These same Piegan and Blood warriors would attempt to fulfill their threats to eliminate the Flatheads, root and branch, in the upcoming spring.

Lemhi Pass Massacre

As winter closed in on the Salish, most Pend Oreilles and some Flatheads returned to home territories. Likewise, a few Nez Perce, having lost many horses to the Piegans, crossed the mountains to the west to obtain remounts from their cousins. The remaining Flatheads, Pend Oreilles and a few Nez Perces again camped on the Lemhi near Bridger's trappers, while a small Nez Perce band made winter quarters at their usual place on the Salmon below its joining with the Lemhi.

The newcomer trader Captain Benjamin Bonneville and a few of his men wintered nearby in crude cabins he built along the river near today's Carmen, Idaho. Piegan horse thieves plagued both encampments, particularly the Nez Perces, who alone lost 127 head in late November.[338] In mid-April 1833, a large Piegan war party attacked the small Nez Perce village on the Salmon River as 22 well-armed braves defended their camp and families from manned trenches dug near individual lodges. Both sides suffered minimal casualties with the enemy coming out worse, largely due to the Piegans' running low on ammunition. After the Piegans stopped firing, they began a war of words. Following a display of insults and ultimatums, the Piegans left, satisfied, with 70 Nez Perce horses,[339] then joined Blood warriors who replenished their supply of ammunition.

The conflict prompted an allied camp-force of Nez Perces and Flatheads on the Lemhi to attempt recovery of the stolen horses and, if necessary, defeat the Blackfeet. Scouts had located the Piegan-Blood camp on upper Horse Prairie Creek below Lemhi Pass[340] but failed to estimate their full

337 [I.S.], Ferris Journal, Ch. 32, October 14, 1832.
338 [I.S.] Irving Journal, Ch. 18, Bonneville.
339 [I.S.] Ibid.
340 [I.S.] Ferris Journal, Ch. 41, July 15, 1833 and Bonneville cite the battle site at Lemhi Pass site.

strength of 300 warriors[341] correctly. Consequently, 42 allied warriors rode off to Lemhi Pass with confidence strengthened entirely by the scouting information. In the rain, and troubled about possible wet powder, the war party approached the pass on May 25, 1833, and proceeded toward the reported enemy camp. Before reaching the pass, the three lead scouts surprised an equal number of Piegans, chased them up a hill and shot them down.[342]

One Flathead, scrambling to catch a Piegan horse, had his own run off, and at the same time, his fellow warriors returned to the main body already engaged with the enemy. The suddenly horseless Flathead ran into the bushes to hide, as a reluctant witness to a battle in which Nez Perce-Flathead allies were outnumbered nearly 10-to-1. Frozen with the horror of bloodshed, he awaited the end. Being the only survivor, he carried the indelible memory back to retell at Nez Perce and Flathead camps. In the fight, the allies sold their lives dearly and killed many enemies, so much so that the Bloods left soon after the slaughter, returning to their home country instead of continuing the war to exterminate the Salish and allies. Relatives and friends in both camps tore off their ornaments, wept and wailed, tearing their hair for two days. Braves went to the battleground to retrieve their dead for burial and found a gruesome scene of headless bodies with their hearts cut out.

Many wounds on each body signified the warriors' valor and the likelihood of numerous Piegan and Blood casualties.[343] Twenty-one Nez Perces, 18 Flatheads, two Iroquois and one Pend Oreille were among the many top warriors to die on that mountain pass.[344] One victim of the carnage had journeyed to St. Louis with AFC Dripps' packtrain in 1831, Nez Perce Tawis Geejumin (Worn Out Horns),[345] and Flathead Paseal's brother, died at the pass in that dreadful encounter. News of the battle traveled north to the HBC Canadian operations at Edmonton House where retelling the tragic events warranted daily journal notations. At the AFC Fort Mackenzie, the home territory of the Piegan participants in the fight, Bear Chief impressed the touring German Prince Maximilian with his casualty count. The Flatheads lost 45 Indians and two white French Canadians versus six of his band killed with "some" wounded.[346] Bear Chief did not account for Blood losses or other allies involved. Reported white men's deaths may have been the mixed-blood Iroquois. The Lemhi Pass carnage

341 [I.S.] Irving Journal, Ch. 18, June 24, 1833.
342 [I.S.] Ibid.
343 [I.S.] Ibid.
344 [I.S.] Wyeth, N. Journal, May 27, 1833.
345 McWhorter Narrative, p. 29.
346 Jackson-Piikani, pp. 124-25.

resembled old battles before the Salish acquired guns, resulting in the most deaths in any single battle in the Salish-allied recorded history.

The Flatheads involved in this atrocity violated a long-standing policy to "never go out and hunt your own grave." Disgusted with constant horse thievery, they joined a desperate and revenge-minded Nez Perce chief who had blood on his mind over recovering horses. The Salish knew of the Piegan threats and the Blood presence but marched anyway; however, valiant action on their part did prevent an attack on their villages by blocking the massive Lemhi-Salmon-bound enemy force.

In the fall of 1835 missionary Samuel Parker and his Nez Perce escort passed by the gravesite of those fallen heroes, five miles north of today's Salmon, Idaho, and stopped to pay silent respects. A year earlier, grave robbers had desecrated their graves, each containing five bodies. The robbers stole blankets, buffalo robes and other personal items buried with the men to keep them comfortable in their long sleep. Plunder-seeking Piegans appropriated clothing for their own use. The Nez Perces had gathered the scattered remains and reburied them in a place where body stalkers could not find them.[347]

One month after the Lemhi Pass massacre, Flathead hunters and a group of fur traders found an "Indian Letter" on carefully leveled ground next to a main trail near Deer Lodge, Montana. Seven Blood warriors boasted of their victory in May by creating a sketch on the earth's surface of the battle site, the river system and their home near Fort Mackenzie, intended to terrify the Salish. Utilizing sticks, bits of cloth and small mounds of red earth, they placed a map of the river system to display the message. Red stickmen flat on the ground depicted the fallen Nez Perces and Flatheads, while more upright sticks represented the fort, and conical mounds of red dirt represented the nearby Blood village. Seven stick men riding stick horses placed partway to the post represented the warriors who had sketched the letter. The Flathead chief, likely Big Face, "shrugged his shoulders with the air of scorning threats and hurled-back defiance, while his eyes flashed fire of inveterate hate and unconquerable courage and grunted 'maybe.' "[348] He turned and walked off to direct camp setup, unfazed by the Bloods' terror tactics.

Meanwhile, on April 30, 1833, 120 lodges of Pend Oreille, Flatheads and a few Kootenais gathered in the lower Bitterroot Valley for the summer hunt.[349] HBC traveling-trader Francis Ermatinger and independent American-trader Nathaniel Wyeth joined them for the pending two-month

347 Parker, pp. 112-13.
348 [I.S.] Ferris, Western Literary Messenger, April 17, 1842.
349 [I.S.] Wyeth, N., Journal, April 30, 1833.

journey to today's Mud Lake, Idaho.

Wyeth and his small party, including naturalists David Douglas and Thomas Nuttall, readily accepted the guide service and protection through hostile territory of a large troop of friendly Indians. Lingering at the Bitterroot Village a week before departing, Wyeth used the time to observe Salish camp life.[350] The following day he wrote: "I find an Indian camp a place of much novelty[;] the Indians appear to enjoy their amusements with more zest than the whites. Although they are simple they are great gamblers in proportion to their means[,] bolder than the whites."[351] Later he continued: "With [t]he absence of quarrells in [an] Indian camp more and more surprise me when I come and see the various occasions[,] which would give rise to them among whites. The crowding together of from 12 to 1800 horses, which have to be driven into camp at night to stake. To load the starting of horses and turning of loads, the seizing of fuel when scarce, which is often the case, the play of men and boys and etc."[352]

A long procession of upward of 1,000 souls, and 1,800 horses loaded with belongings, began a 400-mile trek on May 9, 1833, up the Bitterroot Valley. They wound their way up to Gibbon Pass, following a headwater stream of the Missouri down to the Big Hole River. The trip took 10 days. Here they camped near the willow-lined river that flowed through a wide, grass-covered prairie for five days of spring weather to hunt bull buffalo just coming onto summer range. At that time of year, Indians did not kill calving cows. Led by hunters at a resolute pace, the long procession crossed east over a high open pass into Grasshopper Creek and turned south to Horse Prairie, arriving there May 27, where a few Flatheads were camped. After learning of the recent Lemhi Pass massacre from a sad Flathead, the apprehensive chiefs decided to take the Bannock Pass route to the Lemhi River, believing the enemy had vacated the area. Numerous old signs lingered along the way, but no enemies were sighted. The large group stopped for two days on the Lemhi, waiting for 16 lodges of Nez Perces to join them who had engaged in a skirmish with the Blackfeet on the way. A bit on edge, chiefs assigned scouts in addition to the usual advance group.

Moving down Birch Creek, the hunters found and killed enough bison to satisfy immediate needs around the creek where it narrows near Lone Pine. Continuing downstream for two days to where Birch Creek sinks, the party turned northeast, skirting the foothills through waterless sagebrush country to Warm Springs Creek. Moving north up that creek

350 [I.S.] Wyeth, N., Journal.

351 [I.S.] Wyeth, N., Journal.

352 [I.S.] Wyeth, N., Journal, May 1, 1832.

some miles, the Indians set up camp for five days to chase buffalo, mostly bulls,[353] around the gently sloping hills surrounding the creek. During an early part of the hunt, a galloping horse turned sharply, which threw a Pend Oreille hunter to the ground where a bull gored him in the chest, inflicting a critical wound. Back in camp, while the trader Ermatinger dressed his wound, the incredibly composed brave, breathing through a hole in his chest, dictated his will to attending Indians, who repeated each sentence in unison. According to Wyeth, the man "appeared not the least intimidated by the approach of death."[354] The next day a Flathead scouting for the presence of Blackfeet returned on a slightly wounded horse to report he had barely escaped an ambush by two of the enemy. Two days later, another brave rode into camp to inform the chiefs of a large Piegan camp just 15 miles away on upper Medicine Lodge Creek. That information, plus less than satisfactory hunting results, would cut the hunt short in three days.

All-out battles between large Salish and Piegan forces were rare. Commonly, fewer than 100 warriors (on each side) engaged in a combat that lasted no more than a day. The opponent enduring the greater casualties, experiencing the most difficulty in achieving the objective, quit first. The Jesuit missionary Father Gregory Mengarini described a battle between the Salish and Piegans he witnessed in the spring of 1845.

Mengarini wrote in part: "From the moment when the enemy is sighted the warriors prepare for battle. The poor men stripped down to nothing while the richer ones clothed themselves in calico of flaming colors. Braves led women, children and horses to a safe place. Firing had already begun on both sides and the plain was covered with horsemen curvetting [prancing] and striving to get a chance to kill someone of the enemy. An Indian battle consists a multitude of single combats; there are no ranks, no battalions, no united efforts. Every man for himself is the ruling principle, and victory depends on personal bravery and good horsemanship. ... There is no random shooting. Every Flathead or Blackfoot always aims for the waist."*

This battle lasted all day, killing four Flatheads. They claimed 24 Piegans were killed – likely an exaggeration.

*Mengarini's Narrative of the Rockies, Montana State University, Sources of Northwest History no. 25; Missoula, p. 38.

353 Bull meat was not good table fare and hides made poor robe material, but hides did make excellent moccasins, tepees, cords and saddlebags.

354 [I.S.] Wyeth, N. Journal, June 9, 1833.

Short rations for 1,000 souls necessitated the continuation of the hunt for scattered buffalo in the difficult rolling hills country. Wyeth's party nervously waited for the Indians to move on out of hostile country. His journal entry of June 18 reads: "Same camp, severe hail and snow yesterday afternoon and rain most of last night and until noon today. Camp about out of provisions so we are in hope of moving soon. Nothing but necessity and that immediate need will induce an Indian to do the least thing, any excuse seams [*sic*] to stop business with them and a small party of whites who are not strong enough to move along will find traveling with them occasion for all the patience they may have."[355]

On June 20, the caravan reached the appropriately named Camas Prairie, lush with grass, abundant camas roots and ample buffalo. Over the next 10 days, while camped on the prairie, Indians put up many pounds of dried meat and roots and trapped willow-fringed, serpentine drainages.

On July 1, 1833, 40 lodges of Flatheads and Nez Perces separated from Ermatinger and the Pend Oreilles to pursue buffalo in the Horse Plains area. The latter group and Wyeth's party hunted their way down Camas Creek to Mud Lake, Idaho; as planned, they met up with the American trader Captain Benjamin Bonneville's outfit on July 3 and camped near the lake. In an attempt to compete directly with HBC, Bonneville decided to open trade with the Indians by displaying his packs of merchandise of bright colored cloths, scarlet blankets and everything glorious in the eyes of a warrior or his woman. However, his efforts did not pay off, as the Pend Oreilles remained loyal to HBC, particularly with their trader present.[356] The captain traded for a few furs from free trappers accompanying Ermatinger when he brought forth liquor. Bonneville did receive an invitation from the Kootenais in the group to make a fall hunt in their country, who pledged he would find "abundant beaver." Further conversation indicated the Kootenai Indians' "hallowed friendship" with the Piegans had broken down.[357] Having trouble in establishing his fur business, Bonneville would leave the mountains within two years of this meeting. Wythe and his party joined with Bonneville to trail south toward the Snake River.

On July 7, the Pend Oreilles and trader Ermatinger parted company with Bonneville and Wyeth to begin their journey to home territory. Along the way, the Indians put more beaver on willow drying hoops and added to dried buffalo meat supplies. The hunters and traders arrived in the Big Hole by mid-November, where they lost horses to Piegan thieves. All but a small

355 [I.S.] Wyeth, N. Journal, June 1833.

356 [I.S.] Irving. Bonneville, Ch. 18.

357 [I.S.] Ibid.

band of warriors, left behind to attempt to recover the horses, continued on to the Bitterroot Valley via Gibbon Pass. Within three weeks, the successful war party arrived at the Flathead camp near Hell Gate with 26 of the stolen horses and two trophies from heads of their enemy.[358] Ermatinger put in an arduous but successful trading session with the Salish, exiting Flathead Post with 27 packs of furs and 20 bales of dried buffalo meat and fat.[359]

The Salish and Nez Perce hunting grounds that drained south into the Snake River overlapped into the Shoshonis and Bannocks' traditional home territory they had abandoned a decade earlier due to Blackfeet pressure. Henrys Fork, Camas and Birch creeks, and the Lost and Little Lost rivers supported enormous herds of buffalo in what fur men called the "War Zone." The Shoshonis and Bannocks seldom ventured north of the Snake River into the war zone unless in outsized groups, but instead conducted their hunts south of that river where sizeable herds roamed. The tribes were not immune to Blackfeet horse thieves but nothing like the hunters north of the river. The river corridor provided winter range for bison from which Indians and wintering trappers harvested many. Challenging the Blackfeet, the Salish and allies confined hunts to the summer range, higher up drainages, which fit the enemy's agenda perfectly. With such unmanaged hunting in the region by whites and Indians alike, soon the mighty buffalo herds grazed no more.

In 1833, AFC attempted to break HBC's trading domination with the Salish. The experienced mountain man Robert "Doc" Newell signed on with the firm at the summer rendezvous. Directed to find the Salish and open trade with them, he and company clerk Warren Ferris, six packers and five armed Indians set out. Well acquainted with the route to the Bitterroot Valley, Newell and party found August 15 only 15 lodges of Flatheads headed by a little, old and hardy chief, camped near Hell Gate, still mourning the Lemhi Pass massacre. The Salish welcomed the traders in the usual manner by shaking hands and making prayers for their visitors. After setting up their camp, Newell's crew received gifts of fruits from the Indians that included whortle-, service-, Hawthorne- and snowberries, which the men, dog-like, devoured with relish. Afterward, the chief and lead men went to their camp to smoke. He told them of the Lemhi Pass massacre, dwelling on the virtues of the fallen men. In his closing remarks, the old chief thanked the traders for coming so far through hostile territory to bring munitions and tobacco to them. He then promised to exert his

358 [I.S.] Ferris Journal, Ch. 44, December 29, 1833.

359 [I.S.] Ferris Journal, Ch. 44 and McDonald, A., Historical Memorandum.

influence on his young men to hunt and trade with them, plus supply fruit and other provisions. The next day, the Americans opened their packs of goods and exchanged mostly beads for some beaver and provisions.[360]

A few days later, a mixed lot of Pend Oreilles, Kalispels and Kootenais arrived at the small Flathead camp to form a hunting party. It appears the American traders joined the hunters, traveling with them to the Red Rock River, yet Newell's manuscript and Ferris' diaries are mute on the subject. There is a lapse in Ferris' journal entries for 60 days before he resumed notations, after crossing the sand hills to Henrys Fork, where in October he wrote, "The distance from Pierre's Fork (Teton River) where we left the village to Henrys Fork is about seventy miles."[361] The mileage approximates the regular hunting camp used by the Indians on the Red Rock River. From there the Flathead traders continued downstream to the Teton River where they met Dripps and his trapping brigade establishing winter quarters. During the journey with the Salish hunters, Ferris became acquainted with free trapper Pillet, who also worked part-time for HBC as a packer between Flathead and Kootenai posts.[362] Pillet, six other Indians and seven white free trappers tagged along with the buffalo hunters, most likely linked to HBC's Flathead Post operations. Both the free trappers and Indians resisted trading with traveling companions, from which Ferris concluded the British held trade advantages over the Americans, with equal prices for fur and less expensive goods.

After receiving "encouragement" from Pillet, also a friend of Ermatinger, Ferris quit AFC to join the freemen and Indians back to Salish country. Then, after a speedy, 15-day journey over Monida Pass to the Big Hole, they met Ermatinger at the Bitterroot Forks in late November.[363] During the trek to Flathead Post, Ferris proposed a venture to Ermatinger that involved the company supplying a small party with trade goods to exchange only among the Americans and non-Salish allies. Ferris teamed up with Nicolas Montour Jr. and his family, spending the winter in the environs of the post, while HBC management considered his proposal. Columbia River shipping invoices indicate 70 shirts, 45 gallons of whiskey and other

---

360 [I.S.] Newell Narrative, and [I.S.] Ferris Journal, Ch. 41, October 30, 1833. Ferris' description fits Head Chief Big Face.

361 [I.S.] Ferris Journal, Ch. 42.

362 [I.S.] Ferris Journal, Ch. 44. Pillet was probably the son of François Benjamin Pillet (PFC) and a Kootenai woman. François returned to Montreal after NWC's acquisition of the company.

363 [I.S.] Ferris Journal. The Forks are where the Bitterroot River joins the Clark Fork River.

items went to the Flathead Post for the "Ferris party."[364] In April, Ermatinger arrived at Flathead Post with the trade material, along with a written agreement needing Ferris' signature. The company had refused to engage the two American trappers but instead contracted with them to trade only outside HBC's territory with Americans and Indians living there.[365]

The contract specified that Montour was responsible for the goods and horses but with management vested in Ferris.[366] Finally, HBC had an American capable of quasi-legal trading east of the Continental Divide. With trade goods, terms and prices in hand, Montour and Ferris, a mixed-blood, one Kootenai, two engagees and two Nez Perces, four Pend Oreilles, four women and three children launched their enterprise in May. The trading journey took them east and south until November 23, according to Ferris' journal, when they traded with Ute Indians near Utah Lake.[367] After that, no further information exists on the success or failure of the venture by Ferris or in HBC records. Montour returned to Salish country, while Ferris quit the mountains and returned east.

Newell and nine men returned to the Bitterroots in April 1834 where they met Ermatinger and crew conducting trade with the Salish. Equipped with a grander variety of goods than the previous year, he joined the HBC men and Salish on their jaunt up the Clark Fork and over the Continental Divide to the Beaverhead and Horse Prairie Creek. Newell's trading success at that point is unrecorded, but he separated from the Pend Oreilles and Ermatinger there to go to the Nez Perce-Flathead camp on the Salmon River.[368] Here, he joined Indians hunting south and east through previously described country to Camas Creek. Ever so fleeting is his writing; at Camas Creek 100 Blackfeet attacked the encampment, yet Newell leaves no further words of the fight. During the foray at Salmon, "Doc" Newell met a Nez Perce chief's daughter whom he called Kittie; they would marry at the upcoming rendezvous.[369] Speaking of women, one of Francis Ermatinger's techniques to gain approval of Indian customers involved sponsoring a foot race for Salish women. Afterward, he awarded the winner with an assortment of popular items that included cloth, beads and other trinkets, and gave consolation prizes to all contestants, thus securing tribal goodwill. The two-and-one-half-mile course near the head of Jocko River

364 HBC Columbia River Invoices.

365 Cole, p. 107, Archibald McDonald Letter to Ermatinger, March 6, 1834.

366 Ibid.

367 [I.S.] Ferris Journal, Ch. 49-52, April to July 1834.

368 [I.S.] McDonald, Lois, p. 176 & [I.S.] Newell Narrative.

369 [I.S.] McDonald, Lois, p. 178.

at Evaro hill became known as "Courses des Femmes" to later residents.[370] According to a 1911 Missoulian newspaper article related by Arthur Stone, Iroquois Charles Lamoose's Pend Oreille wife won the first event, in which some 40 women competed.

Ermatinger and American trader Nathanial Wyeth developed a friendship during their long jaunt with the Indians, which led to the exchange of a few letters. In a letter, Wyeth provided his friend with information on American beaverskins' returns brought to St. Louis in a two-year period from the Pierre's Hole and Green River rendezvous. Wyeth personally witnessed the deliveries that included 5 percent land otter carried in 100-pound packs. In 1832, 170 packs came from the Rocky Mountain Rendezvous, and the next year, 153 packs. Just eight years after the American firm began competing with HBC for beaver pelts west of the Continental Divide, the yearly harvest had peaked in 1832, then went steadily downhill from there. In Wyeth's letter from the Green River Rendezvous, he warned Ermatinger of American mountain men's posture toward HBC personnel. Apparently, Ermatinger had expressed interest in trading at the annual affair, which Wyeth cautioned: "I give you this honest opinion which you can communicate to the Co. There is here a great majority of scoundrels. I should much doubt the personal safety of anyone from your side of the house."[371] HBC made its last, company-financed Snake River hunt in that year, relying instead on Ermatinger, who traveled with the Salish and free trappers with a supply of trade goods. The company's return on this operation netted 10 to 12 packs of beaver initially but dropped off steadily due to scarcity of furs. By 1837, HBC had acquired Fort Hall from Wyeth from which it concentrated trading effort with many Americans as customers.

---

370 [I.S.] McDonald, L., p. 209.

371 [I.S.] Wyeth Letter, November 17, 1833 to Jay Baker and son from St. Louis; also his letter to Ermatinger July 18, 1833, from the Green River Rendezvous.

6

Men of God and Rendezvous

1834-1840

Late in the spring of 1834, about 30 Flatheads and Nez Perces traveled from the Salmon area to the Hams Fork Rendezvous with AFC trader Robert Newell to pick up supplies.[372] The event included some 300 trappers attached to three different fur companies: AFC, RMFC and Nathaniel Wyeth's, each with its own supply train from the east and separate campsites eight miles apart along Hams Fork and the Green River, Wyoming. Flathead Little Chief Insula and a large group of Flatheads and Nez Perces arrived and set tents near RMFC, the hub of the event.

Mountain men fancied Insula, considering him a joyful and wise man, distinguished warrior and fine equestrian. He took part in the all-American ceremony of raising the country's flag on the prairie at the Hams Fork. Explorer and journalist William M. Anderson wrote: "[As] I raised the Star Spangled Banner instantly four men were seen darting like Cossacks over the plain, wild with amazement and delight. They screamed and shouted ... and into our tent they rushed . ... Somehow I learned their names. They were Vasquez [a Spaniard], the long lost Vasquez, Fitzpatrick [Thomas, a trader], Gray [John Grey, a half-blood Iroquois], and the Little Chief [Insula]."[373]

This rendezvous marked the arrival of the first missionaries from the eastern United States to the Rocky Mountains. Methodist minister Jason Lee and four laymen convoyed with Nathaniel Wyeth and his supply train from St. Louis specifically to discuss Christianity with the Flatheads and Nez Perces. Wyeth, who a few days earlier had a business deal go sour with RMFC,[374] tried to discourage Lee from meeting with the Indians.

372 [I.S.] Newell Narrative.

373 Alter, p. 146, Anderson Narrative – Insula adopted Tom Fitzpatrick and Robert Campbell as "blood brothers." In 1857, the latter sent Insula a pair of pistols as a gift; also DeVoto p. 199.

374 [I.S.] Wyeth, N., Letter, July 1, 1834, and Journal, June 19, 1834. Wyeth had contracted with RMFC's Thomas Fitzpatrick to supply the 1834 rendezvous, but the latter defaulted by accepting goods from another pack outfit. Left with a variety of trade goods, Wyeth went to the Snake River and built a trading post, Fort Hall, and later sold it to HBC in 1837.

He told them he overheard the mountain men threatening to "give those missionaries hell." Unconcerned, Lee and his party had Wyeth lead them 10 miles to the RMFC camp to meet the Indians and trappers. Lee met briefly with about 10 Nez Perce and two Flatheads and asked the Indians to come again when he had more time. The following day, Sunday, June 22, the Indians returned, and Lee invited as many as would fit inside his tent. Through an interpreter, he explained their reason for coming west, showed them the Bible and recited some of the commandments. Imagine the Indians pressing near as if they might actually see the "strange tracks" jump from the Book of the Great White Spirit into the minds of the missionaries. One Indian asked to have a "house" built at their place and promised they would catch plenty of beaver.

Lee continued through his diary, "One said he was going to St. Louis next year but he would leave his three children with his friend, who was present, and he would give them to us that we might teach them to read and write and be good."[375] The notation is significant, for the man mentioned likely was Old Ignace Lamoose, who went to St. Louis the following year with his two sons. Insula (Little Chief) did his best to convince Lee that his people would welcome him and associates as teachers. As the Indians left the tent, some shook hands "heartily" with the missionaries.

Lee then sent a man to obtain meat from the Nez Perce-Flathead camp, but he returned empty-handed because it was the Sabbath, which impressed the hungry men of God.[376] If Lee's interpretation of the Indians' response to their meeting is accurate, then neither the Flatheads, Nez Perces nor Ignace knew there were several different brands of Christianity. Reverend Lee had made no commitment to the Flatheads or Nez Perces concerning a mission; while packing and preparing to leave on July 4, the Indians paid him another visit. Lee wrote, "The Indians came and informed us that they were about to leave us and wished to know if we intended to come back and stop with the Flathead camp."[377] In a manner of indifference, Lee said he would visit their chiefs sometime that winter or the next winter, or perhaps in the coming year. The get-togethers ended in disappointment for both Indians and missionaries. Concerning the Flatheads, Lee later wrote superiors that he did not bother to explain Christianity to them or plan to establish a mission for them, rationalizing the tribe was small in number and lived in a remote, hostile region.

Lee and his fellow disciples intended to travel to the Willamette

375 [I.S.] OHQ, vol. 17 no. 2, p. 139, Diary of Jason Lee.
376 Ibid.
377 Ibid. p. 140.

Valley in Oregon to set up a mission to benefit more than a single tribe.[378] Insula, other Flatheads and the Nez Perces would return to four of the next five rendezvous, meeting other Protestant missionaries and, finally, a Black Robe, as described to them by their Iroquois friends. The fur traders soon abandoned attempts to discourage the preachers, since the traders' native partners in the fur business eagerly sought the white man's God. In contrast, the Shoshoni and Bannock tribes at these get-togethers showed little interest in anything concerning missionaries.

The Salish tribe's desire for Christian teachers would materialize in due course. Nevertheless, when the rendezvous broke up, the Salmon River-bound Indians accompanied Wyeth and the Lee party to Soda Springs, Idaho, where they separated. The convoy included a renegade Piegan chief who had joined the Nez Perces after instigating serious trouble with his own people. Both the Bonneville and Ferris diaries mention the deserter, who lived with the Salmon River band of hunters to which the allied Flathead Chief Insula belonged. Traveling with this group, John Townsend wrote, "He is a fine, war like looking fellow, and all though [*sic*] he takes part in all the war-songs and sham battles of his adopted brothers, and whoops and howls as loud as the best of them, yet it is plain to perceive that he is distrusted and disliked."[379]

During this rendezvous RMFC dissolved, with Fontenelle and Fitzpatrick forming a new company. In essence, AFC and the former firm joined forces by initiating agreements concerning resupply, trapping logistics and trading posts.[380] Robert Newell's planned return to Flathead country changed only in that he would join James Bridger after the mission. Leaving the rendezvous in August, he and his crew traveled 51 days to the Bitterroot River where he ran across the Salish village in October. Newell's "Memorandum" mentions he delivered supplies to the Indians but failed to give further detail. Did he trade while there or simply drop off items based on vouchers? Whatever the case, the Americans did not return to Salish country to trade and did so only when making contact with them in the field.

Images of Christianity

Indians judged all aspects of life by material results. When prayers failed to save a life, win a battle or relieve starvation, they believed the Great Spirit was displeased or had let them down. They saw the power of the white man's God expressed in guns, ammunition, kettles, iron knives,

378 Paladino, p. 21.
379 [I.S.] Townsend, Ch. 5.
380 Gowans, pp. 118-119.

beads and blankets. The white man seemed to have everything in plenty and showed proficiency in his undertakings; to be so well blessed meant a benevolent and powerful God supported them. Having this kind of power was something Indians felt a profound need to obtain. Instructed at the Caughnawaga Mission from about 1812 onward, Iroquois trappers on the St. Lawrence River in Canada brought notions of Christianity to the Salish.[381] Employed by NWC, Iroquois trappers and French Canadian Catholics interacted closely with the natives and often intermarried. From the time of their arrival until 1821, most inland trapping action originated from trading posts in Salish territory.

When operations shifted to the Snake River, some Iroquois stayed behind to become free trappers and members of the Salish tribes. Catholic trappers conveyed church teachings of prayer and rites, and touted the advantages of having Black Robe missionaries among them. Many Salish adopted some of the practices, such as including morning and evening prayer and observing Sunday as the Sabbath. The chief created a flaglike object attached to a high lodge pole (called "*S'chazeus*" in Salish) as an announcement of the "Lord's day,"[382] on which no hunting, fishing, gambling or travel took place. Captain Bonneville told of meeting four Iroquois hunters in 1832 at his Salmon River winter camp; they were remnants of old Chief Pierre's party that had come to the mountains many years before.[383] These eastern Indian visitors showed up with the Pend Oreilles, indicating they were part of that tribe. Iroquois Pierre Gaucher, also known as Left-hand Peter or Piere Kar-sowata, and old Ignace Lamoose were likely among the visitors. Both men spearheaded efforts to obtain Black Robe missionaries for the Salish. More on such exploits will follow.

From 1834 to 1840, Flatheads, Nez Perces, numerous Shoshonis and a few Bannocks attended annual summer rendezvous in today's Wyoming where trappers resupplied for the upcoming year during two weeks in July. Hardships and perils of the past year led to a relaxed, no-troubles atmosphere. Rich with returns from the hunt, a wild party with watered-down grain alcohol, drunken songs, outlandish stories and grudge fights took up space and filled the air with a scramble of noise. Many trappers raced horses, showed off their marksmanship, and bartered for wives from among the attending Indians. For several years, these gatherings accommodated a single fur trading company, RMFC, but by this time, it involved

381 Palladino, p. 9. Iroquois families had been Catholic for more than 100 years prior to 1812.

382 Ibid. Ch. 2.

383 [I.S.] Irving. Bonneville, Ch. 10.

all American firms and several hundred Indians. Held on the Green River near today's Daniel, Wyoming, the 1835 rendezvous attracted 40 lodges of Flatheads and Nez Perces camping a few miles from its main site. By this time, market demand for dressed buffalo robes had increased to $4 in goods,[384] which the Flatheads had the former and wanted plenty of the latter. Due to the work involved and the bulkiness of dressed hides, trappers let the Indians dress the buffalo robes and transport them to the marketplace. Eighty packs of robes and 120 packs of beaver skins that weighed 90 to 100 pounds each went east after the rendezvous.[385]

Continuing with the missionary trend, the Presbyterian ministers Dr. Marcus Whitman and Samuel Parker traveled with the 1835 rendezvous-bound supply packtrain from Bellevue, Nebraska. Their purpose was to survey the possible demand for missionaries among various tribes attending the event. The two ministers first assembled Indians of the four nations represented to decide where to employ limited workers. After several days of digesting information from veteran mountain men regarding the country and conditions of the people, the two arranged an interview with the chiefs of the Nez Perces and Flatheads to explain their objective of benevolent Christian desires. The ministers concluded their interview by asking who wanted teachers to come among their people to bring the Christian God's word to stimulate their labors. The oldest chief of the Flathead, Big Face, rose first to say, "[I am] old and [do] not expect to know much more; [I am] deaf and [can] not hear, but [my] heart [is] made glad, to see what [I have] never seen before, a man near to God."[386]

Then Chief Insula, as reported by Whitman, spoke of his failed attempt to meet the missionaries along the trail to the rendezvous: "[I] heard, a man near to God was coming to visit them, and [I,] with some of [my] people, together with some white men, went out three days' journey to meet you, but missed you. Then on our way we were robbed by the Crow Indians and I lost a horse I loved very much, but since I had met you I did not lament the loss of my horse. I had been told some things about the worship of God but did not practice them. But now a teacher would come among us, I and my children [band] would obey all that you should say."

A Nez Perce chief then expressed great satisfaction from meeting the men of God, saying, in essence, that he was very simple and ignorant about the worship of the Almighty. He also requested teachers and, along

384 Lepley, p. 274.
385 Gowans, p. 128.
386 [I.S.] OHQ, September 1, 1927, vol. 28, p. 81, Parker, Whitman Journals.

with the Flathead chiefs, promised to help the missionaries.[387]

Overall, the Flatheads gave the missionaries a warm, enthusiastic reception, and paid eager attention to their message. Iroquois, Old Ignace Lamoose and his two sons surely were in camp preparing for their trip to St. Louis. Apparently, Ignace had not given Insula a full description of Black Robes – that the Indians should "expect men of God to wear long black robes, have no wives, who say mass and carry a cross with them."[388] At that time, having a description of a man of God made little difference to at least some of the Flatheads who simply wanted Christian teachers. As it turned out, they would continue to seek missionaries for another five years.

Parker and Whitman then met with fur traders to obtain information on the two tribes' demographics and character of the country they inhabited. They discovered the Nez Perces had two classes: those that stayed home in a fertile country unobstructed by war and a smaller class that hunted buffalo with the Salish and were constantly exposed to war. With that knowledge Whitman decided to return east to convince associates to help establish a mission and return with help in the coming year, while the Reverend Parker would continue west with the Indians. Two Nez Perce boys, one able to speak a little English, received permission from their father to accompany Whitman back to St. Louis, so they could learn each other's language along the way. The missionary promised the boys' father that he would bring them back to the next rendezvous.[389] While at the 1835 event, Dr. Whitman had removed an iron arrowhead from James Bridger's back as several Indians watched closely. Chief Insula was quite likely among the interested. Parker wrote of the operation and Indians' reaction: "It was a difficult operation, the arrow was hooked at the point by striking a large bone and a cartilaginous substance had grown around it. ... The Indians looked on meanwhile, with countenances indicating astonishment when it was extracted."[390]

The eastbound packtrain left the rendezvous August 27 for St. Louis, probably with old Iroquois Ignace Lamoose and his two sons as part of the packer crew. His purpose was twofold: to have his sons baptized by Catholic priests and to ask Black Robes to come to Salish country. After arriving in St. Louis, Ignace contacted Jesuits at the college where a priest baptized his sons Charles and Francis Xavier in December 1835.[391] Then,

387 [I.S.] OHQ, vol. 28, p. 248, Whitman Journals.
388 Paladino, p. 22-23. Paladino contends the Iroquois coined the description.
389 [I.S.] OHQ, vol. 28, pp. 248-249, Whitman Journals.
390 Gowans, p. 123.
391 Paladino, p. 26.

Ignace went to see Bishop Rosati and asked the Black Robe, in French, to send missionaries to the Flatheads. Impressed by the plea, Bishop Rosati supposed it could happen "as soon as possible."[392] This event was the first such request by Salish representatives that priests in St. Louis fully understood. Ignace and his sons would return with the westbound packtrain to the upcoming rendezvous in the spring.

Meanwhile, back at the Green River Rendezvous on August 22, 1835, after recovering from his operation, James Bridger headed north with his 60 trappers, the Reverend Samuel Parker and 300 Nez Perces and Flatheads. The friendly Indians had agreed to guide Parker to the Columbia River and along the way provided many gifts, foodstuff and horses. Bridger led the large column down the Hoback River to the Snake River and west across Teton Pass to Pierre's Hole, where Reverend Parker and most of the Indians separated from Bridger and headed for the Salmon River. After this trip, Parker wrote, "The first chief of the Flathead (Insula) and his family, with a few of his people went with Captain Bridger."[393] With Parker in tow, an estimated 250 Flatheads and Nez Perces journeyed northwest along well-used trails to Henrys Fork, across the dry Snake River Plain, and up Birch Creek, known then as Cote's Defile. Along the way, a band of 200 Nez Perce buffalo hunters and their families came upon the rear of Parker's guides and joined this leg of the trip. Food supplies dwindled quickly on the four-day trek up the creek to the head of the Lemhi River where a large herd of bison awaited.

Parker described the undertaking on September 9, 1835:

> Today we unexpectedly saw before us a large band of buffalo, and halted to make preparations for the chase. The young men and all the good hunters prepared themselves, selected the swiftest horses, examined the few guns they had, and took a supply of arrows with the bows. Our condition was such that it seemed our lives almost depended upon their success. ... They advanced towards the herd of buffalo with great caution, less they should frighten them before they could make a near approach; reserve the power of their horses for the chase, when it should be necessary to bring it into full requisition. When the buffalo took the alarm and fled, the rush was made as each Indian selecting for himself a cow with which he happened to come into nearest contact. All were in swift motion scoring the valley ... a cloud of dust began to arise ... the firing of guns and the shooting of arrows followed in close succession ... soon here and there buffalo were seen prostrate; and the women, who followed close in the rear, began

392 Ibid.

393 Parker, p. 96.

> the work of securing the valuable acquisition; and the men were away again in pursuit of the fleeing herd. Those in the chase, when they came abreast of the buffalo and at the distance of two rods [30 feet], shoot and wheel, expecting the wounded animal to turn upon them. The horses appeared to understand the way to avoid danger. As soon as the wounded animal falls again, the chase is renewed, and such is the alternate wheeling and chasing until the buffalo sinks beneath its wounds. They obtained between 50 and 60.[394]

The Indians had to halt for a day to dry their meat by "jerking," a process Parker described as follows: "The meat is cut into pieces, an inch thick, and spread out on a fixture made with stakes upon which are laid poles, and upon these cross stick. ... Then a moderate fire is placed beneath, which partly smokes, cooks and dries it; until so well free from moisture, that it can be packed, and will keep without injury almost any length of time."[395] On September 11, all but 300 Flatheads and Nez Perces split off from Parker's escort to travel over Bannock Pass to hunt near the Beaverhead.[396] The mostly Nez Perce party continued south to their traditional camp on the Salmon River. From there, Parker and about 20 guides crossed the rugged Salmon River Mountains to the Nez Perce homeland on the Clearwater River in today's state of Idaho. Canoes then transported Parker to the lower Columbia and Fort Vancouver.

Meanwhile, Bridger's crew and Insula's 20 Flatheads trapped their way nearer to the Beaverhead River. Having several encounters with Piegans along the way, the hunters lost a contrary-to-advice Frenchman who got a few miles ahead of the main party. Arriving at the Beaverhead River on September 19, they met the 180-lodge encampment of Flatheads, Pend Oreilles and HBC traders under Francis Ermatinger, who offered a trade for every beaver skin as fast as the Indians dragged it from the water.[397] The following day, the Indians, trappers and HBC men broke camp and moved 12 miles upstream en masse to hunker down with 130 lodges of the same tribes.[398] If the number of lodges is correct, nearly the entire Salish nation camped on the Beaverhead that fall. Bridger and his trappers rested for three days before saddling up to hunt beaver. Insula and his family remained with his people to continue the hunt.

Sometime during this period, Insula's daughter Cora married the

394 Parker, p. 107.
395 Ibid. pp. 107-108.
396 Ibid. p. 108.
397 Russell, p. 33.
398 Ibid.

legendary mountain man James Bridger; unfortunately, the date and place remain unrecorded. Bridger biographer J. Cecil Alter speculates the couple may have been on their honeymoon, riding from the rendezvous to the Beaverhead. He based his premise on Bridger telling General Dodge that his first wife was a daughter of a Flathead chief and his eldest daughter, Mary Ann, age 11, was at the Walla Walla Mission School at the time of the 1847 Whitman Massacre.[399] Coupling this information with records showing Insula attended the rendezvous and camped at least two winters on the Lemhi near Bridger makes his theory plausible. Cora had at least two more children with Bridger before her death a few months after childbirth in the winter of 1845-46 at Fort Bridger, Wyoming. Mary Josephine, born in 1845, was alive in 1850, but nothing more documenting her life appears to exist. Born about 1841, Felix Francis served in a Missouri artillery unit for two years during the Civil War and afterward with General Custer in southwestern Indian campaigns for five years. In 1871, he retired to a farm at Santa Fe."[400]

The Flatheads and Nez Perces trailed to the 1836 rendezvous in early spring by going south to Fort Hall on the Snake River then continuing in that direction to the upper Bear River country. In early May, their 100 lodges joined 400 tepees of Shoshonis and Bannocks and the trader Andrew Dripps and his 100 men on the prairie, lush with spring colors and new growth, on Bear River above the mouth of Smiths Fork.[401] Swelling the throng of humanity, James Bridger's detached trapping outfit of 20 men set up camp there on May 9. In two days, without a blade of grass left standing within a two-mile radius, the entire encampment of about 1,500 souls and 4,000 horses left to cross a ridge west of Hams Fork. At this point, the Indians decided there were far too many people and horses, so each outfit took a separate route to the summer trade fair. The Salish and Nez Perces worked their way east hunting buffalo and before mid-June camped on the meandering Horse Creek, about three miles north of the rendezvous headquarters. Reverend William H. Gray estimated attendance at 100 American hunters, about 50 French packers, five traders, 20 outsiders and the mission party. The Snakes and Bannocks mustered about 150 warriors; the Nez Perce and Flatheads were estimated at 200.[402]

The encampment soon learned of the approach of Thomas Fitzpatrick's supply train from St. Louis that included missionaries and their wives. So about 12 to 15 Nez Perces, Flatheads and others mounted up

399 Alter, p. 156.
400 Ibid. p. 337.
401 Russell, p. 41.
402 Gray, pp. 121-123.

and rode out to greet the men of God, meeting the caravan at two days' distance from the rendezvous site. In the evening, after setting up camp for the night, the missionaries visited the Indians to get acquainted via four languages: English, Iroquois, Flathead and Nez Perce. The arrival of Presbyterian missionaries Dr. Marcus Whitman and his wife Narcissa, Reverend Henry Spalding and his wife Eliza, and William Henry Gray highlighted the annual affair. Reverend Spalding recorded what they said to the Indians, "We … left our friends and home, and come many hundreds of miles to live with [you], to teach [you] how the good white men live, to teach [you] about God and to do … good."[403] The Indians said they were happy they had come.

History claims the wives were the first white women ever seen by Indians. Six days after their arrival, the missionaries received a grand and alarming Indian welcome. Before the "hooting and yelling" natives reached the missionary camp, the weather-stained mountain men explained the about-to-unfold spectacle. Reverend Gray recorded his version.

The procession commenced at the … lower end of the plain in the vicinity of the Flathead, passing from their camps down Horse Creek [where they] joined the Snake and Bannock warriors. [A]ll dressed and painted in the gayest uniforms, each having a company of warriors in war garb, that is naked, except for a single cloth and painted, carrying their war weapons, bearing their war emblems and Indian implements of music, such as skin drawn over hoops with rattles and trinkets to make a noise. When the cavalcade …. of five or six hundred Indian warriors came up the plain (though I noticed quite a number of native belles covered with beads) ... those of us who were not informed as to the object or design of their demonstration began to look at our weapons and calculate on a desperate fight.[404]

Later, Insula, his Salmon River band of Flatheads, and a large delegation of Clearwater Nez Perces met with Dr. Whitman and Reverend Spalding. If the Flatheads were interested in having Protestant teachers live with them, they were out of luck, for Whitman and his superiors had decided before leaving St. Louis that the Nez Perces would be first. After meeting with the Nez Perce greeting party on the trail to the rendezvous, Eliza Spalding wrote, "They appear to be gratified to see us actually on our way to their country."[405] Undoubtedly, Ignace Lamoose, who had just returned from St. Louis, informed the Flatheads of the meeting with the Black Robes and their intention to come to them as soon as possible. It is

403 Rev. Spalding Journal, July 4, 1836.

404 Gowans, p. 142.

405 (I.S.) Eliza Spalding Journal, July 4, 1836.

probable that the Flatheads gave Whitman and Spalding little encouragement to minister to their nation.

The Nez Perces tried to persuade the missionaries to travel with them while they hunted buffalo, then cross the rugged Salmon River Mountains to Nez Perce home territory. However, the fur traders discouraged the already fatigued party from doing so. While the missionaries worried over what to do, HBC trader John Macleod showed up to resolve the problem by agreeing to guide them on the longer but easier route along the Snake River to the Columbia River. On July 18, Whitman and his party broke camp and headed west with Macleod to Fort Hall, and the natives followed along. Both groups arrived at the Snake River and fort on August 3 where the Flatheads and most of the Nez Perces separated to head for Henrys Fork to hunt buffalo. A few Nez Perces stayed behind to help move the missionaries' belongings and stock to Fort Nez Perce on the Columbia.

Dr. Whitman would establish his mission 20 miles up the Walla Walla River among the Cayuse, and their nearby Nez Perce cousins, at Waiilatpu. On November 22 the Spaldings, William Gray and his homesick Indian helpers separated from the Whitmans to complete their journey to the Clearwater River and Lapwai, the future home of the Nez Perce Mission. William Henry Gray, subordinate to Whitman and Spalding, did not have a specific assignment when he arrived on the Columbia, and soon he asked superiors for his own mission among the Flatheads.[406] Gray received a promise from the two missionaries that when buildings reached completion at Waiilatpu and Lapwai, he would get his station.

In late March 1837, with buildings completed, Reverend Gray tied in with Flathead Post trader Francis Ermatinger at Fort Nez Perce to accompany him to Salish country to meet the Indians. The small party traveled up the Palouse River, crossing the prairie to the wooded but still snowbound Spokane River. Here they met Ermatinger's supply train that was dispatched from Fort Colvile, and continued east on Hoodoo Creek trail to the Seneacquoteen portage. At this point, the men and supplies transferred to canoes to paddle upriver to arrive at today's Thompson Falls, Montana, on April 24, where about 200 Kalispels had camped on the small prairie above the falls. In meeting with Reverend Gray, the band's chief said his people would be glad to have missionaries come live with and teach them, but being poor and having nothing, they would do their best[407] to support the missionaries.

406 Josephy, p. 149.
407 Johnson, Donald, p. 25, Gray Journal.

After trading with Ermatinger, the Indians trailed off downriver. The meeting with Gray must have impressed the Kalispels, for on September 18 of the same year, they learned that Reverend Spalding had gone to Fort Colvile for supplies. According to Spalding, a "great number" of Kalispels appeared at the fort to get a sight of the "black coat" and then followed him en masse for two days on his return trip. In the evening camps, the natives sat before him, intently listening to him speak even though they could not understand a word. Separating from the group, Spalding and two chiefs traveled on to Lapwai, where the two Kalispels spent several weeks. While there, the chiefs requested missionaries come live with them; Spalding said none were available.[408] At that time, the Kalispels, like their upriver cousins, thought that all men of God were Black Robes as described to them by white trappers and Iroquois.

Continuing onward for seven days, the trading party and Gray followed the Salish Road to the Buffalo upriver to the Bitterroot Valley. Along the way, the pack string overtook 20 lodges of Pend Oreille moving to join the hunt. These parties continued up the west side of the Bitterroot Valley three days, where they met 80 lodges of Flatheads and Pend Oreilles on the Bitterroot prairie near today's Florence, Montana. After the customary discharging of muskets and handshaking, they set up camp. On May 14, the day being Sunday, the allied Salish devoted themselves to prayers, singing and rest, with Head Chief Walking Bear haranguing the village several times about worship and being good Indians. The wannabe missionary had permission to teach to the natives the Preparation Hymn, which after repetitions they followed along in song without understanding a word. In an afternoon session, the group sang again, followed by prayer, and explanation by Gray in the Nez Perce tongue of why he came to them. The pastor then asked Walking Bear to speak; he accommodated with a 20-minute, animated talk beginning in a sitting position, then on his knees and finally standing up. Ending his talk, the head chief, pointing to Gray, said, "It is all good what he said, it is no bad it is good."[409] Gray ended the services by leading the group in a hymn and prayer, and afterward realized that he must learn their language.

A few days later the camp got word that one Flathead trapper died in the Big Hole and another had a serious arm wound. From a dense willow patch, 15 Blackfeet foot-warriors had ambushed the two. Running for his life, the wounded man kept between his horse and the enemy until he

408 Drury, pp. 177-178.

409 Johnson, Donald, pp. 30-31, Gray Journal, May 14, 1837.

reached another comrade, who had heard the shots. The two men raised their muskets, fired and stopped the Piegans cold. Another duo hurried up with the other horses and all escaped to the Bitterroot camp. The large hunting party continued up the Bitterroot, crossing over Gibbon Pass in a two-mile-long column, arriving in the Big Hole on May 29.

The earlier dispatched hunters greeted the hungry travelers with fresh meat from one of the seven bull buffalo they had killed. That time of year, Indians avoided killing calving cows scattered in the foothills in appreciation of the new additions they brought to the herd. All of the big game were regaining flesh and flavor from a long, lean and hungry winter and needed time to fatten on spring's new growth for more tasty camp meat. Two inches of fresh snow blanketed parts of the 15-mile-wide and 70-mile-long valley by morning when the entire village packed up and moved 10 miles east to camp near the hot springs at Jackson, Montana, near the center crossroads in Big Hole Country.

Twelve lodges of Nez Perces joined the hunters there, swelling their numbers to more than 100 lodges. This favorite resort, where the Indians had dammed the hot springs creek at intervals to create pools for bathing, varied in temperatures from very hot to cold. There, the Blackfeet soon made their presence known by firing random shots near the hunters' camp without hitting anyone; horse thieves struck the first night, getting away with several head.

Early the next morning a Salish war party followed their tracks east up the valley, aiming to retrieve the horses. Crossing the divide into upper Grasshopper Valley, the warriors caught up with the thieves, five Small Robe Piegan braves and one woman. Within minutes, the superior Salish force killed the men, scalped them and took the woman prisoner.[410] The war party returned to the village early in the evening, sans the horses, and held their trophies high. Salish women took into custody "a fair and full bodied, grief-stricken woman with a masculin [*sic*] frame, though not a vicious countenance."[411]

The jubilant warriors paraded around camp, displaying the still bloody scalps, whooping and singing the war song to the beat of drums beneath a fading evening sky. As darkness fell, the first of five consecutive scalp dances began with a line of warriors moving in short steps timed to beating drums, followed by five women, each carrying a scalp attached to

---

410 Ibid. p. 38, Gray Journal, June 2, 1837.

411 Ibid. p. 37. Captured women and children were at the mercy of the aggressor, often forced into slavery, marriage or sold to others. The Salish set these practices aside shortly after fur traders arrived but not the cruel celebration victory over longtime enemies that put female participants in the crime of horse stealing center stage. The uncivilized behavior changed with the Black Robes' arrival.

the top of a long stick held upright. Everyone orchestrated whoops and war yells as the procession stopped at all principal lodges to signal the upcoming scalp dance, thus inviting those interested to join. Fur men called such rituals after an encounter with the enemy "counting coup."[412] The celebrants soon formed a circle and began to dance, with the five female scalp bearers in the center. Onlookers beat drums, rattled jingles and sang. The five women stepped from one side to the other, raising the scalps up and down, striking the sticks to the ground here and there, every act timed to drum beats. Every so often, the dancers stopped and laughed in the most hideous manner.

Soon, escorts led the captive woman into the ring, where the trophy bearers slapped her face with her husband's and brothers' scalps. After what must have seemed forever to the horror-stricken prisoner, an escort roughly took her from the circle.[413] The Salish repeated this dance, with some variations, four more times while on the move to find buffalo. Early the following morning, the entire village broke camp to move 12 miles to the head of Grasshopper Creek. Later in the afternoon, after dwellings were in place and the scalp dance resumed, two young Small Robe Piegans, a female Qánqon and a Salish interpreter arrived at the village with a letter for Ermatinger. The note from James "Jimmy Jock" Bird Jr., an American Fur Company trader traveling with the Piegans, requested a peace council be assembled between the adversaries. Further, he wrote that he would use his influence to bring the council about and that Ermatinger should do the same. He advised the Salish to protect their horses, as stealing horses was the main occupation that made a chief in Piegan camps.[414]

The couriers spent a noisy night until the drumming ended after another scalp dance. Meanwhile, the prisoner endured her last night in that dreadful circle, dressed, face painted and forced to hold a war club, all staged by the female Salish escorts. It was too much for Reverend Gray, who pleaded for the woman to be retired to a lodge. She had suffered with manly fortitude, but her tears and perspiration smearing her painted face, when led from the circle, told a different story. At least the reverend thought so. The next morning, the prisoner asked for relief from her

---

412 Holt, Harry and High, Turney, pp 63-64. Coup, a French word meaning to "strike a blow," assured a Salish warrior's right to wear an eagle feather in his hair after capturing an able-bodied male or proving he killed an enemy in battle. The victor told his story to the chief and displayed evidence of his deed in the form of a scalp, blanket or the testimony of another. Only the first coup honored a warrior with a single feather. After initiation into the elite group of warriors, he "counted coup" by displaying trophies on lodges and lances or, rarely, on his person.

413 Johnson, Donald, Gray Journal, p. 37.

414 Ibid. p. 40.

wretched situation and to accompany the Piegan messengers home, but trader Ermatinger decided he would wait until safer conditions prevailed. He reassured Gray that she would have her liberty in time.

For the next four days, the Salish trailed to Lemhi Valley where they camped at the foot of a canyon trail. In the late afternoon, Jimmy Jock, fluent in both English and Blackfeet languages, entered the camp with three Piegans. He bore news of two camps of northern and Small Robe bands who desired peace and would arrive in the valley the next day. A Piegan chief told Ermatinger and the Salish chiefs that "killing the five men was good enough," because the Small Robes braves had not listened to the warning not to steal horses. Bird went on to say that family and friends of the deceased resisted peace in place of war, but two bands of Piegans wished for peace since they needed to trade with HBC's Ermatinger to resupply for their war with the Bloods. Pondering the proposal, Salish chiefs recalled the many men and women killed and wounded, women raped, hundreds of horses stolen over the years, and several broken peace treaties. The Piegans would try again, even if only for a day, to satisfy their need for supplies. The following morning the Salish and the traders moved their camps a mile downriver with the female prisoner. A great deal of anxiety prevailed in the Salish camp as every man waited with arms ready at a selected defensive position, horses secured and packed. At 11 a.m. on June 9, Salish scouts reported the huge Piegan camp of 200 lodges on the move, and at 1 p.m., intelligence reports said the main northern Piegan march had stopped, and about 25 principal Piegans were proceeding to the Salish camp.[415]

A regular supplier of Salish hunting ventures since 1832, HBC Ermatinger's packtrains contained a complete assortment of goods from ammunition to beads. The natives relished the convenience of their own on-site market, while at the same time, the company thwarted American competition. Set up within the security of an Indian camp, Ermatinger and his small crew utilized a large, circus-like tent where he conducted business. However, the encounter with Bird and peace-seeking Piegans presented a problem. What would happen if they used the ammunition against him and the Salish?

Some comfort existed in Ermatinger's mind as Bird had said the warlike Piegans remained in their Beaverhead camp. Ermatinger and a few Salish chiefs walked out to greet and escort the Piegan head chiefs to the large trading tent, where they sat in a circle on buffalo- and bear-skin mats. Gray wrote about the peace conference: "All went through the ceremony of smoking a big pipe, having a long handle or stem trimmed with horse-

415 Ibid. p. 44, June 9, 1837.

hair and porcupine quills. The pipe filled with the trader's tobacco and the Indians' [Kinnickinick]. The war-chiefs of each tribe took a puff, blew out the smoke, and passed the pipe to his right-hand man, and so around until all the chiefs had smoked the big medicine pipe, or pipe of peace. ... The principle [*sic*] chief in command or great medicine man went through his part of the ceremony by puffing four times and blowing his smoke to each of the four directions, in a circle, from north to east to south to west. This signified a sign of peace to tell all around him."[416]

During the peace-making ceremony, one of the Piegans had the audacity to steal several horses but gave up all but two after a Salish pursuit. Later in the day, the two horses were led into the Salish camp after their owner threatened retaliation if not done promptly. So went the peace council with the Piegans.

The peace parley over, Ermatinger began trading with the Northern Piegans, lead men who had a few beaver. Upon leaving the camp, they told Ermatinger that more would be down in the morning to trade. On June 10, upward of 100 Northern Piegan braves came to the camp to trade, as the Salish stood ready for battle. Most Piegans left the camp after trading, but scouts reported some Small Robe Piegans were on their way, accompanied by James Bird Jr., Qánqon and three chiefs who led the Small Robes peaceably into the camp. The camp's mood changed as the Salish courteously received all, many of whom they had met in peace the previous year. Gray found the Small Robes well disposed compared to the northern band.[417] During the day of trading and friendly powwow, the captive Piegan woman came up missing; she was presumed to have returned to the Piegan camp after the trading session.[418] The Salish moved camp the following day to a more defensible location near the joining of the Lemhi with the Salmon River and went about business as usual. Buffalo had moved up into the foothills of the valley where several men rode up the mountain and chased them downhill to waiting hunters. A good harvest of not-so-fat cows, some downed right in camp, lifted spirits. A blend of the peace confab, secure encampment, and most important, the support of the Small Robes kept the northern Piegan war parties at bay but not the horse thieves. A report on June 13 indicated the Northern Piegans had killed the adventurous female Qánqon, who dressed like a man and traveled with a female companion. Her last venture had been as a messenger between various Piegan camps.[419]

---

416 Gray, History of Oregon gives more details on the peace conference than his journal entries.

417 Donald Johnson, p. 47, Gray Journal.

418 Gray's journal had no more to say about her condition or her whereabouts.

419 Ibid. p. 48.

A photographic reproduction of Alfred Jacob Miller's 1834 watercolor painting "Cavalcade." This depicts the Shoshoni, Bannock, Flathead and Nez Perce procession to welcome missionaries to the 1836 Green River Rendezvous. COURTESY OF WIKIMEDIA COMMONS AND WALTERS ART MUSEUM

On June 15, Reverend Gray, 10 men, two boys, one of which was Ermatinger's son, and four women left the Salish camp and journeyed five days to Fort Hall and eventually to the Green River Rendezvous. They followed the seldom-used, rocky, up-and-down, winding Salmon River trail to the Pahsimeroi and Little Lost rivers to avoid numerous Piegans roaming the Lemhi Valley. Another four days from Fort Hall put them near the rendezvous site and HBC trader John McLeod's camp on June 28, 1837. The traders had escorted three Nez Perce men and a boy from the Lapwai Mission who planned to go east with Gray. Shortly after their arrival, Gray learned that what he called "Spalding's Indians" had disposed of three horses and nearly all their ammunition. In his first meeting, Gray demanded the Indians return Spalding's rifle and horse. He got the rifle but not the horse.[420] Fitzpatrick's supply caravan arrived at the 1837 rendezvous from the states July 5 with many items marked up 2,000 percent above actual cost.[421] Trappers cringed at paying $20 in beaver hides for a blanket and vowed to trade the following year at HBC's Fort Hall. The world market for beaver hides had softened, and now the furnishing and transportation of supplies was the most profitable part of the business.

In a letter to an unidentified business associate, Fort Colvile chief trader Archibald McDonald aptly describes the competitive nature of the

420 Ibid, pp. 54-55.

421 Russell, p. 60.

fur trading business as it stood at the end of 1836: "The trade … is on a more liberal scale than in our early days in the Columbia, especially in the upper company [Flathead and Snake River] both with Indians and freemen in consequence of the number of new adventures now pouring in upon us from the American side of the Mountains. Our profits however continue between 3 and 4 thousand [pounds]."[422] He and HBC had obtained good information on the financial strain American suppliers to the rendezvous faced along with their efforts to make trappers share the burden. McDonald went on to say: "We must now absolutely make a bold stand on the frontiers. … We shall always be able to compete with them [Americans], but the moment an entrepôt [warehouse] is formed by American subjects near the mouth of the Columbia goodbye to our advantage."[423]

Rendezvous arrivals included the sportsman/adventurer Sir William Drummond Stewart and his employee, the artist/writer Alfred Jacob Miller. Having been to the event earlier, Stewart wanted Miller to capture on canvas details of the extraordinary event. Miller not only sketched various activities, which he later painted, but eloquently described a council meeting that could just as well have been a Salish meeting: "Old men generally officiated as speakers, while before them sat the sages and warriors, generally in squatting positions, interspersed with chiefs on horseback, every one as rigid as the statue of Commendatore in 'Don Giovanni.' Each has his turn to harangue amid the most profound silence; and such sentences as were translated to me were short, pithy [meaningful], size, apothegms [proverbial sayings], mixed up with considerable boasting. Their enemies were cowards – serpents with forked tongues, cheat and etc. With a compliment to their own nation – they wish to be at peace and bury the hatchet, one orator would conclude, and the next take the parole [get up to speak]."[424]

After returning east, Miller created an oil painting of a lovely Flathead teenage girl that became a mainstay in his studio business. "One of the belles of the Rocky Mountains" said Miller, had many suitors including his tent mate P – . "She accepted presents from P – , and flirted with him in the presence of her family and mountain men. The confident womanizer among white men could not get her to take an evening stroll with him. P finally learned the Flathead women were not only chaste, but to obtain one as a bride, he must do business with her father. As the rendezvous wound down, a free trapper completed business with her father, struck his tent,

422 WHQ, vol. II, no. 3, April 1908. Text taken from Letters collected by Mrs. Evan Emery Dye's book *McDonald of Oregon*. See also, Cole, Blessed Wilderness.

423 Ibid.

424 Ross, Marvin, Gowan. *The West of Alfred Miller*, p. 159. Marvin Ross, p. 157.

packed his mules and rode off toward the hills, and he took the girl with him."[425] The painting's title is "The Trapper's Bride."

Miller also sketched and later painted a portrait of Shoshoni Chief Ma-Wo-ma, also known to trappers as Little Chief. The simple drawing depicted 15 arrows above a fallen enemy, signifying the number of dead warriors. Reflecting on various Indians met at the rendezvous, Miller and his employer, Stewart, agreed that Flathead Chief Insula, also known as Little Chief, was "in every sense superior to any Indian that we met with."[426]

A photographic reproduction of Alfred Jacob Miller's watercolor "The Trapper's Bride." The trapper had met her father's price and took the Flathead belle as his wife. COURTESY OF WIKIMEDIA COMMONS AND WALTERS ART MUSEUM

425 DeVoto, p. 325.
426 Ibid. p. 324.

The Reverend William H. Gray, who spent a short time with the Salish, so impressed old Chief Big Face, he let two of his sons, one just a boy, go with Gray when he left to return to St. Louis. The old chief had accompanied a small delegation of Flatheads and Nez Perces to the rendezvous. The morning before Gray and party departed, Big Face came to ask that his two sons go east with him to "learn about the white man and their religion." He requested further that Gray should not "make fools out of them by making them drunken and bad men when they returned." Gray told Big Face, who had observed the drunken conduct of white trappers, that he should advise his sons not to drink liquor unless he did and gave it to them. Antsy as usual, Gray began plans to leave the trade fair early without the protection of the eastbound packtrain. Some say that Jim Bridger told Gray just before he left that the grace of God would not carry a man through the prairie! It takes powder and ball![427] July 25, 1837, Rev. William H. Gray and his small party departed for St. Louis despite stern warnings of danger from experienced travelers of the long route. Four Flatheads, an adopted Cree, three Nez Perces, one a chief named Hat, old Iroquois Ignace Lamoose, Francis Ermatinger's half-blood son, and three white men accompanied Gray. Two other Nez Perce chiefs, Ellis and Blue Cloak, excused themselves by saying their horses were too weak to make the long journey, when in reality they heeded the warning.

Gray's party made good time until August 7 when they happened on a large band of Sioux hunters at Ash Hollow on the North Platte River. According to Gray, hostilities broke out after the Sioux stopped the party and insisted, in sign language, they go to their village with them. When the missionary refused their demand, the hostiles attempted to take hold of their horses' reins, which prompted Gray's party to race off in a hail of musket balls. Closely pursued, they crossed the river, returned fire, and sought a defensible position on a nearby bluff. At one point, two Flatheads rushed at 25 Sioux and temporarily stopped the advance, but soon the travelers found themselves surrounded and under a heavy barrage.

Gray suffered two slight wounds to the back of his head and temple area[428] but was conscious and could hear a nearby English-speaking voice call out. Identifying himself as a fur trader, Joseph Papai asked how many Frenchmen were with them. One of the white men answered, three. Papai then advised them to come out and surrender or the Indians would kill them. Gray hollered back that they would meet him at the top of the bluff.

427 Donald Johnson, p. 62, Gray's Journal.
428 Ibid, pp. 68-69.

He, the other white men, and Ermatinger's son took leave of three Flatheads, Nez Perce Chief Hat and guide Ignace, "to await the event of our consultation." Gray explained the party's objectives and identity of the Indians; however, the fur trader told him the Sioux had determined to kill the Indians, to be quiet or they too would die. No sooner did Papai get the words out of his mouth than the hostiles raced past Gray to his five Indians and "butchered them in a most horrible manner." Three Sioux died in the attack, including the head chief's son, and three or four others received wounds.[429]

Conducted to the village, the captive "whites and the boy," the young son of Ermatinger, greeted the head chief, who invited them into his lodge to smoke and to eat a boiled buffalo meat meal. The Reverend Gray noted in his journal that he was "unable to partake of but little" due to "my wound and situation."[430] After spending the night at Papai's lodge, the captives received a few poor horses and essentials to continue their trip east. The majority of their property remained in the hands of the Sioux. When Gray returned to the rendezvous in July 1838 to tell his experience in his own words, many mountain men refused to listen.

After Nez Perce Ellis and Blue Cloak returned early from the rendezvous trip, Reverend Spalding angrily ordered a 50-lash flogging of the men for insubordination, but the Indians refused, leaving Spalding to administer the punishment. In September 1838, Gray returned to Lapwai Nez Perce Mission with details of Hat's death; mission Indians responded by blocking all access to the missionaries' houses for a month. News of Chief Hat's death coupled with the flogging of Ellis and Blue Cloak infuriated the Indians, causing many of them to forsake the mission.[431]

Smallpox

Back in the spring of 1837, AFC's steamboat *St. Peter* made its way up the Missouri River, carrying trade supplies and death in the form of smallpox.[432] Disease-infected clothing carelessly left on board caused some passengers to sicken. They, in turn, spread the malady at each stop upriver. Native peoples, being particularly vulnerable, grew sick as the epidemic raged through the Sioux Nation to the Blackfeet farther west.[433] AFC's Alexander Culbertson at Fort Mackenzie desperately tried to stop the

429 Ibid, pp. 66-67.
430 Ibid, p. 70.
431 McWhorter, pp. 56-58.
432 Lepley, p. 115.
433 Ewers, p. 65.

boat before it reached the fort to let the disease run its course during the winter. Nonetheless, a large encampment of some 500 lodges of Piegans and Bloods camping near the fort raised their voices in loud protest and closed their ears to the warning. Caught up in complete misunderstanding, these obstinate protesters threatened to bring the boat in themselves, so Culbertson gave the order to dock it. Adding insult to injury, the Piegans insisted on opening trade as usual, although two passengers were sick and dying. Within two weeks, smallpox broke out among the Piegans and Bloods. From there, the disease sped to all corners of the Blackfeet Nation and eventually wiped out an estimated half of the population, or about 6,000 people.[434]

Both Robert Newell's and Kit Carson's narratives noted the absence of Blackfeet during the 1837 fall hunts into the heart of that nation's country. Having traversed the lower Rosebud, Tongue and Powder rivers, Newell wrote: "Our camp went through the [Blackfeet] Country last fall without seeing any Indians. We suppose many of them have died with the Smallpox."[435] Trapping farther up the Yellowstone drainage, then penetrating north to the Musselshell River deep in Piegan territory, Carson wrote, "During our hunt we had no fights with the Blackfeet, we could not know the cause."[436] The Small Robe band of Piegans continued to suffer from the epidemic into early summer the next year.

Trapper Osborne Russell, trailing up the Madison River in Jim Bridger's group, noted in his journal: "June 2, (1838) we crossed this fork and traveled up on the West side about 15 miles on a trail made by a village of Blackfeet which had passed up 3 or 4 days previous. They were to all appearances occasionally dying of Small Pox, which has made terrible havoc among the Blackfeet during last winter. Today we passed an Indian lodge standing in the prairie near the river which contained 7 dead bodies."[437] The trappers continued south another four days up the Madison River, crossing the divide toward Henrys Lake, and camped. There they saw 15 lodges of Blackfeet on the southeast side of the lake, directly in their path.

Russell wrote: "The next morning we concluded to move camp to the village and smite it without leaving one to tell their fate – but when within about 2 miles of the village we met six of them coming to us unarmed who invited us in the most humble and submissive manner to

434 Lepley, p. 117.
435 [I.S.] Newell Narrative, 1837.
436 Carson, p. 33.
437 Russell, p. 86.

their village to smoke and trade. This proceeding conquered the bravest in our camp. For we were ashamed to think of fighting a few poor Indians nearly dwindled to skeletons by the Small pox."[438] The epidemic seriously depleted the Blackfeet's will and strength to raid the Salish and fur men for several years. Blood and northern Piegan bands suffered more than did their southern cousins. The Small Robes band of Piegans, with 150 lodges centered at Three Forks, lost half their population.[439]

Normally at war and occasionally at peace with the Salish and trappers, the Small Robes became less of a hindrance to hunters. The Salish took advantage of the Piegan setback in ensuing years by hunting deep in their territory.

News of the death of Big Face's sons and the others who had left with Gray in 1837 discouraged the Flatheads and Nez Perces from attending the 1838 rendezvous on the Wind River near today's Riverton, Wyoming. The deaths struck a blow to the entire tribe because tradition dictated that election of one of his sons fill the hereditary head chief rank. Big Face and the tribe probably did not learn all the details involved in his sons' demise until later, but the mountain men at the rendezous took the matter up with the man who unnecessarily got them in trouble. Gray, with his wife, returned from St. Louis to the 1838 rendezvous, leading three, newly recruited Presbyterian missionaries and their wives, to teach Indians Christianity along the Columbia River system. His presence at the annual affair disturbed the fur men who believed Gray had traded Indians' lives for his own.

Myra, wife of recruit Reverend Cushing Eells, kept an informative diary and described the rendezvous events, writing on July 5: "Last night [we] were troubled exceedingly by the noise of some drunken men. About one was awakened by the barking of dogs, soon we had a rush of drunken men coming directly towards our tent. Mr. Eells answered their inquiries and said little else. They said they wished to settle accounts with Mr. Gray, then they should be off. ... All this while Mr. G. and myself were making preparations for our escape, while Mr. Gray was loading Mr. E's gun, his own being lent."[440] Later when the new missionaries – Eells, Elkanah Walker and Asa Smith and their wives – arrived at Dr. Whitman's mission, the men met to decide on locations for the new recruits. Right away, the three recruits made it clear that after their long journey to Oregon with

438 Ibid. p. 89.

439 Ewers, p. 185.

440 Drury, p. 79 Eells and Elkanah Walker established a mission among the Lower Spokane tribes.

William Gray they "would not be associated with him." Henry Spalding reluctantly agreed to let Gray live at Lapwai Mission, which lasted a little longer than three years before Gray resigned to take up teaching and politics in the Willamette Valley.

HBC's newly appointed Fort Hall manager, Francis Ermatinger, journeyed to the annual event to obtain information on the Americans' current operation and to escort new missionaries west to Walla Walla. Ermatinger found that 125 trappers present had traded only a little more than 2,000 beaver and other hides. American Fur Company attempted to lower the beaver price from $5 per pound to $3 per pound, but the trappers resisted. Ermatinger and the company officials were satisfied the Americans could not make a profit on such a small catch with the large crews they employed to transport 25 loads of goods, predicting it would soon put them out of business. HBC's Fort Hall charged lower prices for goods, which no doubt affected AFC's returns.

Ermatinger's report prompted a long letter from the chief factor, Dr. John McLoughlin of the Columbia, to headquarters, the crux of which read: "It is clearly to our interest to push up the price of goods, on the American side of the frontiers."[441] Scarcity of beaver in the numerous, easily accessed mountain valleys added to the fur men's woes. Yet, company trappers and freemen continued to venture into remote country where only small concentrations of beaver lived, or into hostile Indian country in order to make a living. Lower prices for skins in Eastern and European markets effected a corresponding reduction in value at trading time. These factors coupled with rising prices for trade goods foretold the era's end. At the same time, the mountain man's preferred food source of buffalo was in short supply.

Some American trappers wondered if there would be a rendezvous in the coming year, while others planned to trade at HBC's Fort Hall or to retire from the mountains. Numerous older HBC trappers, traders, voyageurs and freemen began to retire and move to French Prairie in the Willamette Valley of Oregon to take up farming. With most being Catholic, the chief factor of the Columbia Department, Dr. John McLaughlin, requested priests from the Red River area of Canada to serve new settlements and the Fort Vancouver area personnel. In answering the call, priests Francis N. Blanchet and Modeste Demers followed trader trails west across Canada to Fort Colvile, arriving there in November 1838. After six days of conducting mass and baptizing fort personnel and some Indians, the priests resumed

441 Gowans, p. 180. A report from HBC Dr. John McLoughlin to superiors – Nathaniel Wythe sold Fort Hall to HBC in 1837.

their journey to Fort Vancouver to set up shop for saving souls in the area.

Although the Salish realized the downward trend in beaver and buffalo populations on their hunting grounds, they persisted one more year while learning just how weak the smallpox-ravaged Blackfeet were in the Montana Three Forks area. Game populations, particularly buffalo and beaver, were in much worse condition in the Henrys Fork, middle Snake and Bear river drainages. Targeted animals were almost gone. In 1838, after completing a loop from Fort Hall through the previously described country, a sentence in Robert Newell's manuscript defines their condition: "[Times] is hard and peltries low, provisions scarce[,] Indians [Shoshoni and Bannock] in abundance going in all parts in Search of Something to stay their stomachs."[442] During that winter, St. Louis provider Pierre Chouteau decided to send supplies to the 1839 Green River Rendezvous.

Three Protestant missionaries, two with their wives, and Dr. Frederick A. Wislizenus complemented the supply train. While there, the doctor made an interesting note in his journal concerning how Indians traded: "The Indians had for the trade chiefly tanned skins, moccasins, thongs, buffalo leather or braided buffalo hair and fresh or dried buffalo meat. They had no beaver skins. The articles that attracted them most in exchange were powder and lead, knives, tobacco, cinnabar [red earth for pigment], gaily-colored kerchiefs, pocket mirrors and all sorts of ornaments. Before the Indian began to trade he demands sight of everything that may be offered by the other party to the trade. If there is something that attracts him, he, too, will produce his wares, but discovers very quickly how much or how little they are coveted. If he himself is not willing to dispose of some particular thing, he obstinately adheres to his refusal, though ten times the value offered him."[443]

The caravan arrived on July 5 and found some of the regular crowd missing. Beaver prices had dropped to $4 a pound, causing many free trappers to trade at HBC's Fort Hall where they got more goods for their pelts. Francis Ermatinger, chief trader at Fort Hall, was there, and later reported to superiors that AFC shipped only 28 packs of fur, weighing 2,240 pounds or approximately 2,200 beaver pelts, to St. Louis.[444] Purchase of Fort Hall by HBC continued to pay off big-time, with Ermatinger and crew acquiring 3,300 beaver, many from the Americans. Unfortunately, the company had to trade with disgruntled American free trappers – a rough lot. In a letter to his brother, Ermatinger said he had to "deal with as lawless a rabble, the

442 [I.S.] Newell Memorandum.

443 [I.S.] Wislizenus Journal.

444 McDonald, p. 218. HBC James Douglas Report to his superiors.

scum of all nations, as possible to be collected together."[445] After leaving Fort Hall with the furs on November 18 for Fort Vancouver, a messenger caught up with him on the trail with troubling news that scoundrels had stolen company horses and threatened his life while "declaring their forefathers had fought for the country, and the Hudson's Bay Company shall not possess it."[446]

In December 1838 a confrontation occurred between some 50 trappers that had gathered to camp near the fort and company personnel over the customary raising of the British flag for trading events. A spokesman for the trappers' group demanded the American flag be raised alongside the British one. The acting trader immediately denied the request and closed the compound gates behind him. Shots rang out from both sides without doing much damage to either entity, except for the riddled British flag. The aggressors soon forced entry into the fort, where they took down the shredded piece of cloth and replaced it with the Stars and Stripes. The Fort Hall employees had retreated to a storeroom and barricaded the entrance. The trappers demanded their surrender on the following terms: the American flag shall occupy its proper place hereafter and the commandant shall treat his captors to the best liquors in his possession. Unless the offenders comply with these conditions, the captors will consider Fort Hall and its contents as lawful plunder and act accordingly.

After a short parley, the besieged agreed to capitulation and rolled a barrel of whiskey into the front yard. The short but bloodless campaign ended in a wild, frolicking party.[447] When the tough fur trader Ermatinger reached Fort Vancouver, he suggested the company superiors organize and arm some 800 mixed-blood natives of the Columbia Department to resist any takeover attempt by the Americans.[448] Ermatinger overreacted to the threat since most of the lawless trappers had vacated the Snake River country for California, packing off the stolen property, while others quit the mountains. American trapper and trader Robert Newell noted the gang involved about 15; among those he named were Henry Logan and David White.[449]

Meanwhile, back at the 1839 Green River Rendezvous, Insula and his family that included Cora, Bridger's wife, and their child waited, expecting his return from St. Louis. Bridger had left his family with his

445 Ermatinger (Francis) February 6, 1840 Letter to his brother Edward.
446 Ibid.
447 [I.S.] Sage, Rocky Mountain Life.
448 Olga Johnson, p. 235.
449 [I.S.] Newell Memorandum.

father-in-law in the fall of 1837 while he went east. Detained in St Louis, the famous mountain man would not reunite with his family until the subsequent year.[450] After the rendezvous ended, Kit Carson and a trapping outfit fell in with the Flatheads on their way home. Carson wrote in the autumn of 1839, "A chief of the Flathead [Insula] and some of his tribe joined us, and we traveled on to the Big Snake River."[451] Upon separating from the trappers, Little Chief Insula and his small band of 20 Flathead warriors and their families established a camp on the buffalo grounds, possibly on Henrys Fork. In time, a much larger group of Bannock warriors came upon their camp, wherein the friendly Flatheads invited the Bannocks to smoke and exchange news. Insula and others soon felt uneasy about the Bannocks' actions as visitors, as they seemed to be sizing up potential plunder.

Horse security became terribly important. At dusk, after the exchange as the Bannock warriors left, a few Flathead scouts followed them to the Bannock camp. They hid until dark and snuck closer to listen to talk of a raid. Quietly removing themselves from the scene, the scouts mounted their horses and raced back to camp to confirm Insula's suspicion. Insula and his warriors mounted up and rode silently along the trail until they found a suitable ambush position. Sure enough, near daylight, a heavily armed war party came down the trail in the direction of the Salish camp. Insula's small force charged head-on into the enemy column and killed nine warriors, which put the remaining schemers in retreat. The skirmish ended almost as quickly as it began, as Insula realized the new sun brought the Sabbath.[452] Returning to their camp, the Flatheads said their prayers and enjoyed a day of peace without further incident from the Bannocks. Insula would again run into some of the surviving Bannocks in the coming year.

During three decades of living among the Salish, white fur traders had profited at the expense of furbearers and bison populations. By 1840, introduction of modern implements for decoration, domestic use, hunting and warfare had catered to the natives' needs, yet had little effect on their way of life, save the necessity to become more industrious in hunting and gathering. If they desired white man's things, it took more work than the survival mode of earlier years. The Indians quickly grasped the benefits of using metal products over the time-consuming process of honing and carving them from stone, bone, horns or wood. Gun acquisition, primarily

450 Alter, p. 183.
451 Carson, p. 48.
452 [I.S.] Chittenden & Richardson - vol. 1, p. 366, vol. 2, p. 551.

for protection, neutralized the powerful Blackfeet Nation's effort to exterminate the Pend Oreilles and Flatheads. White man's profit motive and hefty competition between trading companies coupled with eager and able native participation had nearly depleted beaver and buffalo in the upper reaches of the Missouri and in southern Idaho by 1840. Salish longtime hunting grounds in high valleys from Lost River east to Camas Creek and Henrys Fork to the Snake River Plain had deteriorated to smaller, scattered bunches of mostly bull buffalo. Far worse conditions existed in river valleys south of the Snake to Utah Lake and portions of the Green River in Wyoming.

While hunting the Portneuf and Bear rivers on November 14, 1841, trapper Osborne Russell noted in his journal: "In the year 1836 large bands of buffalo could be seen in almost every little valley on the small branches of this stream. At this time the only traces ... [of] them were the scattered bones of those that had been killed. The trails ... made in former years deeply indented in the earth were overgrown with grass and weeds. The trappers often remarked to each other as they rode over these lonely plains that it was time for the white man to leave the mountains as beaver and game had nearly disappeared."[453] Russell and most other white trappers quit the fur business for points east or west to Oregon. Right on their heels, thousands of immigrants in wagon trains churned up dust and carved ruts across the plains as way too many headed west.

Demise of buffalo did not fall entirely to exploits of the fur trade. The Salish and other natives who depended on bison for survival outnumbered trappers in the region 20-to-1 or more. An influx of several hundred Blackfeet inhabiting the area known as the war zone added to the overkill and dovetailed with fur men's demand for bison hides, meat and other parts. Foremost, preference for fat cows and unbridled waste devastated the once abundant herds in less than 30 years. Collapse of the buffalo population had an even greater effect on the Shoshoni and Bannock tribes who also occupied the region. As cause begets consequence, they soon traveled to the headwaters of the Missouri to hunt, which gave rise to conflict with other Indian hunters already in the region.

The Salish shifted hunting grounds east to the Small Robe Piegans' Three Forks and the Crows' Yellowstone River areas. Historically, they were friends with the Crows, who shared a common enemy in the Blackfeet Nation. As the next decade progressed, the allies hunted farther into Crow and Blackfeet territory, necessitated by dwindling buffalo herds, which

453 Russell, p. 129.

accelerated conflict between native tribes. Such scarcity resulted in regular winter hunts for the Salish, unheard of in many years when plenty of buffalo roamed the prairies. The Salish timed winter affairs to minimize travel through deep snows, using the Clark Fork River route from the Bitterroot Valley, then crossing grass-covered passes to the plains where they wintered. The buffalo grounds received relatively minor snow accumulations, but freezing temperatures and the ever-present wind made travel and life trying. Under the increasingly difficult conditions, conflicts among Indian tribes intensified on the buffalo grounds.

Depletion of beaver populations in the Rockies and Western plains coincided with a fashion change in men's hats, which lowered demand and prices for beaver fur. Dressed buffalo robes and rawhides replaced the longtime, beaver-driven market as the darling of the business. Demand for laptop carriage robes and men's coats in the Eastern United States and Western Europe opened another period of exploitation of Western plains resources. Nondressed, dried and salted, raw buffalo hides ended up in the East, where mechanized processing equipment prepared and tanned the hides for both robes and leather products. American firms dominated the buffalo hide trade with more than half a million hides shipped down the Missouri River between 1831 and 1858.[454] Blackfeet and other plains tribes exchanged most of those skins, but some Salish robes were included in the totals. HBC did not aggressively compete in the robe market due to weak demand in England.

Indian women provided the labor in a long, arduous process of preparing buffalo robes. After the hunters or women skinned the carcass, a woman took over by first "fleshing" the excess meat and fat from the hide, then stretching it to lodgepole frames or pegging it to the ground to dry. Once dry, the skin was chipped with a steel, hoe-shaped blade to about one-half its original thickness. Using bare hands, the female worker smeared buffalo brains on the fleshless side of the hide, then carefully folded, rolled and put it aside for several days. Afterward a tanner opened each bundle, dampened and stretched the hide to a pole frame, and began the hardest work. The tanner rubbed back and forth against the upright, stretched skin with rawhide thongs until the stiff hide turned as soft and pliable as velvet. This furry, tanned hide brought the Indian $4 to $5 in trade goods[455] – plenty good money back then. The men traded the finished robes for goods that usually included beads and ribbons for their wives.

454 Lepley, p. 275.
455 Ibid.

Beaver hides still had value but at a lower price. The fur market also sought grizzly bear, wolf, lynx, fox, marten and muskrat furs. The Salish traded very few beaver hides but exchanged plenty of buffalo by-products. HBC trading operations moved up to Horse Plains in 1838 and remained the Salish and trappers' marketplace for decades. As resources dwindled in the neighborhood of Fort Hall, many white and mixed-blood trappers of Salish parentage called the Bitterroots home. As the 1840s drew on, small-time, independent traders arrived to barter for Salish horses and furs. Small operations did not hinder HBC enterprises greatly, as they only had a limited supply of goods.

Catholic missionaries venturing into Salish country highlighted the 1840s for the Pend Oreilles, Kalispels, Flatheads and Coeur d'Alenes. The long-sought-after Jesuit Black Robes established missions in the Bitterroot, Flathead, Pend Oreille and St. Joe river valleys, where they taught Christian ideals along with demonstrating white man's ways of survival. Their efforts took hold with some natives but failed with others. Many became lifelong Christians, while as a whole they struggled to maintain old ways of hunting and gathering. As game populations dwindled, conflict with other tribes remained a part of their life on the buffalo grounds, where old friends fought and old enemies made peace.

Trading at Fort Nez Perce in 1841 conducted by Archibald McKinlay. A photographic reproduction of painting by Joseph Drayton, a member of the Charles Wilkes expedition. COURTESY WIKIMEDIA COMMONS

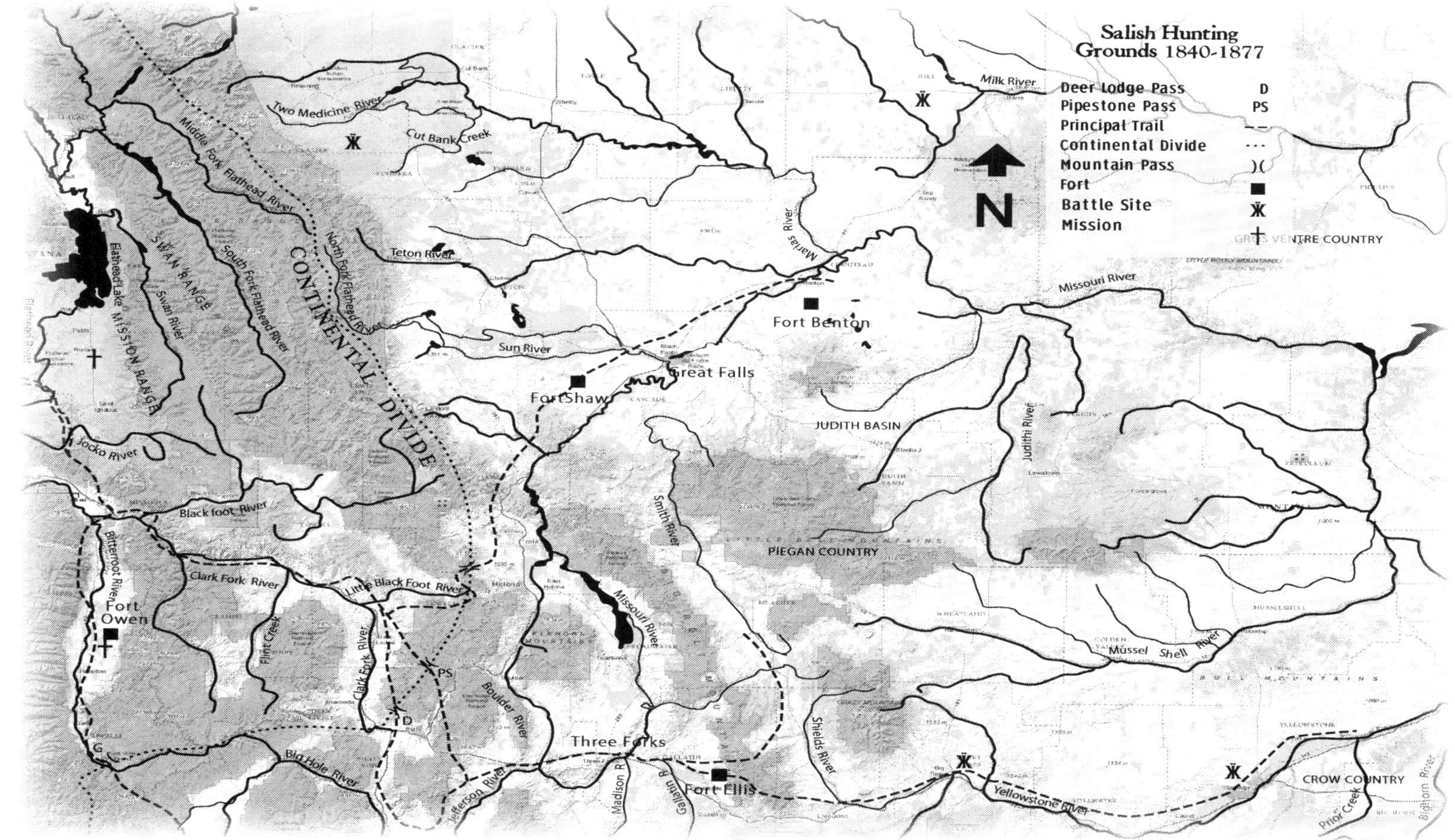

Salish Hunting
Grounds 1840-1877
Deer Lodge Pass D
Pipestone Pass PS
Principal Trail
Continental Divide
Mountain Pass
Fort
Battle Site
Mission
N
CONTINENTAL DIVIDE
SWAN RANGE
MISSION RANGE
Flathead Lake
Swan River
Middle Fork Flathead River
South Fork Flathead River
North Fork Flathead River
Two Medicine River
Cut Bank Creek
Teton River
Marias River
Milk River
Sun River
Jocko River
Black foot River
Bitterroot River
Fort Owen
Clark Fork River
Flint Creek
Little Black Foot River
Clark Fork River
Big Hole River
Jefferson River
Boulder River
Madison R
Gallatin R
Three Forks
Fort Ellis
Missouri River
Smith River
Fort Shaw
Great Falls
Fort Benton
JUDITH BASIN
PIEGAN COUNTRY
Judithi River
Missouri River
GROS VENTRE COUNTRY
Mussel Shell River
Shields River
Yellowstone River
CROW COUNTRY
Prior Creek
Bighorn River
D
PS
G

7

Black Robes Decade 1840-1850

Two French-speaking Iroquois, Pierre Gaucher (Left-hand Peter) and young Ignace Lamoose, departed the 1839 rendezvous with the east-bound caravan in an attempt to obtain Black Robes for the Salish people. They arrived at St. Joseph's Indian Mission near today's Council Bluffs, Iowa, on September 8, where they met with Jesuit Priest Pierre-Jean De Smet at the Potawatomi facility. De Smet's interest deepened as words of the Salish people's virtuous plea for Black Robe teachers touched his heart; he gave the two a gratifying letter of introduction to deliver in person to Bishop Rosati in St. Louis for his approval and decision.[456] Arriving without incident, Gaucher and Lamoose met with the bishop off and on for several weeks.

Rosati felt immediate enthusiasm about the project and was equally impressed with the Iroquois and Salish desires, so he fired off a letter to the Society of Jesus at Rome that included the following: "Of the twenty-four Iroquois who formerly emigrated from Canada, only four are still living. Not only have they planted faith in those wild countries, but they have … defended it against the encroachments of the Protestant ministers. When these missionaries presented themselves among them, our good Catholics refused to accept them. These are not the priests about whom we have spoken to you, they would say to the Flathead. 'These are not the long black-robed priests, who have no wives, who say mass, who carry the crucifix with them.' For the love of God, My Very Reverend Father, do not abandon these souls!" [457]

With the letter in the mail, Bishop Rosati promised young Ignace and Pierre he would send a missionary to the next Green River Rendezvous to meet with the Flatheads. Ignace agreed to winter in the area and join the yet-to-be-selected priest in the spring for the journey west. The Cath-

456 [I.S.] De Smet, p. 6. Report on Indian Missions to St. Louis University, February 4, 1841.

457 Palladino, p. 29.

olic historian Father Palladino wrote that Pierre Gaucher set out alone in the dead of winter to deliver the news to the Salish.[458] This would be a remarkable feat, if indeed it happened.

Despite poor returns in the previous year, Pierre Chouteau dispatched a much larger supply train to the 1840 trading session, which ended up being the last shipment and the last American rendezvous. Jim Bridger and Andrew Dripps led the supply train across the vast prairie, guiding three Protestant missionaries and their wives and the Catholic Priest Pierre-Jean De Smet. An eager delegation of waiting Flatheads greeted the "Black Robe" and their mission delegate, young Ignace. In returning from St. Louis, Bridger happily rejoined his wife, Cora, and their children who came with her father to the rendezvous. The Indian escort had planned to conduct De Smet immediately to Pierre's Hole but changed his mind when the latter requested a four-day stop to rest his horses.

De Smet described the meeting with the Flatheads: "Our meeting was that of children who came to meet their parent, and the effusion of their heart, they bestowed upon me the fondness of names with a simplicity truly patriarchal. They told me of all the interesting particulars of sixty of their men, in a battle against two hundred Blackfeet which lasted five whole days, and in which they killed fifty of their enemies, without losing a single man of their number. The Great Spirit watched over them; they said, he knew that we were to guide you to our camp and he wanted to clear the road of all the obstacles that you might have found on your way. We trust we will not be annoyed any more by the Blackfeet; they went off weeping like women."[459]

The battle occurred on the lower Madison River; the Salish knew it as Tobacco River.[460] The Pend Oreille chief and medicine man, Calax, had predicted the day and place, then led the victorious warriors.[461] Among the many heroes of the battle, Pelchimo single-handedly saved the sizeable Flathead horse herd. On foot, he watched the developing threat of losing them to the enemy. Seeing a mounted woman nearby, he borrowed her horse, grabbed the reins, mounted and galloped to collect the scattered herd and drove them back to camp. Another valiant warrior in the battle, Five Crows (baptized Ambrose) noticed a Piegan on foot armed with a musket. With an eye on the gun, he rode up to the man, who mistook

458 Paladino, p. 30.

459 [I.S.] Chittenden & Richardson, Report on Indian Mission #3, St. Louis, February 4, 1841, Society of Jesuits.

460 Point, p. 167.

461 [I.S.] Chittenden & Richardson, p. 473.

Ambrose for one of his tribe and asked for a ride. Ambrose gave his arm and the enemy swung up behind; the two rode along for a short distance until Ambrose seized the musket, throwing him off-balance to the ground, whereupon Ambrose quickly dismounted and killed him.[462] The Salish claimed they killed 50 of the enemy, while the enemy somehow seriously wounded one of their own, a warrior who suffered five months before dying.

Of the Salish fighting reputation, Father De Smet later wrote Jesuit colleagues in Europe: "It is commonly said in the mountains that one Flathead or Pend Oreille is worth four Blackfeet."[463] However, the Salish loved peace and at every opportunity before or after a battle, they accepted peace offers from the Blackfeet, knowing it would not last. Numerous armed conflicts over the years resulted in some Salish warriors being crippled and scarred for life. In 1841, Father De Smet interviewed seven Flathead men who told their war stories and showed him previous wounds. One man had scars from four musket balls that had pierced his thigh, but he suffered only mild stiffness. Another had his arm and breast pierced by a ball. A third, wounded by a knife and a spear, still had an arrow embedded five inches deep in his stomach, while another had two musket balls embedded in his body. A crippled Flathead among them had had his leg broken by an enemy shooting from a rifle pit; leaping on one leg, he fell upon the enemy, making the place his adversary's grave.[464]

Surrounded by pine boughs and wildflowers, a makeshift altar overlooked the rendezvous site at the first Catholic service in the Rocky Mountains. On Sunday, July 5, 1840, several hundred Indians of three nations, French Canadians, and Americans assembled. On that historic Sunday, during his short stay at Green River, Father De Smet stood behind the altar to conduct mass for a colorful sea of attentive, wilderness congregators, speaking in French and English, which interpreters translated for the Indians. Canadians sang hymns in French and Latin, while the Indians tried to follow in their own tongues. One can imagine the gathered mix, an off-key chorus that camp dogs and distant howling wolves surely joined, although Father De Smet makes no mention of it.

Ten Flathead escorts, De Smet, his friend John de Velder, who had accompanied him West, and 10 French Canadian trappers left the rendezvous July 6 for a meeting with many of the Salish people at Pierre's Hole. The Black Robe party traveled north on customary trails down along the

462 Ibid. De Smet, p. 320.

463 [I.S.] Chittenden & Richardson, vol. 3, p. 1005. De Smet letter to Society of Jesuits, December 1841.

464 Ibid. p. 1013.

Hoback River, crossed the Snake River and over Teton Pass to an enthusiastic encampment. Some 1,000 Flatheads, Pend Oreilles and Nez Perces had trailed 400 miles to meet Father De Smet. Flathead Head Chief Big Face, surrounded by principal chiefs of other tribes and the most renowned warriors, welcomed Father De Smet: "This day Kyleeyou (Great Spirit) has accomplished our wishes; and our hearts swell with joy."[465] After Big Face's address and a response by De Smet, four days of preaching, instruction and baptisms followed. The Salish's own Black Robe baptized 600 Indians, postponing other requests until his return the following year. Among the baptized were principal chiefs, octogenarians Flathead Big Face and upper Pend Oreille Walking Bear, who thereafter missionaries called Paul and Peter, respectively.

Father De Smet recounted an event that took place before 1840 involving Chief Walking Bear while in a hunting camp. The Pend Oreilles had problems with Piegan horse thieves, which prompted the posting of sentries. During a dark night, the guards wounded and immobilized a would-be robber. He sat on the ground and defiantly warned the gathering Pend Oreilles he would shoot anyone approaching him. Walking Bear, though small in stature and advanced in years, courageously ran up to the enemy and, with one strong blow to the head, fell him to the ground. Walking Bear then dropped to his knees and prayed aloud: "Great Spirit! Thou knowest that I did not kill this Blackfoot from a desire of revenge, but because I was forced to it; be merciful to him in the other world. I forgive him from the bottom of my heart all the evil which he has wished to inflict upon us, and to prove the sincerity of my words, I will cover him with my garment."[466]

On July 16, the large encampment packed up and headed north to Henrys Lake where they camped a few days before crossing the divide to Red Rock River – today, the head of Beaverhead River. From this point, the Indians and De Smet traveled seven days down that drainage through former buffalo hunting grounds toward the Three Forks of the Missouri to camp on the Madison Fork. De Smet paid particular attention to foods eaten along the way that did not include buffalo. He wrote: "From Green River to this place, our Indians had made their food of roots and the flesh of such animals as the red and black tailed deer, elk, gazelle [antelope], bighorn, or mountain sheep, grizzly, and black bear, badger, rabit [*sic*], and panther[;] also occasionally such feathered game as grouse, prairie-hen, a

465 Ibid. p. 305.

466 [I.S.] Ibid. vol. 1, pp. 320-321.

kind of pheasant, swan, geese, cranes and ducks. Fish abounded besides in the rivers, particularly salmon trout."[467]

Surrounded by steep, timbered mountain ranges, the vast, gently rolling Three Forks plain stretched 40 miles north and another 40 miles east; it supported many herds of buffalo, the first they had seen in months. The evening of their arrival, they prepared for the hunt; 400 mounted hunters began the chase at daylight while their women erected willow scaffolds near their tepees. Within three hours, they killed 500, mostly fat cows. The hunt and meat drying process continued for two more weeks, resulting in fully loaded packs for home use and trade.[468]

Throughout their stay on the Madison Fork's seemingly endless plain, Father De Smet conducted prayer services and taught Indians the Catholic version of Christianity. On August 27, he began the long journey back to St. Louis to collect the fellow Jesuit missionaries to assist teaching in the coming year. Seventeen Flathead and Pend Oreille warriors escorted Father De Smet through unfriendly Piegan country over Bozeman Pass to the Yellowstone River, which they followed east to friendly Crow Indian country. Six days later the party joined a Crow war party heading east to their village on the Bighorn River.

After arrival at the River Crow camp, De Smet described how a Flathead owning a fine horse, much desired by a Crow chief, conducted trade: "This is how a bargin [*sic*] was concluded before my eyes. A young Crow [c]hief of gigantic stature and covered with his gayest raiment, advanced to the midst of tile [the] gathering, leading his horse by the bridle, and placed in frount [*sic*] of the Flathead, as if to offer it in exchange for his. The latter giving no sign of approval, [the] Crow then laid at his feet his gun, then his scarlet robe, then all his ornaments one after the other, then his leggings too, and finally his moccasins. Then the Flathead took the horse by the bridle, picked up the goods and the bargain ... concluded without a word being said. The Crow chief though despoiled of all his fine clothes and plumage, leaped with joy upon his new horse and ran him around camp."[469]

The next day De Smet and his Salish escorts continued east, traversing the benches above the Yellowstone River for seven days until

---

467 [I.S.] Ibid. vol. 1, p. 231.

468 [I.S.] Ibid. vol. 1, p. 232.

469 [I.S.] Chittenden & Richardson, vol. 1, pp. 239-240. During the fur trade era, the Crow tribe of 12 bands lived in two distinct areas until reservation establishment in the second half of 19th century. The River Crows of some 1,400 people lived along the Yellowstone River from Big Timber to Miles City, Montana. The Mountain Crows of about 2,700 occupied the Wind River to the upper Big Horn River in Wyoming.

finally reaching AFC Fort Alexander on the Rosebud River. There, the Salish turned around and began the long, 400-mile journey to home territory. Utterly alone, De Smet and his friend De Velder rode east overland 200 miles to AFC's Fort Union, from which the Black Robe picked up companions and continued by horse to St. Louis, arriving on January 1. De Smet's journey to the Salish and back to St. Louis covered a 4,300-mile loop.

Meanwhile, the Salish wintered well, all with tight bellies, thanks to the successful hunt on Three Forks and prayers Father De Smet taught. Elated by the power of white man's God from which they credited such good luck, the Salish continued to practice Black Robe prayers and procedures while eagerly looking forward to his return. Just as enthusiastic, the tireless De Smet left Westport on the lower Missouri River for the mountains with Jesuit Priests Gregory Mengarini, Nicolas Point, and three brethren the next year on May 10, 1841. De Smet hired Thomas Fitzpatrick to guide and transport five, mule-drawn carts loaded with missionary paraphernalia to the traditional rendezvous site on Green River. Along the endlessly long prairie trail, the Jesuit party came upon the Bartleson-Bidwell wagon train of 70 people. After more than three months spent crossing the plains, the Black Robes met Flathead Chief Wistilpo's welcoming party of seven. Other greeters included Flatheads Pelchimo, Old Simon and his eight-year-old grandson Francis, Iroquois Ignace (Aeneas), Francis Xavier, and the mixed-blood interpreter Gabriel Prudhomme Jr.[470] The greeters, missionaries and wagon train continued on to Soda Springs, where half the immigrants split off for California, while the others, including the missionaries, went on to Fort Hall on the Snake River.[471] A dozen or so Flathead warriors led by Insula met the travel-weary Black Robes at the fort.[472] Crawling Mountain, known as Moise to the whites and the "Bravest of the Brave" to Father De Smet, had sent along a fine horse with guides for the Black Robe. The latter described Moise, about 45 years old at the time, as the handsomest Indian warrior in his acquaintance, and a superior horseman decked out with a large red scarf worn in a fashion of the Marshal of France.[473] Father De Smet would thank his "adopted Indian brother" after a two-week journey from Fort Hall to the Salish camp on the Beaverhead River.

---

470 [I.S.] Chittenden & Richardson, De Smet p. 292. Prudhomme, experienced trapper and Flathead tribal member, served as De Smet's interpreter. Indians knew Francis Xavier as Francis Saxa.

471 Ibid. Fort Hall, built by Nathaniel Wyeth in 1834 at the junction of the Portneuf and Snake rivers and sold to HBC, became an important stopping point for the Oregon Trail immigrants.

472 [I.S.] Chittenden & Richardson, vol. 1, p. 304.

473 [I.S.] Ibid. vol. 1, p. 305.

After a few days' rest, the party moved on, following trails along the Snake and Henrys Fork river toward Monida Pass. Near the pass, the escorts noticed a small mounted party of Indians on a distant ridge, thought to be Blackfeet. Insula dispatched two braves to see who they were. An hour later, the scouts returned with 12 Bannock warriors, all of whom had been in a fight with Insula's Flatheads. Insula stood face-to-face with the Bannock whose brother's life had been taken by Insula's own hand in the previous year's clash. After a few tense moments, the Flatheads accepted the Bannocks as friends, but refused to smoke with them.[474] Parting without an incident, the Black Robes and escorts continued their journey to the Salish encampment where De Smet and his entourage received a joyous welcome from Big Face (Paul) and assorted Indians. Father De Smet wrote: "In less than half an hour all hearts were united and moved by the same [similar] sentiments. The tribe had the appearance of a flock crowding with eagerness around their shepherd. ... The evening was certainly one of the happiest of our lives." In mid-September, the Indians and missionaries broke camp and took the Deer Lodge-Clark Fork River route to the Bitterroot Valley. On September 29, 1841, the Jesuits and Flatheads erected a cross on an elevated spot 30 miles south of today's Missoula, Montana, to mark the establishment of the first Catholic Mission in the Rocky Mountains, naming it St. Mary's. Construction of cabins for Priests Point and Mengarini and the brethren began immediately, along with fencing in a large garden nearby.

The Jesuits formulated mission objectives for the Salish based on experience gained elsewhere in the world. Rules of conduct involved converting Indian worship of the Great Spirit to a simple, lively faith in Catholic Christianity. Setting goals meant the Indians must have had or developed respect for authority and parents, justice, generosity and individual good behavior, which the Flatheads already practiced. Father De Smet perceived the need to establish "love of labor" among the tribe since idleness was a preponderant vice.[475] The missionaries planned to erect schools and use the Salish language to teach reading, writing, arithmetic and singing.

St. Mary's Mission

Soon after arriving at St Mary's, Father De Smet and 10 Flathead braves set off October 24, 1841, for HBC Fort Colvile to detail Jesuit objectives and purchase food, seeds, tools and livestock. During the jour-

474 Point, p. 38, & [I.S.] Chittenden & Richardson, vol. 1, p. 305 – De Smet.

475 [I.S.] Chittenden & Richardson, vol. 1, p. 329.

ney, he connected with two, wintering bands of upper Pend Oreilles and got to know Chief Hoytelpo, who surprised the Black Robe with the band's knowledge of Christian prayers. Hoytelpo told De Smet he had delegated a young man to the Pierre's Hole welcoming of the Black Robes in 1840 to memorize and bring back prayers to teach fellow tribesmen. The amazed De Smet complimented the young man for his good memory and teaching ability as the Indians repeated them perfectly.[476]

After baptizing most of the band's children, De Smet continued his journey down the Clark Fork River trail, finding small groups of Kalispels along the way, who all requested missionaries come live with them. He met with head chiefs of the tribe's largest campsite at Cusick Meadows, where he promised teachers would come within a few years. Arriving at Fort Colvile in mid-November, De Smet received a gracious welcome and generous hospitality from Archibald McDonald, the chief trader, who encouraged the missionary's endeavors. With winter approaching fast, De Smet stayed only a few days, then loaded the party's 14 horses with tools, provisions and seeds; he also made arrangements to take possession of four cows with calves, a heifer and a bull, in all costing him $400 in American currency.[477] Fort Colvile personnel had built up their cattle herd from a bull and two cows in 1826 to 196 head by the time De Smet arrived in 1841.[478]

Father De Smet returned to St. Mary's on December 8 to find the missionaries and Indians had constructed a chapel and four, smaller cabins for staff housing of cottonwood logs chinked with clay and a roof of poles covered with reeds and soil. The three brethren had used only ax, saw and auger, and Indians' strong backs to face the chapel with a pediment and colonnadeand finish the inside with a choir area, altar and benches.[479] The chapel measured 25 by 30 feet with two 8-by-30-foot galleries, large enough to hold 400 souls.[480] While work on the building continued, the Indians had cut and set posts around a parcel of land set aside for planting crops in the spring. The Flatheads provided the missionaries with buffalo robes and 70 packs of dried buffalo meat (80 pounds each), along with roots and berries, leaving little trade stuffs for themselves. On Christmas Day, Father De Smet baptized 115 Flatheads and three chiefs, 30 Nez Perce and their chief, and a Piegan family in a 10-hour session at the new chapel. Earlier, Fathers Mengarini and Point had baptized 350 Indians.

---

476 [I.S.] Ibid. vol. 1, p. 346.

477 Cole, p. 196. Archibald McDonald's Letter of October 15, 1841, that intercepted De Smet en route to Fort Colvile, said there were no oxen (work cattle) to spare.

478 Oliphant, WHQ, 1925, vol. 116, p. 43.

479 Ibid.

480 [I.S.] Chittenden & Richardson, vol. 1, p. 329.

Initial instructions from Mengarini and Point involved translating into Salish the Lord's Prayer, the Hail Mary, and the Ten Commandments with the acts of Faith, Hope, Charity and Contrition. Placing all ages of Indian pupils in a circle, the priests taught each one a different commandment, or one sentence of a prayer. By rotating lessons to different pupils in the circle over the course of three days, young and old alike had memorized the basics.[481]

The day after Christmas, De Smet solemnized 24 marriages in what he called a "heroic sacrifice." Some men had two wives. Each had agreed to retain the wife whose children were most numerous. With the greatest respect, the husbands dismissed their other wives, generously giving them things they needed. A few nights later, one husband went to the chapel, still filled with people, and publicly asked what to do, since he had followed priestly instruction by dismissing his younger wife and reuniting with his first, whom he had earlier forsaken. Unfortunately, De Smet gave no solution to this man's dilemma. Multiple marriages required resolution before a man qualified for baptism because no man, under God, could be married to more than one woman at a time.[482]

On December 29, 1841, the Pend Oreilles and Flatheads, along with a few Spokanes, Coeur d'Alenes and Kootenais, assembled at Hell Gate to make a winter hunt. Priest Nicolas Point, who had accompanied the Indians, left a record of the venture.[483] After following the trail up the Clark Fork River and over Deer Lodge Pass, the party arrived on the Beaverhead plains January 11. There, the Pend Oreilles and other tribal participants separated from the Flatheads due to "their hearts not in harmony," as Father Point put it. Five days later a large party of Nez Perce joined the Flathead camp and made all there feel more comfortable in the dangerous country. Pend Oreille Head Chief Selpisto and Hunt Chief Kous Kous Kaemi found acting Flathead Head Chief Smoire too bossy. The two parties spread their camps five to 10 miles apart and both hunted east, where they eventually found buffalo on the Madison River. While on the trail and on the hunting grounds, the Salish steadfastly adhered to a fixed routine to protect life and property and assure hunting success.

Upon arrival at a suitable campsite, the women pitched their lodges in a tight circle under the direction of a chief, a process that took no more than 30 minutes, and then prepared the evening meal. At nightfall, in enemy territory, prize horses were tethered or hobbled near lodges with

481 [I.S.] Ibid, vol. 1, p. 344-56.
482 [I.S.] Ibid, vol. 1, p. 344-56.
483 Point, pp. 147-152.

guards posted. All rose with the sun, when the men led their horses to the pasture with rifle in hand, remaining there until the women broke camp and were ready to depart. The men then scattered in groups of three to 10 in the general direction of the march, at the same time searching for game and for the enemy. Upon locating buffalo, the scouts returned to camp to tell leaders to get ready for the hunt, while the women followed their routine. Under direction of the chief, the men moved quietly to assigned positions from which the chase began at full gallop. While racing alongside the stampeding buffalo, a hunter selected a cow and aimed his arrow at a spot just behind the last rib, to pierce forward through to the heart or lungs. A true shot usually put the buffalo down within two hundred yards.

Camps remained in one place for several days after locating game concentrations; women, children, elders and an occasional, older chief maintained the camp, as scouting and hunting took place. Young and mature women gathered firewood, built horse corrals, dried meat and dressed hides. Elderly men and women braided bison hair ropes and made horn drinking vessels and toys for the children. Guarding and herding the horses on nearby, open and unfenced pasture fell to boys too young to hunt or scout. An addition to the routine was Father Point's conducting of catechism class in the evening, through an interpreter, for the children and adults preparing for baptism. By hunt's end, 60 mature people had become Catholic.

Flathead hunters had not located a large buffalo herd by January 22, bringing back to a hungry camp only four cows, which lifted spirits slightly. During 17 days of unsuccessful hunting, the camp dogs picked up anything that looked like meat and ran off with it. Father Point used his driest meat pack as a pillow, thinking it safe from starving canines. Nevertheless, one night, a large white dog tried to steal his pillow and interrupted his slumber. Finally, after the 17 days had passed, the hunters located a large herd, killing 150. The timely event was topped off with many fish caught from the Jefferson River.[484] On February 9, Chief Smoire's camp welcomed a friendly visit from a band of Small Robe Piegans. The parley between former enemies went well and Smoire invited the Piegan Chief Nicholas and his band to dinner and to dance. Afterward, Nicholas passed several nights in his host's tent. During the latter's stay, Flathead guards killed a Piegan leading four horses out of camp, but the thief belonged to a different band of the tribe. When the friendly visit between the two ended, the Small Robe Chief Nicholas announced that he and his band of 30 would journey

484 Point, p. 154.

to St. Mary's in the spring for baptism.

A Coeur d'Alene scout dispatched from the Pend Oreille camp rode into the Flathead camp February 13, 1842, to report his band would arrive soon. The scout also described a battle they had had with the Blackfeet that began when four scouts, three Pend Oreilles and one Coeur d'Alene, topped a ridge and startled an enemy war party sneaking on foot toward their Pend Oreille camp. Reacting quickly, the scouts killed the Piegan chief, which instigated the still-surprised warriors to disappear into a nearby ravine to avoid what they thought was a large force readying for an attack. Gunshots heard at the Pend Oreille camp sent hunters racing to the conflict, led by Kuiliy, a young but fearless Pend Oreille woman. Upon arrival, the Pend Oreille reinforcements surrounded the pinned-down Blackfeet Piegans, killing and scalping 30, as the remaining four escaped. Four Pend Oreilles in the allied troops received wounds.[485]

The next day the Pend Oreille group appeared on a ridgeline five miles away and came toward the valley floor, whereupon they made camp some distance from the Flathead camp. On February 15, a scout sent by Selpisto went to the Flathead camp with news that they had discovered a huge herd of buffalo and killed many. The hunters who had had bad luck earlier rushed off with the scout to help with the slaughter.

By March 15, the Indian camps had come together but still harbored differences. Chiefs Selpisto and Smoire worked them out by agreeing that Pend Oreille Hunt Chief Kous Kous Kaemi would lead the entire party until they reached Hell Gate. To demonstrate their accord, Smoire and Selpisto set up their tents next to each other when they reached the Bitterroot Valley in mid-April 1842.[486] With the Flathead tribe back in the St. Mary's neighborhood, spiritual instruction resumed, as did baptisms and the solemnization of marriages.

In the spring, the brethren planted a garden and taught farming principles to interested native bystanders. At least one of the observers thought it foolish to dig up the prairie, ruining good pasture to plant seeds they could have eaten instead. Nevertheless, five different groups of Indians decided to try, but due to mostly rocky, arid soil, they needed to relocate plots in creek bottoms spread over a 16-mile area.[487] The Indians who stayed put until harvest time enjoyed potatoes, peas, carrots and turnips, but they turned up their noses at onions. Camas and bitterroot digging in spring, instead of farming, continued to occupy most of the tribe's time.

485 Point, pp. 158-161.

486 Point, pp. 162-163.

487 [I.S.] *First Roots*, p. 25.

For six years, beginning in 1841, HBC Fort Hall on the Snake River traded supplies for worn-out cattle from immigrants on the Oregon Trail. St. Mary's Jesuits obtained their stock from HBC's Fort Vancouver, as did the company's other forts.[488] As the number of settlers increased along the trail, small operators opened businesses to replace oxen and horses worn down by fatigue. One animal in good shape traded for two gaunt ones. Then over the next year, they fattened them on nature's bountiful grasses. Traders camping along the trail with rejuvenated livestock nearby soon accumulated large herds and would become the Far West's first cattle barons. Besides Fort Hall, other HBC posts along the Oregon Trail also provided a great advantage to some 10,000 trail-weary pilgrims. Located at intervals along the route, Fort Boise on the Snake River and Fort Nez Perce across the Blue Mountains served as resupply stops for many wagon trains. Upon arrival in the Willamette Valley, settlers found all the items they might need at the company post at Fort Vancouver. The company's huge farm provided a variety of groceries, all types of vegetables, flour, butter, cheese, fish and meat. It also sold lumber and hardware for building houses and outbuildings. After 2,000 miles along wilderness trails, the newcomers found a small but civilized oasis.[489]

•••

Tagged "apostles" by Father De Smet, two of the old Salish headmen passed from history in the initial years of St. Mary's. The first was Chief Tjolzhitzy, baptized Paul, also known as Big Face, or Grand Visage, the latter name used by certain fur traders. He died in 1841 or 1842, well into his 80s. Through strong leadership and devotion to the Great Spirit, the Flathead chief endured decades of strife with the more numerous Blackfeet during which he survived 65 battles.[490] In his final years, Big Face prepared himself and his followers to accept and practice Christianity. Apparently, he had no eligible sons to fill the usual hereditary chief position, a traditional practice among the Flatheads. Research shows he lost two sons to the Sioux in the ill-fated trip to St. Louis. Easy-to-Get-Horses, baptized Victor and called Mitt-to by tribesmen, succeeded Tjolzhitzy as the Flathead head chief. The 46-year-old son of a former head chief, Three Eagles, Victor was a minor chief at the time of his succession by the tribe. According to Father De Smet, Victor showed diplomatic qualities of both

488 McLoughlin Letter to De Smet, September 28, 1841.

489 [I.S.] Sage, Ch. 26.

490 [I.S.] Chittenden & Richardson, vol. 2, n.p. and Point Letter #28, 1847.

heart and head, and he conveyed adequate communication skills in a simple, smooth and non-boastful manner.

The second, Pend Oreille Principal Chief Walking Bear, baptized Peter, and called Guignon (Bad Luck) by white fur men, died or vacated his post due to infirmities of old age by 1842.[491] He was more than 80 years old. Missionaries traveling to and establishing St. Mary's never mention him again. According to Father Point, Kous Kous Kaemi led the tribe in 1841. Father Point in 1842 and 1846, and Father De Smet in 1845, refer to Selpisto as the head chief of the Pend Oreilles.[492] De Smet neglected to record Selpisto's baptized name, but it appears to have been Constantin by Father Point's account.[493] He led the tribe for five years before abdicating his post to Pierre George after losing two sons in a battle with the Blackfeet. Referred to by Point as the Pend Oreille great chief and leader of the tribe in late 1846, Pierre George served in that position only a short time. Indian agent Peter Ronan wrote after a campfire confab with War Chief Big Canoe that Joseph advanced as the next head chief. By tribal election in 1848, Alexander became the headman.[494]

Meanwhile, the 1842 summer hunt got off in July with Victor and Insula leading the way along the Bitterroot trail to the Big Hole Valley. Accompanied by Father Point, the Indians stopped in the valley to dig camas and hunt antelope and deer. Their primary objective was buffalo; however, after finding none, they continued on to the Three Forks area and camped several days on Tobacco Fork (Madison River).[495] Buffalo there, too, were scarce, undoubtedly hunted or killed by Nez Perces who got there first. After putting up just enough meat to sustain the party for a few weeks, Victor's company moved eastward to cross over the later-known Flathead Pass[496] in the direction of Shields River where it meets the plains. Moving down through the foothills toward the valley floor, they caught sight of many buffalo quietly grazing below. The hunters soon went to work killing 344 fat cows over the course of several days.[497] Processing the bountiful

491 [I.S.] Chittenden & Richardson, vol. 1, pp. 318, 369 & 482.

492 [I.S.] Chittenden & Richardson, vol. 2 p. 47; Point, p. 158.

493 [I.S.] Chittenden & Richardson, vol. 2, p. 47, p. 206.

494 Ronan, p. 73.

495 Point, p. 170.

496 [I.S.] Rockwell, pp. 140-141. Lieut. Maynader, of a U.S. Army exploration in 1859, followed a well-beaten lodge trail from the Sweet Grass area on the Yellowstone River he thought was the Flatheads' trail. The recently traversed trail turned up Shields River 20 miles, then west along a meandering, willow-lined creek to the timberline top out at the pass. Descent to the Gallatin River cut through a narrow, rocky canyon confined to a single horse width in places.

497 [I.S.] Chittenden & Richardson, Point Letter No. 27, n.d., an extract from his journal.

harvest took a week or more, during which time a small band of Crows, accompanied by an American Scotsman trader and two Shawnees, visited their camp.

After a friendly meeting of several days, the Crows moved on, leaving the Scotsman's party with the hunters who had planned to travel west with the Flatheads. After a few days during which the Scotsman made repeated passes at Salish women, he and his comrades received orders to leave. It seems the white man had become accustomed to the Crows' practice of allowing inexpensive purchase of a woman's favors.[498]

With morning frosts and occasional blowing snows, the Salish loaded packhorses with dried meat and hides and began the nearly 30-day-long ride back to the Bitterroot. The Indians had just two months before the winter hunt began to continue their Christian education at St. Mary's Mission. Just before leaving on the winter hunt, the Flatheads asked the Jesuits for morning and evening prayers that applied directly to their upcoming endeavors. They received five: 1. to the heart of Jesus, as protector of the brotherhood; 2. to the Blessed Virgin, patron of women's companionship; 3. to St. Michael, model of the brave; 4. to St. Raphael, the guide of travelers; 5. to St. Hubert, the patron of hunters.[499] Time would tell if the Black Robe medicine produced better results than the Great Spirit.

In early January 1844, the Pend Oreilles and Flatheads directed a 24-day march in cold, rainy weather up the Clark Fork River toward the Three Forks area before finding a buffalo. Of the painful and hungry journey, Father Point, who accompanied them, said the Indians showed no "sign of discord, discontentment or impatience."[500] The hunters, after having fair success in the Three Forks area, crossed over to the Yellowstone Plains, way deeper into the hostile Blackfeet country. On March 12 while trailing home, Victor suddenly stopped and reversed the entire procession back four miles to the top of a treeless, snow-covered ridge. From that point, what Victor thought were buffalo turned out to be 37 Piegans on foot, working their way up a wide and open grassy slope, hidden from view of the Salish camp.

Victor and five others moved swiftly to where they figured the potential horse thieves should appear. Soon after, Victor's horse came up lame. Thunder (Fidel) and Five Crows (Ambrose) were in the lead of the 50 mounted warriors riding hard toward the Piegans. Surrounding the enemy, they shouted, "Surrender or die!" The Piegans threw down their weapons in utter fear. Winning without firing a shot or losing a man surely

498 Point, p. 170.
499 [I.S.] Chittenden & Richardson, Point Letter No. 28, December 1846, at Ft. Lewis.
500 [I.S.] Ibid.

calmed Flathead hearts. Shortly, both sides sat together on a circle of robes spread over freshly fallen snow to have a friendly smoke. Afterward the subdued robbers returned to the Flathead camp.[501] Upon arrival, Salish reception threatened to get ugly, but after the shaken Piegans flocked around the Black Robe, Ambrose talked to the crowd and everyone calmed down. All smoked the peace pipe again, and as night fell, the Piegans left for their camp. In leaving, they assured Victor and Father Point "the prayer of the Flatheads would be their prayer."[502]

The next day, a skeptical Victor guided his people on a long march to distance themselves from the Piegan camp. The same night, four horses came up missing, stolen by six raiders coming and going from a different direction than that of the would-be thieves' camp. A few days later, on the trail to home, Small Robe Piegan Head Chief Chetlesmalakas (Three Crows) paid the Salish a visit in an attempt to understand the benevolent pardon of the 37 horse thieves. After smoking with all the Flathead chiefs in the missionary lodge, Ambrose explained their religion, and the old Piegan chief nodded in comprehension of such strange behavior. The following morning, after spending the night in Victor's tent, he informed Father Point of his decision to seek baptism for himself and 28 lodges of his people.[503] During the Small Robe's visit, five horses disappeared from the Flathead camp, which led to the killing of one of the raiders. The thief did not belong to the Small Robe's band. Heeding Christian instruction, the Salish buried the Piegan thief unscalped, showing they had willingly abandoned the barbaric practice.

St. Joseph Mission

The Catholic Jesuits order, headquartered in Belgium, provided most of the financial support for the expanded mission operations in Oregon country. In Father De Smet's area of responsibility, four missions were established among Salish tribes during the Jesuits' first decade in the region. Through reassignment of personnel from St. Mary's, the Jesuits opened a second mission among the Coeur d'Alenes. At the end of November 1842, a few buffalo-hunting Coeur d'Alenes familiar with the Flatheads' Christian training left St. Mary's for home territory with Father Nicholas Point and a lay brother to establish a mission. The party arrived at a large encampment engaged in netting fish at the outlet of Coeur d'Alene Lake. In November of each year, Indians barricaded the outlet with wicker screen baskets joined together with traverse poles. Several young men stood in

501 [I.S.] Ibid.
502 Point, p. 185.
503 Ibid.

breast-deep water, next to the baskets, and when the baskets were full of fish, dumped them into waiting canoes. The system resulted in a huge catch, later divided equally among the participants.[504]

Deciding on the mission's location took a few days, as Father Point waited for chiefs representing 27 scattered places to arrive at the fishing camp. The 90-year-old Head Chief Circle Raven led the discussion once all the leaders appeared. Other leaders or future chiefs in attendance included Circle Raven's son Stellam, or Thunder, of the Coeur d'Alene Lake band; Balsa, baptized Vincent, of the Hayden Lake Band; and Seltice, baptized Andrew, who lived at Seltice Lake.[505] Once all the leaders appeared, a lengthy discussion commenced regarding the mission. At length, the oversized council resolved to establish St. Joseph Mission on the St. Joe River near present-day St. Maries, Idaho.

During the several days of conferences, Father Point recorded personal characteristics of the Coeur d'Alenes he met there: "Dirty faces, hair in disorder, hands serving as a comb, handkerchief, knife, fork, and spoon."[506] Foul sounds from the nose, throat and other parts of the body while eating added to the Black Robe's pity for the poor souls. Besides the Indians' visual squalor, Point noted their love of gambling to the extent of giving up sleep time. Criticizing their work ethic, he wrote, "They emerged from

Flathead Head Chief Victor – Mitt-to (1795-1870) – outfitted in a military coat given to him by Washington Territorial Governor Isaac Stevens, circa 1865. COURTESY MANSFIELD LIBRARY, UNIVERSITY OF MONTANA

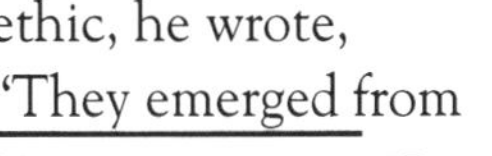

504 Point, p. 175.
505 Fry, p. 299.
506 Point, pp. 50-51.

sloth only when hungry." Father Point's European background naturally caused him to frown on the Coeur d'Alenes' personal cultural practices; he would attempt to "civilize" them according to white man's standards.

The Coeur d'Alenes experienced little exposure to Christianity from Catholic fur men, and they only recognized such evils as lying, stealing and fighting among themselves. They had learned moral standards from their fathers and from the nearby Spokane Chief Garry. Father Point worked with the Coeur d'Alenes on their Christian shortcomings for three years, baptizing many in the tribe. He accompanied the Indians on winter deer hunts to the south end of Lake Pend Oreille that required ideal climate conditions for success: deep snows in the mountains and snow on the valley bottom deep enough for the deer to bog down, yet firm enough to hold the Indian up on snowshoes. On one such hunt, most of the animals fell to clubs and arrows; the 100 native hunters accredited their success in killing 600 deer to their prayers.[507] Protestant missions among the Nez Perces and lower Spokane-Colville tribes had functioned seven years when, in the middle of November 1845, 10 lead men of the Nez Perce tribe arrived at St. Joseph Mission to request instruction. The Indians told the Black Robe they were disgusted at "everything to do with" the Lapwai Mission guided by Reverend Spalding.[508]

The Black Robes jumped at the opportunity to teach Catholic procedures and prayers. Over the course of 10 days of instruction, the Nez Perces mastered their lessons and then departed. Upon returning to their wives and camps, two kinds of prayers went into use, one in the manner of Presbyterian and the other of Catholic. With Father Point's reassignment a few months later, St. Joseph closed down due to yearly spring flooding and moved to the Coeur d'Alene River near Cataldo, Idaho, where Father Anthony Ravalli began construction in 1847 on a new mission complex named Sacred Heart.

Beginning in 1838, Methodist missionaries Cushing Eells and Elkanah Walker and their wives established "Tshimakain" on a small prairie north of today's Ford, Washington. Situated along the main route from Fort Nez Perce to Kettle Falls, the location served the lower bands of Spokanes and a few Colville natives. Upon arrival, the ministers went first to Fort Colvile where they met with chief trader Archibald McDonald, a Catholic, who discouraged them from establishing the mission among the Colville (Kettle) tribe. Before traveling south to the eventual mission site,

---

507 Point, p. 178.
508 Point, p. 99.

they stopped briefly to conduct services among the Colvilles but found the natives oriented toward the Catholic faith due to their close association with local Canadian trappers and mixed-bloods. The missionaries built a church, quarters and a gristmill while at the same time teaching them prayers and farming methods. The Eellses and Walkers closed the mission during the aftermath of the Whitman massacre in 1847 due to fear of distant tribes' wreaking havoc on whites. Natives living along the mid-Columbia River and Yakamas attempted to recruit warriors from among local tribes in their war against the white man with little success.

A band of the Shwoyaopi known locally as Colvilles (that spoke a Salish dialect) occupied the Colville River valley to Kettle Falls where they lived in mat and skin lodges, subsisting on roots, dried salmon and local deer. An explorer passing south through the river valley from Fort Colvile in June 1841 observed a camp of some 70 families with tons of camas roots stored in "neatly woven sacks of netting" made from tule grass matting,[509] drying for winter use.

The Colvilles got their own Black Robe about 1845 when Jesuit Father Pierre De Vos built a small chapel on a bench overlooking Kettle Falls. Two years later, he oversaw construction of a large, hewn-log church, St. Paul Mission, of which a replica stands today. The mission operated until 1869 and served the Colvilles and other Indians that congregated each year at the falls to fish for salmon. Catholic employees at nearby Fort Colvile also worshipped there.

509 Barry, WHQ, vol. 20, pp. 57-60. Dr. Picking's diary, 1841 Wilkes Expedition.

Indians drying fish at the "commons" in Kettle Falls near Fort Colvile by Paul Kane, circa 1847. Kalispel, Colville and Sanpoil tribes used this location as an annual camp. COURTESY WIKIMEDIA COMMONS

Old St. Ignatius Mission

In the summer of 1844, Jesuit Fathers Pierre De Vos and Adrian Hoecken, part of De Smet's team, started St. Ignatius Mission on the north bank of the Pend Oreille River, downstream from today's Newport, Washington. Due to flooding in the spring runoff, they abandoned the site for higher ground downriver near Usk, Washington. Soon after assuming duties, Father Hoecken found the Kalispel society animated, labeling them a "Happy Family" devoted to the Great Spirit. Especially in difficult times, the people neither complained, murmured nor backbit; and blasphemy did not have a word in their language. The Kalispels divided habitation between the large camas meadows on either side of the river from Usk to Locke, Washington, moving about in canoes. Other major campsites included a hunting area on the north bank of Priest River where it joins the Pend Oreille River at the town of Priest River, Idaho, and another at Furport, Washington.[510]

A south-facing bench below Albeni Falls on the Pend Oreille River provided winter camp for a large portion of the tribe. The site

510 PNWQ, Ray, vol. 27 pp. 128-129.

afforded protection from the wind with abundant firewood at hand. The Jesuit priests found the Kalispels (lower Pend Oreilles) poor by white man's standards and nomadic, in the sense that, Indians fished for salmon on the Columbia and below Box Canyon in early summer, followed by a portion of the tribe hunting buffalo on the upper Missouri. Other Indians remained in the area to hunt and fish the waters of the Clark Fork and Pend Oreille rivers by utilizing sturgeon-nosed bark canoes to travel from place to place, all living in peace with neighboring tribes. Thousands of deer dropped down from the mountains when snow reached 2 to 3 feet deep, making easy camp meat. Father De Smet, who wintered there in 1843, wrote that on a single day 40 hunters killed 300 deer.[511]

The Kalispels shared great love, obedience and respect for their chiefs. Effective in leadership, Head Chief Grizzly Bear Standing, baptized Loyola, and subchiefs spoke calmly but never in vain; with guidance, the followers initiated the "task" forthwith.[512] The Indians even consulted their head chief before marriage for sanction or disapproval. A man with an impairment would not receive permission to marry, because the head chief believed his condition might pass on to his children.

Each chief regulated hunting, fishing, and the gathering of roots and fruits. Upon delivery to his lodge, he divided the foodstuffs into equal shares, making sure each family received its share based on the number of mouths in that household. The old, infirm and widows all received an equal share of the hunt and the harvest. According to Father De Smet, by July in the second year of St. Ignatius, missionaries and Indians had erected 14 log houses and a barn and prepared logs for a church. They had 300 acres of grain growing enclosed by a pole fence, 30 head of horned cattle, a few hogs and some domestic fowl. The women had learned to milk cows and churn butter.[513]

In early 1845, Jesuits at St. Mary's founded a station south of Flathead Lake among the upper Pend Oreilles called St. Francis Borgia.[514] Little information exists on the place, but it appears meetings took place at various Indian encampments. St. Mary's missionaries traveled four days north from the church to teach and conduct services with Indians. Such infrequent meetings proved fruitful for the Jesuits. Some 300 Upper Pend Oreilles, mostly adults, traveled to St. Mary's for Easter services conducted by Father De Smet. The same day, working into the night, he baptized an

511 [I.S.] Chittenden & Richardson, vol. 2, p. 469.
512 [I.S.] Ibid. vol. 2, p. 458-59.
513 [I.S.] Ibid. vol. 2, p. 471.
514 Palladino, p. 12.

entire group that amounted to a majority of the tribe. Among the five Pend Oreille chiefs, the most distinguished of all were Selpisto, the head chief; Stiettiedloodsho, the war chief; and Chalax, a chief and medicine man of the lower Flathead River band.[515] Another leader of 30 lodges at Horse Plains, Hoytelpo, who had met Father De Smet for the first time in his earlier fall trip to Fort Colvile, undoubtedly received baptism by him that Easter.

Father Nicholas Point's engraving of old St. Ignatius Mission at Kalispel Bay on the Pend Oreille River, circa 1848. COURTESY WASHINGTON STATE UNIVERSITY LIBRARIES

•••

Indian migration north from the Snake River Plain began midway through the decade due to diminishing game populations in the area and the steady summertime flow of immigrants on the Oregon Trail. Many Shoshonis and Bannocks went north in the already over-hunted upper Missouri to find game. A number of bands made the Beaverhead their annual resort from which they hunted farther into Blackfeet country only to find violence and few buffalo. Subsisting primarily on local deer, elk, antelope and fish, the southern Indians resupplied by trading skins and horses to trappers and Fort Hall traders. The tribes' propensity to steal horses troubled the Salish who passed by the Beaverhead on their way to the buffalo. The Flatheads first experienced the shift of southern tribes in the winter of 1845 on the upper Missouri when attacked by a large force of Bannocks. The short engagement ended in a rout, as the aggressors fled and left three

515 [I.S.] Chittenden & Richardson, vol. 2, p. 472. The war chief's English name was likely Big Canoe.

dead warriors on the battlefield.[516] Victor and Selpisto, Flatheads and Pend Oreilles joined forces on the 1845 summer hunt to the Missouri plains, accompanied by Father Mengarini.

The chiefs had learned of a planned ambush by an organized contingent of Blackfeet along the path to the hunting grounds. Nearly out of food, the hungry procession cautiously trailed along, with lead scouts well in advance of the main body; nearing a potential ambush location, the Salish set up camp in a protected canyon. The next morning, women, children, baggage and Father Mengarini stayed in camp while the warriors rode off, preceded by the two scouts, toward the point of danger. The scouts had just made it to the timbered pass when a Blackfeet chief and a French Creole trader stepped out of the woods, displaying a peace pipe and signaling with their hands in a friendly manner.

Within minutes, a shot rang out from the nearby woods, and one Pend Oreille scout fell dead while the other raced back in a hail of balls to the nearby main force, as the Blackfeet chief and a French Creole retreated to their stronghold. Chiefs Victor and Selpisto quickly formulated plans to draw the enemy out by a rushing attack followed by a hasty retreat. The entire Salish force attacked the Blackfeet close enough to draw heavy musket fire and swiftly feigned their escape. The Blackfeet took the bait. When they were completely out in the open, the Salish whipped around and bravely attacked head-on. The effort rapidly worked its effect. At the conclusion of the clash, 25 Blackfeet lay dead, while two sons of Selpisto and a Snake brave married to a Flathead woman died.[517] After the battle, the Salish warriors returned to their camp to waiting families and the priest. The grieving Selpisto, with revenge on his mind, pressed for renewing the conflict in the morning, but Father Mengarini managed to discourage both chiefs. A day or so later, the above-mentioned French Creole came to the Salish camp, representing the Piegan tribe, and asked the priest to visit their camp, as they were "eager to hear his words." Father Mengarini accepted the invitation, but the chiefs, particularly Selpisto, would have none of it. The Salish chiefs told the Jesuit that if he went to the enemy's camp, they would follow him and "fight so long as one of them (Blackfeet) remained standing"; they were so angry, they threatened to abandon him.[518] Mengarini stayed put, but neither the Indians nor Father Mengarini ever

516 [I.S.] Chittenden & Richardson, vol. 2, p. 570 - De Smet Letter #23, September 6, 1846.

517 Palladino, pp. 52-53, De Smet Letter #23, September 1846; tallied 23 Blackfeet, 3 Pend Oreille and 1 Flathead dead.

518 Paladino, p. 53.

forgave the episode, and the priest abstained from joining future Salish hunting parties.

•••

Not long after the event, Selpisto demonstrated his Christian education when he pardoned a Piegan involved in the battle in which his two sons fell. During Easter time back in home territory, the Flatheads delivered a Piegan prisoner, who had killed one of their own, to the Pend Oreille head chief. Selpisto took the panic-stricken man into his lodge, followed shortly by several of his own young men who desired to put the Piegan down. It being Holy Week, Selpisto said: "Another time I might have consented to your desire, but today I shall not." He told his people, since God had shown great mercy toward him, "I must do for this unhappy man what has been done for me."[519] Selpisto not only granted the Piegan life but also saw to his safe return home.

The fortunate St. Mary's Mission complex had many of the trappings of civilization by the end of 1846. Built right on a nearby stream, the small gristmill could grind 10 to 12 bushels of wheat into flour a day. Next to the complex, fenced-in farmland produced abundant crops of oats, potatoes and wheat. Construction to divert two small streams for irrigating crops had begun. An on-site sawmill turned out planks and beams for a 30-foot-by-60-foot chapel under construction and for 12 new buildings with bastions on opposite corners of the log-walled compound. The security measures were meant to discourage sporadic Blackfeet raids during the Flatheads' absence.

The Flatheads and many of the upper Pend Oreilles had learned Catholic prayers and practices well; confession, communion and crossing themselves before meals were integrated in a regimented routine. The Indians adopted Christian ideals well during their five years of instruction and abandoned brutal practices of the past. Father De Smet reported to superiors in late 1846 that some Flatheads had entirely abolished polygamy and capricious disregard of wives. Young Indian maidens could choose mates for life rather than be sold for horses by their fathers. The Flathead men's vindictiveness that led to war evolved to a Christian sense of justice that displaced unjust aggression for the defense of inherent rights.[520]

The missionaries also had 40 head of cattle, a fast-growing herd

519 Point, p. 189.
520 Ibid.

of hogs and numerous varieties of fowl. According to Father De Smet, these amenities "contributed to ... increasing wants of the surrounding country [dwellers] along with a charitable objective to feed the hungry and strengthen the helpless."[521] Such white men's improvements satisfied needs of the missionary staff moreso than for the Flatheads. Most Indians wanted no part of farming or raising livestock, until after the buffalo were gone.

A few free trappers living at HBC's Fort Connah put together a group of young, well-armed Pend Oreilles and Kootenais to hunt the Blackfeet's homeland they thought was uninhabited. In the spring of 1846, some 40 Pend Oreilles, Kootenais and a few half-blood trappers entered the dangerous country of the Canadian plains south of Calgary to hunt and trap. It had been 40 years or more since any of the Pend Oreilles had hunted the area. They likely used Crowsnest Pass to access the plains while hunting north, skirting the rolling mountain foothills, for beaver and buffalo. South of High River on June 16, 1846, a detached party collided with 28 young Piegan warriors that started an immediate fight. They quickly gained the field, killing two Pend Oreilles without a loss before returning to their camp. The next day, accompanied by James Bird Jr., 20 of the over-confident warriors returned singing war songs and rode into an ambush. The five-hour battle ended with the allies forcing the badly beaten Piegans into retreat; a Piegan chief and three of his followers were killed. Four Pend Oreilles died in the costly victory.[522] The mixed group abandoned their risky hunting venture to sneak back to home base with little to show for their efforts.

End of Friendship

On course to return to St. Louis during the summer of 1846, Father De Smet traveled to the Coeur d'Alene St. Joseph Mission to join up with Father Point and then on to St. Mary's Mission. He planned to travel with Salish hunters to visit the River Crows band he had met four years earlier. Arriving too late to join the hunters, De Smet instead formed a 12-man escort that included interpreters Gabriel Prudhomme and Pend Oreille Charlie. The party left the mission August 16 to follow the well-beaten trail up the Clark Fork River toward the Yellowstone River and Crow country. They caught up with the Salish on about September 5 to learn of a fight between the former allies, in which Small Robe Piegans supported

521 [I.S.] Chittenden & Richards, De Smet Letter #23 from Flathead Camp Yellowstone, September 6, 1846.

522 Rundle Journals, pp. 264-65. As told to Methodist minister Robert Rundle by his guide James Bird Jr. during an 1847 trek through Blackfeet country where Bird pointed out the site.

the Salish. The Salish hunters left the Bitterroot Valley in early July 1846, making a beeline for the Yellowstone River and buffalo. Along the trail, 12 lodges of 76 men, women and children of the Small Robe Piegans joined the Salish ranks on their own request, an amazing occurrence considering past hostilities between the two tribes. The party continued east, crossing a pass to the Yellowstone River along the trail on the north side of that river to Square Butte and Crow country.

Near today's town of Laurel, Montana, they happened upon a camp of 30 Nez Perce lodges on the opposite bank of the Yellowstone,[523] whom they joined. The Salish and Small Robes had set up camp nearby and, at the same time, learned of a large Crow camp downriver. Seeing the chance to renew their longstanding peace, Flathead Chief Victor sent emissaries to invite the Crows to their camp for a reunion. When the well-armed Crows arrived at the joint encampment and laid eyes on bitter Small Robe enemies, the latter forgot all about the peaceful invitation and began shouting at the Salish greeting party, "They must leave!" The large Crow delegation belligerently spewed their own added insults: "One Crow armed with a stick would be enough to make 100 Flathead flee."[524] There stood before them the calm Salish whose very demeanor stopped the immediate conflict dead in its tracks as the unexpected Gabriel Prudhomme and Pend Oreille Charlie, who had just arrived, stepped into the middle of the fray to announce the imminent arrival of Black Robes De Smet and Point. Even such a warring Crow party did not wish to offend the missionaries. Gabriel and Charlie's interference quickly and smoothly settled tempers temporarily. This scalp-tingling ordeal dropped the hammer on Victor's hope for a peaceful reunion as the party broke up before it started.

Having displaced peace, and stiffly departing for their camp, the Crows snarled at the Salish that no peace could come between them so long as a Piegan remained in their camp. True to their word, on the following day, Crows stole 30 horses from worried Salish, who were busy fortifying their camp and stationing women and children safely out of harm's way. At the same time, a unit of the Nez Perce camp under Flathead Crawling Mountain (Moise) took up a forward position some distance from the Salish camp.[525] At 10 o'clock the next day, a cloud of dust announced the Crows galloping attack on Moise's advance line but pulled up short of musket range. Within minutes, the Crow line moved cautiously forward, led by a chief who fired the first shot that ended the life of a Nez Perce chief's

523 [I.S.] Chittenden & Richardson, p. 574, De Smet Letter no. 23.

524 Point, p. 189.

525 [I.S.] Chittenden & Richardson, vol. 2, p. 576, De Smet Letter no. 23.

young son. The allied forward line opened fire with great efficiency, dehorsing several Crows in the first volley, causing the rest to back off and begin racing their horses in all directions in a spectacular show of horsemanship.

Watching from their fortified camp, Chief Victor perceived the Crows' horses would soon tire and ordered his braves to mount up and attack. The Salish and allies pursued the enemy for two miles, fighting until nightfall. Even the women got involved by gathering spent arrows for warriors whose own had run out. One old woman got between a warrior and her son, who was tending his horse; with a hatchet in her hand, she caused the warrior to leave quickly. After the fight ended, a younger woman said, "I thought these great talkers were men, but I was wrong, they're not even worth pursuing."[526] Amazingly, in nine hours of fighting, the Nez Perces suffered two deaths and one wounded; the Crows had 10 killed and 14 wounded.[527]

Father Point, in his memoirs, noted that Indian fights are similar to mock warfare that lasts a long time without spilling much blood: "We shall have 'sport' rather than fight."[528] De Smet and party arrived at the Salish camp a day after the battle to find everything ready to repel another attack. He sent a messenger to the Crow to camp to request a visit. The messenger returned shortly with word that the Crows grievously declined. Following this setback, after calling on the Small Robes for help, the Jesuit Black Robes hoped to have better luck introducing the Northern Piegans to Christianity. The morning after celebrating victory with a dance, the Salish, Nez Perces, Small Robes and missionaries broke camp to trail north toward the Blackfeet homeland over a route of miserably dry plains devoid of fresh, clean water. Many got stomach sickness from sipping alkali-rimmed, putrid, stagnant ponds and creeks. Along the way, the few scattered bulls killed were scarcely enough to feed the large camp.

Judith Basin Council

During the journey through the arid climes, the Nez Perces refused to smoke the peace pipe with the Piegans, stubbornly hanging on to old animosities. Even the words of a caring Small Robes woman introducing her 20-year-old adopted stepson to his rightful Nez Perce father did not break the ice. Finally, the Nez Perces could no longer keep up appearances and quit the camp on the morning of September 10, 1846, only to return

526 Point, p. 191.
527 Ibid.
528 Ibid. p. 192.

in the afternoon, fearing an attack by the Crows.[529] The following day, the apprehensive allies reached the Musselshell River where the Salish and Nez Perce separated from De Smet's party and the Small Robes. Entering their longtime enemy's homeland, Victor, and probably De Smet, thought it best to part company. The missionary party continued north four days, arriving at the headwaters of the Judith River on September 14, not far from Piegan Chief Big Lake's camp near today's Garniell, Montana.[530]

Meanwhile, Victor had dispatched messengers to tell the Piegan chief he would like to visit their village and trade on friendly terms. In a show of courage and faith in De Smet's peace-making ability, and without a definitive answer from the Piegans, the Salish and Nez Perces rode up to the missionaries' camp soon after Big Lake's band had arrived. The meeting of adversaries, though initially tense on the Piegans' part, soon relaxed into friendlier discourse. During the two-day assembly, according to Father De Smet, the Salish chiefs' simplicity and cordiality won the affection of the Piegan chiefs.[531] Soon the gathering swelled with Blackfeet, Blood and Gros Ventre representatives of about 2,000 Indians, including the Salish and Nez Perce. On the morning of September 15, Father De Smet stood before the large assembly to conduct mass, and afterward a trading session began. He later wrote: "It appears as if their ancient deadly feud has long since buried in oblivion. ... How long will this last?"[532] The next day, the Salish and Nez Perces packed up their camp, said goodbye to the Black Robes, and trailed off in search of buffalo.

Charles Larpenteur, on his way to trade with the Flatheads, said the peace lasted a little longer than a year. Some of the young men of the Small Robes picked a fight with the Salish in which a few in each party perished. After learning of the hostile situation, Larpenteur's Piegan guide advised it would not be safe for him to travel west to enemy homeland as they planned to continue their war with the Salish.[533]

The Salish and Nez Perces left the Judith Basin Council, disappointed in the Black Robes for catering to perennial antagonists. They perceived a slight when the missionaries provided tobacco to the Piegans and excluded them. Fathers De Smet and Point accompanied the Blackfeet to the AFC Fort Lewis on the Missouri River, where De Smet boarded a steamboat bound for St. Louis. Father Point stayed the winter and taught the Blackfeet Christianity; he baptized some 600, while young men in Big

529 [I.S.] Chittenden & Richardson, De Smet Letter #24, January 1,1847.
530 Ibid.
531 Ibid.
532 Ibid.
533 Larpenteur, Ch 14.

Lake's band conducted horse-stealing raids in Salish home territory with some success. Big Lake did not approve the foray, which cost about 10 of his raiders' lives "by the hands of the Pend Oreilles."[534] All of this added to an earlier dispute when Father Mengarini's aspiration to visit a Piegan war party created an open rift between the Salish and St. Mary's Jesuits. Father Ravalli, a missionary at the time, gave his reason for such rancor against the priests. He thought Father De Smet might have upset the "spiritual balance of power" by sending Father Point to the Blackfeet.[535] The Flatheads returned from the hunt in an unfriendly mood and flatly refused to sell dried meat to the mission staff. The once-fervent and sizeable congregation began to shrink as members simply moved away from the mission settlement in small numbers.

The Crows sought revenge a month after their drubbing by the Salish and Piegan allies on the Yellowstone River. Launching a massive force, they attacked a major Small Robes village, probably in the Three Forks area, killing many and taking women and children captive. Word of the reported massacre and capture spread rapidly across the plains. On his return trip to St. Louis, De Smet received a report in October 1846 that said Crows had killed an entire band of 50 Small Robe families, save 160 women and children taken captive.[536] Shortly after capture, Crow children came down with scarlet fever, yet the Small Robe captives who had survived an earlier bout with the malady went unaffected. Asked by their captors how they had survived the illness, they told the Crows to soak in the cold waters of the river. The fever-stricken people accepted their supposed remedy that only hastened their death, as Father De Smet put it, "in the dark spirit of vengeance."[537] A short time later, Father Point, then with the Piegans at Fort Lewis, learned that half of the Small Robe band had survived the vicious attack.[538] Midway through the 19th century, the Small Robes band numbered some 30 lodges, but it never regained its prominence in the Piegan tribe.[539]

---

534 [I.S.] Chittenden & Richardson, vol. 3, p. 952. Fort Lewis was abandoned a few years after De Smet's visit, for a better location nearby called Fort Benton.

535 Ravalli letter to Roothaan, February 29, 1847.

536 Ewers, p. 188, De Smet Letter.

537 [I.S.] Chittenden & Richardson, vol. 2, p. 504.

538 Point, p. 188.

539 Ewers, p. 188.

Fort Connah

About 1834, the location of Flathead Post's fall and winter trading sessions moved seven miles upstream to Horse Plains and assumed the old name. The new site eliminated the need for Indians to pass over Bad Rock and gave HBC easy water transportation to and from Thompson Falls. Lower prices for the scarce beaver skins and the resulting trade volume gradually led to less company staff at the site. The traders at the new location had little need for substantial structure since they returned to Fort Colvile for the winter. Tents provided shelter for men and trade goods for the short time they spent there during the spring and fall trading session. From April until mid-November, HBC men trailed with the Indians and free trappers on buffalo hunts.

Francis Ermatinger led the successful trading venture until his 1838 promotion to chief trader at Fort Hall. Even though the beaver market had weakened along with the very resource itself, HBC aggressively sought the furry animal. Trapping and location changed when the Salish shifted hunting grounds in 1839 to the Three Forks quarter that organized American trapping parties had abandoned. Remembering prior troubles with the Blackfeet, the few American trappers remaining in the mountains did not venture that far north and concentrated efforts to a 200-mile radius of Fort Hall. Donald McLean assumed the job as traveling trader with the Salish well into American lands. In a letter to John McLoughlin, Fort Colvile trader Archibald McDonald wrote, "Mr. McLean returned from the plains with 1,000 beaver short of last year."[540]

John McPherson, who followed McLean as Flathead Post trader, had returns that declined slightly each year for several years. The abandoned Flathead Post's seven connected buildings protected upriver by Bad Rock became a firewood source for wintering Pend Oreilles. The old site served HBC well for 16 years and consistently produced the highest returns on the company's Columbia Department. HBC trader Angus McDonald later poetically captured the old site as it appeared in 1849: "Many a fine buffalo tongue and many a glass of the finest brandy that ever crossed the Atlantic were served in that sylvan (wood) building; not a vestige of it now remains. Where the stirring yell of Gillie Crubach and the solemn strains of the Flowers of the Forest were whistled and sung. … We were glad to hear once a year from Europe, though seldom if ever from the United States, Montana's rye grass and the cock of the hills and meadow dance there, but we say with the old bard, 'When will it be morn in the grave to

540 Cole, p. 166. Archibald McDonald Letter, January 4, 1848.

bid the slumberers awake?' "[541]

HBC had directed apprentice clerk Neal McArthur in 1846 to begin construction on a new Flathead Post 40 miles east of Horse Plains on Post Creek in the Mission Valley. Framed to the east by the lofty Mission Mountains, the setting positioned the company trading operation in the heart of Pend Oreille homeland and closer to the Flatheads. Water transported goods on the Flathead River to the mouth of Mission Creek where a six-mile-long packhorse trail to the post made the location feasible. Moreso, the new post would put the company in a better position to intercept Salish trade from increasing numbers of individual American traders frequenting the area. Indians fancied the new site since it was closer to home and eliminated 40 miles of trailing, fording the Flathead River and negotiating a mountain to reach Horse Plains. Scotsman Angus McDonald's transfer from HBC Fort Hall to the Colvile District soon led to his appointment as Flathead Post's clerk trader.

McDonald, stationed at Fort Colvile, replaced McArthur as Flathead Post clerk trader. Angus, his Nez Perce wife and young family traveled to the Mission Valley in the spring of 1847, where he completed construction on the trading post McArthur began. McDonald named the post Fort Connen after a Scottish river valley, but the approximately 20 French-speaking free trappers that set up camp nearby had difficulty pronouncing the word. Thus, the new Fort Connen became "Fort Connah"; however, with no protective walls surrounding it, the post could hardly stand as a fort. Workers had constructed four buildings all with bark roofs, a 24-by-16 foot residence, one 14-foot-square bastion and two storerooms each 10-foot square. A 60-foot square, log corral completed the scene, all of which set out in the open prairie near Post Creek. Roving Blackfeet thieves stole two kegs of powder and two bags of shot before the trading post was completed. Further cutting into company profits for 1847, raiders took 29 company horses without a shot fired.[542]

Late in September a band of 60, well-armed Piegans surprised McDonald and four men as they broke out of the timber on the upper end of Horse Plains where the men had turned their horses out to graze. Armed with only two guns, the traders surrendered all the stock. As McDonald later put it, "They didn't bother with scalps."[543] A few days after the robbery, Pend Oreilles killed four of the thieves but did not recover the horses.

541 McDonald (Angus), Manuscript written after 1871.

542 PCNWQ, vol. 30, no. 4, 1939, Partoll, pp. 401-402. The son of Governor Simpson and a native woman, George Simpson Jr.'s Letter to his father, October 31, 1847.

543 WHQ, vol. 8, 1917, A Few Points on the Old West. McDonald.

More Piegan raids occurred in the winter of 1849-1850 in the Mission Valley where an attempt to rob Fort Connah failed, but three miles from the post a company employee was shot, stripped and scalped, he being the half-blood son of naturalist David Douglas. The Pend Oreilles lost a whopping 334 horses during the raid."[544]

Colvile District trader Anderson considered trade material acquired at Fort Connah "indispensible and required." The Indian production of dried buffalo meat, tallow and particularly buffalo skin accessories were most important. Items such as provisions, fur-on-one-side saddle blankets, rawhide and woven buffalo fur cords were unavailable and needed on the west side of the Rockies. Fort Colvile personnel transported these materials to other HBC posts. The Jesuits at St. Mary's Mission hampered HBC's quest for dried buffalo meat and fat by purchasing powder and shot, usually from Fort Vancouver, which they traded to the Indians for provisions. Fort Colvile aside, the Post Creek people obtained ample meat from the Indians and supplemented that by cultivating 2 acres of ground for provisions.[545]

Angus McDonald relished his job at Connah Post and enthusiastically mixed with the Pend Oreilles as they prepared to leave for dangers of the buffalo grounds. By tradition, the tribe held a departing ceremony that involved a feast dance and emotional song *San-ka-ha*. On at least one occasion, McDonald stripped to the waist, painted his upper body with vermillion, and mounted his black buffalo horse, wearing his full eagle feather bonnet while cantering around with the Indians. He wrote: "To hear it, [*San-ka-ha*] sung by 500 to 600 voices in a calm starry night on the plains – is a rare exception. … The mothers and sisters – always the most tender – could not stand its thrilling notes, and they wept loud and deeply for those that were and were not."[546]

Back at St. Mary's, priests either refused or perhaps were uninvited to accompany Indian hunters after 1845. Troubled by prior issues, the Flatheads began to question Black Robes' "medicine." Influenced by longtime Nez Perce hunting partners and blood relatives, the Flatheads learned of that tribe's disappointment with the Lapwai missionaries. Many Nez Perces, particularly the buffalo-hunting faction, rejected Christianity by reverting to original beliefs in the Great Spirit. Such campfire sessions furthered separation of many Flatheads from the Jesuits. Some Salish resumed gambling while on seasonal hunts, one of the first prohibitions established

544 Anderson Letter to Gov. Simpson, April 18, 1850.
545 PCNWQ, vol. 30, no. 4. 1939, Partoll. George Stevens Jr., Letter.
546 McDonald, Angus, Manuscript.

by Father De Smet.

By 1847, St. Mary's Mission compound had completed two bastions at opposite corners linked by an upright and pointed log wall, making it well fortified. The newly constructed 30-foot-by-60-foot chapel and staff quarters tied together to form one end of the complex.[547] Flatheads off hunting half the year and episodes of intermittent raids made the fortification necessary. During the initial nine years of St. Mary's operations, not one of the missionaries sustained a serious wound. Yet, Blackfeet and sporadic Bannock horse thieves habitually raided the Bitterroot Valley, robbing Indians and missionaries alike.

In his first of three years at St. Mary's, Father Anthony Ravalli told of an incident that took place in September 1847 after the Indians left on the fall hunt. The priest, one brother, one old man, two boys, and some old women and children were occupying the stockade, when early one morning, ear-piercing yells announced the presence of Blackfeet. Without knowing how many people were inside, they dared not attack. One of the Indian boys ventured outside, which cost his life. The murdering thieves then drove off all horses in the vicinity.[548] Not only Blackfeet troubles concerned the mission staff, but also St Mary's remoteness made obtaining supplies and mail difficult.

Distant Forts Hall and Colvile supplied various needs of the mission but did not offer wine for mass. Once a year, the priests traveled to Fort Vancouver with Salish packers for wine, mail and other items unavailable at other outposts. HBC Fort Hall had geared up to provide goods for settlers passing on the Oregon Trail, so the mission acquired particular hardware there; however, the jaunt passed through dangerous country. At least twice in five years, Flathead packers had all possessions stolen and wore the scars to prove it.[549]

Missionaries abhorred Indian contact with white men and mixed-blood trappers, believing the latter corrupted converts and ridiculed missionaries. About 1846, a band of "wolfers and trappers whose only religion was whiskey and women," all married to Indian women, settled in with the Flatheads during late fall, according to Father Ravalli.[550] Between hunts in 1847, Flathead Little Faro and his followers moved across the river from the mission and camped with two American trappers. The following year,

547 Discovery writers, p. 27.

548 Palladino, Ravalli Manuscript, p. 7. Father Ravalli served as St. Mary's missionary and as Father Mengarini's assistant from the fall of 1845 to 1850.

549 Palladino, p. 6.

550 Palladino, p. 7.

Father Mengarini gave the mission just two years to survive. The missionaries suspected the renegades circulated "vile, nasty stories" amongst the Indians. Blaming Indian discontent on these men, Fathers Ravalli and Palladino wrote, "Flathead[s], who had been thus far, so willing, so docile and so affectionate towards the Fathers, became careless, indifferent, insolent and pretentious to a degree, that from then on, all the exertion of the missionaries in behalf of these Indians availed little [or] nothing."[551]

Five years later, Priest Michael Accolti blamed Angus McDonald for the mission closure, and wrote Father De Smet: "Some time ago these Indians underwent a change of heart in regard to the Fathers through the machinations [artful scheming] of a certain Mr. McDonald an agent of the Bay Company [Hudson's Bay Company], of some Nez Perce and a few whites."[552] Fathers Mengarini and Accolti also thought the passing away of older leadership of the tribe a reason for mission failures. The priests, in following a well-defined pecking order, had trouble coping with Indian methods of operation. Varied in size, each clan or band had its own chief with each leader making independent decisions. Only during tribal hunting excursions or war did participating bands have centralized leadership. Father Point wrote that Pend Oreilles and Flatheads living at 27 different sites and under separate leaderships were obstacles to successful missions.[553] For these reasons and more, the missionaries and Flatheads drew further apart, spelling the eventual closure of St. Mary's. The former mountain man Thomas Fitzpatrick, a blood brother of Insula, concluded in 1847 that Indians would submit to ceremonies of "the medicine" with good grace until they discovered that those who passed through all the ceremonies of religion had no better luck in hunting and war than before. The only conclusion Indians could fall back on was that "the white man's medicine is not as strong as his own."[554] The Indians' mode of survival, both physically and economically, had not changed during the mission years as they had once expected. Spiritually, a portion of the Flatheads would continue to practice the Catholic faith while others reverted to their Great Spirit and old customs.

Father De Smet, referring to former Salish hunting grounds, wrote in an 1849 letter: "I resided a long time among the Flathead[s] and Kalispels, I have visited at different epochs the Kootenais at the North, and the

---

551 Palladino, p. 8.

552 Garraghan, G. J., vol. II, p. 382. Accolti Letters to De Smet, May 5, 1851.

553 Mengarini, pp. 117-18.

554 Ibid, p. 120, Fitzpatrick Letter, to Thomas H. Harvey October 19, 1847. Upper Platte Agency where Fitzpatrick was the agent.

Shoshonis or Snakes at the South. Their vast territories, watered by the principal branches of the upper Columbia and the Rio Colorado [Green River] of the West ... formerly abundantly provided ... every variety of game, which furnished them with clothing and nourishment. But now that the buffalo have disappeared from these lands, the poor Indians are obliged to go and pass a portion of the year east of the Rocky Mountains in search of their only means of subsistence."[555] During the next decade, buffalo hunting conditions deteriorated due to quantity of animals and competition among the tribes.

After the Flatheads' falling out with the Black Robes in 1847, few details of their activities exist. Records show bison herds in the Three Forks area dwindled further, causing the Salish and Nez Perces to travel farther north and east along the Yellowstone drainages, putting them at odds with the Crows and Big Lakes band of Northern Piegans. The long-abandoned route to the Missouri River via the Little Blackfoot River and over the future Mullan Pass once again echoed with sounds of horse hooves and the Salish. It became increasingly difficult and equally dangerous for the Salish and allies to find fat cows as in the past.

Through an interpreter, L.V. McWorter's interview with Two Moons in 1909 provides some information on Salish activity during this time frame. Two Moons (Hessemdooka), son of a Flathead warrior and a Nez Perce mother, told of his intertribal warfare during an 80-plus-year lifespan. He took his grandfather's name, "given him by the power of the sun and moon, the two," and wore his grandfather's spirit charm, a crane wingbone from a bird that "flies high in the sky."[556] Neither man ever received a serious wound. His Flathead father, Five Blue, also a noted warrior, is supposed to have died before the son's teen years. Two Moons lived with his mother in the combined Nez Perce-Salish camp. At age 15, he probably did not think about doing battle when answering the call to chase after an early morning, horse-thieving Crow; yet, without thought for his own safety, he instinctively demonstrated superior bravery in the ensuing fight.

Rising at sunup, Two Moons had gone to the corral and was saddling his horse when he heard the shout, "The enemy has our horses!" Quickly, he mounted and tore off down the valley dappled with many allied tepees. As he passed Flathead Chief Baldhead's tepee,Two Moons caught sight of a Crow driving five horses.[557] Leaning forward to urge his

555 [I.S.] Chittenden & Richardson, vol. 4, pp. 1187-88. De Smet Letter to Association of Lyons, June 10, 1849, St. Louis.

556 McWorter, pp. 561-65.

557 Ibid.

horse to put on some speed, Two Moons shortened the distance between himself and the hard-riding thief. Catching up, he spotted a large group of dismounted Crow warriors bearing arms. Putting heels to his horse, Two Moons caught up with the robber, musket raised. The enemy forgot the horses, frantically trying to reach the safety of his partners in crime. Two Moons gathered the horses and drove them toward camp, meeting fellow Flathead warriors whose mounts were breathing hard as they stopped near him; the brave youngster then joined the war party to experience his first combat. The allies then drove the Crows out into the open plain where the chief warrior sent Two Moons to a position at the end of the battleground.

As the fight escalated, Two Moons had difficulty holding his post against the advancing Crows, but at a critical moment, the enemies' line collapsed on the opposite side, drawing off the attackers on his side. Then a lone, mounted Crow warrior rode head-on toward Two Moons, bent so low over the saddle his painted face blended with the flowing mane and forward pricked ears of his mount. As the Crow rose up to aim and shoot at close range, Two Moons fired from a standing position. The Crow warrior never knew what hit him and dropped on the spot. At the same instant, a Flathead warrior at a greater distance fired and subsequently claimed he had downed the enemy. Two Moons ignored the warrior and went about scalping his dead enemy, before seizing his horse and gun.

With the first part of the battle over, the young warrior rode to the command center, a cave-like indenture on the rolling prairie floor. There, Nez Perce War Chief Three Feathers was taking off his war bonnet and blanket, mumbling about how they made him an easy target. Two Moons asked to put the feathers on, and a Flathead chief granted permission. With bonnet in place, he rode through enemy lines three times. Not one shot hit Two Moons in the hail of musket balls that followed. The battle ended at nightfall when the Crows slipped away. From that day on, the young brave warrior, Two Moons, always made three rounds in a war dance to signify the good medicine of his first real battle experience.

The old warrior told of a fight the Salish got into with the Blackfeet in about 1849 at an unidentified location. On the hunting grounds, Two Moons camped with Flatheads, "mostly my own blood," at the edge of a canyon. Messengers brought word of a party of strange Indians a distance off. A war party formed and sped off to the reported location, a short canyon with high, steep bluffs. The warriors encircled the canyon mouth and a portion of the rim with the Flatheads occupying the most likely escape route. However, the Blackfeet had climbed out via a different break in the canyon wall and entered a timber stand on top. On his own volition, Two Moons rode hard to circle the canyon rim, looking for signs of the enemy's escape route. Finding their tracks at a certain place, the young warrior stopped his hard-breathing horse to signal the Flatheads by waving his blanket. The Blackfeet had not known he was alone. Soon the Flatheads attacked from the opposite direction, chasing them down and killing 28 of the 30 Blackfeet war party. Two Moons, the lone scout, did not engage in the fight as "the Flathead warriors did the best fighting" that day.[558] The Flatheads let an old man and a boy go free. One Flathead received a leg wound, but none died.

The upper Pend Oreilles changed leadership in 1848 with the election of 45-year-old Tum-cle-hot-cut-se (No Horses), baptized Alexander. Supported by St. Ignatius Jesuits, Alexander united various bands of that tribe. During his two decades as head chief, he developed a reputation of being courageous, aggressive and strict, yet just. As a devoted Christian and friend of the Jesuits, Alexander struggled with some members of his tribe that hung onto old ways counter to missionary teachings, particularly as more white settlers came to the area. His decision to ignore hunting boundaries set by treaties with the U.S. government ended in tragedy.

Boundary Settlement

Although the Salish played no part in the International Boundary Settlement, nor would they have understood why such was necessary if asked for an opinion, the arrangement would cause them serious consequences in a few years. Beginning in 1837, a few former HBC trappers and their families took up farmsteads near Indian missions' sites in the Walla Walla and Willamette valleys. The joint occupancy treaty of 1818 between the United States and Britain had not addressed the settlement issue. Within a few years, Americans joined these former trapper families as Eastern outsiders in covered wagons. HBC soon realized they needed to import Canadians to these regions to improve their proclaimed rights to portions of the Columbia country. In 1841, Governor Simpson ordered James Sinclair to guide 200 mixed-blood, French-speaking settlers from the Red River colony to the Fort Vancouver area. These people mixed well with the fur men and their families; however, this combined population majority would soon end.

Dr. Elijah White, a missionary physician, completed a census in 1841-1842 of families living near Walla Walla and the Willamette val-

558 McWorter, p. 567.

leys.[559] He enumerated nearly 250 people, noting heads of households; females and children; acres under improvement; bushels of grain; and numbers of horses, cattle, sheep and hogs. Joseph Rivet appears as having 80 acres under improvement and harvesting 400 bushels of wheat in 1841 and 210 bushels of grain in 1842. He also had 50 head of horses, 11 cattle and 45 hogs. The sons of 80-year-old François and wife Teresa Flathead, Joseph and Antoni Rivet, actually farmed their father's land claim.

At the same time, Dr. White conducted the census of settlers in the Willamette; the Valley settlers began holding meetings to discuss organizing a government for the area. Simultaneously, more Americans, former trappers, and upward of 1,000 immigrants traveled the Oregon Trail to arrive in the region in 1843. These new settlers joined the discussions, and in the same year, local residents created the Provisional Government of Oregon. By a slim margin, a "civil community" formed with elected officials, an executive committee of three men, and a supreme judge. Robert "Doc" Newell, Joseph Meek and Osborne Russell were among American trappers mentioned in this text, all three taking part in the provisional government. Meek became the sheriff and collected voluntary taxes from citizens. Robert "Doc" Newell was elected to the provisonal legislature.[560] Russell became the supreme judge by appointment of the executive committee, after the voters' choice declined the position.[561]

The United States and Great Britain had operated in the Columbia drainage since the Anglo-American Treaty of 1818, which called for joint occupancy for a 10-year period. Settlement of the international boundary between the two nations went unresolved during this time frame. A second round of negotiations from 1825-1827 failed to settle the issue. The treaty was renewed; however, an added stipulation required either party intending to abrogate the agreements to give a year's advance notice. Originally, the United States demanded the boundary be located on the 49th parallel, while Great Britain argued for its location in the center of the Columbia River. In 1845, the issue became highly politicized in the United States when some congressional representatives demanded moving the boundary farther north to "54° - 40' or fight." At the end of that year, the U.S. Congress passed a resolution notifying the British of intent to terminate the old agreement. Representatives of both governments met in early 1846 to determine the boundaries of the "Oregon Country." Terms of the final product established the entire Columbia River system south of

559 White, 1842 Oregon Census, National Archives microfilm 607.
560 Jackson, p. 160.
561 Russell, p. ix, preface by editor Aubrey L. Haines.

the 49th parallel as a U.S. Territory and allowed the British government navigation rights for 12 years on the Columbia River. The Inland Salish tribes acquired a new ruler in the deal. Settlement of the boundary issue had little effect on the Salish way of life for several years to come; however, Indians living close to the Oregon Trail, where settlements began springing up, suffered miserably from measles and typhus epidemics brought by American migrants. The United States delayed employment of troops in Oregon Territory until 1849, taking action only after receiving news of the Whitman Massacre.

Whitman's Waiilatpu Mission

Unrest among the Cayuse and other Indians living near the Waiilatpu Mission operated by Dr. Marcus Whitman and his wife, Narcissa, occurred for several reasons. The ever-increasing stream of Willamette Valley-bound settlers passed through or remained in the Indians' homeland, some infected with measles and cholera. These diseases spread rapidly through local Indians, killing two sons of the local chief, of whom Dr. Whitman had unsuccessfully treated. A disgruntled, half-blood, ex-HBC employee living with the Indians tempted Cayuse chiefs to pick up the tomahawk, reinforcing the belief that Whitman had "bad medicine." The whites Whitman treated mostly got well, while many of the sick Indians died. A swarm of Indians attacked the mission of 72 settlers, mission staff and schoolchildren on November 29, 1848, murdering and scalping 13 people, including the Whitmans and most of the men.[562] The Cayuse captured 54 women and children and held them for ransom. HBC Peter Ogden, then a guest in America, immediately sent two large canoes loaded with blankets, shirts, knives, guns, ammunition and other items upriver to Fort Walla Walla to buy the freedom of American prisoners. By the end of December, the Indians had released these prisoners, less five who died of the measles while in captivity. HBC rushed the released to the safety at Fort Walla Walla. It took the U.S. government nearly a year to place military and judicial personnel in Oregon Territory before white men's justice could be served. In December 1847, the provincial legislature of Oregon called for immediate and prompt action by authorizing the raising of 50 volunteer soldiers to go into Cayuse country. A month later, 500 militiamen joined the volunteers and together they marched toward the Whitman's mission.

At Sand Hollow, the Oregon men engaged the Cayuse in battle, pushing the Indians east toward Walla Walla. For the next year and a half,

562 [I.S.] Flora, Stephanie, Manuscript of Flora, Whitman Massacre.

the militiamen worked out of a fort they had built on the Columbia, provoking both friendly and hostile Indians in the region. In 1849, U.S. troops joined the fray, pursuing the Cayuse to the Blue Mountains, and later, north across the Snake River. A restless sort of peace occurred when the hostiles turned over five prominent chiefs most instrumental in the mission murders. A trial conducted by U.S. military officials with a citizen jury found the five men guilty and ordered them hanged. On June 3, 1850, the ex-mountain man Joseph Meek, then U.S. Marshal, carried out the hangings. The harsh military action against the Cayuse and the measles epidemic throughout the Columbia area increased unrest among all the natives. The disease spread to the Spokanes and north to Indians living near Fort Colvile. During the winter of 1847-48, measles and "blood flux" dysentery led to 83 Indian deaths in the fort's vicinity.[563] During the same period, Flathead missionary Mengarini reported 86 people died of smallpox.[564]

Four settlers who had ventured up to the Bitterroot from Fort Hall spread disease among the elderly and young Nez Perces and Flatheads camped near Hell Gate. There is no record of smallpox among Oregon Trail immigrants during that year, so it appears to have been measles or typhoid fever. Whatever the case, when Salish buffalo hunters returned in the spring, they discovered many relatives had died of disease. Father Mengarini learned of the calamity after the fact, as his headquarters was 40 miles from the Indian encampment. Unlike the Cayuse and other Columbia River Indians, the Salish remained peaceful rather than take up arms against the American immigrants and missionaries; however, Spokanes and their neighbors, the Palouse and Sanpoils, considered joining the Cayuse in the war against the Americans but backed off when the Protestant missionary Cushing Eells discouraged them in an all-night council meeting. According to Peter Ogden: "1848 brought 4,000 souls to the Columbia if they have any. ... As traveling companions they carried with them the measles, a killing dysentery and typhus fever."[565] Ogden estimated 1,500 Indians along the Columbia had succumbed to diseases.

The border settlement creating the Oregon Territory in 1846 changed the status of HBC from that of magistrate of territory inhabitants to that of a foreign company. The firm had supplied ransom goods to free American prisoners taken by the Cayuse, but afterward refused to advance credit for needed supplies to Oregon militias. HBC moved its headquarters from Fort Vancouver to Vancouver Island (Victoria, British Columbia), rel-

563 John Lewis Letter to Walker, January 4, 1848.

564 Mengarini, p. 195.

565 Ogden Letter to Paul Kane (artist), March 12, 1848.

egating the old hub to a supply depot and trading post for settlers moving into the area. The treaty allowed British subjects to keep their land claims, subject to becoming American citizens. Former HBC employees, mostly mixed-blood, French-speaking Catholics (Métis) with native wives, had settled the best land in Willamette Valley. According to the non-native U.S. Census, by 1850, more than 13,000 people lived in today's Oregon, of which only 1,144 admitted a foreign birth. Across the Columbia River, 2,749 people resided in the future Washington Territory.[566]

Some Métis had struck off for the California gold fields before the census, while others relocated later to Walla Walla and Salish country. The new, white man-dominated Oregon City (today's Portland) had nothing to offer the young people who had grown up in the wild country of the Northwest. During the next decade, many Métis sold their land claims to the pilgrims and relocated to Spokane, Colville and the Bitterroot Valley. The agreement guaranteed HBC the right to conduct business in Oregon Territory until 1858, subject to that company paying customs duties on all goods brought in from Europe. After the boundary settlement, substantial profit came from supplying emigrants, particularly at Fort Hall, where more than 270,000 people passed on trails bound for California and Oregon. Likewise, Fort Vancouver became the general store for settlers until competing American firms encouraged its closure in 1860. The Salish trading post, Fort Connah, continued to conduct business through 1871, even though the treaty called for earlier closures. HBC Fort Colvile conducted fur trade business and provided a resupply point for settlers and miners along the main trail to Canadian gold discoveries until it closed in 1869.

HBC claimed indemnity from the U.S. government for the loss of 14 fort trading posts because of the boundary treaty. After years of haggling over the value of HBC's property in old Oregon Country, the United States agreed to pay $650,000 in gold bullion, which included $200,000 for the company's agricultural land around Puget Sound.[567] Not surprising, the firm had filed claims for more than they finally received. At a joint meeting of the claims commission in 1865 at Fort Victoria, British Columbia, Duncan McDonald testified on the company's valuation of Fort Hall. A U.S. commissioner asked McDonald what could possibly justify America's payment of a million dollars for the Fort Hall site. The wry fur trader with 25 years of service with HBC said, "To use it as a game preserve."[568]

Back in St Mary's, Father Mengarini and his mission staff had lost

566 Jackson, p. 226. Washington Territory established 1853.
567 WHQ, p. 96. J. Orin Oliphant finalized September 10, 1869.
568 Jackson, p. 268, Report of Claims Commission.

effectiveness among the Flatheads by 1850. In the spring of that year, he traveled to the Willamette Valley in Oregon to present his case for closure of the mission to Supervisor Michael Accolti. Making a hasty decision, Accolti directed Father Joset to proceed to the mission and close it, at least for the time being, "so the Indians might discover the value of missionaries by losing their services."[569]

Father Joset arrived at St. Mary's in October, as the process of shutting down the mission began, and negotiated a conditional sale-lease with a newly arrived independent trader, Major John Owen.[570] Improvements on the site sold November 9, 1850, to the major for $300, with a provision they revert to the missionaries if so requested in a three-year period. In late November, Father Joset and Brother Claessons loaded four wagons and three carts with St. Mary's effects and began the journey to the Kalispel mission, St. Ignatius, on the shores of the Pend Oreille River. Thirty lodges of the most devout Flatheads and Pend Oreilles accompanied the Jesuits to the joining of the Flathead and Jocko rivers, where all set up their winter camp together.

In the spring, during high water, the missionaries launched rafts they had built during the winter to continue on to the Kalispels. Unknowledgeable of rapids and rocks on a raging river, Joset, Claessons and Indian helpers loaded the crude craft. By the time they reached Thompson Falls, all cargo had been lost and the rafts lay wrecked among the rocks. Alone, the two Jesuits found their way to the mission.[571] The missionaries' plan to introduce and ease the Flatheads into white men's culture failed miserably, both from lack of the Jesuit order's financial backing and moreso due to missionaries encouraging the Indians to abandon habits and their traditional way of life. The priests certainly demonstrated the most appropriate way to incorporate the white man's sense of civilization in building permanent houses, raising crops and animals for food, and constructing gristmills and sawmills, but very few Flatheads embraced that way of life. Spiritual education and Catholic practices taught by the missionaries remained intact with many Flatheads and Pend Oreilles who practiced Christianity, while others reverted to the "Great Spirit" in their beliefs, or a combination of the two. These free, pious and friendly peoples would remain faithful to their ancient, nomadic lifestyle until the end of untamed buffalo.

569 Davis, p. 66.

570 Ibid. Major John Owen Journals & Letters provides Salish information; he withdrew as a permitted trader to serve the new military post along the Oregon Trail at Fort Hall and guided a two-wheeled wagon full of trade goods north to the Bitterroots in 1850. How he got the handle "Major" is unknown.

571 Davis, p. 67.

8

Treaty Making
1850-1856

Until the time of the 1846 Boundary Settlement, the Inland Salish tribes ruled their home territory, carved out centuries ago from what Americans vaguely termed Oregon Country. Fur traders who lived and worked in native territories did not interfere in their affairs or culture, which, along with the introduction of European trade goods, created a favorable impression of white man among the natives. Not far behind flowed a disturbing influx of emigrants from the East, dragging wagons and possessions and trailing livestock. Almost in tandem came white leaders, political and military, eager to explore the country for development of white settlements and to deal with the mix of unruly native tribes.

The American leaders dispatched a survey party, led by a newly appointed governor, to examine a potential railroad route from the Mississippi River to the Pacific Ocean and a military road from the coast to the Missouri River. During his trek to the West, Governor Isaac Stevens and his staff met with Indian tribes along the way, listening to problems and explaining why they had come. Treaty negotiations with most tribes from the Pacific Coast to the Missouri River led to the initiation of reservations, a concept neither comprehended nor wanted. The naturally free, simple-lifestyled natives tried to adjust to boundaries being set on traditional hunting and gathering grounds. The denial of treaties to some of the tribes on the Columbia Plateau was one feature that contributed to unrest and war. The survey of the railroad and military road involved major travel routes throughout the entire Inland Salish realm, during which the natives found the majority of the reconnoitering personnel aloof and far less friendly than were the fur men before them. Taking major changes in stride, the Salish continued to hunt and gather as if their lifestyle would continue forever, without knowing just how much change the white man's culture would demand.

Provisional purchase of the St. Mary's Mission site by Major John Owen in 1850 provided the Flatheads with a good neighbor and trader. In the summer of that year, the ex-merchant, serving a U.S. Rifle Regiment operating out of Fort Hall on the Oregon Trail, went to the Bitterroot Valley.[572] Over time, as its trader, Owen transformed the mission site into a productive farm while building the adobe-walled "Fort Owen" with a residence, storage building and livestock pens, all within the enclosure. The Flatheads esteemed and trusted Owen, who not only provided them with a nearby trading outlet, but also opened his compound to them for root and meat storage. The Salish, when first meeting him, called him *I-mool-tzen* because his facial hair resembled a bison drinking cup each Indian carried strapped over his shoulder.[573]

After Owen had the fort wall covered with adobe (a mixture of clay, water and grass), the place became known as Sumeh-tah-oo, or "house of dirt." By adding a herd of cattle, hogs and fowl, he gradually expanded agricultural operations. Like the Black Robes before him, he attempted to alter Indians' way of life by turning theirs into a settled life tending fields and livestock, but he met with limited success. Owen's diaries and letters describe Salish activities from 1851 to 1867.

Leadership of the Salish buffalo hunting elements during the period fell on the shoulders of either Flathead Chief Victor or Pend Oreille Chief Alexander. Participants from neighboring Kalispel, Spokane, Coeur d'Alene and Kootenai tribes accompanied one of the chiefs, who late in the period, conducted hunts to different areas. Flatheads and Nez Perces penetrated farther each year into Crow and Blackfeet territory, thus escalating hostility and resulting casualties. Victor's second-in-command, Moise, whose sturdy, independent and outspoken nature contrasted his leader's quiet courage and sincerity, blended in a leadership team necessary to the hostile hunting environment. Victor's strong Christian ideals had prompted him to abandon the tribal cultural practice of using the whip as an instrument of maintaining discipline among his people. As a result, he lost respect among some members of the tribe.[574]

Alexander (Tum-cle-hot-cut se) No Horses united the various bands of upper Pend Oreilles in 1848 by his election as head chief. Under his leadership the tribe, their Kootenai allies and the Kalispels returned to their once traditional hunting grounds above the Missouri River. Some Piegan bands tolerated their return, while others reacted violently by murdering and stealing horses. However, with many well-armed warriors, the

572 It is unknown how John Owen obtained the title of "Major," for he did not hold a military rank. He came to the Bitterroot with his Snake Indian wife, Nancy, and brother Frank.

573 Dunbar. Owen, p. 11.

574 Bigart and Woodcock, p. 61.

allied force stood up well until the 1860s and beyond.

Unbeknown to the Salish leaders and allies, the first government agreement made with Western Indians, known as the Laramie Treaty, initiated territorial boundaries unfavorable to buffalo hunters. In the summer of 1851, some 10,000 Plains Indians assembled at Fort Laramie to hear the words of the American government. The government desired to delineate territories of rival tribes with the purpose of securing the Oregon Trail by inhibiting roaming Indians. Tribes west of the Continental Divide were not invited. Superintendent of Indian Affairs David Mitchell, who arranged the council, sent word to AFC Alexander Culbertson at Fort Union to select delegates from the upper Missouri tribes. The message arrived too late for him to contact representatives from the Blackfeet and Gros Ventre tribes.

The Laramie Treaty became history when three old, white friends of the Blackfeet – Mitchel, Culbertson and Father Pierre-Jean De Smet – defined that nation's territory. Neither the Blackfeet nor the Salish learned of that agreement, and if they had, it would not have changed their adversarial relationship one bit. Father De Smet sketched a map designating Blackfeet lands as east of the Continental Divide from Canada to the upper Missouri. Consequently, the Laramie Treaty fixed traditional Salish-allied hunting grounds from the Big Hole east to Three Forks as Blackfeet territory, which legitimized their claim to the land and resources therein. However, four years later, boundaries established at Laramie became an issue for the Salish and other Western tribes at the Blackfeet Treaty session.

One of the several Métis who participated in the California gold rush, François Benetsie Finlay, returned to Salish Country in 1851, bringing horses to the Gold Creek tributary of the upper Clark Fork River where he set up shop as a small-time trader. One day he decided to work the gravel bar behind his lodge, which produced a small amount of gold. After accumulating about a teaspoonful of the precious metal, he rode off to Fort Connah to show Angus McDonald his find. The trader advised Finlay that, as a British citizen, he could not prove a claim and had better keep his find and its location quiet.[575] Apparently, both men kept lips sealed, for it took a decade before others made a discovery there. Finlay, one of the growing numbers of minor traders, stayed with the business but continued to search for gold throughout the region.

The primary trading outlets in upper Pend Oreille and Flathead

575 Jackson, Children, p. 254. Benetsie Finlay, son of Jaco, participated in several HBC trapping brigades.

country, Forts Connah and Owen, supplied the Indians' needs for European goods. Fort Connah dealt primarily with the Pend Oreille, Kootenai and Métis free trappers that camped near the post. Besides dealing in furs, buffalo parts and meat that commanded a good value, HBC did not aggressively trade for buffalo robes, as the market in Great Britain never reached the proportions it did in America.

In early 1852, Angus McDonald moved to Fort Colvile as chief trader, a position he held until the fort's closure in 1869. Michael Ogden, half-blood son of Peter Skene Ogden and Julia, assumed the head trader's position at Fort Connah and served until 1861. Salish family ties through his marriage to a Pend Oreille woman, and his longtime interaction with Métis free trappers and the Indians, enhanced his success as a trader. Trader John Owen's fort was located 35 miles south of the Flathead main encampment near Hell Gate and dealt primarily with the Flatheads, plus a few trappers and white men who drifted into the country from the Oregon Trail or elsewhere.

Ogden and Owen, though competitors, exchanged frequent visits in a friendly relationship. After 1853, Fort Owen became a place for white men and their Indian wives to congregate when trading labor for supplies, and at the end of three years of operation, five mixed-blood families had settled near the fort. In Owen's second year, Blackfeet raiders broke into the fort and stole four horses. Apparently, the Flatheads, with their large horse herd, were off hunting and made slim pickings for horse thieves.

Three days after the heist, the Blackfeet brutally murdered and scalped a young white man named Dodson, who had been putting up hay within sight of the fort.[576] That event, along with poor returns in the first half of 1853, induced John Owen, his staff and his brother Frank to vacate the fort for safer, more prosperous opportunities along the way to Fort Vancouver. By chance, Owen met up with Lieutenant Rufus Saxton and 18 soldiers leading a long packtrain of supplies near the Spokane River crossing. Saxton carried orders to deliver the goods to the Bitterroot Valley, where he would rendezvous with the Washington Territorial Governor Isaac Ingalls Stevens' railroad survey crew.

The Owen brothers quickly revamped plans, realizing the likely economic boost the Pacific Railroad Survey would bring to the Bitterroot Valley, so Frank Owen accompanied the soldiers back to the abandoned fort, while John continued on to Walla Walla with his crew to obtain supplies for the trading post. The soldiers and Frank traveled north to

576 [I.S.] First Roots, p. 88.

Seneacquoteen portage on the Pend Oreille River, where an HBC canoe facilitated movement of supplies to the opposite bank and the Salish Road to the Buffalo. Trailing east on August 12, 1853, they met 100 Kalispels on their way home with 300 horses and many loads of dried meat and robes.

It was Lieutenant Saxton's first meeting with a large group of Salish. He commented in his report, "They were perfectly civil and seemed to feel proud, rich and independent."[577] Continuing on to the mouth of the Clark Fork River, the lieutenant met HBC Duncan McDonald and Michael Ogden, who said they would find no grass for the next five-day journey as the Indians had torched the countryside. The green lieutenant thought the fires were started "to retard their progress," not realizing the Indians burned heavily timbered areas periodically to encourage regrowth of the brush needed for game feed. The troops and Owen broke into the fire at Trout Creek, where they endured smoke, hot ashes and flames at intervals along the trail to Thompson Falls.[578]

The newly appointed Governor Stevens, an ex-military officer and civil engineer, managed hefty responsibilities that included exploring the northern transcontinental railroad route, serving as superintendent of Indian affairs, and organizing the government of the newly formed Washington Territory. The extensive assignment involved a massive amount of land that encompassed the present state of Washington, northern Idaho and western Montana. From the Cascade Mountain range east, inhabitants were nearly all natives with whom treaties would become necessary before construction of a railroad might actually happen. Governor Stevens began that process by holding council meetings with various tribes during his journey across the plains to the Pacific Coast. The "war-like" Blackfeet nation presented a particular problem for the government, as they had continued unofficial war against the Americans since the Lewis and Clark expedition had passed through the area.

Isaac Stevens' party arrived at Fort Union, near the mouth of the Yellowstone River, on August 1, 1853, after exploring a potential railroad route west from St. Paul, Minnesota. The AFC chief trader Alexander Culbertson and his native wife greeted the governor, who soon realized Culbertson could be of great assistance in brokering peace with the Blackfeet. Not only was he a knowledgeable Indian trader, he knew how to obtain the Indian interest by providing gifts and tobacco to Blackfeet chiefs, which he provided along with a message from Governor Stevens asking for a general

577 Lieutenant Saxon Report, pp. 257-258.

578 Ibid.

council meeting at Fort Benton.

It took nearly eight weeks to connive and confirm a council of some 30 Blackfeet chiefs who would attend. Culbertson's Blood Indian wife, Medicine Snake Woman, insisted on accompanying him to the meeting. According to 1854 reports of the commissioner of Indian Affairs, she told Stevens: "My people are good people, but they are jealous and vindictive. I am afraid they and the whites will not understand each other, but if I go, I may be able to explain things to them and soothe them if they should be irritated. I know there is great danger."[579] The council with the Blackfeet came off without incident, likely due to Medicine Snake Woman's participation; however, Stevens made slow progress in his peace-treaty makings.

Stevens dispatched Lieutenant John Mullan from Fort Benton on September 14 to locate the Salish buffalo hunters and arrange a council meeting with their chiefs in the Bitterroot Valley. Expecting to find the Indian camp on the Musselshell, Mullan and two men, guided by the Piegan White Crane, found only a deserted campsite and a clear trail leading south. Leaving all but two of his men behind, the lieutenant and Piegan guide tracked them some 70 miles southeast into the Yellowstone drainage where they found the encampment of 150 lodges of Pend Oreille, Flatheads and Nez Perces. After a friendly reception, Mullan met with the chiefs, who, to his astonishment, offered prayers before taking up business.[580] Victor consented to send four of his principal men with the lieutenant to his waiting men, then all would depart for the Bitterroot Valley. The Piegan guide deserted on reaching the Musselshell, but the Salish knew the way home.

Governor Stevens met with the four Salish and one Nez Perce chiefs, all delegates at Fort Owen on September 30 and October 1, 1853, all of the "old sages" mentioned in his report.[581] After referring to himself as a representative of the "Great Father" (president of the United States), Stevens explained the government's objective of making peace among all natives and white people, with rights to jointly use Indians' lands.

The Salish people were more concerned with murders and horse stealing committed by the Blackfeet than with the ability to provide for themselves. The chiefs pointed out six or seven orphan boys whose fathers the Blackfeet had killed within the last three years. Stevens responded that Blackfeet chiefs desired peace but had little control over their young men who committed the acts. He added that he believed all their (Blackfeet)

579 Ewers, p. 209, Annual report of the Commissioner of Indian Affairs, 1854.

580 Railroad Route Survey Report, p. 124.

581 Ibid. Survey Report, p. 126.

chiefs and principal men would control their young men if necessary.[582] At least one Flathead chief could not relate to the control issue, explaining that when one of their people does wrong, "We talk to them and they mind what we say." The council ended with Stevens proposing a conference at Fort Benton the following year to establish peace among the Blackfeet and their neighboring tribes, an event that failed to occur.

Two years later, at a briefing before the Hell Gate Treaty Council, Victor harshly informed the governor, "The Blackfeet have troubled us very much."

Stevens replied, "I have heard of your troubles before and have done all I can to get this matter arranged in time."

Victor persisted: "I am going to tell what happened since you were here. Twelve men have been killed when out hunting – not on war parties. I fear[ed] the whites and kept quiet. I cannot tell how many horses have been stolen since. Now I listen and hear what you wish me to do. Were it not for you I would have had my revenge ere this [by now]. They [Blackfeet] have stolen horses seven times this spring."[583] After the exchange, the Hell Gate Treaty Council convened.

Stevens departed for his post at Olympia, Washington, in early October 1853 and left Lieutenant John Mullan in charge of the railroad survey group and 10 soldiers. Mullan selected for his camp a meadow 10 miles south of Fort Owen and named it Cantonment Stevens. The soldiers constructed four, crude log structures for winter quarters – one for storage, two for housing and a corral for horses. Among the soldiers, Gustavus Sohon put his linguistic skills to developing a Salish word and phrase list. During the survey and later road construction years, he also sketched many pictures of events and Indian chiefs. Lieutenant Mullan spent the winter gathering data on the geography of the country between the Bitterroot Valley and AFC Fort Benton on the Missouri River. Much of his information came from the mixed-blood Gabriel Prudhomme, who had traveled with and interpreted for the Jesuits.

On March 1, 1854, Mullan, Prudhomme and crew left their camp for Fort Benton, following the well-beaten Salish trail up the Clark Fork River where they turned northeast up the Little Blackfoot River. Crossing the Continental Divide at a place later called Mullan Pass, the surveyors descended to Little Prickly Pear Creek, then north, where they picked up Indian roads that led to the fort.

582 Ibid.

583 Bigart and Woodstock, pp. 22-23.

At Fort Benton, they outfitted two-wheeled, horse-drawn carts for the return trip to the Bitterroot Valley then retraced their route, arriving there after 14 days' travel.[584] The Mullan road soon became a portion of a military road later named after him, from Walla Walla to Fort Benton and eventually following the Northern Pacific Railroad route. Because of this preliminary survey, Congress made its first appropriation of $30,000 for construction of the road. Iroquois Aeneas (or young Ignace Lamoose) told Mullan of a potential route from the Bitterroot Valley west over the Coeur d'Alene Mountains to Spokane Valley, and he helped locate a portion of the road nearly to the divide. Major Owen's trading business flourished because of the survey team's close proximity; he was no longer entirely dependent on Indian and trapper trade items, as Mullan associates paid in American dollars.

St. Ignatius Mission

At the same time Lieutenant Mullan explored the potential Fort Benton route, another member of the railroad team, Army surgeon Dr. George Stuckley and two men launched a canoe at the mouth of the Jocko River. Their task was to examine the navigability of the river system to Fort Vancouver on the Columbia River and report on native inhabitants along the waterways. His first contact with Indians came on the wet, snowy day of November 7, 1853, when Stuckley paddled ashore a few miles above the Marshal Lake outlet below today's Newport, Washington. The cold and wet men planned to set up camp with a family group of Kalispels under the patriarch Chief All-ol-sturg. The old man invited them into his mat-covered lodge and fed them dried camas roots, berries and raw tallow. However, before eating the scant meal, the chief rang a little bell that, directly, filled the lodge with others from the small encampment. Immediately everyone fell to their knees and chanted a long prayer in their language to the Creator. A few pious sentences and a hymn closed the exercise, and then the men could eat. Father Hoecken of the St. Ignatius Mission, seven miles downriver, was their teacher.[585] The next morning after a breakfast of dried fish and berries, the men bid farewell and paddled to the mission where they stayed two days, gathering information on the Kalispels.

Father Hoecken graciously greeted the surveyor Stuckley and his party, gave them a sleeping room, provided meals, and answered questions regarding the Kalispels. Stuckley marveled at the accomplishments of the

584 [I.S.] Mullan Report.

585 Stuckley Report, p. 294, U.S. Railroad Survey.

Jesuits, both with the people's progress in learning Christianity and the mission complex itself. The site included 16 buildings constructed from squared logs sawed by a hand-turned mill that also converted to a gristmill, and the large church that held the entire tribe of some 420 people. Other buildings included residences, a blacksmith-carpenter shop operated by Brother Francis (a true jack-of-all-trades), and sheds for the variety of livestock. Implements, tools, seeds and clothing came directly from Europe to Fort Vancouver then up the Columbia to Kettle Falls for pickup. The brothers fashioned a grindstone from native stone that the Indians powered by hand, which processed three bushels of wheat a day for flour to make bread. The self-sufficient mission produced soap and candles made with livestock by-products and vinegar from apples grown in their orchard, all cared for on their 160-acre farm managed by Brother Mageau.

Each Indian interested in farming had a parcel of land allocated to him, but the success of such enterprise varied each year depending on climate conditions and river water levels. Stuckley learned that only 2 acres of rich, deep soil in a drained swamp consistently produced good crops, while soil on higher ground had a mere 2-inch mantle of good dirt overlaying blue clay that, after a few years of cultivation, quit producing. A huge problem arose due to annual flooding of farmland that did not subside until July in some years, too late for planting most any crop.

The missionaries had wanted to move to the Spokane Valley or upriver to Horse Prairie for several years, but the Kalispels were unwilling to go. They said: "This is our country; here are the graves of our forefathers; here we were born, and here we wish to die. We do not want to leave our country, poor as it is."[586]

Out of necessity, the Kalispels hunted, fished and gathered over a hundred-square-mile area from the mission site, east to upper Lake Pend Oreille and west to Kettle Falls. Many traveled exclusively in sturgeon-nosed, cedar-framed canoes covered with white pine bark to fishing and gathering places along waterways. The Clark Fork River delta, where the northernmost, shallow channel flowed rapidly into Lake Pend Oreille, provided annual fish for a small portion of the tribe. Indians camped nearby and constructed a fence across the channel that guided fish into a weir or rack that captured many. A larger number of Kalispels trailed on horses to Kettle Falls to spear salmon in late summer. Camas roots were dug in early summer by women and prepared for winter use across the river from the mission site. In autumn, most Kalispels hunted and dried the meat of deer

586 Stuckley Report, pp. 295-298, U.S. Government Railroad Survey.

and bear for winter use, while others cut rushes the Indians called "flags" for mats used to cover lodges. Mat preparation involved laying the cut material parallel and threading the rushes together at the ends before rolling the mats in cylindrical bundles for easy transportation on horses or in canoes.

In conversation with Stuckley, Father Hoecken told how he taught the Kalispels his understanding of the Creator and the meaning of the word *soul*, a word that did not exist in their language. After hearing the Christian definition of *Creator* and *Savior*, the Kalispels came up with their own word that translated in English as "the man who made himself." In adding the new word soul to the Indian's vocabulary, Hoecken, through a translator, further explained that each of them had a "gut that never rotted" and this was their living principle or soul. Prior to Christian instruction, the Kalispels considered themselves as animals close to beavers but greater, because they said, "The beaver builds a house like us, and he is very cunning, true, but we catch the beaver, and he cannot catch us; therefore, we are greater than he."[587]

Troubled by winter food shortages and flooding, the Kalispels and missionaries began talking about moving the St. Ignatius Mission to a more suitable farming country. Before his death, old Head Chief Standing Grizzly Bear (Loyola) told the missionaries, "God gave them their land; they ought to keep it,"[588] but the great chief would not see another growing season.

Soon after Loyola's death in April 1854 and the election of a new head chief, Victor (Pitol), the Jesuits decided to move their mission 190 miles east to the Upper Pend Oreille country at today's St. Ignatius, Montana. Upper Pend Oreille Chief Alexander had shown the missionaries the site of a tribal meeting place several miles distant from any regular campsite.

In September 1854, Father Hoecken arrived and found "a beautiful region, evidently fertile, a variety of woods and prairies, lakes and rivers"[589] six miles from Fort Connah and two days from the main Flathead encampment near Hell Gate. Indeed, the more centrally situated mission would now better serve the majority of Salish and the neighboring Kootenai tribe. Many of the Kalispels moved to the new St. Ignatius location and set up their lodges around the mission site. The buffalo hunters were now four days closer to their prey.

The Jesuits, with the Indians' help and design advice from Lieutenant John Mullan, went to work making improvements on the site. Construction of a chapel, two houses, and carpenter and blacksmith shops

587 Stuckley Report, p. 297.

588 [I.S.] Ellersick Manuscript.

589 [I.S.] Chittenden & Richardson, Hoecken Letter, October 18, 1855.

began immediately, in order for all to be finished and ready for use by mid-winter. By spring, the Indians had cut and placed 18,000 rails around land designated for crops. Around Easter time, the mission had the appearance of a large village with more than 1,000 Indians that included the Kootenais, upper and lower bands of Pend Oreilles, and Flatheads.[590]

At the new St. Ignatius, the Lower Pend Oreilles (Kalispels) felt a growing disappointment with mission conditions and began returning home in the following year. Head Chief Victor (Pitol) and several others had property at the mission by 1857 but refused to move there on a permanent basis. Jesuits emphasized taking up farming and ranching, which concerned most of the tribe whose old home territory had better fishing resources acessed by canoes rather than by horseback. They desired the Christian God to strengthen their lives as Indians, not to become like the whites.[591] Within two years, only a dozen very poor Kalispels remained near the mission after the move.[592] Even a group of buffalo hunters led by Michael had moved back to make their winter quarters on the Hope Peninsula on Lake Pend Oreille,[593] having found a more peaceful setting there than the congested new mission site.

In the process of organizing the Hell Gate Treaty Council meeting in 1855, Dr. Richard Landsdale, frontman for Governor Isaac Stevens, wrote that the Kalispels were too "poor in horses and having frail bark canoes only, and compelled to hunt and fish for subsistence the tribe was unable to reach the mission"[594] to attend the treaty session. Plainly, the Kalispels graciously declined the treaty council invitation because they did not want to move from their homeland. After their return home, life for the Kalispels went well until the Northern Pacific Railroad began construction through the eastern section of their lands in 1883.

Some Kalispel family groups wintered miles apart from the main concentration at the mission, on and above upper Lake Pend Oreille along the Clark Fork River. While reconnoitering the railroad route from Hell Gate to the Spokane Valley in February 1854, Lieutenant Mullan and his crew met several wintering groups of Kalispels along the route and noticed evidence of old camp sites. About eight miles below Thompson Falls, he passed five low, poorly built mat lodges occupied by old men, women, naked children and yelping dogs that he termed "the most desti-

590 Ibid.
591 [I.S.] Ellersick Manuscript.
592 [I.S.] Chittenden & Richardson, Hoecken Letter, April 15, 1857.
593 Fahey, Kalispel, p. 36.
594 Ibid.

tute, squalid, miserable looking human beings I think I ever saw."[595] Those poor Indians sold Mullan 20 pounds of venison – all they could spare – for powder and balls.

Continuing downriver the next day, the Mullan-surveying outfit found an abandoned village site below Deep Creek, Montana, as evidenced by skeletons of their lodges still standing. The old camp held a mud structure 6 feet long by 3 feet wide with an arched top and a lining of white pine boughs inside. Mullan thought it a "dormitory for some bachelor Indian," but it likely was a sweat lodge used by Indians. From there on, snow depth reached up to 2 feet of crusted snow. The horses broke through the crust repeatedly, cutting their legs and causing them to collapse – noses on the crust, breathing hard. The poor animals had nothing to eat for two days, which added to their exhaustion. The men continued on foot to Swamp Creek, struggling, encouraging their horses not to give up, until reaching a camp of 11 mat lodges, whose inhabitants were "cleaner and better clad" than the upriver people, according to Mullan. Near Swamp Creek camp, the men felled cottonwood trees to feed branch tips to the horses.

The next day, after purchasing venison, the party abandoned the undefined, snow-bound trail to pick their way along the shore of the Clark Fork River. A few miles from their previous camp, they came on another old Kalispel camp where a four-pole scaffolding with a platform 8-feet high held the poorly wrapped body of an Indian. Nearby, they discovered a log cabin 7 feet long by 4 feet wide and 4 feet high that appeared to Mullan as a chapel used by the Indians. The explorers continued on another two days along the riverbank, sometimes trailing on shoreline ice through the broad valley of the river, until reaching Clark Fork, Idaho, where they put up a day in less snow with sufficient grass for the horses and mules to eat and rest.

A Kalispel man clad in an old, worn buffalo robe visited the camp the next morning to smoke and eat, but he quickly learned that those white American men differed from the fur men. After receiving a cold welcome and no smoke, he watched Mullan skin a pine marten. When he started to throw the carcass away, the Kalispel asked if he could have it to eat. After roasting and eating the meat, he hung around camp until the surveyors started dinner, and when not invited to join them, he stalked off with a "great show of offended dignity." His band of likely buffalo hunters were wintering on the Hope Peninsula about four miles from the surveyors' camp, where horses could find grass on southern exposures.[596] The Kalispel

595 [I.S.] Mullan Report, p. 507. U.S. Government Railroad survey.

596 [I.S.] Mullan Report, pp. 508-509.

people Mullan found upriver from this camp undoubtedly had traveled by canoe and made a living on deer forced down to the valley due to deep snows on the mountains. The Mullan survey party continued on to Sandpoint and crossed the Pend Oreille River at Laclede without passing any more native camps. The surveyors continued through the Spokane Valley exploring the railroad route to Puget Sound.

That fall, the Spokane and Coeur d'Alene tribes experienced firsthand white settlers traveling through their country, a preview of what would follow in just two years when the rush to gold fields in Canada began. John V. Campbell's memoirs provide information on the Spokane and Colville valley's inhabitants in 1854-1855.[597] Campbell and 64 other white folks, recruited by HBC to settle in the Willamette Valley of Oregon, had trailed fully loaded, two-wheeled carts from the Red River area of Canada and arrived, exhausted, at Spokane Prairie. Much to their surprise, Frank Owen (John's brother), and a man named Gibson had set up camp along with six other, white hired hands to winter 500 head of cattle on the prairie right in between two large Indian encampments. The settlers, overjoyed to rest and converse with English-speaking people, stayed a week at Owen's camp before moving on to Walla Walla. Campbell and another man remained behind to winter their fatigued and footsore livestock on the prairie eight miles upriver from Owen's location where they built a log cabin. One can only imagine the Indians' reaction to this invasion by whites and their herds of animals denuding the countryside of grass needed by the wintering Indians' sizeable horse herds.

The mixed-blood Antoine Plante and his Pend Oreille wife named Mary had settled at a ford on the Spokane River in 1852 (Trent) where he built a ferry crossing in anticipation of wagon traffic from settlers and miners. Downriver three miles from his place, a large band of Spokanes led by Chief Garry and Big Star maintained an annual winter camp. The cattlemen had centered their operation on the north bank of the river on today's Idaho-Washington state line. A few miles above there, near Post Falls, the majority of the Coeur d'Alene tribe under Chief Stellam made their winter quarters. The white men must have made peace with the natives, for in the spring Campbell went to Fort Colvile by himself along Indian trails to obtain supplies. Along the way, he observed up to 30 Métis families operating farms adjacent to the mid-Colville River valley down to the Meyers Falls flour mill. All but two of the Métis men, with native wives, were past

597 WHQ, Campbell, pp. 194-201. William S. Lewis prepared Campbell's Manuscript from his Letters & Memoirs. HBC's James Sinclair led the second group, 1854 emigration party to Oregon.

HBC employees, including three of Jaco Finlay's sons. Fort Colvile had all the trappings of a small town located next to a large farming operation with several buildings for employees and storage structures nestled near the walled trading post. At the nearby Kettle Falls, a large encampment of Colville Indians had a tent village. Campbell returned to his stock and partners, then continued on to Walla Walla, herding the refurbished animals. Possibly the rent for Owen's and Campbell's pasturage was cattle to augment or start a herd, for a few years later the Coeur d'Alenes, in particular, had a sizeable number of cattle.

Back in the Bitterroot Valley, seven bold Blackfeet raiders snowshoed into the valley in late winter and built a fort not far from Hell Gate, where they could watch the main trail near the river ford for potential victims. During their vigil, they killed two stray cows in the valley, butchered them and took them back to camp for drying. The right opportunity for a raid arose on April 12, 1854, when trader Caleb Irvin and some Pend Oreilles arrived at the ford with 50 horses en route to Fort Hall to trade along the emigrant trail. The raiders jumped the unsuspecting bunch and, without a fight, robbed them of all their horses and personal belongings, forcing Irvin and his Indians to wait for help. Leaving behind their snowshoes, the Blackfeet promptly exited the scene with dried meat in newly acquired saddle packs and a leader destined for chiefdom when they arrived home. Fortunately, Lieutenant Mullan and his survey crew came by three days later to transport the victims across the river to a Flathead camp. Seventeen Flatheads and Pend Oreilles took pursuit a few days later but did not catch up with the "hell-hounds," as Mullan called them.[598]

The U.S. government directed the Washington Territorial Governor Isaac Stevens to form a treaty commission to negotiate with the various tribes in that territory. The huge influx of white settlers in the western half of the territory had prompted such action. One of the commission's goals was to "concentrate the Indians upon a few reservations and encourage them to cultivate the soil and adopt settled and civilized habits."[599] In late May 1855, the process dropped like a hammer on Salish allies, the Nez Perce, when 35 mediators met with upward of 1,000 Nez Perce people on a knoll near Walla Walla, Washington. The large body of anxious Nez Perces waited three days for the reluctant Yakama, Cayuse and Palouse tribes to arrive.

Finally, with all tribes present, the council got under way with the governor and other commission members laying out their objectives. Three

598 [I.S.] Mullan Report, pp. 516-517. U.S. Government Railroad Survey. Caleb Irvin, ex-military officer, a close associate of John Owen who moved to the valley in 1851.

599 Stevens, Hazard, vol. 1. He attended the conference with his father, Isaac.

reservations were designated: a large area in the Lapwai area in Idaho for the Nez Perces; a smaller one for the Cayuse and Umatilla tribes around Walla Walla; and another on the Yakima River for the Yakama tribe. The commission expounded benefits Indians would receive for giving up much of their traditional hunting and gathering lands. Such things as mills, schools, livestock and assorted goods sounded good to the Nez Perces.

Walla Walla Treaty

An aggressive bargaining session took place on the second day in which reservation boundaries commanded the discussions. The Nez Perces took a more active part in the session than did the Yakamas and Palouses, who listened with a skeptical ear. Nez Perce Chief Lawyer of the Kooskia band assumed a leading role in the negotiations by proposing an amendment to the treaty, which required the government to keep white men from encroaching upon the reservation. Governor Stevens assured Lawyer with a sincere-sounding and poker-faced verbal commitment to that effect; however, within five years, gold discoveries on their reserved lands brought many unwanted white trespassers to their promised land.

On June 8, 12 days after the council began, three elderly Nez Perce chiefs arrived at the gathering after a long ride from the buffalo grounds over the snow-covered Coeur d'Alene Mountains.[600] Chiefs Looking Glass Sr., Cloud Piler and Yellow Bird had just returned from spending three years on the upper Missouri and Yellowstone plains. When learning of the boundaries agreed to in his absence, Looking Glass Sr. became furious: "My people, what have you done? While I was gone, you sold my country."[601]

Over the next few days, Governor Stevens made some compromises that satisfied most of the Nez Perces, and Looking Glass Sr. signed the treaty. Only Cloud Piler refused, as he and his Snake River Band lost their home territory in the deal. The rest fixed their X on the treaty. The Walla Walla Treaty session that Nez Perce historian L.V. McWhorter labeled "the War Creating Council" broke up in mid-June, and the treaty commissioners gathered up their things and went east to meet with the Flatheads, Pend Oreilles and Kootenais in the Bitterroot Valley.

The treaty agreed to by chiefs of the Yakama, Cayuse, Umatilla and Walla Walla tribes lasted just four months. Chief Kamiakin (Yakama) boiled over and led 300 allies in an attack against U.S. troops near today's

600 Doty, pp. 19-20.
601 Josephy, p. 328.

Yakima, Washington. Having lost nearly 6 million acres of hunting and gathering lands, and the white man's deliberate trespass on new lands, caused the revolt. After a pitched battle with U.S. troops, the allied natives led by Kamiakin fled with their families across the Columbia River into Palouse and Spokane territory.

Hell Gate Treaty

The Hell Gate Council got under way July 7, 1855, at Council Grove about six miles west of Missoula on the north bank of the Clark Fork River. Some 500 Flathead, Pend Oreille and Kootenai people folded their arms and legs and sat on the ground in a semicircle around the treaty commission table as Governor Stevens presented opening remarks through interpreters. About a thousand eyes fixed on the white chief as he began to explain his version of establishing peace between all tribes and land cession. Early in his opening remarks, the governor proposed a reservation that would include all three nations so Indians "could live on one tract of land – large enough for your cattle and farms; the climate of that tract to be mild enough for your animals to graze in winter."[602] Furthermore, he said the U.S. government would purchase the remainder of their land and make "certain payments" through an agent who would live with them. Payment for ceded land provided for schools, blacksmiths, farmers, wheelwrights, saw and gristmills, and the governor promised the Indians would be safe on the reservation from attacks by the Blackfeet. Stevens added, you "will govern yourselves according to your laws, but will respect the white man's laws as they will respect yours." He continued, "The first year a large amount of clothing, of cooking utensils and everything to start your farms and you will have an addition of the same things every year for 20 years." He then asked, "Will such a treaty suit you?" and concluded by asking for comments from the head chiefs.

The first to speak, Flathead Chief Victor suggested two possibilities for a single reservation, one on the Bitterroot near Hell Gate and the other "yonder" in the Flathead Valley, but wanted to think about it and withheld further comment for the time being. When it came Pend Oreille Chief Alexander's turn, he offered thoughts on those portions of the governor's speech that dealt specifically with white man's laws but hedged an opinion of a location for a specific reservation site. Red Wolf, living with the Flatheads, a son of a Flathead mother and Kootenai father, pointed out the need for two

---

602 PNQ, vol. 29 no. 3, Patroll, Albert J., pp. 283-321. The Flathead Indian Treaty Council of 1855. Proceedings of Hell Gate Treaty that follow are part of this publication. Patrol got his information from the original source: U. S. National Archives microfilm.

separate reservations, but he, too, would have to think about it. The council continued at 2 p.m. on the second day, with Governor Stevens asking the assembled what they thought about a single reservation for all three tribes.

Two Kalispel men in their traditional sturgeon-nosed bark canoe, photographed circa 1906. The man in front is believed to be John BigSmoke, who was the last formal Kalispel chief.
COURTESY OF SPOKANE PUBLIC LIBRARY, NORTHWEST ROOM

Pend Oreille War Chief Big Canoe began a long and penetrating speech by asking why there had to be a treaty, as the tribes had always been friendly with the whites. He held that all the country spoken of belonged to the Indians, and the whites, as their friends, could use it. Big Canoe and other Indians believed treaties were intended to resolve disturbances, battles and injury, or in this case, to form an alliance with the U.S. government.

Not getting the answer he desired, Governor Stevens asked again if the Indians understood his address of the previous day. Without responding to Big Canoe's input, Stevens changed his words around and repetitiously asked the head chiefs if the three tribes represented what everyone thought. Whereupon, Big Canoe stood up and said, "I do not understand you right." Again ignoring him, the governor invited other head chiefs to comment.

Victor said, "I am willing to go on reservation, but I do not wish to go over yonder."

Alexander nodded, "It is good for us all to stop in one place."

The Kootenai Chief Michelle agreed, "I am with Alexander."[603]

A short discussion of agricultural potentials on the two sites

603 Michelle and his band lived seasonally on the shores of the upper Flathead Lake. A few years after the Hell Gate Treaty was in effect, he left his people and moved to the Columbia Lakes region in Canada. Michelle represented a minority of the Kootenai Nation's bands.

ensued. The conference ended by Stevens again persisting in outlining advantages of living on a joint reservation.

Wednesday's council meeting began at 11:30 a.m. with Governor Stevens making a condescending query: "My children, have you agreed upon the place you will live? I ask the chief, I ask Victor."

Victor said, "I am content with the valley (Bitterroot)."

Alexander said, "The Kootenai and Pend Oreille and Kalispel will come to my place [Mission Valley]."

The governor then told Alexander that he did not represent the non-attending Kalispels (lower Pend Oreilles) and followed with a long lecture on the virtues of choosing one location for the three tribes' reservation. Alexander did not want to leave his land near St. Ignatius Mission, but he would if Stevens said, "[Alexander] could not go to heaven at his own place." Stevens reiterated the necessity of one reservation in one place, in order to receive government support, and the council ended for the day after Stevens directed Victor and Alexander to discuss the matter. The next day, no council meeting occurred, as the commissioners provided a grand feast of two beeves, coffee, sugar and tobacco for the Indians. The rest of the day, the chiefs and their people discussed the proposed treaty among themselves.

At noon on Friday, July 13, Governor Stevens questioned the Indians again. Had they decided which reservation location they desired? He repeated the benefits for the tribes and described government's annuities for clothing, tools and housing for chiefs, and emphasized $500 each year to the three head chiefs. After dangling that carrot a moment, the governor asked, "Are you ready to sign the treaty?" Sadly for him, exasperation prevailed. Alexander and the Kootenai chief, Michelle, in one accord wanted to remain in the Mission Valley. Stevens perhaps needed to believe the Flatheads had agreed to the location. He again went over the terms of the treaty and without a pause, barked: "Now we will sign the treaty."

Victor had had enough and interrupted: "Where is my country? I want to speak ..."

The governor cut him off indignantly, "When I call upon you to sign the treaty, you can make your objections."

Victor retaliated, "I have not agreed to accept this land [Mission Valley]."

Stevens ignored Victor by doggedly staying his course and squared off with, "I was talking to you and I told you no." At this point, the meeting erupted in a heated debate between Stevens and Victor and joined by

Flatheads Ambrose, Red Wolf and Bear Track.

Stevens' next words ended the debate: "Or is not Victor a chief? Is he as one of his people has called him, an old woman? Dumb as a dog? If Victor is a chief, let him speak now." Victor responded by passing the discussion to his people and walking out. Saturday came and went without a council meeting, after Victor informed the governor he had yet to make up his mind. The next meeting took place on Monday, July 16, at 11 a.m. with Stevens gearing up to exercise his authority to settle this ordeal.

No longer passive, Victor interrupted to state his case: "I am going to talk; I was not content – you gave me a very small place; then I thought, here they are giving away my land. That is my country over there at the mission; this [Bitterroot Valley] also, I think so; plenty of you say Victor is the chief; you white people say so too. ... The place you pointed to me [map] above is too small." (The governor had proposed the land from Lolo Creek south in the Bitterroot drainage for the reservation.)

After poking a finger at the map, Victor continued: "I believe that you wish to help me and that my people will do well there. If you want, we will (send) this word to the Great Father (president of the United States), our chief (too) will come and look at it. When you look at Alexander's place and say the land is good, and say, come here Victor – then I would go. If you think this above (Bitterroot) is good land then Victor will say come here Alexander. ... That is the way we will make the treaty, my father." Victor's overture satisfied the Pend Oreilles and his people but by no means settled the issue of one reservation for both tribes.

Realizing the Pend Oreilles and Flatheads did not intend to leave their homelands, Governor Stevens hastily agreed to add Victor's proposition to the treaty, and the signing process began: first, the three head chiefs put their X next to the finger by their name, then 11 Flatheads and upper Pend Oreilles signed, followed by four Kootenais.

When asked to sign the treaty, Flathead War Chief Moise refused, stepped forward, and in a bitter tone, said: "My brother is buried there [near Hell Gate]. I did not think you would take the only piece of ground I had. Here are three fellows [head chiefs], they say get on your horses and go [either to the upper Bitterroot or to Mission Valley]; they never say talk. If you would give us a big place, I would not talk foolish. If I go to your country and say give me this, will you give it to me? Maybe you know it – here is all of these people – that have only one piece of ground. Now their mouths are all shut – sewed up. Last year when you were talking about the Blackfeet you were joking." A short, testy exchange between Governor Stevens and Moise ended after the latter pressed for an answer to his question, "Will you give me land if I go to your country?"

Stevens callously replied, "Yes, as much as you choose to buy."

These recorded exchanges indicate that at least Big Canoe understood their new rulers were imposing hardships upon their people. Victor's proposal became Article II in the treaty agreement. This part of provision describes the area: "The Bitterroot Valley, above the Lolo Fork, shall be carefully surveyed and examined and if it shall prove, in the judgment of the President[,] to be better adapted to the wants of the Flathead tribe than the general reservation provided for in this treaty, then such portions of it as may be necessary shall be set apart as a separate reservation for the said tribe. No portion of the Bitterroot Valley, above the Lolo Forks, shall be open to settlement until such examination is had and the declaration of the President made known."[604]

Gustavus Sohon drawing titled "Big Canoe; Or-tunta tle-a or Nek-hal-tsa; Pend d'Oreilles Chief," July 12, 1855. COURTESY WASHINGTON STATE HISTORICAL SOCIETY

Therefore, the conditional Hell Gate Treaty would become history. The Salish resistance to leave their homelands won the battle with the commission, for a while at least. Both the Flatheads and Pend Oreilles stayed put on portions of their homeland and maintained their lifestyle as though there had been no treaty council. The same applied to the Kootenais as most remained in their old haunts. Hoping the Stevens commission would forge a peace agreement at the upcoming Fort Benton Blackfeet council, the Salish and their allies made plans to focus on the summer hunt in that direction.

Incredibly, before the Blackfeet Peace Council convened, two young Piegans stole four horses from the Pend Oreilles as they neared the

604 PNQ, vol. 29 no. 3, Partoll, Albert J., pp. 283-321: Partoll Proceeding of Hell Gate Council.

280 lodges of Indians gathered for the event. A bad omen perhaps, but when the Piegan Chief Little Dog learned of the disgrace, he ordered the culprits to go get the horses and return them pronto. Although one of the young men returned three of the mounts, the other, more rebellious lad rode north on the fourth dandy steed. In a gesture of goodwill and peace of mind, Little Dog gave the victim a good horse from his herd.[605] This rare occurrence surprised the Salish and sparked hope among the peace commissioners for a successful council.

Lame Bull Treaty

A few days after the Hell Gate Treaty Council, Governor Stevens and his party packed up to go east to Fort Benton for a parley with the Blackfeet Nation. Upon arrival and hearing about the delay of a boat loaded with $10,000 worth of presents for the Indians, they had to move the meeting place 100 miles down the Missouri River, below the mouth of Judith River, at Head Chief Lame Bull's camp.

The council opened at 1 p.m. on October 16, 1855, with commissioners and interpreters situated under a pole and canvas structure. The Indians sat on their own blankets in a semicircle with 26 principal Blackfeet chiefs in the front row, the lesser chiefs behind them and 15 Salish chiefs and 12 Nez Perce leaders in the rear. Governor Stevens' opening remarks stressed the need for peace among all tribes of the region and with the whites. He called a rumor that had circulated among the Blackfeet a lie – that white men would take their land and drive them north to Canada.

Stevens outlined the commission's objective of establishing farms stocked with cattle on the new reservation in the Blackfeet's own country and closed with: "We hope through the long winters the Blackfeet would not be obliged to live on poor buffalo meat but would have domestic cattle for food. You know the buffalo will not continue forever. Get farms and cattle in time."[606] One can imagine what the attending native peoples thought of Stevens' statement.

The commissioners then proceeded to explain each article of the treaty. Articles III and IV angered the Salish, for they put boundaries on their hunting grounds in line with those established in the 1853 Laramie Treaty, of which they knew nothing. Article 3 designated an open hunting area for all tribes, including the Blackfeet, from Medicine Rock (north of Helena, Montana) east to the headwaters of the Musselshell River, on to

605 [I.S.] Railroad Survey Report, p. 116.

606 Ewers, p. 216.

the mouth of Shields River,[607] up the Yellowstone River to its northern source, and along the Continental Divide back to its beginning at Medicine Rock. Furthermore, signees of the treaty would not establish villages within 10 miles of the northern line of the common hunting ground.

The Shields River and the Musselshell River became the boundary separating the Crows and Blackfeet territories. Article IV described the boundary of the Blackfeet Nation – Gros Ventre Reservation, with allowance for the Assiniboines to hunt eastern portions to the Milk River. The huge piece of real estate allocated to the Blackfeet included some of the Salish and Nez Perces present and long-past hunting grounds.

After being shown a map of the boundaries, Pend Oreille Chief Alexander objected to his peoples' exclusion from traditional hunting grounds north of the Musselshell River. Asserting ancestral rights, he said: "A long time ago our people used to hunt above the Three Buttes [Sweet Grass Hills north of Chester, Montana] and the Blackfeet lived far north. When my father was living, he told me that was an old road for our people."[608]

Piegan Chief Little Dog offered Alexander the right to hunt there, but the commission squashed that offer by reminding the western allies of their small numbers compared to the Blackfeet Nation's larger numbers. Again, Alexander pressed to have traditional rights to hunt country assigned to the Blackfeet.

Big Canoe followed by questioning the commission's concept of setting boundaries to the governor: "I thought our roads would be all over the country. Now you tell us different. Suppose we do not stick together and do make peace. ... Now you tell me not to step over that way. I have a mind to go there."

The irritated Piegan Head Chief Lame Bull spoke for the first time to remind the Salish and Nez Perce: "[T]he white chief wrote the treaty." Pointing toward the commissioners, he said: "Look at those tribes, they are the first to speak making objections this morning. We intend to do whatever the Government tells us. … Let us listen. … I hope these Indians [Salish and Nez Perce] will make friends with us and that it may be shown

607 Rockwell, pp. 140-141. Lt. Maynader, as part of an U.S. Army exploration party in 1859, took a well-beaten "lodge trail" from the Sweet Grass area on the Yellowstone River he thought to be the one used by the Flatheads. His recently traveled trail turned up Shields River 20 miles then west along a meandering willow-lined creek to the timberline, topping out at the pass. Descent to the Gallatin River went through a narrow, rocky canyon, in some places, confined to single horse width. Point's earlier description of their route closely matches this.

608 Ewers, p. 218, from Albert J. Partoll's "The Blackfoot Indian Peace Council." Alexander's father, a Shoshoni, probably referred to his father's tribe. In ancient days, the Pend Oreilles may have gone that far east, but original sources do not verify his statement.

by friendly exchange of property."[609]

The treaty council adjourned for the day after they discussed half of the articles in the document, mainly those most objectionable to the Salish. The next day, the commissioners went through the remainder of the treaty without protests. Appearing much satisfied with the treaty, 14 Piegans, eight Bloods, eight Gros Ventres and three Blackfeet put their marks on the document. Expecting that peace would come about with the treaty, 15 Salish chiefs signed the agreement, led by Victor, Alexander, Big Canoe and Moise, who refused to accept his tribe's treaty but signed this one. Likewise, 12 Nez Perce chiefs marked the document, all representing the buffalo hunting bands from areas of the Clearwater and Snake rivers in Idaho.

A modicum of peace followed the Lame Bull Council on the buffalo grounds, even though the Salish and allied hunters largely ignored the hunt boundaries set by the commission. Perhaps stealth was involved, for during winter hunts the Salish expected the Blackfeet to be snug up north in their winter camps, while leaving outlying bison for Salish use. In addition to Little Dog's band, the Small Robes and other friendly Piegans tolerated Salish hunters trespassing on the Blackfeet tribe's private reserve. However, the Blackfeet chiefs had little control over their young men who appropriated horses from Victor's party while returning home from the peace conference. Iroquois Francis Saxa, old Ignace's son, lost 22 head to a Piegan and six Blood thieves on the Musselshell River. Apparently impressed by the words of government officials at the peace council, the Iroquois asked Agent Owen to obtain restitution for his loss. A letter to that effect sent to Olympia received no answer.[610] Problems with horse stealing on the plains and at home had not been resolved at the Lame Bull Council.

However, peace on the buffalo grounds seemed possible in 1855 before the Lame Bull council convened. Piegan War Chief Three Suns, in relating his various battles over the years, tells of 10 lodges of Pend Oreilles joining his 60 for a hunt in the Sweet Grass Hills north of the council site.[611] While there, a force of 400 nomadic Sioux raiders, not a party to the peace agreement, overran half the camp in the dark of night and killed or stole most of the horses. Three Suns rallied the camp, holding off the raiders until morning when the Sioux withdrew. The joint camp killed 16 of the enemy while losing 11 of their own.

After leaving the Lame Bull council meeting, Chief Alexander, with 20 lodges of his people, hunted west to the Helena Valley on the

609 Ibid. Ewers, p. 218.

610 Dunbar, vol. 2, p 168, June 23, 1856.

611 Jackson, Piikani, p. 206.

Missouri River in Montana. In early March 1856, being low on ammunition and faced with deep snows on approaches to Mullan Pass, the Indians spent several days breaking trail with their horses bucking belly-deep snow. John Owen and a party of railroad surveyors on their way to Fort Benton struggled through the similar snow for the last mile to reach the pass from the Little Blackfoot River side. Much to their good fortune, they broke through to tie into the Pend Oreilles' trail a mile from the ridgetop. Seven miles down the trail, Owen found Chief Alexander's camp in a nearly snow-free prairie.[612] Alexander with his two sons and another Indian then accompanied Owen for the four-day journey to Fort Benton to trade for ammunition.

After completing their transaction at the fort, the chief and his small party left for home just as Piegan Chief Lame Bull and his band rode into that area. Along the trail home through Piegan country, Alexander's party helped themselves to nine buffalo cows. Upon reaching his people's campsite in the Helena Valley, he found they too had packed up and gone home, leaving a well-packed trail in melting snow over the pass to the Little Blackfoot River where he and three men joined his people.[613] Snow in the Clark Fork Valley had nearly melted by April 1, putting the Salish hunters on the move for home. Deep snows on passes and the Clark Fork River canyon had forced Victor's people to wait on the Beaverhead prairie for better traveling conditions.

After crossing Deer Lodge Pass and trailing to the mouth of the Little Blacktail River, their heavily loaded horses needed rest before completing the journey home. A huge traffic jam occurred on the Clark Fork River trail when the vanguard of the Flathead's Five Crows (Ambrose) band got in file behind Alexander's Pend Oreilles. They created a nearly five-mile-long string of mounted horses for the three days it took to reach the Bitterroot Valley. Three weeks earlier, 30 lodges of Nez Perces had experienced a similarly difficult time passing through the same stretch of trail due to deep snows. The Salish and allies enjoyed a good hunt, losing one man killed by the Gros Ventres on the Missouri plains.

The Kalispels regularly took advantage of deep snow years that forced white-tailed deer to yard up, making it difficult for them to escape hunters. Utilizing snowshoes, Indians surrounded sheltered deeryards, shooting and even clubbing them to death until none stood or managed to flee. A large number of the slaughtered deer were in poor shape, mostly skin and bone, hardly edible. In the winter of 1852, the Kalispels killed

612 Dunbar, Owen Journal, vol. 1, pp. 119-120.

613 Ibid. vol. 1, pp. 120-121.

800 deer, just enough to meet their needs. Yet, the Commissioner of Indian Affairs worried about Indians killing too many and expressed his concern, "They hunt over the whole section so thoroughly as to exterminate these animals in that location leaving none to breed."[614] They were effective hunters for sure, but during severe winters the Indians did not exploit the entire region, as conditions hampered long-distance mobility.

The newly appointed reservation agent, Dr. Richard Landsdale, went to work shortly after the Hell Gate Council to prepare a budget according to terms of the treaty, functioning from a tent near St. Ignatius Mission; he prepared a thorough report to Governor Stevens in October 1855. Landsdale estimated costs of preparing land for agriculture, building houses, mills, blacksmith shops, hospitals and schools and administrators to the tune of $78,400 exclusive of agency employee salaries.[615] It is unknown what the governor did with the funding request, but little would happen until Congress approved the treaty some four years later. Landsdale had a small amount of government funds, for he hired in November seven men and a woman in the Bitterroot Valley, loaded a wagon with essential tools, and hauled them to the joining of the Jocko and Flathead rivers. Selecting a site just north of there on higher ground, the men began cutting cottonwood trees for 10 huts measuring 14 by 16 feet, each seven feet high and spaced six feet apart. One 14-by-14 hut was the cook's house and office. All huts were chinked with a mud-grass mix and had doors and windows. A 72-foot roof sloped in an eastward direction covered all buildings.[616] In his December 1, 1855, report to Governor Stevens, Agent Landsdale noted the Flatheads and Chief Victor were hunting on the Musselshell where they planned to winter. Alexander and the Pend Oreilles had hunted their way home from the Lame Bull Treaty Council. All of Chief Michelle's Kootenais had moved to the Tobacco River in British territory for the winter. Many of the Kalispels and a few Spokanes traveled to St. Ignatius and then moved up the Jocko River to camp near the falls. Kalispel Head Chief, the other Victor, had not arrived at his intended new home at the mission before Landsdale sent his letter off.

The new Jocko Agency on the Flathead Reservation lay a great distance from supply sources, requiring Dr. Landsdale to be away from his station for long periods, and he needed somebody to manage affairs

---

614 Annual Report of the Commission of Indian Affairs from Stuckley Report, p. 296. The U.S. Government Railroad Survey did not reference excessive deer kills.

615 Montana State Historical Society, "National Indian Service Archives," Dr. Landsdale's October 3, 1855 report.

616 Ibid. Dr. Landsdale report, December 1, 1855.

in his absence. Returning from a supply excursion to Salt Lake in the spring of 1856, he met newlyweds Henry and Minnie Miller at Fort Hall. The couple had fled Salt Lake to avoid the wrath of her Mormon family for marrying a nonmember. Landsdale hired the couple on the spot and returned to the reservation with them.[617] Minnie, only the second white woman to arrive in the area, presented quite a spectacle to Pend Oreille onlookers as she rode by, perched sideways on her horse. The Millers left the agency after Dr. Landsdale turned management of the reservation over to John Owen in 1858.

St. Ignatius Mission had many of the basic needs of civilization, which they loaned out to neighbors at the Jocko Agency and HBC Fort Connah personnel. Father Hoecken's 1856 journal notes the loan and return of salt, a small churn, butter keg, washtub and washboard to Dr. Landsdale, who later borrowed 10 pints of coffee, a small tent and a mule named Rose. Michael Ogden at Fort Connah also borrowed a few pounds of salt and 20 nails, commodities he could easily replace from Fort Colvile shipments.[618] However, the Jesuits and reservation agents had to travel hundreds of miles to either Salt Lake City or Fort Benton to obtain most items.

New St. Ignatius Mission in 1863. COURTESY WASHINGTON STATE HISTORICAL SOCIETY

St. Ignatius Mission began to take on the looks of a small, multination Indian village by the end of 1856. Lodges of some Flatheads, Nez Perces, Kootenais, Coeur d'Alenes and Spokanes had sprung up around the

617 Helena Independent Newspaper, January 20, 1875. Also, Dunbar, vol. 1, p 132; Owen Journal June 16, 1854.

618 Gonzaga University Special Collections – Hoecken Diary, May 23 and June 30, 1856.

mission along with Iroquois young Ignace and the family of the deceased Pierre Gaucher.[619] The 160-acre mission farm and garden produced crops of wheat, potatoes, cabbage and other edibles. The few Indians that worked the fields found their labor worthwhile enough to take up farming. Northern Piegan Chief Little Dog, participant in the Lame Bull Council, paid a visit to the Bitterroot Valley and St. Ignatius. The Piegans entered the mission in early June with the American flag unfurled, marching to a lively song accented by many tiny bells. Father Hoecken held several conferences with them and concluded that, "all the old difficulties are forgiven" between the chief's people and the Salish. While in the area, Little Dog's party called on Major Owen before proceeding up the valley to meet with Victor's people who were digging roots.[620] During the summer, Crow thieves ran off with 20 head of mission Indian horses. A few days afterward, a group of friendly Crows entered the village only to face an attack by excited victims of the recent theft, who forgot the law of nations that secured protection to enemies who stepped into their camp. Two of the Crows fell before cooler heads stopped the shooting to allow the friendly Crows to escape.[621]

By the summer of 1856, the Salish began to feel the effect of many white settlers to the south and west of their territory. The huge Mormon migration to Salt Lake had begun to spread out into southeast Idaho to the Lemhi Valley. This invasion, coupled with scarcity of game in their quarter, compelled elements of the Shoshoni and Bannock tribes to go north to Salish hunting grounds in search of food. Known as expert horse thieves, the natives moved en masse to the Beaverhead and Deer Lodge areas to winter. Taking advantage of the open hunting grounds provided in the Lame Bull Treaty, the Snakes trailed deep enough into the new Blackfeet country to come in conflict with that nation.

---

619 [I.S.] Chittenden & Richardson, Hoecken Letter 24, April 15, 1857. In fall of 1855, Iroquois Pierre Gaucher died from a broken neck when he fell from his horse while hunting elk in the Big Hole area.

620 Dunbar, Owen Journal, pp. 123-125, V. 1. John Owen noted the visit of five lodges of Blackfeet led by Sarta, Sartra or Sartria to his fort. The name may equate to Little Dog in English. Little Dog, then chief of the Black Patched Moccasin Band, became head chief of the Piegans in 1857 after the death of Lame Bull. As a young man, he had many encounters with the allied Salish hunters. The Piegans under his leadership remained peaceful until his death in 1866.

621 [I.S.] Chittenden & Richardson, Hoecken Letter 24, April 15, 1857.

9

Indian Wars and Change

1855-1866

War clouds covered the Columbia plateau region when the Governor Stevens party of some 25 men arrived at Fort Colvile in late August 1855. A courier brought the governor news that the Yakama and Cayuse tribes had declared war on the whites, killing several passing miners and an Indian agent who went to investigate the crime. Poorly armed and fearing he might have to fight his way through the hostile country to reach Olympia, Stevens sent a detachment to Fort Benton for arms and ammunition. The governor pondered the question: How could this happen when he had just completed a treaty with the hostiles four months ago?

With that weight on his mind, the governor and his remaining staff traveled to the Bitterroot Valley where he planned to meet the supply train and then proceed via the Coeur d'Alene mission trail to the Spokane Valley for a council with area tribes.

While Stevens waited for the munitions, Nez Perce buffalo hunters entered the valley on their return trip home, and he quickly set up a meeting with the three head chiefs, Spotted Eagle, Looking Glass Sr. and Three Feathers, to advise them of the hostile situation on the Columbia. Afterward, all three chiefs volunteered to escort the Stevens party, along with a few warriors, to Walla Walla and safety. On November 25, 1855, the party arrived at the Coeur d'Alene mission where Stevens found the Indians "excited" and balancing either peace or war with Americans, which could go either way.

The governor's party arrived at Antoine Plante's place for the council meeting on the Spokane River in the afternoon or evening of November 27. While waiting for the Indians to appear, Stevens met with a few miners who had organized a volunteer company of soldiers, "The Spokane Invincibles," which he authorized on the spot. On December 3, the Colville tribe, accompanied by HBC Duncan McDonald and four miners, joined the Spokanes and Coeur d'Alenes to begin the council meeting. Stevens was not prepared, nor in the mood, to offer a treaty at this meeting, particularly after the hostilities that took place during the past two months in which Kamiakin's 300 Yakama and Cayuse warriors had engaged U.S. troops in two battles; the last ended with the Indians retreating across the Columbia River into Palouse and Spokane territory. The native council attendees, disturbed by the war that some blamed on the Walla Walla Treaty, feared they might be next.

The governor opened the proceeding by defending his actions at the Walla Walla Council and pointedly reminded them that the Yakama and Cayuse chiefs had signed the agreement. He called the Indian rumor of soldiers coming to take away their lands a lie. Stevens then told the assembly he did not think it the proper time to talk about land: "When you talk about your lands, you want time to think of selling it. I want time to think of it. We want to think together." After realizing that hostiles living in their midst had sparked anxiety, Steven closed his remarks by emphasizing they need not become involved in the present war. Then he decided to feel out the chiefs on the issue of war or peace by asking those present "to speak their hearts."[622]

Spokane Head Chief Garry opened the session saying, "It's peace I want." Then in a long speech in fluent English, he reviewed the events that caused the conflict between the white and red man, even the Whitman massacre, which he blamed on a white worker employed by Dr. Whitman. Garry spoke at length of the Indians' fear of the Americans stealing their land as they did in the case of the Cayuse and Yakamas. He stressed the necessity of keeping the soldiers out of his country and concluded his remarks by telling Stevens, "When you talk to the soldiers and tell them not to cross the Snake River into our country, I will be glad."[623] Mixed-blood Baptiste Peone, who maintained an HBC post north of Plante's place, translated the following portion of that council.

A principal chief of the lower Spokanes began his talk: "A long time we have not known our hearts. Together, all the chiefs would not be bad," meaning they did not want war with the whites. The chief thought the Coeur d'Alenes a "little sore" but were not enemies of the whites or Americans. He complained when the Americans stopped trade of ammunition to the tribes: "You stabbed our hearts. We do not know what to make of it. We are not Blackfeet." Going further, the chief said, "It was as if you had put up a fence between the Indian and the whites," complaining about

622 Doty, pp. 39-66. James Doty, aide de camp and adjutant, kept the governor's journal that he signed at intervals. The testimony at the Spokane Council follows in the above numbered pages.

623 Doty, p. 48.

the whites bringing smallpox into their country. He concluded: "Since the word of God came into our country we have always been afraid to disobey it. That is why I threw away all my arms. We have arms only for hunting now."[624]

Speaking directly to governor, Chief Stellam of the Coeur d'Alenes said: "We have not yet made friends … all the Indians are not yet your children. You have not yet made friendship." The chief then expressed his displeasure at the Yakama war, which he thought the government leaders could have prevented by peaceful means rather than sending soldiers to try a forceful solution. "You have many soldiers and I would not like to have them among my people," he said. He expressed concern over the shooting of each other in the whole of the region and suggested white man could stop it entirely by controlling their people. If the whites "dry the blood," the Coeur d'Alenes would "take you for a friend."[625] Schlat-eal, a Spokane, continued the theme that his children would spill no blood, but the Americans should stop the war against fellow red men along the Columbia. He noted the Yakamas were at the forks and he would not like the soldiers to cross the river in pursuit. Sternly, the chief protested: "We have not made friendship yet. When we see the soldiers don't cross the Columbia, we believe you will take us for your friends. When you stop … the fighting now going on, we shall believe you intend to adopt us for your children. Then I will believe you have taken us for your friends, and I will take you for my friend."[626]

Spokane Chief Garry (1811-1892) in photograph taken in 1888. COURTESY OF SPOKANE PUBLIC LIBRARY, NORTHWEST ROOM

Colville Chief Peter John expressed his wish for peace and friendship and also issued the complaint, "They have stopped the ammunition and made us poor."

624 Ibid, p. 58.
625 Ibid, p 56.
626 Doty, p. 58.

Sanpoil Chief Sho-homish, of the lower Spokanes, elaborated on the friendship and peace his people had with the French (fur traders) back to his grandfather. Then, expressing his peaceful nature he said: "I never loved bad Indians nor war. I never believed in making war against the Americans, the side of good I do love. I wish they would stop all the whites and Indians from fighting."[627]

In sharp contrast, the upper Spokane Chief Big Star blamed the governor for the current war and for passing through their country three times without making a treaty with them; yet, he made such with others. "The reason I am talking now is that all the Indians did not like what you said at the Walla Walla Council. They put all the fault on you [for] the trouble since. ... My heart is very small toward you. My heart is the same as the others for you."[628] The next two native speakers advocated peace.

Bear-Upon-His-Back, a Spokane, gave his perception of where the natives and the governor stood on the issue of war or peace: "I am an Indian. I myself have in my heart two writings [thoughts] and you, governor, have the same. You have in your heart a writing that is bad [war] and so have I, and those two letters [words meet and that troubles us. You want to know our hearts and we to know yours and now it is nothing else but war we are talking of. When you will listen to us, and we to you, then we will take all the bad writing and throw it [to] one side. ... When we are done talking, we will all be friends and the heart of the Indian will follow you."[629]

Finally, after the session and with light snow falling, a grim-voiced Head Chief Garry gave his take on the difference between the Indians and white Americans: "See how everybody is red and you are white. The Indians think they are not poor [inferior]. When you look at yourself, you see you are white. You see the Indian is red. What do you think? Do you think they are poor when you look at them that way? When you look at those red men, you think you have more heart, more sense than those poor Indians. I think the difference between us and you Americans is in the clothing; the blood and body are the same. The Indians are proud, they are not poor. If you talk truth to the Indian to make peace, the Indian will do the same to you."[630]

Governor Stevens told the chiefs he would return the following year, early if possible, to negotiate a treaty. The council adjourned, and Stevens and the miner volunteers departed for Walla Walla accompanied

627 Ibid, p. 60.
628 Ibid.
629 Ibid, p. 64.
630 Ibid, p 66.

by the Nez Perce escort. The Coeur d'Alenes, Spokanes, Colvilles and Sanpoils remained without a treaty for years to come. Stevens did not keep his word.

News of Indian unrest in the West arrived in the Bitterroot Valley via a letter from the Nez Perce Indian agent William Craig directed to John Owen.[631] Craig reported the war-inclined Nez Perces in his region were not looking for presents as provided in the Walla Walla Treaty. Old Chief Looking Glass, Three Feathers and Joseph, bystanders at the Spokane Council and the primary leaders of the faction said the "whites must leave the country." Craig felt he, too, might be obliged to leave the area.[632]

The provoking event was an attack on a council meeting of 300 Walla Walla, Yakama, Cayuse, Umatilla and Nez Perce warriors and families near today's La Grande, Oregon, by 150 Washington Territorial volunteer soldiers from Walla Walla. Thirty Indians and three soldiers lost their lives. On July 17, 1856, soldiers had surrounded the peaceful camp, wherein the Indians requested a peace council, but the commanding officer suspected treachery and ordered his men to move in. The Indians, in an indefensible position, had no other option than to flee in different directions, leaving 30 dead behind. Afterward, the volunteers captured 200 horses, gathered up a variety of provisions, 100 pounds of powder, and then piled and burned over 100 lodges. Details of the event spread rapidly among the native brethren, inciting shrill war cries among braves of the Spokane, Palouse, Coeur d'Alene and Nez Perce.

The Coeur d'Alenes, Spokanes and neighboring tribes talked of war while they waited for Governor Stevens to fulfill his promise to convene a treaty council and settle the land issue. One can only speculate why the government took no action, but surely the mass of miners and land-hungry settlers had their eyes on the rich lands east of the Columbia River. Over the next two years, warrior natives of the Inland Northwest aligned themselves with one of two sides: those who waited for peace toward whites and those whose nostrils flared for war. For a time, there was much discussion among the Indians over what to do and what would result from their decisions.

A leading recruiter for the natives' war cause, Yakama Chief Kamiakin, then living with the Spokanes, approached the Sanpoil and Colville tribes and, while in that area, paid a visit to Duncan McDonald

631 Dunbar, Owen Journal, p. 137, vol. 1. William Craig, a former American trapper married to a Nez Perce woman, lived 10 miles south of the Lapwai Mission, where he reared his family.

632 Ibid.

and his family at Fort Colvile. Conversation at an evening meal included the chief's worry over white Americans' disrespect of natives while trying to overrun Indians' homelands. McDonald listened patiently and finally told Kamiakin, "It is hopeless for the Indians to fight the white man: to kill a white man is like killing an ant and hundreds more pour out of the hole." The hostile leader received similar advice from Spokane Head Chief Garry, who had managed to convince many of his people to remain peaceful.[633] Recruitment for the Indian war moved west to the Bitterroot Valley.

When the Pend Oreilles returned home from a successful winter hunt, waiting Nez Perce and Spokane recruiters tried hard to goad them to take part in a planned war. However, the Pend Oreille and Flathead chiefs wanted no part of such a rebellion, which furthered tensions among the furious. During the spring, many Coeur d'Alenes and Spokanes shielded themselves from their hostile brothers and went to hunt buffalo, only to find violence. While wintering on the hunting grounds, they clashed with the Bannocks, losing five of their own and killing six in return.[634]

Fort Connah traders paid dearly for what little meat and fat they bargained from the Indians. The Flathead hunters returned home in March 1856 loaded down with meat, after hunting the Musselshell on their way home from the Lame Bull Treaty Council.[635] Earlier, Owen noted in his journal of the Kootenais at the St Ignatius Mission as "absolute objects of poverty" and issued them a small ration of beef from his herd,[636] which he supplemented later by purchasing buffalo meat from the hunters for the reservation Indians. In late March, the Bannocks killed a Flathead, provoking younger members of that tribe to get ready for war. Many Snakes and Bannocks had taken up residence in the Deer Lodge area, where they helped themselves to Salish horses. War Chief Moise discouraged the young men after learning the Blackfeet had planned a large, revenge-minded party against the Snakes and Bannocks for killing 26 of their hunters on the buffalo grounds.[637] Others noted the planned assault, such as Mormon settler Joseph Hauber in his June 23, 1857, journal notation of 500 Blackfeet waiting on the Beaverhead to kill off the Bannocks and their allies.[638]

Governor Stevens, in his July 5, 1855, letter about the Peace Council proceedings, estimated 450 Flatheads, 350 Kootenais and 600 upper Pend Oreilles having a combined 1,000 head of cattle. Cattle in the

633 WHQ, vol. 13, no 2, p. 108. Christine McDonald Memoirs.
634 [I.S.] Chittenden & Richardson, Hoecken Letter No. 15, April 15, 1857.
635 Dunbar, vol. 2, p. 168, Owen Letter, June 22, 1856.
636 Ibid.
637 Dunbar, vol. 1, Owen Journal, April 30 and 31, 1857.
638 [I.S.] Gray, Victor, ed.

Bitterroot Valley originated from the Jesuits, Owen and Fort Colvile's small herds. The number of animals seems unusually high, as the primary source for stock came from traders along the Oregon Trail, but few had ventured north before that time. Several men operated trading businesses along the trail, but the former HBC chief trader at Fort Hall, Richard Grant, and his son Johnny had the most success. In 1855-1856, the two men and several others wintered cattle on the Beaverhead and Blacktail Deer Creek on former Salish hunting grounds.[639] By 1857, the elder Grant had built a three-room log cabin at the mouth of Ruby River. A large, mixed-blood group of some 18 men, most with families, had accompanied him and set up lodges nearby. The Grants and others traded for horses from small groups of wintering Snakes, Bannocks, Nez Perces and Flatheads. The stockmen grumbled about adventurous Americans driving up the price for an Indian horse to more than double in the past 10 years. It cost two blankets, one shirt, one pair of cloth leggings, one small mirror, one knife, one paper of vermillion and other trifles for a horse.[640] Two years later, Johnny Grant drove his livestock to the lower Deer Lodge Valley where he built a cabin near the mouth of the Little Blackfoot River, thus beginning the area's cattle industry.

By 1857, ever-increasing and expanding Mormon populations compounded problems facing the Salish. Without the benefit of a treaty with the U.S. government, the Fort Hall area Bannocks and Shoshonis continued migrating north to the Bitterroot Valley. Dwindling game herds and the Mormon missionary settlement prompted the movement. Utah Territorial Governor Brigham Young had visited the location outside his jurisdiction in 1857 and determined to transform the settlement into an adobe-walled fort, later known as Fort Lemhi. Young intended the fort to be his "refuge" if he lost the governorship appointment in a struggle with U.S. authorities. The governor had declared martial law in Utah Territory, prohibiting the U.S. armed forces or any person without a permit to pass or repass into and though the territory. Posters to that effect went up in the Washington Territory, on main trails in the Beaverhead and in the Big Hole.[641]

This proclamation put federal troops in motion; a year later, they restored order in Utah Territory where Young made peace and remained as its governor.[642] Built among the largely transient Shoshonis and Bannocks,

639 Meikle, p. 63. Johnny Grant Memoirs.

640 Meikle, pp. 69-70. Granville Stuart's Journal.

641 Dunbar, vol. 2, p. 186. Owen Letter.

642 [I.S.] Svignen, Prof., History: Fort Lemhi Survey and Assessment. Washington Territory at the time included portions of today's western Montana and all of Idaho.

the Lemhi mission failed from the beginning as agriculture took top priority among the settlers. Brigham Young's settlement policy was it is "manifestly more economical and less expensive to feed and clothe them than to fight them."[643] The Indians objected to establishing any walled fort, plowing ground, fencing pasture for large herds of livestock and, particularly, transporting large amounts of pickled salmon to Salt Lake. Violence broke out in 1858 when a Bannock-Snake war party stole a large number of horses and cattle and killed two settlers in the process. The Mormons abandoned Fort Lemhi after that incident.

Appointed special agent for the Flatheads in 1856 and, two years later, as the agent for the U.S. Interior Department, John Owen[644] accepted additional responsibilities as agent for the Flathead Reservation and self-appointed advocate for the Mountain Snakes and Bannock tribes. The $1,000-a-year position entailed many problems, not the least a fledgling but under-funded service to Indians that spanned the entire Pacific Northwest during his watch. Owen constantly wrote superiors of local problems and suggested solutions for them. After the U.S. Congress ratified the Hell Gate Treaty, he became increasingly critical of the government's handling of reservation annuities. The agent assisted Bannock and Shoshoni migrants to the Deer Lodge valley with provisions and blankets out of his own pocket and with material designated for the Flathead Reservation. Owen's clamoring for creating a reservation for those tribes near Fort Hall took root a few years after he departed service. Central to Agent Owen's problems was the remoteness of the area he served that required hundreds of miles of mountain trails to transport commodities from the nearest sources at Salt Lake City, Fort Benton and Walla Walla.

Hostilities Begin

After waiting more than two years for Governor Stevens to return to negotiate a treaty, the Coeur d'Alenes and Spokanes thought the Americans would leave them alone. Unbeknownst to the natives, Stevens had departed the territory as a U.S. congressman in 1857, leaving the Indian problem for others to solve. At the same time, the United States' West Coast military leadership changed, and with it came a more aggressive approach to dealing with unruly Indians. In the winter of 1857, after Palouse Indians stole government horses from Fort Walla Walla, military officials ordered Colonel Edward Steptoe and his troops to move across

643 Madsen, Northern Shoshonis, p. 33.

644 Dunbar, vol. 2, p. 187, Owen Letter from Commissioner J. W. Denver, November 17, 1858.

the Snake River, find the thieves and examine affairs at Fort Colvile. When the soldiers neared Spokane and Coeur d'Alene country, the natives realized Stevens had broken his promise, and the soldiers had come to take their land. War it would be.

In May 1858, the mounted U.S. officers and soldiers began their show of force. They veered in an easterly direction across the prairie through Palouse country rather than taking the direct route to Fort Colvile. Upon reaching Pine Creek near today's Rosalia, Washington, mounted Indians appeared in a line along hilltops on either side of the column, keeping pace with the soldiers' every move. As the troops began to descend through a canyon toward the Spokane River, Steptoe realized the Indians were not a welcoming party. He ordered his troops to backtrack to Squaw Creek about 20 miles south of the river and set up camp in a defensible position.

On the morning of May 15, Coeur d'Alene Head Chief Vincent (Balsa) and the missionary Father Joseph Joset went to Colonel Steptoe's camp for a conference. Vincent demanded an explanation of why his troops were trespassing on their land. Steptoe explained his mission as peaceful; they were en route to see their Spokane friends, then continue on to Fort Colvile. Vincent abruptly told the colonel, "We are not Spokanes but Coeur d'Alenes." Not wanting a battle, Steptoe said the soldiers were in the process of turning back to Walla Walla, which immediately relieved the tension for both men. No sooner had the conversation turned peaceful when a Nez Perce scout, employed by the troops, struck Vincent with his whip and shouted: "Steptoe speak with forked tongue! Why don't you fight?" Soldiers immediately took the scout under custody, but he later joined up with the Indians. Vincent rode to the front to catch five Palouse warriors embroiled in an argument over who would take the first shot, when a Yakama leaped astride his horse and raced down the hill, firing his musket into the column. Bugles sounded and troops returned fire.[645] The allied force of 150 Spokane, 200 Coeur d'Alene, 45 Palouse and 172 Yakama warriors attacked the soldiers wielding short-range muskets with much the same weapons. In no time, the allies had forced Steptoe and his men with some of their baggage to a barren prairie knob.[646]

A different version from an unnamed Spokane participant in the above battle described the mobilization and initial attack: "In May, the upper- and middle-Spokanes and some Coeur d'Alenes were camped in small groups on the prairie digging roots in the vicinity of Spangle [Washington] when hunters discovered soldiers moving in the direction of the

645 Kowrach, ed., pp 102-104. A Coeur d'Alene Indian oral history of the Steptoe battle.

646 Glassly, pp. 144-145.

Spokane River. After a short parley, they decided they should kill the white men. The warriors from the valley joined with the others that lined the hills above the mounted lead column of troops. The Spokanes found the old chiefs trying to restrain the young men as the angry Coeur d'Alene Chief Tsitsiuhsimu and Chief Paschall Stellam ... rode forth and shot at the troops. The firing became general on the part of the Coeur d'Alenes, but the Spokane chief succeeded for a time in holding us back. Before long we engaged in the fighting ... three Coeur d'Alenes were killed and I saw four soldiers['] bodies. ... Kamiakin took no part in the fighting; he was camped in Coeur d'Alene country."[647]

The soldiers assembled on a barren hilltop with only clumps of grass or baggage for cover but managed to hold off the Indians until nightfall. Steptoe, low on ammunition, ordered a hasty retreat under cover of darkness and headed for home to their post at Fort Walla Walla. Seven U.S. soldiers lost their lives, with several wounded, while varied accounts indicate nine Indians died, with numerous wounded. The victorious allies had absolutely no idea of the consequence that would follow but paused long enough to glean the battlefield of government property left behind by Steptoe. They rounded up the horses and returned to their Spokane River camp with spirits bolstered.

Not long after Steptoe's defeat, John Owen went to Fort Colvile on business. After learning of the event, he took it upon himself to arrange a council meeting with the rebellious allied Indians in mid-July. Owen described his meeting with "500 fighting men" as the "darkest" ever held on the Pacific slopes. Indians parading around the soldiers captured their horses to the tune of the scalp and war dance. A rebellious chief told Owen they looked at him as a spy for Steptoe but added their own people were watching the latter's fort. During the council meeting, the warriors told Owen that when he returned to the Flatheads, he had better not try to keep them from joining their allied cause.

From the beginning of the council, Owen found it apparent that the Indians would reject all peace talks unless the Americans agreed to leave the country. "Tell Steptoe to come, we dare Steptoe to come."[648] The hostiles had no concept of the white man's military strength, believing the entire white tribe with all members and their families had already moved from the east to the west. After five days of war talk and the theft of three pack horses, Owen asked for permission to pass through Coeur d'Alene

647 Curtis, pp. 18-19. The hilltop is now called Steptoe Butte.

648 Dunbar, vol. 2, pp. 181-182, Owen Letter, July 16, 1858.

country to the Seneacquoteen portage on the Pend Oreille River to return home. The chief denied his request. The trader-agent took the longer route to the Pend Oreille River and lost several horses while passing through the Colville Valley in a night raid by hostiles. After crossing a mountain range to the old St. Ignatius site, friendly Kalispels loaded his goods on canoes and, for a price, transported them to the head of Lake Pend Oreille.[649]

During Owen's failed attempt to broker peace, the victorious allies sent messages out to neighboring tribes to gather at Spokane Falls, where war dances went on each night and mounted war practice during the day. A Spokane warrior participant said: "About 20 Kalispels joined us, but the lower Spokanes took no part in war. ... Kamiakin joined the fight as did a few Nez Perce[s]."[650] The war-like faction of Spokanes, Coeur d'Alenes, Palouses and Yakamas[651] got their wish when Colonel George Wright and 680 soldiers, armed with new long-range rifles and howitzers, attacked their camp at Four Lakes by today's Cheney, Washington. Armed only with short-range trade guns, the Indians soon realized their error in judgment and, after sustaining casualties, retreated north. Five weeks later, on September 5, Wright attacked the hostiles on the Spokane plains with similar results that wasted four chiefs. Howitzer fire put the Indians on the run, to separate into small groups and disappear in timbered ravines nearby. Chief Spotted Coyote and his small group of Kalispels engaged in the battle but balked at the first cannon shot, telling Chief Stellam: "There is no use of us fighting. We can do nothing against cannons, we must give up fighting and make peace or leave the country."[652] Most of the upper Spokanes fled to Coeur d'Alene country, while the middle Spokanes fled north to Kalispel country.

Two days later, as the troops moved east on the north bank of the Spokane River, Spokane Head Chief Garry and a few lead men met the column to ask for peace. Colonel Wright said: "I did not come into this country to ask you to make peace, I came here to fight. … I will tell you what you must do: You must come to me with your arms, with your women and children, and everything you have and lay them at my feet – you must trust in my mercy. Surrender or fight on!"[653] Since he had not participated in the battle, Chief Garry could not provide the answer Wright expected, and a few days later, the former sent several other chiefs with warriors to the Colonel's camp to discuss the matter.

---

649 Ibid. p. 184, Owen Letter, September 18, 1858.
650 Curtis, p. 20
651 Kowrach, p. 122.
652 Ruby and Brown, p. 132. The story of Stellam.
653 Glassley, p. 149.

The killing of 800 Spokane and Coeur d'Alene horses after the battle of Spokane Prairie in 1858. COURTESY WASHINGTON SECRETARY OF STATE

Without submitting to surrender, the hostiles began quietly to move their horses east toward the mountains – an unspoken sign of continued war. Wright responded promptly by burning lodges, haystacks and storage buildings; he captured 800 horses and killed all but 130 mounts retained for the soldiers, an act that totally demoralized the Coeur d'Alenes and Spokanes.[654] Unbeknownst to Wright, most horses and destroyed property belonged to peaceful Indians. On September 15, 1858, a council began on Latah Creek where the colonel dictated terms of the surrender; the Spokanes and Coeur d'Alenes marked their X. The Indians were required to return all articles taken from Steptoe and give up the man who started the battle. Wright took several families hostage from the Coeur d'Alene and Spokane tribes to hold for a year at Fort Vancouver, to be released if the tribes remained peaceful and allowed miners to pass through their country. Later, Colonel Wright hanged or shot down two Yakama chiefs and seven Palouses. Clearly, life for Coeur d'Alene, Spokane and Palouse tribes changed forever.

A principal leader in the war movement, Yakama Head Chief

654 Ibid, p. 150.

Kamiakin avoided punishment for his part in the war effort when a howitzer shell dislodged a large tree limb that hit him. Afterward his wife carried him from the battlefield to safety in a canyon. Once again, the longtime warrior eluded death or capture by American soldiers, this time by fleeing north to Canada. A short while later, he went to St. Ignatius Mission among the Pend Oreilles, where he lived for three years before returning to his people at Yakima.

Back in the Bitterroot Valley, Chief Victor fell ill in the fall of 1858 and took to his bed, where Owen found him upon returning to the valley in September. In a visit with him, Owen delivered a query from the superintendent of Indian Affairs in Oregon regarding the Flatheads' perspective of the Spokane Indian War. Victor [655] urged Owen to "tell my white Father that he should need never fear the firmness and friendly feeling of the Flathead Nation." Owen asked how the old chief would like to spend a $1,000 gift to the tribe. The old leader said to get half in ammunition and tobacco and spend the rest for a plow so they could open a field to raise grain "as buffalo are growing scarce." Chief Victor then thanked Owen and reminded him of Governor Stevens' promise of three snows ago, to help his poor nation. In June of 1859, Owen placed the order with Pierre Chouteau for all but the costly plow. Victor's illness lasted nearly two years, during which time Moise took over as second chief to lead the buffalo hunts. As the Flatheads headed out for the winter hunt, Victor and three lodges of families stayed home to look after the sick and such. The agency provided food for him and his Nez Perce wife during the hunters' absence. Fortunately, Victor recovered to resume his post as the leader of the next fall hunt.

St. Ignatius, by 1859, looked down on elongated fields and fenced gardens that blossomed under the direction of a young, white Kentuckian hired by Father Hoecken. Situated on higher ground, the site embodied several log houses and a church, with a second larger edifice for worship under construction. A gristmill and sawmill completed the improvements made by the Jesuits in just five years. Scattered around the houses of veneration were lodges of the greater part of the upper Pend Oreilles and those of a few Kootenais. From August to December, or longer, most of the Indians went to the buffalo, leaving behind a few old men, women, children and mission staff.[656] Most of the Kootenais resided off the reservation north of Flathead Lake and Tobacco Plains on the Kootenai River. Until white settlers and miners forced the move, the Kootenais hung on to traditional lands.

655 Dunbar, vol. 2, pp. 184-185, Owen Letter, September 18, 1858.
656 [I.S.] Mullan Report, 1860.

HBC's Fort Connah and St. Ignatius personnel maintained an agreeable relationship until October 1859 when Michael Ogden filed a complaint with Indian agent John Owen against the new head priest, Father Menatry. The accusation involved the priest using his influence with the Indians, much to the detriment of the Indian Service and white settlers in the country. In the prior year, Chief Alexander's Pend Oreilles burned down the cabin built by HBC deserter Louis Brown near the Jocko River, supposedly at Father Menatry's urging. The matter came to a head when the priest confronted a Mr. Van Etten along the trail to Hell Gate and forbid him to establish a winter camp on the plains near today's Arlee, for which he held a permit from Agent Owen. This turf battle between church and state came to an agreeable solution after Father Menatry understood Owen managed the reservation, and HBC Fort Connah had rights guaranteed by the U.S. government. Owen told Menatry, "It is my wish and intention to remove from the reservation, when once permanently fixed, all persons obnoxious to the Indians as well and those who in my estimate exercise a deleterious influence by example or otherwise."[657]

In the fall of 1859, livestock operator Johnny Grant had a surprise visit at his Deer Lodge residence from Head Chief Little Dog and some 50 Piegans.[658] Particularly vexed over the security of his 250 horses and more than 800 cattle, Grant invited them to smoke, have dinner and camp by his dwelling.[659] During their visit, he learned the Piegans had made peace with the Snakes and together were en route to barter with the Salish. There is no record of the Piegans meeting with the Salish at that time, but at the Lame Bull Treaty session, Little Dog did invite Big Canoe to come hunt in the Sweet Grass Hills. Presumably, the Piegans met with the Pend Oreille chiefs, which is precisely where Alexander led his hunters into trouble with a different tribe in the consequent year. Johnny Grant's memoirs contain a humorous story involving the shrewd Little Dog and Blackfeet Indian Agent Alfred Vaughan. The latter had ordered the great chief of the Piegans, Little Dog, to pour out any white man's firewater he saw in use, without exception. The great chief then reached under the agent's bed and pulled out a two-gallon keg of whiskey, threatening to "spill it out." Vaughan hollered, "Not that one!" Afterward the also fond-of-strong-drink Little Dog said: "Well, other white men like their whiskey as well as you

657 Dunbar, vol. 2 p. 197. Owen, October 12, 1859, Letter to H.M. Chase, the assigned investigator.

658 Ewers, p. 223. At the time, Little Dog commented he was chief of the Black Patch Moccasin band and succeeded to head chief after the death of Lame Bull in 1858.

659 Meikle, p. 72.

do. If I cannot spill that one, I will not spill theirs either." Order revoked, the two men settled the issue by sampling the contents of the keg.[660]

Snows in the winter of 1858-59 blocked the Flatheads and lower Pend Oreilles from returning home from the hunt until late March. The Kalispels' jaded horses needed three weeks to rest before continuing downriver to their homeland. Later in 1859, Richard Grant drove 300 head of cattle and horses into the Bitterroot Valley, aggravating the Flatheads and jogging Owen's mind over short pasturage. Victor repeated treaty rules to Owen that banned settlers from entering the Bitterroot Valley above Lolo Creek. Earlier, the Flatheads had put some cows and calves on that range to ready calves for market. The same year, the Indians fenced in more than 100 acres of wheat and potatoes with Owen's help.[661] Some Salish realized such an investment of time and trouble would help feed the tribe in poor hunting years. Buffalo populations continued to decline, and it took longer to find small, scattered herds.[662]

Father De Smet journeyed to St. Ignatius in the spring of 1859 to invite tribal leaders to renew peace treaties with a general and superintendent of Indian Affairs at Fort Vancouver. The eight men who agreed to accompany De Smet were Head Chiefs Alexander, upper Pend Oreille; Victor (Pitol), Kalispel; Dennis (Thunder Robe), Kettle; Kamiakin, Yakama; and subchiefs Adolphe, Flathead; Francis Saxa, an Iroquois adopted into the tribe as a Flathead; and Coeur d'Alenes Andrew (Seltice) and Bonaventure. The party left in April from the new St. Ignatius by canoes only to encounter ice jams on the Clark Fork River that required laborious portages. Transferring to horses near Old St. Ignatius, they rode through deep snows on the mountain pass. After 30 grueling days, they rode the overland route safely into Fort Vancouver.

During their three weeks at government expense, the Indians toured industrial establishments and gaped at steam engines, forges, manufacturing plants and printing businesses. The strange white man's wonders brought forth few questions or comments, but the visit to Portland's prison captivated many. The chiefs asked what bad things prisoners did to make them wear chains inside crowded cells without fresh air. They wanted to know the causes, motives and duration of imprisonment. Most influenced by the visit, Chief Alexander returned to St. Ignatius and immediately gathered his people to tell them the story of his visit.

First, he named the wonders of white man's civilization and then

660 Ibid, pp. 90-91.

661 Dunbar, vol. 2, Owen Letter, August 16, 1859.

662 Ibid.

detailed the severe punishment he witnessed in their society: "We have neither chains nor prisons, and for want of them, no doubt, a great number of us are wicked and have deaf ears. As chief, I am determined to do my duty; I shall take a whip to punish the wicked; let all those who have been guilty of any misdemeanor present themselves. I am ready."[663] Thereafter, known guilty parties and others feeling the need for chastisement came forward voluntarily as individuals to accept punishment according to the offense. At the end of the proceedings, the tribe celebrated with a feast.

Father De Smet and Salish delegation to Fort Vancouver in 1859. Top left: Bonaventure (Coeur d'Alene), Dennis Thunder Robe (Colville), De Smet, Francis Xavier (Iroquois-Flathead). Bottom left: Victor Pitol (Kalispel), Alexander (Pend Oreille), Adolphe Red Feather (Flathead) and Andrew Seltice, (Coeur d'Alene).

Salish rules of conduct were passed down by each generation and had no need for police officers to enforce, as the victim reported the offense or crime directly to his or her chief. Whipping, administered by the chief, served all infractions, with the number of lashes doled out according to its degree of severity. He used a leather whip, sometimes loaded with stones, in public, where victim and villagers witnessed the criminal's shame. The whipping seldom caused serious injury and/or death, as the case of 100 lashes was rare. Uncommon in pre-alcohol days, murder and theft within the village or tribe constituted the most serious crimes and their resulting

663 [I.S.] Chittenden & Richardson, vol. 2, pp. 766-68. De Smet Letter.

punishments.[664] From the time of accusation to judgment to punishment, the process began with the chief lecturing the offender (as in a court proceeding) in the presence of the victim and interested observers. Afterward, the entire assembly moved to the victim's lodge, where the criminal made restitution and received the lashes according to the harm inflicted.[665]

Jesuits among the Flatheads discouraged the age-old practice of using the whip for discipline, but the Pend Oreilles, Kalispels and Spokanes maintained the custom as an integral part of their justice system.

After the Lame Bull Treaty designated an open hunting area, the Salish no longer formed large alliances to hunt buffalo with the Nez Perces, as the latter's tribal participation significantly increased. About 30 Nez Perce families residing in the Bitterroot Valley continued to hunt with their Flathead relatives. The Flathead group, often supplemented by members of the Spokane and Coeur d'Alene tribes, formed a large force for security purposes. The upper Pend Oreilles regularly hunted as a tribe with downriver cousins and a few Kootenais. By 1859, neither the Salish nor the Nez Perce hunters paid much attention to treaty hunting boundaries, as buffalo numbers were, for all practical purposes, gone in the area open to them. The Nez Perce concentrated hunting efforts on Yellowstone herds, pressing well into Crow territory, while the Flathead group encroached on Piegans' reserved hunting grounds. The Pend Oreilles worked Piegan country in the Sun River region and farther east.

Unrestrained hunting areas coupled with peace agreements with the Blackfeet opened the floodgates for other Western tribes that included the Cayuses, Walla Wallas, Palouses and Colvilles. Additional tribal turnout increased among customary hunters like the Kalispels, Spokanes, Coeur d'Alenes and Nez Perces. According to Chiefs Looking Glass and Three Feathers, the Nez Perces had 1,000 people on the Yellowstone River in pursuit of buffalo in December 1855.[666] Then, on March 10, 1860, the once-again healthy Chief Victor led his Flathead hunters home into the Bitterroot Valley on very poor horses, after being absent seven long months that included spending a bitterly cold winter on the snow-covered Musselshell River. Victor figured they made out fairly well with an excess of five bales of meat and many bison tongues for trade. Even though the hunt took place in Piegan territory, no hostility occurred, probably because the Piegans never wintered there.[667]

664 High, Turney and Holt, Harry, pp. 46-47.
665 Ibid.
666 Farr, p. 17.
667 Dunbar, Owen Journal, March 8, 1860.

Once ratified by the U.S. Congress and the president, the Hell Gate Treaty called for annuities to be paid to the Salish and Kootenais. The process of delivery began in 1859, with Indian Affairs' officials in the East deciding what the Flathead Reservation would receive in the initial installment. Disregarding specific requests for wagons, carpenter tools, plows, and machinery for a gristmill and sawmill, the government invoice listed tons of coffee, rice and hard bread – foreign to the people – delivered to Fort Benton for pickup. John Owen bitterly complained in a letter to the superintendent of Indian Affairs in Portland about the quality of blankets, shawls, knives and other essential items shipped. His pen told the department to keep the hard bread, rice and coffee as the Indians "know very well the lands they sold were not to be paid for in hard bread and the like."[668]

To make matters worse, when the Owen crew started for Fort Benton to pick up the goods, a lead man from the fort turned them back along the trail as the Blackfeet Agent Vaughan flatly denied release of the commodities without a written order from the Portland office. Adding insult to injury, after the Salish had left on their winter hunt, the Fort Benton Agency decided to pack the annuity items over the mountains to Fort Owen, costing the government 10 cents per pound to a tune of $13,000. The goods ended up in the Fort Owen warehouse until March, when the Indians returned from hunting. The few Kootenais living north of the reservation received word they could pick up their allotment anytime. Again, in a letter to the Portland office, Owen protested the inventory of spoiled coffee and inferior quality of other items he could have bought in Portland for a third of the price.[669] The expensive machinery the Flatheads needed did not materialize because the Hell Gate Treaty called for a government survey before determining the status of lands above Lolo Creek. Fortunately, the Flatheads could use Owen's farm equipment and mill to carry out limited agricultural activities. At St. Ignatius on the reservation, the Jesuits provided an on-site farmer and eventually added hospital and education facilities with minimal government assistance.

Many years would pass before the Flatheads and Pend Oreilles received fair compensation for some 12 million acres surrendered to the United States – worth $5.3 million in 1859. The total amount paid the tribes in goods and cash up to September 29, 1965, came to $593,377.82. The Indian Claims Commission finally settled with the reservation natives in March 1967 for $4,016,293.[670] Attorney fees and other processing

668 Dunbar, vol. 2, p. 209. Owen Letter to Portland, May 25, 1860.

669 Dunbar, vol. 2, pp. 238-239. Owen Letter to Portland, December 21, 1860.

670 Bigart and Woodcock, pp. 149-150.

expenses made up the difference.

In the fall of 1859, the Indian Agency employed two men to fence, break ground and sow 15 acres of grain on the Flatheads' conditional reservation land above Lolo Creek on Burnt Fork. Owen's farmer and head of the project, Thomas Harris, reported in the June 14, 1860, fort journal that the wheat crop looked good. However, agency personnel had to harvest and mill wheat because the Indians decided it was a good time to go hunting.

Owen's 1859 Annual Report had suggested the need for a military post in the area, citing frequent horse-stealing raids to the Salish homeland since the Hell Gate Treaty. Native people did not understand why they had to submit to wrongs committed against them and not take the matter into their own hands. On the hunting grounds, Bloods had taken the warpath against whites and friendly tribes. Taking the issue further, Owen wrote that outlaws and fugitives from justice who traded alcohol to the natives infested the country, and "take special care to cater to the vices of the Indian."[671] Other than the soldiers assigned to hacking out the military road (Mullan Road), the requested fort would just have to wait for its establishment until 1877. A few years after Owen's request, miners and settlers formed vigilante groups to deal with the outlaws that committed crimes against the white miners and settlers.

In 1860, Jocko Agency relocated its reservation headquarters to a broad flat about one mile north of the original site that provided ample space for future development. Initial construction during the years included one double dwelling for farmers and assistants, a millwright cabin, and blacksmith and millwright shops near Jocko Falls.[672] Owen purchased Richard Grant's 300 cattle that ran free on the Bitterroot conditional reservation for a $105,000 credit account, a nice retirement fund for Grant, if he ever received the money.[673] Owen split the livestock equally between the Flatheads, the upper Pend Oreilles and those Kootenais on the reservation. Most Kootenais did not benefit from annuity goods as they lived off the reservation. The treaty involved only one small band of Kootenais who inhabited the north end of Flathead Lake. The remainder of that tribe lived in small bands scattered along the length of the Kootenai River to its headwaters in Canada.

In the fall of 1860, Chief Alexander led the Pend Oreilles deep into the Blackfeet's exclusive hunting grounds on the Milk River, likely by invitation from Piegan Chief Little Dog. After the long jaunt to near

671 Dunbar, vol. 2, p. 216. Owen Letter, 1859 Annual Report, June 30, 1860.

672 Ibid. vol. 2, pp. 263-264. Owen Letter, 1860 Annual Report.

673 Ibid. vol. 2, p. 265. Owen Letter, October 3, 1861.

the Sweet Grass Hills, they found many buffalo. In fine spirits, they set up camp and prepared for the morning chase. In the evening on bended knees, the entire camp thanked God for the opportunity before them; afterward, Alexander told everyone "to secure his fastest horse, for tomorrow we will make our winter meat and return home."[674] Unencumbered by family, lodge or horse, some 200 Assiniboine and Cree warriors surrounded the sleeping camp. One hour before daylight, they began a steady barrage of rifle fire into outlying lodges.

Trader Michael Ogden, from camp center, described the chaotic rifle reports, sheeting fire from around their positions, women wailing and horses neighing in panic as the enemy cut open lodges in search of plunder. At daylight, a nearby camp of Piegans heard gunfire and hurriedly sent warriors to the sound. Arriving at the battle scene, the Piegans aptly ran off Assiniboines protecting comrades who were ambitiously plundering portions of the undefended Pend Oreille camp.[675] Saved by a former enemy, Alexander's people gathered surviving horses and camp gear and put the wounded on travois for the long trip home. Apparently, the allied Assiniboine war party had plunder in mind, regardless of the tribe's identity. The Pend Oreille tally of the 20 killed included Alexander's 20-year-old son, and of 25 wounded, five later died. With the loss of 290 horses, many had to walk the 400 miles home without provisions, clothing or shelter. Women carrying babies on their backs were completely exhausted. Alexander, tears in his eyes and thirsting for revenge, told the agent he must return to visit the "sleeping place" of his son.[676] A doctor traveling with the International Boundary Survey team that wintered in the area performed some 15 difficult surgeries to extract arrow points and bullets from the wounded. Owen gave four head of cattle to surviving Pend Oreille hunters and their families.

In mid-September of 1860, a Pickney City resident and Washington Territorial census taker made a trip over the mountains to count white and mixed-blood residents of the Bitterroot Valley and St. Ignatius area.[677] Below Lolo Creek in the Bitterroot Valley to Hell Gate he counted 126 individuals in early stages of permanent settlement. The residents included

674 Ibid. vol. 2, pp. 138-139. Owen Letter to Portland Office, December 21, 1860.

675 Jackson, Piikani, appendix ix, p. 257. Piegan historians began a count of personal events in 1830. The winter count began in October, the Indian new year, and ran through the following season. Several different Piegans drew the events on dressed hides over a span of 30 years, ending in 1882. Blue Plume interpreted the painted buffalo hide to a northern Piegan missionary.

676 Ibid.

677 1860 U.S. Census reporter George Taylor for the Spokane District, Washington Territory.

57 white men listed as married who had Indian or mixed-blood wives and children. Occupations embodied 16 farmers, numerous laborers, a few carpenters, packers and teamsters, one each grist miller, blacksmith, tinsmith and carriage maker – or most of the professions in a small community at the time. C.P. Higgins and Frank Worden established a new trading post mercantile at Hell Gate, near the under-construction Walla Walla Road to Fort Benton, that soon became the centerpiece for Montana's first town. Two other small-scale traders and the John Owen operation established the Washington Territorial count of non-Indian heads of household. In a separate census taken by Owen's assistant, Thomas Adams, in March 1861, the Flathead tribe population residing in the area part-time included 90 families, or 548 people.[678] By the next census, the new white settlers would outnumber the Flatheads. The May 4, 1871, Missoula Plains newspaper estimated the population of Missoula County at 2,555 people.[679]

In contrast, the reservation that embraced St. Ignatius and Fort Connah had but 14 white people considered inveterate at the mission site. Some 139 mixed-blood, trapper-hunter families, many being descendants of Jaco Finlay, lived in tepees around the HBC post.[680] As time moved on, many of these people would become permanent reservation residents. Thomas Adams counted 895 upper Pend Oreille in 184 families with 604 adults. Moving west, the Spokane County census taker found no whites living on the Kalispel, Spokane or Coeur d'Alene tribes' home territory due to Indian unrest.

However, the ex-HBC squatter-Métis families of Antoine Plante and Baptist Pione operated, respectively, a ferry and trading post farm and lived among the Spokanes who had returned to their home country after their decisive defeat by U.S. troops. Moving farther north to the Colville River, still in the Spokane District, some 275 whites resided at a newly constructed American military post in the lower valley. The census taker counted a small colony of 55 ex-HBC Métis families with established farms but noted the district had yet to open for land claims.[681] To the east in Kalispel country, only a few white and Métis trappers appeared in the census.

Because of the Indian wars, Colonel Wright ordered a fort built on the lower Colville River valley to protect transient miners from potentially

---

678 Dunbar, vol. 2, pp. 262-263. Owen's 1860 annual report December 12, 1861.

679 PNQ, vol. 30, p. 415. Partoll, Missoula County included both Bitterroot and Missoula valleys at the time.

680 1860 U.S. Census Report, Spokane County, Washington Territory.

681 Ibid. U.S. Census Report.

hostile Indians. Its construction began in 1859, which accounts for all the whites counted on the previous year's census. Along with the soldiers came merchants, a few farmers, blacksmiths, etc., who established a community, Pickney City, nearby to supply the needs of soldiers, miners, the American International Boundary Survey crew and local Indians. Merchants at Pickney promptly built a still to produce alcohol from grain grown in the valley by Métis farmers to satisfy the demand of soldiers and other roughshod customers. The fort hosted a Christmas dinner in 1860, complete with the mind-altering merchant drink, which British members of the International Boundary Survey team attended. Afterward, Lieutenant Samuel Anderson wrote of the nefarious affair: "The Americans at the garrison celebrated the Christmas in their usual way – one man stabbed, another shot, several heads broken and eyes broken, accompanied with several other incidents of minor character, such as their military surgeon breaking his fist in some pugilistic encounter with a citizen"[682] The post commander shut down the still a few days after the fact and future events, some attended by as many as 400, were alcohol free.

In 1863, Stevens County was created, with Pickney City designated its seat of government in the huge division of Washington Territory that included all land east of the Cascades, northern Idaho and the western part of Montana. The little settlement next to the fort thrived but did not spread out, as government land surveys were necessary before opening the region for homesteading. After the fort closed down, the community moved a few miles south to form the present town of Colville.

Back in the Bitterroot Valley, Agent Owen summed up conditions of Indian affairs in his area of responsibility. In a series of letters beginning in August 1859, he wrote that some Bannocks stole 100 head of horses belonging to Indians and whites, and he "planned to visit" them near Fort Hall "to straighten them out." The Indian was becoming daily more and more unsettled, some alarmingly so. "There used to be one enemy – Blackfeet – but now the enemy grows between once friendly tribes," Owen wrote. He listed the natives' concerns that included "inroads made by white man in their country ... fear they will be swallowed up by whites ... Roads being made through their country ... game becoming scarce ... The promises made in treaties were not complied with."[683]

In May 1860, allotment goods shipped from Washington, D.C., arrived at the reservation, of which Owen noted numerous useless items

682 Graham, Patrick, p. 14. Book Z, Military, Fort Colvile, 2006.

683 Dunbar, vol. 2, p. 192. Owen Letters.

"forced upon the Indians in payment for their land." Omitted from a previous request were guns, ammunition, knives, tinware, wagons and a blacksmith shop. Again, in September he noted his "goods were delayed" at Fort Benton, causing the Indians to leave on their hunt without adequate guns, knives, tobacco and blankets. "Lodges will be cold this winter," he wrote. In December destitute Snakes, among the 300 lodges camped in Deer Lodge valley, killed 20 head of cattle belonging to settlers and, when confronted, readily admitted to the attack.[684] On December 30, 1860, he wrote: "The Flatheads … repulsed the overtures of Kamiakin in 1858 with manly firmness … might yet be prompted to change their friendly position; they are Indians and have their sympathies in common with their Red Brethren. I have no hesitation in saying that the united tribes of this mountains' locked section could muster and put in the field 10,000 warriors, well mounted, well armed, ... and could with all ease sustain themselves on game."[685] Owen's string of comments demonstrates his frustration with his overwhelming job and the new, understaffed Bureau of Indian Affairs. His straightforward reports ruffled the feathers of equally swamped superiors in Olympia, Portland and Washington, D.C.

Owen's $105,000 credit purchase of cattle, approved by a post superintendent, Geary, no doubt hit the cash-strapped U.S. government agency hard and had a lot to do with his dismissal two years later. However, John Owen, the first Indian agent in the wilderness of Montana, conscientiously did his best to carry out the Hell Gate Treaty terms. Owen's problems in obtaining important requisitions caused hardships for his charges but nothing like the challenges faced by the buffalo hunters on the prairies.

Twice each year, Salish hunters passed right on by Johnny Grant's livestock operation along the Clark Fork River. Other Indians used the main trail also, including the terrorizing Blackfeet. In June 1861, the veteran raiders stole 15 head of Grant's horses and drove them over Deer Lodge Pass toward the prairie, only to suddenly happen upon a Flathead camp. Realizing their terrific mistake, the Blackfeet released the horses, saving a few of the best, and fled to the hills. The honest and good-natured Flatheads recognized Grant's brand and appointed a few men to drive the horses back to him.[686]

In 1861, the Pend Oreilles, still smarting from the Milk River disaster, conducted their hunt in the White Sulphur Springs area where 60 hunters crossed the designated treaty hunting-boundary into Blackfeet

684 Dunbar, vol. 2, pp. 192, 209, 232. Owen Letters.

685 Ibid, p 233.

686 Stewart, p. 173.

territory. The group began hunting north into the Smith River Valley where they surprised 11 Piegan raiders led by War Chief Three Suns, whose plan was to steal horses from the Pend Oreille camp.[687] Several miles north of the treaty boundary, caught in the open and badly outnumbered, the Piegans hastily disappeared in a brushy draw with the chief's brother, who received a wound in the first volley of fire. The trespassing Pend Oreilles' cost was one man killed. In another incident, 13 Northern Piegans traveled 100 miles to the Judith Basin to harass 60 lodges of Pend Oreille hunters camping there. In the night, Three Suns crawled into the hunters' camp to cut loose prized buffalo horses, but an alert guard put him on the run while shooting holes through his coat, miraculously missing all body parts.

A year earlier while seeking revenge for the Milk River defeat, Pend Oreille raiders returned to the area to recoup horses lost in the disaster. Finding no Assiniboines, only their allied Gros Ventres with plenty of mounts, the Pend Oreilles helped themselves to all they could handle. Quickly leaving the scene, the Pend Oreilles drove their booty west, but the Gros Ventre victims took to their trail in hot pursuit. As the Pend Oreille raiders passed a Piegan village near the Marias River, they left a few ponies nearby without breaking stride. Unaware of the thieves' identity, the pursuing Gros Ventres attacked the Piegan village without pausing to ask their friends how their ponies had gotten there.[688] It is unknown whether this was a planned ploy or if the Pend Oreilles just discarded some horses in surprised flight, but it worked. The raiding party may have originated from the Judith Basin hunting party.

By 1862, a small, growing community of white traders, packers and farmers had sprung up around the Higgins-Warden Mercantile operation at Hell Gate that initiated trade from the Indians. An incident caused Flathead Chief Ambrose (Five Crows) to complain to Agent Owen over a business there selling liquor to Indians, who got their snoots full and nearly caused "serious difficulty." In a letter to an unspecified trader at Hell Gate, Owen vented on the evils of offering liquor to Indians for trivial pecuniary gain.[689] Evidently, the letter did not dent the practice, because his journal continued to note inebriated Indians over the next several years. Owen recorded incidents such as cattle having their legs slashed and a Pend Oreille killing a white man, which he attributed to one or more drunken

687 Jackson, Piikani, p. 207: Three Suns, son of Bear Chief of the Marias River band, painted his battle record on an elk skin that he used later in retelling the event to an Indian agent and writer.

688 Jackson, p. 174.

689 Dunbar, vol. 2, p. 276. Owen Letter, July 17, 1862.

Indians.

The Flatheads conducted their 1862-1863 hunts on the Yellowstone River, eventually going deep into Crow country. A report received from a trapper with the hunting party indicated that up until Christmas, when he departed, only a few scattered bulls had been located. He assumed Victor would probably move camp north to the Musselshell. Victor and his half-starved, weather-beaten village returned to the Bitterroot on April 24, 1863, after nine months on the hunt. The disheartened chief had lost a few men and many horses to the Crows, and he returned with barely enough meat to get them home.[690]

Meanwhile, Flathead Faro and his small party passed a miner's camp on Gold Creek on the Clark Fork River trail on February 4, 1862, herding a band of horses. At about 9 a.m. the next day, Bannock warriors went by the same camp, following Faro's trail downriver. They returned the next day with two scalps and a band of horses. After setting up camp near Grant's place, the Bannocks danced all night,[691] apparently to celebrate killing Faro and a woman at his camp on Flint Creek. The elderly Faro had appropriated horses from the Bannocks' herd to compensate for animals he had lost to their past thievery. Faro and his family group, somewhat loners, hunted the Beaverhead for elk and deer, which at the time was overrun by Bannocks. Surviving members of Faro's party returned to the Bitterroot Valley, where they attempted to raise a war with the Bannocks, but Owen figured they had better wait until their chiefs returned from the hunt. The young men believed the thieving Bannocks got some of their own medicine by Faro's raid. Having only part of the story, the young Flatheads blamed Johnny Grant for harboring 12 lodges of Snakes and Bannocks at his place, the greater part being Grant's relatives by his several wives. When Victor returned home, he quickly put the matter to rest, reminding the angry people of the dangers involved in stealing horses.[692]

In 1863 to 1864, Moise and Ambrose led a hunting expedition deep into the contested Crow-Piegan Lake Basin area that lasted nine or 10 months. Passing through the Gallatin Fork on their way to the Yellowstone, the hunters observed white men building a town that would later become Bozeman, Montana, right in the middle of old haunts. Once on the Yellowstone, the Crows attacked their hunting party's camp and killed a man. That was bad enough, but by late January, not one buffalo, not even a recent sign, existed. In desperate straits, the camp moved north to the

690 Stuart Journal, vol. 1, p. 203.

691 Ibid.

692 Dunbar, vol. 2, p. 247. Owen Journal.

Musselshell where they found buffalo and Piegan horse thieves. The windy, bitterly cold winter brought on sickness, which caused a few deaths on the dismal plains. On their trip back home, the hunting party was struck by Bannock horse thieves at Flint Creek, who drove off 70 horses belonging to Pelchimo, the well-respected horse doctor. Pelchimo died at the hands of one Bannock thief in his attempt to recover his property.[693]

As the returning Flathead hunters neared Johnny Grant's place, Chief Victor arranged a meeting with the livestock operator, Grant, and a miner that had Bannock and Shoshoni wives. On April 7, the chief told them of probable trouble with the Pend Oreilles because of the Bannock and Shoshoni's many horse-stealing relatives who camped near Grant's place.[694] Victor warned the stockman to keep the Snakes and Bannocks away from his place. During the summer, Grant moved his operation from the mouth of the Little Blackfoot River, adjacent to the primary travel route of the Salish and allies, to Cottonwood (Deer Lodge).

Earlier, in July 1862, John Owen wrote: "The Mullan Road is lined with people going to the Deer Lodge mines."[695] A community of prospectors and merchants to serve them boomed for several years until placer mines played out. Left behind, the settlers and cattle ranchers formed the second-oldest town in Montana and named it Cottonwood, now Deer Lodge, Montana. Some of the new Mullan Road travelers took up claims in the upper Bitterroot Valley without knowing anything of the area's conditional reservation status. Flatheads, alarmed over treaty violations, made it known to Agent Owen, but before he could do anything about the trespassing palefaces, the Shoshonis raided and ran off the settlers' and Flatheads' livestock. In October, a hopeful Flathead party rode south to take the Snakes to task for depredating their animals, degrading their lands and disrupting their lives.[696]

In August 1862, the aging Chief Victor stayed home from the hunt, and John Owen's Flathead Reservation agent days were numbered. In his last official act, he provided the old chief with a cabin and designated a field for his use in the spring. In December, Owen turned over his job to an agent bureaucrat sent from Olympia, Charles Hutchins, who was utterly unfamiliar with local natives' problems but very aware of the Indian Affairs Agency's funding problems and of Owen's critical correspondence. The ex-agent Owen received criticism from superiors because he had not

693 Dunbar, vol. 1 pp. 278-79. Owen Journal.

694 Stuart, vol. 2, pp. 203-204.

695 Dunbar, vol. 1, p. 254. Owen Journal.

696 Ibid, vol. p. 262.

firmly established agriculture among the natives; yet, they disregarded headquarter's refusal to fill specific requests for farm implements. During the incoming and outgoing agents' meeting, Owen received the news that his benefactor, ex-Governor Isaac Stevens, had lost his life in the Civil War. Later, he penned frustration in his journal over the government's lack of understanding regarding natives' ability or their willingness to take up farming: "[They] are Indians and Indians they will remain. To Christianize, Civilize and Educate the Indian is a farce long since exploited. The Department at Washington knows no more about the management of the Indian tribes than Indians do about the cause of the present war."[697]

By January 1865, the new agent Hutchins had no better luck encouraging agriculture endeavors among the reservation Indians, even though annuity shipments included many tools. The Olympia superintendent complained of parting with such a "large outlay for only 35 acres of cultivation." Most of the Indians continued to hunt as buffalo parts, particularly meat, brought high prices from white miners and settlers.[698] Before leaving his post in two years, Hutchins began a crusade to remove the British Fort Connah and replace it with an American-owned trading post on the reservation. In a letter to the Montana Territory governor, he suggested that an American trader sent to the reservation would receive little competition from Fort Connah and would better serve travelers in the area.

A new agent in 1866, A.H. Chapman, took up the cause and brought the commissioner of Indian Affairs into the fray, who after several months of study and consultation with the Montana governor, ordered Chapman to evict the HBC post personnel. When confronted, Connah Postmaster Napoleon Fitzstubbs told the Indian agent, "I was sent here by the Company [HBC] with orders to remain here and trade until I was forcibly ejected from the reservation." Stymied by Fitzstubbs' protest against his removal, the agent shifted the matter to higher authorities,[699] which resulted in no action, due to the claims settlement commission agreement.

Both Pend Oreille and Flathead chiefs had lost control over some of their younger men. Incidents of horse stealing, outside the realm of retaliation for a similar crime against them, became more common. Poor, young Salish men stole from tribes that had pillaged their people in the past, namely the Crows, Blackfeet, Bannocks and Shoshonis. At the same time, Salish men began trading for firewater at Hell Gate and from miners along the main Clark Fork trail to the buffalo. Despite such shortcomings,

697 Dunbar, p. 262, Owen Journal, December 13, 1862

698 Hale, Robert C. Report, pp. 244-245.

699 PNQ, vol. 30, No. 4, Patroll, p. 411.

the Salish remained honest in their dealing with friends and whites. One such incident occurred on July 20, 1863, when 16 Flathead and Pend Oreille horse thieves passed Granville Stuart's camp on Gold Creek with horses stolen from the Crows. Two animals among the booty had a white man's brand, which the Indians returned to the owner who rewarded their trouble.[700] The few Indians among the Salish who committed crimes against white men received no support from their chiefs. In May 1863, a Pend Oreille and another man killed a white man on the Clark Fork canyon trail, stole his horses and outfit, then joined Flatheads returning to the Bitterroot Valley. A group of white miners who found his body tracked the Flatheads to their village and demanded the chief turn over the murderer. At first, the chief refused, as the Indian was not of his tribe, but further discussion helped him decide in favor of the unhappy miners, who conducted a short trial and hung the guilty party at Hell Gate.[701]

Education had also been added to the mix, for early in 1863, St. Ignatius received an $1,800 government grant to establish a reservation school for children at the mission. Four Montreal nuns arrived the following year with credentials as teachers, some with medical backgrounds. The sisters immediately set up a boarding school for girls, while the priests attempted the same for the boys with limited success. The Pend Oreilles, still stuck in their old ways, did not readily take to this program. Seven years after initiation of the school, just six boys and 23 girls enrolled. When the buffalo were gone in 1882, the school's enrollment had jumped to 186. The nuns also began a small hospital soon after they first arrived that served the reservation until 1914. St. Ignatius provided much assistance to the Pend Oreilles and a few Kootenais during the early years of government reservation management.

Population growth of miners, merchants and settlers in the Rocky Mountains brought on political boundary changes initiated by the U.S. Congress in 1863 and 1864 that created the Idaho and Montana territories. They were subdivisions originating from Washington, Oregon and Nebraska territories, each of which represented current state boundaries.[702]

Mullan Road provided the thoroughfare for a flood of gold seekers cutting across Inland Salish country, some of whom stopped along the way to farm or begin small communities, which cropped up in the Spokane, Gallatin and Bitterroot valleys. At Fort Owen, part-time post manager Tom

700 Stuart Journal, vol. 1, p. 252.

701 Ibid. pp. 242, 245-246.

702 Idaho Territory originally included parts of Wyoming and western Montana from the Continental Divide east to its current boundary.

Harris lamented in 1865 that more and more settlers passed by Hell Gate: "The country is overloaded with goods and whiskey, which they sell for less than St. Louis prices. Drunken Indians were everywhere."[703]

In Spokane and Coeur d'Alene quarters, Antoine Plante operated a ferry on the Spokane River below today's Post Falls that linked overland traffic with the Mullan Road. The crossing became obsolete after bridge construction near the current Idaho line in 1864, soon followed by a small settlement called Spokane Bridge.

South of the Mullan Road, the town of Lewiston sprang up in 1861 in the wake of gold discoveries near Pierce; both places were within the Nez Perce Reservation set by treaty just three years earlier. Soon Lewiston was the largest town in the newly created Idaho Territory, and it stood as the capital until Boise-area population surpassed the short-lived boomtown a few years later. The fur trade era all but passed into history in 1866, brought on by a decline in markets and dwindling resources. Exploration of the region by the fur industry people had laid the groundwork for development and permanent white settlement that already had begun. Former mountain men turned to locating wagon roads and providing guide service for newcomers to promising places for settlement and mining, just as the natives had done for them in their search for beaver. The Inland Salish would remember the friendly, cooperative years between themseves and white fur men. The American Indians' attempt to maintain ancient lifestyles under the pressure of mass immigration, invasion and mandatory changes by government buckled under the movement that white leaders in the East called Manifest Destiny. The United States of America now spread from coast to coast, and all things the demoralized native peoples held dear went underground or disappeared.

703 Dunbar, Tom Harris kept Fort Owen Journal in the absence of John Owen.

Epilogue
1864-1875

White mining and settlement rapidly replaced the fur trade barter system with a medium of exchange that involved gold and American greenbacks. To earn the new currency, one needed to produce something useful for white man's consumption, such as foodstuffs, building materials or a service to provide such needs – enterprises natives took years to grasp. Caught up in the huge economic and cultural change, the Inland Salish and other natives struggled to survive in the new environment. Inadequacies of new reservation systems and dislike of white man's survival methods compelled the natives to hunt and gather until those resources were exhausted or beyond reach, due to white settlement.

A few words of closure are necessary to describe the Inland Salish plight during the immediate aftermath of the fur trade age. The once-vast wilderness rapidly lost its original character to developments; lush bottomland turned into pastures, farm fields and placer mines, all connected to communities.

The U.S. government dealt with this activity, starting in 1862, by initiating the Homestead Act that allowed American citizens to file claims on vacant lands up to 160 acres for agricultural purposes, subject to a token fee. Just four years later, the U.S. Congress authorized the Chaffee law that granted rights to the applicant to stake mining claims subject to legitimate mineral production. As a result, these laws opened the floodgates for opportunistic Americans to swarm into Indian country to take up claims on longtime hunting, camping and root-digging lands. Initially, white settlement affected the buffalo-dependent natives bound for the plains more than it did the stay-at-home Inland Salish tribes, who still had fish, roots and wild game.

During the white dash for land and minerals, only two Inland Salish tribes had reservations to fall back on, the Pend Oreilles-Flatheads and one band of Kootenais, which protected a small portion of their original homelands. The Coeur d'Alene and Spokane tribes, both without reservations, managed to dodge excessive settlement, but many people continued to pass through their country on the Mullan Road to points west.[704] How-

704 According to Coeur d'Alene oral history, Mullan never asked the tribe for permission to build the road, which is likely the case with the Spokanes.

ever, the door to whites taking up land swung wide open in 1873 after the government and the Coeur d'Alene tribe agreed to a reservation about one-quarter the size of its original territory. Homesteaders soon poured into the surrounding countryside, taking up claims that included lands in the Spokane tribal quarter.

The upper and middle Spokane bands inhabiting the Spokane River Valley area continued to present a problem for the government regarding settlement of the valuable land along the river. With the transcontinental railroad about to pass through the valley, something had to be done about Indians in the way. A potential solution came as a presidential order in 1881 to establish a small reservation on the river's north bank in a portion of lower Spokanes' original territory; however, the upper and middle bands of Spokanes refused to move there. Finally, after more strained negotiations, and with Fort George Wright in their midst, the holdouts ceded their lands and moved either to the Coeur d'Alene, Flathead or Colville reservations at government expense. The displaced made their choice based on friends and relatives already located at particular reservations, except for Spokane Chief Garry, who refused to move. The old chief moved from his farm to a white man's abandoned log cabin on Latah Creek, where he and his family lived until a different white man claimed the property.

One day during Garry's absence, the new owner burned the cabin to the ground. Garry moved his family upstream, where a kindly white settler allowed him to live on his property until his death. A few years before he died, Garry said to a newspaper reporter, "Inside us humans there is the same color of blood, so we should treat each other equally under the God of ours."

Friends and neighbors to the north, the Kalispel tribe, experienced white man's advance when in 1883 the Northern Pacific Railroad began construction through the eastern part of their lands. Contesting the encroachment on their lands, the Kalispel tribe and the U.S. government began treaty negotiations at Sandpoint in 1887, with both the upper and lower Pend Oreilles' lead men present. Chief of the upper Pend Oreille tribe, Michael, Alexander's replacement, signed the faulty document, but Masselow, as the leader of the Kalispels, declined the terms. Congress's refusal to ratify the treaty resulted in the government confiscating all Kalispel lands and opened the way for settlement and the railroad. Railroad construction spurred the development of communities along its route, such as Clark Fork, Hope and Sandpoint, which displaced some Kalispels from their hunting and gathering places. Many families chose to vacate their homeland to live with relatives on the Coeur d'Alene and Flathead Reservations while others moved in with Kalispels living near the old mission site and root meadows. By executive order in 1914, President Woodrow Wilson authorized 4,600 acres for a reservation along a 10-mile stretch of the Pend Oreille River at Usk, Washington.

The mass of white miners and settlers in parts of Montana Territory led to a clash of cultures between newcomers and Indians traveling through their communities on their annual treks to hunt the Yellowstone or north to the Missouri River. Either destination guided the natives through Missoula on the main Mullan Road, which eventually took northern hunters through the mining town of Helena. Those natives going to the Yellowstone forked off the Mullan Road and passed by the settlements of Deer Lodge and Bozeman. The Flatheads and Pend Oreilles, along with other Columbia Plateau tribes, used those roads to travel to the buffalo, which led to a variety of problems for both Indians and whites. One can understand the settlers' agitation caused by successive groups of 500 or more Indians dragging travoises on dusty roads, trailing twice as many horses that disturbed crop lands adjacent to the road.

White residents' complaints to government officials became exaggerated in suggesting the pitiful Indians had no means to support themselves and must beg or steal to survive. A rising flow of complaints over "roaming Indians" resulted in the U.S. military establishing a series of forts near population centers and along travel routes. Fort Shaw sprang up near the Mullan Road on Sun River, midway between Fort Benton and Helena, to protect the supply route from hostile Blackfeet. At the same time, Fort Ellis arose in the Gallatin Valley, and a satellite post at Camp Meagher helped keep the peace during native migrations to and from the Yellowstone River country.

Often, one group of Nez Perces, Spokanes and Colvilles would follow another of the Pend Oreilles, Kootenais and Flatheads. Adding to settlers' disfavor and anxiety toward Indians, the Piegans and Crows assaulted white settlements, stole horses, wounded cattle with arrows and committed isolated murders from 1866 to 1869. In all cases, soldiers or white citizen groups pursued the raiders, recovered stolen property and put down many thieves. In addition to harassment from white settlers, Salish people traveling to the buffalo had to deal with the Blackfeet, often face-to-face, in competition for diminishing herds of buffalo. Utilizing the Mullan Road in 1866, the Pend Oreilles returned early from their hunt, devoid of meat and travoising 27 wounded men, due to a Blood, Piegan and Blackfoot attack on the hunting party that killed 20 men and women on the spot. Father Ravalli went to St. Ignatius Mission hospital where his surgical skills saved many of the wounded. Later in the year, Flatheads arrived home with loads of meat, unscathed by hostile tribes.[705] The new military posts did little to resolve grievances between native tribes that earlier treaties had addressed, but they left the Indians alone to resolve intertribal grievances the old-fashioned way – by hostility. Military personnel primarily protected settlers, miners and supply routes from hostile attacks.

Elsewhere in early July 1867, a party of Flathead hunters on the move to the Yellowstone camped about 10 miles west of the developing town of Bozeman, where a young Indian had stolen some horses from a nearby settler. A captain and squad of soldiers from nearby Fort Meagher went to the camp and recovered the horses. The captain demanded the chief turn over the thief and met no resistance, but the Indians could not find him. Soldiers returned to the Flathead camp the next day, where the chief handed over the guilty young man. The captain declared his intention to hang the thief, but, after a pause, offered a reprieve if the chief so requested. The chief called the thief a very bad Indian who caused much trouble and wished him to die. The soldiers hung him in the presence of the camp.[706]

Some Flatheads particularly concerned over the Bozeman hanging called for a tribal council meeting to consider ordering the white man to leave the country. Area settlers, upon hearing of the meeting, readied their guns, and nervously awaited the outcome. The council convened on August 20, 1867, at the mouth of Lolo Creek where Flathead leaders convinced their tribe's majority that an attempt to force the foreigners away was a bad idea. Yet, after the meeting broke up, six disgruntled and drunken Indians fired five pistol shots at a white man without effect as he passed them five miles below Fort Owen.[707]

The Third Judicial District of Montana Territory met in 1869 at Helena to convene a grand jury to address the problem of "roving" Indians. Settlers had accused the Pend Oreilles of stealing horses, setting prairie fires and possibly committing murder while on their way to the hunting grounds. Members of the grand jury, hoping to expose conditions of the white people, recommended that the military and Territorial Bureau of Indian Affairs authorities should prohibit Indian passage through settled

705 Chapman Letter, p. 315, August 31, 1866.
706 Stuart, vol. 2, p. 66.
707 Dunbar, vol. 2, p. 68. Owen Journal.

valleys.[708] Neither took immediate action on the jury's recommendation, since Indian treaties had not restricted them to reservations.

Unsuccessful with the grand jury process, communities put pressure on the new Montana Territory superintendent of Indian Affairs, who issued instructions to his agents in an 1871 letter that, in "all cases," friendly Indians desiring to pass through white settlements shall apply for permission. "If granted," a military guard would accompany them through said settlement. Permits were available from either the reservation agent or a military post authority, whereupon unhappy pony soldiers guided them through settlement areas. The loosely enforced edict had limited success in quelling complaints, as most Indian groups did not bother to obtain a permit. On one occasion, Pend Oreille Chief Big Canoe's party of 500 "assorted Indians" returning from a winter hunt obtained soldiers to escort them through Blackfeet country and Helena. The officer in charge later explained, "They were 11 days out from Fort Shaw, were hard to herd and lazy to travel."[709] Spokanes, Coeur d'Alenes and Kalispels, all without reservations, traveled with either the Pend Oreilles or Flatheads, whose agent and treaty placed no restrictions on leaving the reservation at their pleasure. Such trifling actions satisfied neither Indians nor settlers.

Two giants in the fur trade industry, HBC and AFC, closed down Western operations in 1869 and 1871 respectively, leaving the diminishing business to small operators. Both Forts Colvile and Connah closed their doors after finalization of the international claims committee between the United States and HBC. Duncan McDonald Jr., the final manager of Fort Connah, moved to the newly founded town of Missoula, where he independently resumed business. There, he capitalized on strong demand for buffalo meat and certain by-products from settlers. Out of necessity, the enterprising and efficient Salish hunters maintained their lifestyle in order to supply themselves with white man's merchandise. One such group of 600 Pend Oreilles, Coeur d'Alenes, Kootenais, Spokanes and Colvilles, hunting in three heats, killed about 600 animals in two hours. Some made out exceptionally well in the region's new economy, according to a January 1875 letter sent by McDonald to the Weekly Missoula newspaper. He reported five individuals singlehandedly killed 104 fat cows that were sold to McDonald for many white men's goods and new currency.

Most Salish and other native hunters refused to alter lifestyles to merge with the developing new economy, and they clung tenaciously to old

708 Farr, U. S. Grand Jury Report, October 9, 1869.
709 Farr, Part 2, vol. 54.

but proven and familiar ways. However, torment from the new white citizens and violent deaths by fellow Indians gradually motivated more to bend toward the white man's ways. Cultivation on the Flathead Reservation increased production from 35 acres to 145 acres by 1870. That year, Indians produced, in bushel measurement, 500 wheat, 2,800 potatoes, 25 peas and 50 beets.[710] Two years later, Jocko Indian Agent C.J. Jones reported that some 105 Pend Oreille men had taken up farming and ranching, or about 25 percent of the heads of household. Each owned 13 acres on which they collectively produced 5,000 bushels of wheat, 1,650 of potatoes and 160 of corn. At the same time, the Spokanes, and to a lesser extent the Kalispels, also increased their agricultural production. The dedicated buffalo hunting factions of the Inland Salish stayed their course until the last animal fell.

Newspapers reported antagonistic and ugly stories about the always-on-the-move Indians. The Helena Daily Herald wrote of a nearby Flathead and Pend Oreille camp in 1873: "Bucks and Squaws are to be seen at all hours on our streets. ... They are an excellent substitute for hogs about a slaughterhouse, and garbage and offal disappear under their manipulation with a suddenness and dexterity."

Elsewhere, in 1872, The Missoula Pioneer complained bitterly about the Nez Perces' annual passage through their town "to trade in firewater, steal and rob white settlers of their horses and mules, destroy grain fields with their band of horses, lay waste and pillage unprotected farms and farmhouses, assault frightened defenseless women and children." The newspaper demanded the government keep the Nez Perces on their reservation and "urged similar steps ... taken to keep the Pend Oreille and Kootenai upon their reservation in the Jocko."[711] The same paper published an indifferent story in March 1877 of Sioux and Crow that had "cleaned out" Big Canoe's Pend Oreilles on the Yellowstone. "We will soon have them back here ... in a destitute and dilapidated plight on their return home where starvation awaits them."

Two years later, the Deer Lodge News Northwest declared, after a large body of Flatheads, Pend Oreilles and Nez Perces moved through their town: "Some several hundred warriors remained behind to engage in the semi-annual set-to with the Sioux by way of keeping up the spirit of their forefathers. A courier had arrived from the field bearing the joyful news ... that hostilities had actually commenced and that the Flatheads were already in possession of 50 head of Sioux ponies and some hair. Let

710 Danilson, vol. 1, 1870 Annual Report, Bureau of Indian Affairs, p. 189.

711 Farr, Part 2, vol. 54. Newspapers articles, October 24, 1873, and September 21, 1872, respectively.

'em fight."[712]

Such commentary continued for another three years until the buffalo were all but gone, when newspapers turned their attention to the promotional grand opening of the Flatheads' conditional reservation as the solution to a steady increase in numbers of white settlers wanting their lands. The Flatheads, with many horses and some cattle and crops, occupied the most fertile land in the valley above Lolo Creek, complete with a mission church.

The new St. Mary's church and mission that took root in the fall of 1866, a mile south of the Fort Owen site among the Flatheads, served the Indians until the last of them moved to the Jocko Reservation. The priests' vital records reflected the struggle for survival the Flatheads endured from 1866 to 1891. During that time, three women and 60 Flathead men met violent deaths, which amounted to 35 percent of adult male deaths during the period. Flatheads' forcible deaths included seven by the Crow, five by the Blackfeet, 22 by the Sioux and three by white men.[713] Most fatalities occurred on the buffalo grounds before 1879 when intertribal competition for the diminishing resource caused disputes. Pend Oreille losses of this nature surely equaled or exceeded their numbers, while few Spokanes, Coeur d'Alenes and Kalispels suffered violent deaths on the contentious plains due to smaller numbers participating in hunts.

Traditionally, the Flatheads avoided encounters with the Sioux as the latter tribe's domain laid many miles to the east of Flathead hunting grounds. White man's inroads into Indian country and depleted buffalo herds caused large numbers of Sioux to drift north and west into Crow country. The largest loss of life during this period occurred July 11, 1871, at the hands of the Sioux. According to H.H. Tourney-High's 1930 interview with the old Flathead warrior named Sam Resurrection, the fight began when a large force of Sioux attacked a small, detached Flathead hunting party mounted on fatigued horses. The disadvantaged hunters lost several men as they raced toward their well-protected camp of several hundred Indians. The Sioux attacked the Salish position but were unable to break their defensive line. At nightfall they retired to their camp, less 24 warriors downed by the Flatheads. In the night, the Flatheads slipped away with their wounded and horses, leaving 18 brave men on the battlefield without burial.[714]

During such difficult years of upheaval and change, the Salish lost four longtime, strong Christian leaders to death. Upper Pend Oreille Head

712 Ibid. News articles, November 17, 1870, and March 16, 1872, respectively.

713 Bigart, Life and Death, pp. 29-30.

714 Holt, H. and High, H. Flatheads of Montana.

Chief Alexander went first in 1868, followed by Flathead Second Chief Moise in the same year, who had suffered illness for some time. Head Chief Victor passed away of sickness in 1870 while hunting near Three Buttes on the Sun River. His quiet courage and determination in the compromise at the Hell Gate Treaty deliberations rejuvenated his tribe's respect for him. Ambrose, who succeeded Moise as second chief, died in 1871. All four great leaders, all 70 or older, lived throughout the fur trade era with the Blackfeet as their largest problem in a period of great change brought on by a new ruler and white settlement.

Coming on the heels of the Flathead-Sioux conflict, a government commission headed by James Garfield, a U.S. congressman and future president, met with the Flathead tribe in 1872 to negotiate their movement to the Flathead Reservation. Citizens in the Bitterroot Valley pressed government officials to solve the "Indian problem" which caused President Ulysses S. Grant to issue an executive order to remove the Flatheads to the Jocko Agency, even those who held land patents. Following his orders, Garfield told tribal leaders the valley above Lolo Creek had been "carefully surveyed and examined" in accordance with the Hell Gate Treaty and found inferior in value to the Mission Valley site (Jocko Agency). To encourage the move on these premeditated fabrications of the truth, Garfield offered the Flatheads $50,000 for the sale of the Bitterroot country and farm implements, cattle and land for their relocation to the reservation.

Flathead Head Chief Charlo, a son of Victor, refused to move his people. The final document contained his mark, those of Nez Perce-by-birth War Chief Arlee and Adolphe, and Garfield's signature. The latter packed up to return East and added the X next to Chief Charlo's name, which attending chiefs later said Charlo never signed. Arlee and his people moved first to the Flathead Reservation, followed by Adolphe a few years later, leaving Charlo and some 450 of his people behind in the Bitterroot Valley.[715] Soon after Garfield's treacherous deed, homesteaders swarmed into the valley and took up claims on all lands but the Flatheads' seasonal land-use area and improvements. After the demise of the buffalo, the two diverse cultures lived side-by-side for a few years, with the natives struggling to survive by white man's ways.

In 1884, the government invited Charlo and his lead men to Washington, D.C., hoping to convince them to move their people to the reservation. After nearly a month in the Great White Father's place, Charlo yielded only that his people were free to move if they so desired. As for him-

715 Hungry Wolf, p. 96.

self, he wished to live and die in the valley his ancestors called home.

Upon Charlo's returning to the Bitterroot Valley, 21 families decided to move to the reservation without Charlo and 350 others.[716] One by one, other families began leaving, motivated by changes that took away ancestral home locations and left troublesome young men with no buffalo to hunt.

One can imagine the chiefs' cynicism and amazement when they boarded the "Iron Horse" at Missoula in 1884 for their journey to council with the Great White Father in Washington, D.C. The depot from which they boarded stood near their ancestors' primary camping grounds. As the engine chugged its way up the old Clark Fork River trail at a full gallop, they surely reminisced going to the buffalo not so long ago. Cutting through rocky canyons bypassed in earlier days, they crossed bridges over rivers at one time forded on horses. They passed through prior hunting grounds that rekindled memories of successes and conflicts, all in a matter of days instead of weeks. Traveling farther east to their destination, the chiefs surely marveled at the size and power of the white tribe.

After returning home, most of these great leaders rejected traditional lifestyles and reluctantly accepted white man's living conditions. They built homes, acquired livestock, and changed from hunting and gathering to staying in one place and farming.

In 1891, after many of Chief Charlo's people left, another General and Indian Agent Peter Ronan met with him to convince him to move to the reservation. After a long pause, Charlo looked Ronan in the eye and in a quiet but firm voice said: "I will go – I and my children. My young men are becoming bad; they have no place to hunt. I do not want the land you promise. I do not believe your promises. All I want is enough ground for my grave. We will go over there."[717] Earlier, in 1876, the Montana Territory legislature had proposed a tax on land occupied by Chief Charlo's band in the Bitterroot Valley. The chief's response to the matter, printed in a Missoula weekly newspaper, reflected all Northwestern Indians' sentiments toward white man at the time.

A part of Charlo's eloquent speech is worth mention: "Seven times ten winters ago," when Lewis and Clark's party arrived unexpectedly at Ross Hole camp, "what is he? Who sent him here? We were happy when he first came; since then we often saw him, always hear him, we first thought he came from the light, but he comes like the dark of the evening now, not like

716 Ronan, pp. 62-71.
717 Ibid. p. 96.

the dawn of the morning. He comes like a day that passed and night enters our future with him."[718]

It was the beginning of the end for some and a beginning for others.

718 Weekly Missoulian, April 26, 1876.

Appellations

White men's journals during the fur trade and missionary periods designated places, people and things much differently than did the Salish. For example, the Salish word for today's Bitterroot River translates as "waters of the red osier dogwood." The Salish described the trail up the Bitterroot River from their campsite as from Grass Valley (west Missoula) the road passed the Trail to Nez Perce (Lolo Creek), Big Cottonwoods (Stevensville), Rams Head (above Darby) and Big Open (Ross Hole) to mention a few. Journalists used miles to mark features along the road, useful in guiding fellow fur men through the country to beaver. Few Indian names for places are in use today, while a larger number of fur traders' titles have spanned the years. The author has used modern-day appellations in most cases.

Many early accounts refer to the Flathead, Pend Oreille and Kalispel tribes as Flatheads, whom all spoke the same language and joined to hunt buffalo, which made group distinction difficult. The term Salish, used frequently in the text, refers to a combination of the tribes mentioned above when participating in an event or cultural practice. Some of the Spokane, Coeur d'Alene and Colville peoples spoke a similar Salish dialect and joined them on buffalo hunts.

Columbia Plateau: The Columbia and Snake River drainages east of the Cascade Mountains in Washington, Idaho and Montana.

Fort Colvile: A Hudson's Bay Company trading post. Original spelling corrupted to Colville.

Oregon Country: An American term for a disputed region of the Pacific Northwest.

Southeastern Idaho: The region from Lookout Pass south along the Continental Divide, then south along the Idaho state line to Utah, then west to Raft River, then in a northerly direction to the point of beginning.

Inland Salish: The Pend Oreille, Kalispel, Flathead, Spokane, Colville and Coeur d'Alene tribes.

Upper Pend Oreilles: Ear Pendants or Ear Bobs

Kalispels (Lower Pend Oreilles): Ear Pendant, Camas People

Colvilles: Kettle

Coeur d'Alenes: Pointed Hearts

Blackfeet Nation: In order to differentiate between the nation's three tribes, a conflict with proper English occurs in this text when referring

to the nation as a whole.
Blackfeet: Blackfoot People (Siksika)
Bloods: Bloody Indians (Kainaa)
Piegans: Muddy River Indians, Meadow Indians (Piikani), Blackfeet Plains neighbors
Assiniboines: Stone Indians
Gros Ventre: White Clay People or Falls Indians (Atsiina)
Cree: Southern People
Nez Perce: Pierced Noses
Shoshoni: Snakes

Very few names of Salish people appear in source material or in their English translation, if mentioned. Fur traders gave names to principal natives in the French language, but when translated to English, a given name often described a physical feature of the person. Catholic missionaries added another name through the baptismal process. Selected chiefs' names in Salish, English or French translation, and baptismal follow:

Kalispel: Etsowish-simmege-itshin, Standing Grizzly Bear, Loyola
Pend Oreille: Tum-cle-hot-cut-se, No Horses, Alexander
Flathead: Insula, Red Feather, Little Chief, Michael
Spokane: Unknown, Sun Chief, Spokane Garry
Coeur d'Alene: Balsa, unknown, Vincent
Coeur d'Alene: Stellam, Thunder, not baptized
Pend Oreille: Unknown, La Buche, Rough Hewn
Pend Oreille: Unknown, Gros Pied, Big Feet

Names of waterways in use during the fur trade period follow:
Pend Oreille River: Saleesh, Flathead
Pend Oreille Lake: Kalispel
Upper Clark Fork River: Courtins, Piegan and Hell Gate
Snake River: Lewis
Salmon River: Salmon
Lemhi River: South Fork of Salmon
Ruby River: Stinking Water
Beaverhead River: Jefferson
Big Hole River: Wisdom
Birch Creek, (Idaho): Cote's Defile
Little Lost River: Days Defile
Lost River: Godins Defile

Abbreviations

NWC: North West Company
HBC: Hudson's Bay Company
PFC: Pacific Fur Company
RMFC: Rocky Mountain Fur Company
AFC: American Fur Company

Abbreviations in footnotes
OHQ: Oregon Historical Quarterly
PCNWQ: Pacific Northwest Quarterly
WHQ: Washington Historical Quarterly

Bibliography

Books and Periodicals

Alter, J. Cecil. *Jim Bridger.* University of Oklahoma Press, Norman, OK, 1962.

Anonymous Fur Trader. *Traits of American Indian Life and Character.* Smith Elder and Company, London, 1853.

Baker, Burt Brown, ed. *Letters of Dr. John Mcloughlin 1829-32.* Bruford and Mort, Portland, Oregon, 1948.

Barry, J. Nellson. *Wilkes Expeditions to Fort Colville.* WHQ Vol. 20 June 1929.

Belyea, Barbara. *David Thompson Columbia Journals.* McGill-Queen's University Press, Montreal, 1993.

Bigart, Robert and Woodcock, Clarence. *In the Name of the Salish and Kootenai Nation.* Salish Kootenai Press, Pablo, MT, 1996.

Bond, Trever J. "History of Fort Lemhi." *Magazine of Western History Vol. 53, August 30, 2010.*

Boas, Franz and Teit, James. *Couer d'Alene, Flathead and Okanagan Indians.* Ye Galleon Press, Fairfield, WA, 1930.

Campbell, John V. *The Sinclair Party Emmigration to Spokane, Washington.* WHQ Vol. 7 July 1916.

Carson, as dictated to Col and Mrs. O.C. Peters abt 1856. *Kit Carson's Own Story of His Lifetime.* Santa Barbara, CA, 2001.

Catlin, George. *North American Indians.* Edited by Peter Mathiessen. Penguin Books, London, 1989.

Cebula, Larry. *Plains Indians and the Quest for Spirit Power 1700-1850.* University of Nebraska Press, Lincoln, NE, 2003.

Chance, David H. *Infuence of the Hudson's Bay Company on the Native Cluture of the Colville District.* Northwest Anthropologic Research Notes; Vol. 7 No. 1, part 2.

Chittenden, Hiram M. and Richardson, Albert T. Pierre De Smet Bicentenial. *Life, Letters and Travels of Father Pierre Jean De Smet 1801-1873.* Vol. 4 Iraneis Harper, New York, 1905.

Chittenden, Hiram Martin. *The American Fur Trade of the Far West.* 2 volumes: University of Nebraska Press, Lincoln, NE, 1933-1937.

Cole, Jean Muray,ed. *The Blessed Wilderness.* Archibald McDonald Letters Columbia Press Victoria, B.C.

Coues, Elliott. *Alexander Henry and David Thompson Journals.* Vol. 1 and 2.

Ross and Haines, Inc, Minneapolis, MN, 1965.
Cox, Ross. *Adventures on the Colombia River*. H. Collburn, R. Betly, London England, 1831.
Curtis, Edward S. *The North American Indians*. 20 vols. copyright, North Western University, 1907-1930.
Davies, John, ed. *Douglas of the Forests, Journal of David Douglas*. University of Washington Press, 1980.
Davis, Rev. William L. *St. Ingatius Mission*. C.W. Hill Co., Spokane, WA, 1954.
Dempsey, Hugh A.,ed. *The Rundle Journals 1840-1848*. Historical Society of Alberta, Calgary, Canada, 1977.
Devoto, Bernard. *Across the Wide Missouri*. Houghton-Mifflin Co., Boston, 1975.
Discovery, Writers. *First Roots – Montana's Oldest Community*. Stoneydale Press Publishing Company, Stevensville, MT, 2005.
Donnelly, Joseph R.translation. *Wilderness Kingdom*. The Journal and Paintings of Nicolas Point J.J. 1840-47, Rinehart and Winston, New York, 1967.
Drury, Cliford M. *Henry Harmon Spaulding*. Caxton Printers, Caldwell, Idaho, 1936.
Dunbar, Seymour,ed. *The Journals and Letters of Major John Owen*. Two Volumes, Edward Eberstadt, New York, 1927.
Ellersick, Steven Donald. "Ellersick." Remembering St. Ignatius Mission on the Pend Oreille River. 1994.
Elliott, T.C., ed. *Alexander Ross 1824 Snake Rriver Expedition*. Oregon Historical Quarterly (OHQ) Vol. 14, 1913.
—. *John Work Journal September 7 - December 14, 1825*. Washington Historical Quarterly (WHQ),Vol. 5 No. 3, 1914.
—. *Journal of David Thompson*. September 26 to October 16, 1809, WHQ Vol. 23, July 1932.
—. *Journal of David Thompson*. 1812,WHQ Vol. 19, October 1918.
—. *Journal of David Thompson*. 1811, WHQ Vol. 23, January 1932.
—. *Journal of David Thompson*. 1809 WHQ Vol. 11, July 1920.
—. *Journal of John Work*. December 15, 1825, to September 15, 1826 WHQ Vol. 15 No. 4, 1914.
—. *Journal of John Work -Snake River Expedition 1830-31*. OHQ Vol. 13 No. 4, 1912.
Ewers, John. *The Blackfeet*. Oklahoma University Press, Norman, OK, 1958.

Fahey, John. *The Flathead Indians*. Oklahoma University Press, Norman, OK, 1974.

—. *The Kalispel Indians*. Oklahoma University Press, Norman, OK, 1986.

Farr, William E. *Going to Buffalo*. Montana Magazine of Western History Part 2 Vol. 54, Spring 2004.

—. *Going to Buffalo*. Montana Magazine of Western History Part 1 Vol. 53, Winter 2003.

Fry, Rodney. *Landscape Traveled by Coyote and Crane*. McLellen Book, University of Washington Press, Seattle.

Glassley, Howard. *Pacific Northwest Indian Wars*. Binford and Mort, Portland, OR, 1953.

Gowan, Fred R. *Rocky Mountain Rendezvous*. Gibson Smith Publisher, Layton, Utah, 2005.

Gray, William Henry. *A History of Oregon*. Harris and Holman, Portland, OR, 1870.

Hafen, Leroy. *Mountain Men and Fur Traders of the Far West*. University of Nebraska Press, Lincoln, NE, 1965.

Harris, Burton. *John Colter*. University of Nebraska Press, Lincoln, NE, 1993.

Harris, Francis. *Northwest Spread of Horses to the Plains Indians*. American Anthropolist 40, No. 3, 1938.

Hodge, Frederick Webb. *Bureau of American Ethnology, Smithsonian Institute Bulletin*. U.S. Government Printing Office, 1907.

Holt, Harry and High, Turney. *Flathead Indians of Montana*. Vol. 56 Menoin of Amercian Anthropological Association, Montana State University, Menasha, WI, 1930.

Hopwood, Victor G. *David Thompson's Travels in Western North America 1784-1812*. McMillan, Toronto.

Hungery, Wolf, Adolf and Beverly. *Indian Tribes of the Northern Rockies*. Good Medicine Books, Skookumchuck, B.C., Canada, 1989.

Jackson, John C. *The Piikani Blackfoot*. Mountain Press Publishing, Missoula, MT, 2000.

Jackson, John. *Children of the Fur Trade*. Oregon State University Press, Corvallis, OR, 1996.

—. *Old Rivet*. article Columbia Road Magazine, Vol. 54 No. 2, 2004.

Johnson, Donald R, ed. *Journal of William Henry Gray of a Journey East 1836-37*. Ye Galleon Press, Fairfield, WA, 1980.

Johnson, Olga Weydemeyer. *Flathead and Kootenay*. Arthur H. Clark Co., Glendale, CA, 1964.

Josephy, Alvin M. *The Nez Perce Indians*. Abridged Edition, copyright Yale University, University of Nebraska Press, 1965.

Kinston, C.S. *Buffalo in the Pacific Northwest*. WHQ, July 1923.

Kowrach, Edward I. *Saga of the Couer d'Alene Indians*. Ye Galleon Press, Fairfield, WA, 1999.

Lee, Jason. *Diary*. OHQ Vol. 17 No. 2 , 1916.

Lepley, John G. *Blackfoot Fur Trade on the Upper Missouri*. Pictorial Histories Publishing Co., Missoula, MT, 2004.

Lewis, William S. and Phillips, Paul C., ed. *The Journals of John Work 1831-32*. The Arthur H. Clark Co., Cleveland, OH, 1923.

Lewis, William S. *Old Fort Colville*. WHQ Vol. 16 No. 2, 1923.

MacGregor, Carol L. *The Journals of Patrick Gass*. Mountain Press, Missoula, MT, 1997.

Madson, Bringham D. *Northern Shoshoni*. Caxton Press, Caldwell, ID, 2000.

—. *The Bannock of Idaho*. University of Idaho Press, Moscow, ID, 1996.

—. *The Lemhi: Sacajawea's People*. Caxton Press, Caldwell, Idaho, 2000.

Malouf, Richard T. *Life and Death at St. Mary's Mission Montana*. Edited by Robert Bigart. Salish-Kootenai College Press, Pablo, MT, 2005.

McDonald, Angus. *A Few Items of the West*. Montana State Historical Society Resources, Helena, MT and Washington Historical Quarterly Vol. 8 1917, 1893.

McDonald, Christina. *Christina M.M. Williams*. WHQ Vol. 13 , April 1922.

McDonald, Lois Halliday. *Fur Trade Letters of Francis Ermatinger*. Arthur H. Clark Co., Glendale,CA, 1980.

McWorter, L.V. *Hear Me My Chiefs*. Carton Press, Caldwell, Idaho, 2001.

Meikle, Lyndel. *Very Close to Trouble-Johny Grant Memoirs*. Washington State University Press, Pullman.WA, 1996.

Mengarini, Rev Gregory. *Recollections of the Flathead Mission*. Edited by Gloria Ricci Lanthrop. Arthur Clark Co., 1977.

Merk, Frederick, ed. *Fur Trade and Empire, George Simpson Journal and Letters*. Belkap Press, Harvard University, Cambridge, MA, 1968.

Morgan, Dale L. *Jedediah Smith*. University of Nebraska Press, Lincoln, NE, 1953.

Moulton, Gary E, edi. *The Journals of Lewis and Clark Expedition*. Vol. 2 and 5. University of Nebraska Press, 1988.

Nisbet, Jack. *The Mapmaker's Eye*. Washington State University Press, Pullman, WA, 2005.

—. *Spokane House Journal April 15, 1822, to April 1823 kept by Finan*

McDonald and James Birne. Transcription of, HBC microfilm record, Manitoba, Canada.

—. *Spokane House Report 1822-23*. By Alexander Kennedy, Transcription of HBC microfilm records, Manitoba, Canada.

Oliphant, J Orin. *Old Fort Colville*. Washington Historical Quarterly Vol. 16, 1925.

Paladino, Rev L.B. *Anthony Ravalli – 40 Years a Missionary*. George E. Boss and Company, 1884.

—. *Indians and Whites in the History of the North West*. Wickersheim Publishing Co., Lancaster, PA, 1922.

Parker, Rev. Samuel. *Journal of an Exploration Tour Beyond the Rocky Mountains*. Mack Andrus and Woodruff, Ithaca, NY, 1842, reprint University of Idaho Press, 1940.

Partoll, Albert J. *Fort Connah: A Frontier Trading Post 1847-1871*. Pacific Northwest Quarterly Vol. 30 No. 4, October 1939.

—. *The Flathead Indian Treaty Council of 1855*. By Isaac I. Stevens, Pacific Northwest Quarterly Vol. 29 No. 3 p 283-314, July 1938.

Ray, Verne F. *Native Villages and Groupings*. Pacific Northwest Quarterly Vol. 27 , 1936.

Rich, E.E., ed. *Peter Skene Ogden's and Wilhau Kittson's Snake Country Journals 1824-25*. The Hudson's Bay Record Society, London, 1950.

Rockwell, Ronald V. *The US Army in Frontier, Montana* . Sweetgrass Books, Helena, MT, 2009.

Ruby, Robert H. and Brown, John A. *Children of the Sun*. University of Oklahoma Press, 1970.

Russell, Osborne. *Journal of a Trapper.* Edited by Aubrey Haines. University of Nebraska, Lincoln, NE, 1965.

Salish, Culture Committee and Elders of the Confederated Salish and Kootenai Tribes. University of Nebraska Press, Lincoln, NE, 2005.

Stevens, Hazard. *The Life of Isaac I. Stevens*. 2 Vol., Houghton-Mifflin Co., New York, 1900.

Stuart, Granville. *Forty Years on the Frontier.* Edited by Paul Phillips. Journals 2 Vols original publication 1925, Univesity of Nebraska Press, Lincoln, NE, 1977.

Thompson, David. *Narrative*. The Champlain Society, Toronto, 1902.

White, M. Catherine ,editor. *David Thompson Journals Relating to Montana and Adjacent Regions 1808-1812*. University of Montana Press, Missoula, MT, 1950.

Wood, W. Raymond and Thiessen, Thomas. *Early Fur Trade of the Northern*

Plains. University of Oklahoma Press, Norman, OK, 1985.

Young, F.G. *Dr. Marcus Whitman Journal and Report of Exploration with Rev. Samuel Parker*. Oregon Historical Quarterly Vol. 28, September 1927.

Internet Sources

Ball, John. Library of Western Fur Trade Documents. Across the Plains to Oregon 1832. Autobiography: Dean-Hicks Co. 1925. http://www.mtman.org

Boner, T.D. Library of Western Fur Trade Documents. Life and Adventures of James P Beckwourth. Harper and Brothers, New York 1856. http://www.mtman.org

Campbell, Robert. Library of Western Fur Trade Documents. A Narrative of Colonel Robert Cambell in the Rocky Mountains. William Kay St. Louis, July 1886. http://www.mtman.org

Eddin, O. Library of Western Fur Trade Documents. Spanish Colonial Horses and Plains Indians Culture. Afton, WY. http://www.mtman.org

Ferris, Warren Agnus. Library of Western Fur Trade Documents. Life in the Rocky Mountains 1830-35. Western Literary Messenger. Buffalo, NY, 1842-44. http://www.mtman.org

Flora, Stephenie. Whitman Massacre. www.oregonpioneers.com

Grey, Victor, ed. Joseph Harker Diary. lemhi.idgenweb.org.

Irving, Washinton. Library of Western Fur Trade Documents. The Adventures of Captain Bonneville. George P. Putman. NY and London, original publication 1849. http://www.mtman.org

James, General Thomas. Library of Western Fur Trade Documents. Three Years Among the Indians and Mexicans. War Eagle Press. Waterloo, IL, original publication 1846. http://www.mtman.org

Larpenteur, Charles. Library of Western Fur Trade Documents. Forty Years a Furtrader on the Upper Missouri. Francis A. Harper, New York 1898. http://www.mtman.org

Leonard, Zenas. Library of Western Fur Trade Documents. Narrative of Adventures of Zenas Leonard. Clearfied PA D.W. Moose, 1839. http://www.mtman.org

Newell, Robert. Library of Western Fur Trade Documents. Travels in the Territory of Missouri. Edited by Dorothy O. Johnson. Champoeg Press, 1959. http://www.mtman.org

Ogden, Peter Skene. Library of Western Fur Trade Documents. Journal of the Snake River Expedition 1825-26. Edited by T.C. Elliott. http://

www.mtman.org

—. Library of Western Fur Trade Documents. Expedition to Utah in 1825. Edited by David E. Mills. http://www.mtman.org

Ross, Alexander. Library of Western Fur Trade Documents. Adventures of the First on the Oregon and Columbia River. Smity Elber Co., Cornell Hill, 1849. http://www.mtman.org

—. Library of Western Fur Trade Documents. Journal of Snake River Expedition 1824. Edited by T.C. Elliot. 1913. http://www.mtman.org

Sage, Rufus. Library of Western Fur Trade Documents. Rocky Mountain Life. Wentworth and Company, Boston, 1853. http://www.mtman.org

Spalding, Eliza. Library of Western Fur Trade Documents. Extract from Mrs. Eliza Spalding Diary. June 15 - July 6, 1836. http://www.mtman.org

Spirit Talk News, The Indian Horse, Spirit Talk News, Vol 14 Number 6 Nov-Dec 2008 Spirittalknews.com 6/1/2009. (Website temporarily unavailable.)

Townsend, John K. narrative of. Library of Western Fur Trade Documents. Journey Across the Rocckey Mountains to the Columbia. Henry Perkins Philidelphia, 1839. http://www.mtman.org

Wislizenus, F.A. Library of Western Fur Trade Documents. A Journey to the Rocky Mountains in 1839. http://www.mtman.org

Wyeth, John H. Library of Western Fur Trade Documents. Oregon or a Short History of a Long Journey. Cambridge, MA, 1833. http://www.mtman.org

Wyeth, Nathaniel. Library of Western Fur Trade Documents. The Journals of Captain Nathaniel Wyeth's Expedition to Oregon Country from 1831-36. Oregon University Press, 1899. http://www.mtman.org

U.S. Government Publications

Commissioner. *Annual Report of Commissioner of Indian Affairs*. 1859.
—. *Report of Commissoner of Indian Affairs*. 1853.
Danilson, W.I. and Galbrith, Major A.S. *Annual Report 1869 and 1870, U.S. Bureau of Indian Affairs*.
Hale, Rorbert C. *Report of Superintendant of Indian Affairs, Washington Territory*. 1863.
Mullan, Captain John. "Mullan Report." *Construction of Military Road from Walla Walla to Fort Benton*. U.S. Government Printing Office, Washington, D.C., 1863.
Oregon. "White Census of Oregon 1841-42."
Raynolds, W.E. *Report on the Explortation of the Yellowstone River*. U.S. Government Printing Office, Washington, D.C, 1868.
Report, Government. *Exploration and Survey of Railroad Route from Mississippi River to the Pacific Ocean*. Vol. 7, Book 1 Washington, D.C., 1860.
Mullan, Lt. John. "Fort Benton to Fort Owen." 20 January, 1854.
Mullan, Lt. John. "Report of Exploration of Clark Fork River." 3 January, 1855.
Mullan, Lt. John. "Report of Exploration of Kootenai River." May 1855.
Saxton, Lt. Rufus. "Report on Journey from Puget Sound to Fort Owen." February 1854
Stuckley, Dr. George. "Report on the Navigatability of Rivers from the Bitteroot to Dalles on the Columbia River." 19 December 1853
Washington. "Washington Territorial Census 1860."

Unpublished Material

Doty, James, Aide de Camp. "Journal of Operations." Governor Isaac Stevens, December, 23 1819, Northwest Room, Spokane Public Library.
Father Adrian Hoecken Diary at St. Ignatius, 1856, Gonzaga University Special Collections.
Landsdale, Dr. Richard, Letter dated October 3, 1855. *Report of Operation Flathead Agency*, Montana Historical Society, Helena, Montana.
Thain White Research Collection. *Howse of Hudson's Bay Co*. Montana Historical Society, Manuscript box 5 No. 2

Index

An *f*, *p* or *m* indicates footnote, photo or map respectively.

C

G

H

I

M

N

O

P

T